The Queer Fantasies of the American Family Sitcom

The Queer Fantasies of the American Family Sitcom

TISON PUGH

Rutgers University Press

New Brunswick, Camden, and Newark, New Jersey, and London

Library of Congress Cataloging-in-Publication Data

Names: Pugh, Tison, author.
Title: The queer fantasies of the American family sitcom / Tison Pugh.
Description: New Brunswick, NJ : Rutgers University Press, [2018] | Includes bibliographical references and index.
Identifiers: LCCN 2017012061 (print) | LCCN 2017027760 (ebook) | ISBN 9780813591735 (E-pub) | ISBN 9780813591759 (Web PDF) | ISBN 9780813591728 (hardback) | ISBN 9780813591711 (paperback)
Subjects: LCSH: Situation comedies (Television programs)—United States—History and criticism. | Homosexuality and television. | Homosexuality on television. | Sex role on television. | Television programs—Social aspects—United States.
Classification: LCC PN1992.8.C66 (ebook) | LCC PN1992.8.C66 P84 2018 (print) | DDC 791.45/617—dc23
LC record available at https://lccn.loc.gov/2017012061

A British Cataloging-in-Publication record for this book is available from the British Library.

∞ The paper used in this publication meets the requirements of the American National Standard for Information Sciences—Permanence of Paper for Printed Library Materials, ANSI Z39.48–1992.

www.rutgersuniversitypress.org

Manufactured in the United States of America

To my most beloved fellow *Brady Bunch* fans:

Betsy Lefeaux Beaird
Maggie Devlin Landry
Jennifer Jane Lefeaux
Kellianne Moller
Beth Ann Techow

Contents

Introduction: TV's Three Queer Fantasies 1

1 The Queer Times of *Leave It to Beaver*: Beaver's Present, Ward's Past, and June's Future 26

2 Queer Innocence and Kitsch Nostalgia in *The Brady Bunch* 51

3 No Sex Please, We're African American: *The Cosby Show*'s Queer Fear of Black Sexuality 79

4 Feminism, Homosexuality, and Blue-Collar Perversity in *Roseanne* 107

5 Allegory, Queer Authenticity, and Marketing Tween Sexuality in *Hannah Montana* 134

6 Conservative Narratology, Queer Politics, and the Humor of Gay Stereotypes in *Modern Family* 161

Conclusion: Tolstoy Was Wrong; or, On the Queer Reception of Television's Happy Families 190

Acknowledgments 197

List of Television Programs 199

Notes 205

Works Cited 227

Index 241

The Queer Fantasies of the American Family Sitcom

Introduction

TV's Three Queer Fantasies

While starring in popular family sitcoms, Kirk Cameron of *Growing Pains* (1985–92) and Angus T. Jones of *Two and a Half Men* (2003–15) fulminated against the lax morality depicted in their fictional households, biting the hands of producers who were very generously feeding them. Cameron skyrocketed to fame and teen idol status in his role as Mike Seaver yet complained to the producers and writers about transgressions against his sense of Christian morality—such as a fantasy sequence implying that Mike had consummated his relationship with his girlfriend—stating that such a scene "crosses the line in my conscience . . . and since I'm the guy who has to get up there and do this in front of millions of people, I don't want to do it."[1] Jones, while earning roughly $8 million annually, lambasted *Two and a Half Men* as "filth" and urged viewers not to watch it, stating, "It's the number one comedy, but it's very inappropriate and its themes are very inappropriate. I have to be this person I am not."[2] One would presume that these actors, notwithstanding their deeply held religious convictions, would understand that their occupation requires them to play roles that might not accord with their personal views. The inherent ridiculousness of Jones's proclamation—"I have to be this person that I am not"—is true of every actor in every part, and his assumption of the role of teen regulator of American morality smacks of righteousness rather than rightness.

But while it is easy to dismiss Cameron's and Jones's diatribes for their sincere yet grandiose moralizing, might one concede that, on a historical and narratological level, they have a point to argue about the nature of the family sitcom in the United States and its trajectory from the 1950s to today, as well as about the fluid protocols of the networks' programming in relationship to the chimerical concept of "family-friendly programming"? In his autobiography, Cameron argues that "a TV series has an unspoken agreement to be what it has been from the beginning. A sitcom shouldn't become a drama. Nobody wants to see a homicide investigation on *Mr. Belvedere*."[3] In some ways, Cameron's discomfort with his program's escalating treatments of sexuality reflects his understanding of an inherent contradiction in the generic structure of the family sitcom, as it faces the challenge of creating fare appropriate for all family members, no matter their ages. His argument about the suitability of certain story lines for television programs—that narrative paradigms construct protocols for writers and producers, as well as expectations for viewers—is a reasonable assessment of the utility of aesthetic genres. These issues of genre and interpretation foist vexing pressures on family sitcoms because they, in many ways, are expected to capture for viewers a nostalgic, ostensibly timeless view of American domestic life rather than its shifting realities.

In their laments against television's lax morality, Cameron and Jones tacitly advocate the three fantasies that underpin this study—the genre of the family sitcom, the long-standing and historically recurrent marketing concept of family-friendly programming, and children themselves—while overlooking their inherently queer potential. To discern queer potential in these televisual texts is to argue against their historical and generic facade of smiling, feckless, American normativity. In brief, queerness as a critical concept fractures cultural constructions of gendered and erotic normativity, dismantling rigid binary codes of licit and illicit desires and identities. *Queer* refers to contested sexual and gender identities but extends further to include identities that challenge regimes of normativity. More so, queerness exposes how deeply heteronormative narrative frameworks, such as that of the family sitcom, are structurally incapable of suturing over their aporias and contradictions, such that their surface normativity cannot withstand the steady erosion of their symptomatic queerness. David Eng, Jack Halberstam, and José Esteban Muñoz state that queerness and queer theory "challenge the normalizing mechanisms of state power to name its sexual subjects: male or female, married or single, heterosexual or homosexual, natural or perverse."[4] In this light, queer theory serves as a preferred tool for querying any genre or social practice that valorizes normality, as family sitcoms, virtually by their existence, attempt to accomplish—or, more potently, have been conscripted to accomplish in their reception. Such an approach does not simply cement a long-standing binary between the queer and the normative but instead depicts their radical intertwining, such that the normative cannot, in the final analysis, obscure the queer at its heart.

To describe the disparate entities of a televisual narrative structure, an advertising ploy, and young humans as queer fantasies does not deny their effect or reduce them to gossamer ephemeralities, of course, yet doing so highlights the ways in which they serve, and concomitantly subvert, ideological objectives outside themselves. Individually and collectively, domestic sitcoms, family-friendly programming, and children act as discursive concepts through which television narratives are staged, marketed, and consumed but also through which cultural battles are waged over the fate of America's moral condition—primarily to bemoan a coarsening of the entertainment industry but, through other eyes, to celebrate increasingly candid depictions of sexuality as an integral part of the human experience. So discussions of family sitcoms often touch on issues of morality and pseudotheological attempts to define what American families should both be and see—as Cameron, Jones, and cultural commentators of their ilk demonstrate.

As is readily apparent by even a cursory overview of the featured programs of this volume—*Leave It to Beaver* (1957–63), *The Brady Bunch* (1969–74), *The Cosby Show* (1984–92), *Roseanne* (1988–97), *Hannah Montana* (2006–11), and *Modern Family* (2009–)—family sitcoms from the 1950s to the 2010s record America's changing sexual and social norms, but it is not my objective to chart the history of sexual depictions—the first married couple to share a bed, the first gay kiss, the first teen character to lose his or her virginity. Instead, this study examines how the families of domestic sitcoms simultaneously resist and display sexuality's cultural shifts transpiring throughout the United States at various historical moments, for the purported innocence of children necessitates complex and conflicting strategies for addressing the eroticism ostensibly shunted to these programs' margins. Neither narrating a downward spiral into vulgarity nor applauding increasingly graphic depictions of sexuality, *The Queer Fantasies of the American Family Sitcom* instead analyzes the ways in which children, families, and sexualities interact in relation to a host of other cultural issues, for sexuality serves as a preferred, if obscured, site of ideological power. As Michel Foucault so powerfully observes of sexuality's meaning: "Sexuality must not be thought of as a kind of natural given which power tries to hold in check, or as an obscure domain which knowledge tries gradually to uncover. It is the name that can be given to a historical construct: not a furtive reality that is difficult to grasp, but a great surface network in which the stimulation of bodies, the intensification of pleasures, the incitement to discourse, the formation of special knowledges, the strengthening of controls and resistances, are linked to one another, in accordance with a few major strategies of knowledge and power."[5] Of particular concern to children's genres, which include family sitcoms within their purview, Foucault notes the "pedagogization of children's sex" and the "psychiatrization of perverse pleasure" as key tactics in the ideological construction of sex. Early family sitcoms (mostly) refrain from addressing sexuality and "perverse" pleasures, yet what they attempt to hide inevitably bleeds through into story lines otherwise cleansed of such fare. And so they must: a foundational irony of family sitcoms emerges from their tendency to camouflage or otherwise cloak sex, thus overlooking the foundational role of sex in building the families depicted onscreen.

Such narrative tensions result in queerness, in the disruptions of gendered and (hetero)sexual normativity ostensibly encoded in these TV narratives that invariably cannot prevent fissures from subverting their surface presentation of the American family in the throes of domestic bliss. Queerness, as Alexander Doty argues in his landmark study of gay representations in popular media, serves "to mark a flexible space for the expression of all aspects of non- (anti-, contra-) straight cultural production and reception. As such, this cultural 'queer space' recognizes the possibility that various and fluctuating queer positions might be occupied whenever *anyone* produces or responds to culture."[6] Various studies have traced the history of gay portrayals on television from virtual absence to a vibrant presence, as they have also noticed the ambivalence of many such depictions.[7] As Lynne Joyrich cautions, "It's the ambivalence, though, of how queerness can be both the electrical spark and the grounding against any possible shock that remains the paradox and the problem—indeed, I'd argue, *the* problematic—for queer television studies."[8] This book contributes to this ongoing discussion by exploring how the fantasies of genre, of marketing, and of children can never fully cloak the queerness lurking within the plucky families designed for American viewers' comic delight. Queer readings of family sitcoms demolish myths of yesteryear, demonstrating the illusion of American sexual innocence in television's early programs and its lasting consequences in the nation's self-construction, as they also allow fresh insights into the ways in which more recent programs negotiate new visions of sexuality while remaining indebted to previous narrative traditions and long-standing generic conventions. Simply put, queer readings of America's domestic sitcoms radically unsettle the nation's simplistic vision of itself, revealing both a deeper vision of its families and of a television genre overwhelmingly dismissed as frivolous fare.

The Queer Fantasy of the Family Sitcom

Within the world of narrative analysis, genres stand as trivial yet essential constructions: trivial, because they divulge so little; essential, because they establish a framework for understanding and digesting a cultural work. As Jason Mittell explains of television genres, "Genre definitions are no more natural than the texts that they seem to categorize. Genres are cultural products, constituted by media practices and subject to ongoing change and redefinition."[9] For example, to label a television show a mystery is to give only the barest hints of its contents or its aesthetic quality, for the form ranges from modern classics, such as Helen Mirren's gutsy performances in the *Prime Suspect* series (recurring from 1991 to 2006) to kitschy flops, such as Loni Anderson's and Lynda Carter's stars fading in the short-lived *Partners in Crime* (1984); it includes as well the subgenre of procedurals (e.g., *Law & Order* [1990–2010], *CSI: Crime Scene Investigation* [2000–2015]), in which plot takes precedence over character development and emotional depth. In this light, genres represent little more than collective fantasies, a helpful yet inconsequential attempt to organize art into conceptual categories—categories that the creators of these works, according to their unique visions, then dismantle or, more optimistically, reconstruct. Within the television economy, genres emerge through the complex interactions of creative talent, producers, and audiences, with each exerting their influence on which programs are created, aired, and renewed, both in regard to individual shows and the genres of which they serve as constituent elements.

Of the various television genres, the situation comedy towers as a resiliently popular form, reborn in successive generations and capturing various aspects of its zeitgeist. Richard Butsch observes that the "situation comedy is built around a humorous 'situation' in which tension develops and is resolved during the half hour. In episode after episode the situation is re-created."[10] Many sitcoms succinctly establish their foundational comic premise in their titles: lost on a tropical paradise in *Gilligan's Island* (1964–67), or the continual delay of answering the apparently simple question of *How I Met Your Mother* (2005–14). Even sitcoms named for their eponymous protagonist disclose their situational plotlines once audiences understand his or her identity: a white couple adopting a young African American child in *Webster* (1983–89) or the neurotic nothingness of *Seinfeld* (1989–98). Moreover, sitcoms typically adhere to formulaic plots that do not advance their foundational premises. As Paul Attallah explains: "It is a narrative necessity of situation comedy that the 'situation' must remain unchanged. If the program is to be repeated week after week, the characters and their mode of interaction must not be allowed to evolve. Were they to acquire experience, then evolution would occur and the show would not continue."[11] Attallah's point is clearly evident in the vast majority of sitcoms, for most episodes of a series can stand alone without the scaffolding of past narratives. The genre's popularity is matched by its lucrative payoffs, for, as Lawrence Mintz notes, financial incentives abound owing to the fact that the sitcom "reigns supreme in the syndication market and as an exportable commodity"—which further explains its resiliency despite the various programming fads over the decades since television's rise.[12] If a sitcom can remain in production long enough to be distributed in syndication—typically, for five seasons, or approximately one hundred episodes—a financial bonanza awaits.

Under the wider rubric of situation comedies, the subheading of family, or domestic, sitcoms stands as one of its most durable, even beloved, forms. Lynn

Spigel states that the genre's traditional parameters include "a suburban home, character relationships based on family ties, a setting filled with middle-class luxuries, a story that emphasizes everyday complications, and a narrative structure based on conflicts that resolve in thirty minutes."[13] Horace Newcomb distinguishes between situation comedies and domestic comedies, with the latter taking as their domain the daily activities of a given family, which, as he argues, results in programs with "more warmth and a deeper sense of humanity" than standard sitcoms.[14] The names of many of TV's families resonate with an appeal both nostalgic and iconic: the Nelsons of *The Adventures of Ozzie and Harriet* (1952–66), the Ricardos of *I Love Lucy* (1951–57), the Cunninghams of *Happy Days* (1974–84), as well as the six primary clans examined in this monograph: the Cleavers of *Leave It to Beaver*, the Bradys of *The Brady Bunch*, the Huxtables of *The Cosby Show*, the Conners of *Roseanne*, the Stewarts of *Hannah Montana*, and the Pritchetts, Tucker-Pritchetts, and Dunphys of *Modern Family*. These fictional families have influenced countless viewers' perception of American domesticity, even when filtered through such lenses as irony, nostalgia, or incredulity.

The narrative structure of family sitcoms favors pat conclusions for their plots, and most of these programs end with a touch of moralizing, summarizing the lessons learned from the transgression against the family's rules. Many story lines involve only a minimal disruption of the family's unity, which George Burns suggests sardonically in a moment of metadiscourse in his *George Burns and Gracie Allen Show* (1950–58): "We try to strike a happy medium. We have more plot than a variety show, and not as much as a wrestling match" ("Chapter 3").[15] Whatever the extent of the transgression, all is forgiven by story's end, as is evident in—to take one example out of the thousands of narratives constituting sitcom history—the "Body Damage" episode of *Family Matters* (1989–98). Rachel (Telma Hopkins) damages her brother-in-law's car, and the family conspires to keep it a secret from him. When Carl (Reginald VelJohnson) learns the truth, he is more upset about the secret than the car: "But guys, remember, we're a family. Your problems are my problems. But I can't do anything about them unless you let me know what they are, okay?" His wife, Harriette (JoMarie Payton), agrees, speaking for herself and the rest of the family: "Right, baby. From now on, this family sticks together." David Marc describes the plotlines of family sitcoms as "illustrat[ing], in practical everyday subphilosophic terms, the tangible rewards of faith and trust in the family,"[16] so even in family sitcoms that flagrantly rewrite the codes of domestic life into gleeful odes to dysfunctionality, the family unit remains sacrosanct: Al and Peg Bundy of *Married with Children* (1987–97), despite apparently loathing each other, could never divorce, for doing so would sever the program's foundational premise of familyhood.

But defining the apparently simple genre of the family sitcom conjures a foundational hermeneutic conundrum, for what configuration of individuals and consanguinity constitutes a family? The American family persists as a vibrantly amorphous entity, one that shifts in accordance with the prevailing zeitgeist, and further along these lines, prominent subgenres of family sitcoms rewrite the significance of children to the family unit or construct childhood according to varying parameters. For instance, *All in the Family* (1971–79) features bigoted antihero Archie Bunker (Carroll O'Connor) and his wife, Edith (Jean Stapleton), in its lead roles, along with their daughter, Gloria (Sally Struthers), and son-in-law, Mike "Meathead" Stivic (Rob Reiner). While Gloria is indeed Archie and Edith's child, she is hardly one in the sense of an innocent naïf; on the contrary, she resists her father's prejudices on numerous occasions and denounces him accordingly: "You are so sick," she asserts after one of his antiethnic rants ("The Joys of Sex"). In complementary contrast, *Everybody Loves Raymond* (1996–2005) reverses the standard intergenerational dynamic of most family sitcoms, with its plotlines addressing the rocky relationship of Ray (Ray Romano) and Debra Barone (Patricia Heaton) with Ray's overbearing parents, Frank (Peter Boyle) and Marie (Doris Roberts). Thus, the variability of children and their ages affects—sometimes multiplying, sometimes restricting—the register, themes, and audiences available to a particular sitcom.

As this brief overview of family sitcoms and their shifting parameters attests, this genre is amorphous, as are all genres, and it is in the end, I think, unhelpful to construct a definition of the term that unnecessarily delimits it in light of its protean variations—one, for example, that would embrace *The Brady Bunch* for its focus on six young children but omit *All in the Family* because of Gloria's early adulthood. Rather, the variability of familial relationships for each of these programs requires viewers to examine how a particular construction of kinship complements its narrative investments in other issues and the ways in which queer themes seep into a genre overarchingly conveying the fundamental sexual normativity of its members. For in so many instances, any promise of seamless heteronormativity is inevitably complicated, if not undone, as a program broaches topics it otherwise promises to eschew through its generic affiliation, thus rendering queer the very concept of the family-sitcom genre. At the same time, for the purposes of interpretive clarity, this volume focuses on programs that include young teen and preteen children as primary cast members, for these programs stake their appeal to viewers of all ages—even if their narratives are sometimes deemed too provocative for the fantasy of family-friendly programming. Television's funny families with young children must tacitly address the issue of how to depict sexuality in a manner that will not alienate real-life parents tuning in to watch a program with their kids, so the marketing concept of family-friendly programming attempts to assuage parents' concerns about television content through this ultimately meaningless designation.

The Queer Fantasy of Family-Friendly Programming

"You know, FOX turned into a hardcore sex channel so gradually I didn't even notice," sighs Marge Simpson in *The Simpsons* ("Lisa's Wedding"), in a satiric jab at network television's increasingly graphic depictions of sexuality over the years. Marge's words exaggerate yet echo recurring criticisms of television's shifting mores, particularly in relation to the chimerical concept of family-friendly programming. From television's early days, when the majority of families who owned a set owned only one and gathered together to watch it, domestic sitcoms were built on the foundational premise of appealing to the various members of their audiences, with the assumption that each member of a viewing family would identify with his or her corresponding role in these narrative families. As Lawrence Laurent notes in his classic 1956 study, family sitcoms enhance their commercial value through their multiple points of audience identification: "In some ways, commercial sponsorship is directly responsible for the kinds of programs which are seen on television. If the sponsor is trying to win 100 percent acceptance of his product, he is likely to prefer a program which will appeal to 100 percent of the audience. This fact accounts, in large part, for the plethora of 'family situation comedies' which fill the TV schedules."[17] Early television advertisers also saw the benefit of appealing directly to child viewers, as Vance Packard charges in his 1957 anti-propaganda classic *The Hidden Persuaders*, in which he quotes a contemporary advertiser to reveal the industry's unscrupulous methods and pecuniary aims: "Think of what it can mean to your firm in profits if you can condition a million or ten million children who will grow up into adults trained to buy your product as soldiers are trained to advance when they hear the trigger words 'forward march.'"[18] In sum, advertisers have long relied on family-friendly programming, little more than a marketing ploy based on an ecumenical appeal to various demographics, as they urge audiences to purchase their wares. This strategy bears the side-effect that viewers will inevitably compare themselves and their ideal vision of the American family to the images seen onscreen, with these sitcom families validating certain forms of kinship and overlooking others. Such a simplistic assessment cannot account for the multiple and contradictory viewing positions any given individual may stake in relation to a program, nor did most early television families recognize the diversity of the American family in relation to race, gender, and other identities excluded by the normative assumption of suburban whiteness. Nonetheless, this marketing foundation of universality imbues domestic sitcoms with accompanying values and appeals, thus virtually assuring their queer collapse under these inherent contradictions.

Recurring controversies over the chimerical concept of the "family hour" showcase the queer and hazy parameters of any real commitment to family-friendly programming on the part of the legacy networks and cable channels. A staunch defender of this fantasy, television critic Thomas Johnson proposes that "shows airing in that hour should not merely entertain children, but be good for them; they should reinforce traditional values, not subvert them," citing *Little House on the Prairie* (1974–83), *Happy Days*, *The Cosby Show*, and *Full House* (1987–95) as examples of appropriate family-friendly fare.[19] A family hour was unnecessary during television's early years when the networks censored themselves to the extent that on *I Love Lucy*, Lucy (Lucille Ball) and Ricky Ricardo (Desi Arnaz) avoid the word "pregnant"—preferring instead the euphemism "expecting." By the 1970s, however, concern had mounted increasingly over programs' candid depictions of controversial topics, including racism, violence, women's reproductive rights, and homosexuality. The 1971 report "Television and Growing Up: The Impact of Televised Violence," submitted to Surgeon General Jesse Steinfeld, concludes that "The Department of Health, Education and Welfare would do well to consider increased involvement in this field, not just in relation to the possibly harmful effects of television, but also to develop the experience and professional relationships needed to consider and stimulate television's health-promoting possibilities."[20] The federal government, identifying a moral scourge on the television screens of the nation's families, charged itself with the improvement of the American mind.

Seeing the handwriting on the wall, and responding to additional pressure from Congress and the Federal Communications Commission, the networks embraced and codified family-friendly protocols in 1975, agreeing that the first hour of prime-time scheduling would consist of shows appropriate for all ages. Arthur R. Taylor of CBS Entertainment endorsed the "Family Hour" plan, which, as Richard Blake attests, "was adopted into the Code of the National Association of Broadcasters in April, 1975, and became policy at the start of the 1975–76 season."[21] Unsurprisingly, the family-hour policy proved exceedingly unpopular among the creative forces behind network television. Norman Lear, producer of *All in the Family*, *Maude* (1972–78), *Mary Hartman, Mary Hartman* (1976–77), and other popular programs, asked Robert D. Wood, president of CBS Television (1969–76), to clarify its parameters but received only equivocations and so replied with cheeky exasperation, "Well, how can you think of moving [*All in the Family*] out of the Family Hour unless you know what it is? . . . Is there something you can read to me so I'll know what it is you want me to conform to?"[22] Additional creative voices expressing outrage over the tyranny of the family hour included George Schlatter, executive producer of *Rowan and Martin's Laugh-In* (1967–73) and *Cher* (1975–76), who tersely jibed, "The family hour sucks," and Paul Junger Witt, executive producer of *The Partridge Family* (1970–74) and *Soap* (1977–81), who agreed that it was "an outrageous pain in the ass."[23] Rebelling against the restrictions it imposed, television programs of the era employed the family hour as fodder for sarcastic humor, such as in *One Day at a Time* (1975–84), when petulant daughter Julie (Mackenzie Phillips) snipes at her mother, Ann (Bonnie Franklin), for treating her like a child: "I didn't think the family hour ended 'til nine!" ("Chicago Rendezvous").

Victory for family-hour advocates was short-lived, and in the ensuing court case, the Writers' Guild of America, the Directors' Guild, and several production companies (including Norman Lear's Tandem Productions) sued ABC, CBS, NBC, the Federal Communications Commission, and the National Association of Broadcasters. On 4 November 1976, Judge Warren J. Ferguson of the Federal District Court in Los Angeles ruled the "Family Hour" policy unconstitutional for violating the First Amendment, so after one fleeting season, its family-friendly standards were jettisoned.[24] Even if the family hour had survived this legal challenge, it is difficult to imagine its guidelines being strictly enforced year after year. Much as film ratings have shifted over the decades, necessitating the addition of the PG-13 and NC-17 designations, so, too, would any protocols for family-hour programming have likely stretched with the passing of time. Counterfactuals are, of course, impossible to prove, yet it appears likely that any attempt to codify programming protocols for the networks would have faced increasing subversions over the years.

Beyond the immediate realm of the television networks, their programming schedules, and this skirmish over the "family hour," the fantasy of family-friendly narratives invites political grandstanding in the so-called culture wars, for, as one unidentified source from the National Association of Broadcasters lamented in a 1997 interview, politicians "can never lose a vote bashing broadcasters and Hollywood."[25] The cultural legacy of the 1970s family hour and accompanying calls for family-friendly programming have regularly erupted as flashpoints in debates addressing the United States' moral character over the decades. Despite the fact that the "family hour" no longer existed in the 1990s as part of network protocols, L. Brent Bozell, chairman of the conservative Media Research Center, derided the loss of this phantom construction while bemoaning television as a "moral wasteland," decrying *Spin City* (1996–2002) as "hyperlibidinous" and *Ellen* (1994–98) as "homosexually obsessed."[26] Across the partisan divide, Senator Joe Lieberman (Democrat, Connecticut) agreed: "The safe haven that we once counted on has turned into a broadcasting bordello. Much of this material seems about as healthful and suitable to kids, frankly, as a plate full of lead paint."[27] Similar to the controversies of the 1970s that resulted in the short-lived family hour, on 1 January 1997 a system of parental guidelines, proposed by the United States Congress, the major television networks, and the Federal Communications Commission, began notifying audiences of the appropriateness and content of various fare with the markings TV-Y (appropriate for all children), TV-Y7 (appropriate for children seven and older), TV-G (suitable for all ages), TV-PG (unsuitable for younger children), TV-14 (unsuitable for children under fourteen years), and TV-MA (mature audiences only). The guidelines also include content labels: D for suggestive dialogue, L for vulgar language, S for sexual situations, V for violence, and FV for fantasy violence.[28] These guidelines purportedly assist parents in determining whether their children should watch a given program, yet it is quite likely that the many combinations possible from this array of labels—e.g., TV Y7 FV, TV-14 DLS—confuse rather than clarify its subject matter. The guidelines did little to mollify lawmakers: two years later, U.S. Senators Sam Brownback (Republican, Kansas) and Byron Dorgan (Democrat, South Dakota), with several colleagues from the House of Representatives, sent a letter to the network presidents, urging them "to reverse course and reinstate the family hour, once again making that time slot suitable for children."[29]

Unsurprisingly, neither the family-hour debates of the 1970s nor the institution of parental guidelines in the 1990s have squelched the fantasy of the family hour, with tempests regularly swirling over allegedly inappropriate content in the ensuing decades. A minor brouhaha arose following "The Baby Monitor" episode of *According to Jim* (2001–9), which depicts a neighbor consoling her husband over his small penis (notably, the stature of Jim's penis—and thus of star Jim Belushi's penis—does not trigger these anxieties). Stephanie Leifer, ABC's vice president of comedy series, batted away the controversy: "We felt it wasn't too graphic—it was done with a lot of double entendre. We're trying to walk a fine line. We want adults to stay interested *and* feel comfortable enough to watch a show with their kids."[30] The "MILF Island" episode of *30 Rock* (2006–13) likewise generated a minor stir over its plot, as Jack Donaghy (Alec Baldwin) produces a *Survivor*-like reality program based on horny adolescents determining which sexy mother will win the contest—"Twenty-five super-hot moms, fifty eighth-grade boys, no rules"—both hiding and trumpeting its sexual humor with the acronym MILF ("Mother I'd Like to Fuck"). NBC's responses to the hullabaloo constituted a masterful medley of obfuscation and doublespeak. Executive Ben Silverman endorsed the family hour as "the 8 to 9 p.m. block of programming that . . . would consist of shows a family could watch together," while Mitch Metcalf, NBC's executive vice president for program scheduling, countered that the family hour suggests a proper "direction for program development" but should not be construed as establishing "black-and-white expectations" for viewers: "There are not going to be hard and fast rules," he added.[31] The family-hour culture wars flared anew with CBS's short-lived *$#*! My Dad Says* (2010). Fuming at the vulgarity encoded in its title, media critic Jeff McCall lambasted it as "a poke in the eye for that large part of society that is, indeed, concerned about the role television plays in our national culture. Our culture has coarsened, of course, but that is in no small part because of television redefining acceptable standards."[32] Responding to such cultural pressures, the cable network ABC Family was renamed Freeform in 2015, in large part to escape the moral standards implied by its name. This domestic appellation was undercut through numerous controversial and sexually daring programs such as *Pretty Little Liars* (2010–17), which features teen girls as its protagonists in a variety of sexually suggestive and murderously vengeful scenarios.[33] As Emily Yahr notes in a *Washington Post* article whose title captures her exasperation—"*Pretty Little Liars*: When Will the Show Stop with Its Creepy Underage Relationships?"—this program "has always been a disturbing teen drama, the kind that makes people say 'It's on ABC *Family*?'"[34]

As these recurring controversies over the family hour from the 1970s to the 2010s indicate, the queer fantasy of family-friendly programming has proved resilient, for it continues to haunt discussions of television programming and its protocols. Many viewers believed then—and continue to believe now—that the legacy networks and certain cable channels should air programs consistent with the nebulous parameters of "family values" during this time slot, and they often expect that the contents of this hour should reflect their personal sense of morality. With the rise of children's networks in the 1980s and 1990s, primarily Nickelodeon and Disney Channel, many parents expected the original programming on these channels to adhere to family-friendly protocols as well, only to be surprised by their occasionally candid depictions of teen sexuality. Further confusing the fantasy of family-friendly programming, the legacy and cable networks, when it appears financially advantageous to do so, often highlight their kid-friendly fare, thereby reminding viewers of yesteryear's code and its spectral descendants to which they do not formally adhere.

Beyond the financial motivations of the networks, ever-changing viewing habits have contributed to the erosion of family-friendly programming. As I have mentioned, during television's early days, most families gathered together to watch their single console, but as prices fell over the decades, households began owning multiple sets, with viewing fragmenting along age lines: "Kids are watching something in their room, and parents are watching something else in *their* room," noted media analyst Betsy Frank, which resulted in the further fragmentation of advertising demographics.[35] Moreover, with the explosion of cable networks in the 1990s and 2000s, and with the rise of Internet entertainment and viewing devices such as electronic pads, audiences have increasingly segregated themselves not merely by the programs they watch but by the channels or websites to which they turn. A cherished illusion throughout TV's history, the fantasy of family-friendly programming continues to pervade discussions of network programming and its suitability for audiences of all ages—even when a given sitcom evinces little interest in appealing to "innocent" young viewers, who some believe must be protected from the culture around them. Family-friendly programming, a fantasy rendered queer through the impossibility of its call for children's eternal innocence, cannot fully inoculate programs from the surrounding culture, nor can it quarantine children from that which they cannot be quarantined: themselves.

The Queer Fantasy of Innocent Children

"And if you are going to take a stand, perhaps the best one possible is the one good for the child." I picked this quotation virtually at random, knowing that I would need someone to make this point as I wrote this book, knowing that someone would oblige, for various politicians, pundits, and cultural commentators are always defending their viewpoints through an appeal to pathos predicated on the image of the child.[36] In the realm of family sitcoms, such pleas are parodied in the repeated cries of Helen Lovejoy on *The Simpsons*—"Oh-h-h, won't somebody please think of the children?" ("Much Apu about Nothing")—always with the objective of winning whatever argument is at hand. For who can argue against children, against children's needs, against children's innocence? When we think of children, we think of the cultural fantasy of children—young, fresh-faced naïfs in need of parental and community guidance to nurture them into adolescence and then adulthood—an often true yet strikingly simplistic assessment of their maturation process. Of course, this is not to deny the obvious fact that children require nurture, support, and affection during their upbringing and that the category "children" represents real human beings. At the same time, the children examined in this study are fictional characters who, by the very fact of their design to fit into a commercial entertainment product and thus to generate revenue, advance particular ideological fantasies of childhood. Similar to race, sex, and sexual orientation, children and childhood reflect an unremarkable condition, yet these cultural markers often become the defining, if not overriding, aspect of a young person's identity. "Childhood is thus to a considerable degree a function of adult expectations," opines historian Colin Heywood.[37] Furthermore, the concepts of children and childhood in Western culture have radically shifted over the centuries, which highlights the ways in which children must live their lives at the intersection of their biological reality and cultural constructions of what they represent. Within a television show's story lines, children *always* serve as cultural scripts that illuminate how and why they are so constructed and to what ends they are deployed: there is no "real child" in a fictional program. The ideological construction of the Child overwrites children's individuality, amalgamating them into an undifferentiated collective in need of nurture and protection—and often, as Helen Lovejoy's cry attests, through sentimentally moralistic appeals on their behalf.

In this regard, children's sexual innocence is not an inherently natural state of human development but a collective fantasy that attempts to protect and regulate the social order. Gary Cross and David Buckingham, in their groundbreaking studies of children's depictions in various cultural texts, argue that children's innocence merely cloaks adults' need of children's innocence for their own designs. Cross avows, "The child increasingly has borne the obligation of imposing cultural standards on a society that is at war with itself over such standards. . . . Sheltering innocence may be more about the deep moral conflicts among adults than the needs of children."[38] For Buckingham, the figure of the Child, in its role as a signifier of social innocence, demarcates normative behaviors and pleasures for adults: "The idea of childhood serves as a repository for qualities which adults regard both as precious and as problematic—qualities which they cannot tolerate as part of themselves; yet it can also serve as a dream world into which we retreat from the pressures and responsibilities of maturity."[39] Childhood innocence stands as virtually an unquestioned social good, for innocence's opposite is guilt, and who wants a guilty child? Here again the faulty logic of binaries reveals itself, for the opposite of innocence need not be guilt but instead knowledge, awareness, or simply comprehension. Preserving children's innocence on television, however, requires regulating adult actions, including those of the producers, actors, and consumers of television programs straitjacketed by network censors demanding a rigorous submission to normative codes of social and sexual behavior and the nebulous parameters of "family-friendly programming." Coded with so many conflicting and variant meanings, the fictional children of numerous narratives often ironically emerge as queer figures who highlight, rather than dampen, the tensions of depicting their eternal innocence.

Family sitcoms with young children in their casts construct these characters as they are needed for their narratives, yet the child actors selected for these roles inevitably mature, thus continually testing the foundations of youthful innocence on which a given program is built. Moreover, as much as the producers of a family sitcom might prefer for their show to resist evolving in order to generate more episodes and greater profits, these programs by necessity must recognize the maturing bodies of their child actors in their story lines. The jokes and plots appropriate for five- or six-year-old children, including both actors and audience members, will no longer be appropriate when they turn ten or eleven and will be even less so when they turn fifteen or sixteen. Live-action family sitcoms thus face the conundrum of seeking the stasis of their narrative frameworks while also acknowledging that the child actors and child viewers jointly responsible for their success will one day outgrow their current interests—and more so, outgrow their current bodies—as they proceed into adolescence and beyond. As producer Dan Guntzelman of *Growing Pains* and *Just the Ten of Us* (1988–90) explains, "Most successful sitcoms have a life of five, six, or seven years, then the pressures start to mount: Actors want to move on, the show gets top heavy. (How many executive producers does it take to screw in a light bulb? About 10 in the fifth year of a series.) A family sitcom has an even greater incentive. (Kids grow up and there goes the family.)"[40] No television family can fully resist the ravages of time, which is registered in the faces of even the youngest stars.

In the annals of American television history *The Adventures of Ozzie and Harriet* most successfully navigated this challenge in its fourteen-year run, whereas many other popular family sitcoms—including *Diff'rent Strokes* (1978–86), *Silver Spoons* (1982–87), *Punky Brewster* (1984–88), *Full House*, and *Home Improvement* (1991–99)—ended after about five to eight years, when their child stars were no longer children. In contrast, an animated program like *The Simpsons*, which has run more than twenty-five seasons and shows little sign of imminent cancellation, demonstrates the elasticity available to a family sitcom whose members will never mature beyond their current ages: Bart, Lisa, and Maggie look and act the same today as they did during their first season in 1989. Furthermore, as their child actors grow and their ratings sag, numerous family sitcoms have attempted to generate renewed interest and a ratings bump by introducing young cast members, as did *The Brady Bunch* with Cousin Oliver (Robbie Rist), *Family Ties* (1982–89) with Andy (Brian Bonsall), and *Growing Pains* with Luke (Leonardo DiCaprio)—a ploy rarely successful but that evinces a desire for the stasis and popularity of the past, as well as its impossibility as time passes and children grow.

Children's innocence may appear to be a timeless value—or, more precisely, its advocates attempt to present it as a timeless value—yet images of children's innocence have shifted remarkably within television's relatively short history, which further adumbrates the queer potential of the child. Today no television program would depict a naked child, yet young Buffy Peterson-Davis (Anissa Jones) is shown naked from the waist up while preparing for her bath in *Family Affair* (1966–71; "Jody and Cissy"), and when demonstrating where she received her vaccines, she lifts her skirt and reveals her bare buttocks ("The Matter of School"; see figs. I.1 and I.2). In the 1960s a nude child simply represented an innocent child, and these shots of Buffy call to mind photographs of unclothed toddlers in family photo albums of the era. From the 1980s onward, in the wake of the numerous child molestation scandals involving the Catholic Church and the Boy Scouts of America, including as well the notorious McMartin preschool trial, a naked child has become the intolerable vision of a molested child.[41] Television of more recent vintage might display infants' behinds, such as when Jesse and Joey bathe baby Michelle in *Full House* ("Our Very First Show") or in *Everybody Loves Raymond* when Ray and Debra bathe

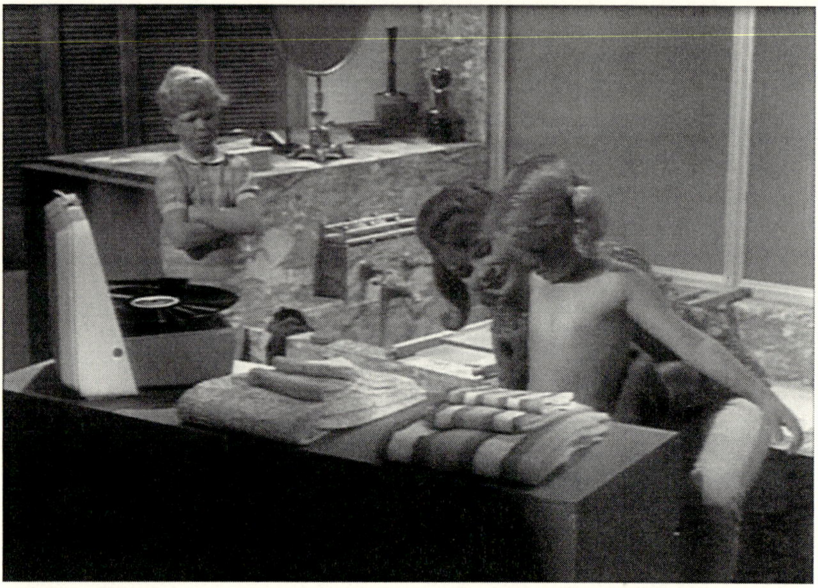

FIGURES I.1 AND I.2 Innocent or perverse? Children's nudity registers the fluid vision of cultural innocence, as these images of Buffy in *Family Affair* attest. Unremarkable in their day, these images, or ones similar to them, simply do not appear in today's family sitcoms.

their twin infant sons, but notably, not their kindergarten-age daughter, Allie ("I Love You"). In this light, Buffy's nudity highlights the ways in which depictions of childhood innocence alter according to changing cultural and historical circumstances and thus also the queer ways in which family sitcoms construct children to mark their narrative space as concomitantly innocent, despite the semiotic instability of children to achieve this goal.

Beyond this semiotic instability of the figure of the child, many young actors in family sitcoms do not want to be seen merely as children, realizing that typecasting will jeopardize their future careers. Thus, as these actors mature, many take on sexually provocative roles or discuss their sex lives candidly in an attempt to cast aside the mantle of childhood. As the ensuing chapters address, Eve Plumb from *The Brady Bunch*, Lisa Bonet from *The Cosby Show*, and Miley Cyrus from *Hannah Montana* took on risky, sexually frank roles to shed their good-girl images. Also, numerous child actors who have faded from public view exploit the titillation factor of child stars growing up into sexually active adults. Frank Bank, who played "Lumpy" Rutherford on *Leave It to Beaver*, titles a chapter of his autobiography "Speaking of Lots of Beaver,"[42] and Dustin Diamond, who played Samuel "Screech" Powers on *Saved by the Bell* (1989–93), employs a similar tactic in his tell-all account of the show, with such chapters as "I'm Going to Disneyland . . . To Get Laid" and "Screech Is a Born Cougar Hunter."[43] Family-sitcom innocence can curtail a young actor's career, whereas sexually charged roles demand audiences to see these stars anew—thereby displaying the utility of sexuality in rebranding a young star's celebrity persona. In both instances, sexuality defines a given actor's career arc, with the lost aura of youthful innocence influencing casting directors' perceptions of their appropriateness for more mature roles.

Beyond these issues surrounding child characters and child actors in family sitcoms emerge similar concerns circulating around the children in their audiences. Commentators have long fretted over children's exposure to the media, whether through their tendency to overindulge in its pleasures or to select inappropriate fare. Marie Winn's *The Plug-In Drug* advises parents to "make their children's childhood a rich and distinctive experience, one that will serve as a resource for the rest of their lives"—and to accomplish this objective by putting "television under control."[44] Even educational children's fare raises its own set of dilemmas, similar to those bedeviling family sitcoms, as Brian Simpson observes: "Children's programming, it is said, must be 'educational and informational,' although few can agree on what this means. Quality programming seems to be desirable, yet commercial broadcasters bemoan the difficulty of producing such programming in a commercially viable manner."[45] Further along these lines, many critics castigate television shows for modeling antisocial behavior yet without paying sufficient attention to the structures of narratology that require some type of conflict to motivate a plot. In her analysis of sibling relationships in sitcoms, Mary Strom Larson documents that "very few examples of the support and loyalty described as key elements in siblingship exist. The sitcom siblings observed do not appear to illustrate [the] claim that television tells viewers 'families are the best things we've got.'"[46] Siblings arguing with one another is immediately recognizable as the basic structure of a plot; children getting along together, however much parents might wish for it in their personal lives, makes for less compelling television. Even the children of the homey families of the 1950s disagree with one another—sometimes rather violently—more often than nostalgia might lead one to believe.

In sum, the queer fantasies of the family sitcom, of family-friendly programming, and of children themselves establish protocols of viewing that, through their inevitable self-contradictions, frequently corrupt creators' and viewers' attempts to circumscribe their cultural meaning as insistently guileless. This is not, of course, to argue that all family sitcoms cloak within their narrative structure a flouting of ideological codes of normativity, for a large share of these programs are truly as innocuous as one would presume. At the same time, a successful family sitcom can run for more than two hundred episodes, with numerous producers, directors, and writers all contributing their unique visions—and their unique subversions—of the genre's prevailing surface of innocence. So family sitcoms have a queer story to tell about sexuality in the United States of America as the decades have passed, with their insistent innocence camouflaging deeper investments in questioning the cultural meaning of family, as the following chapters attest. To see family sitcoms as an ultimately queer genre is to reconceive America's conception of itself, as portrayed through its defining television programs, in light of these programs' impossible innocence and conflicting depictions of sexuality's significance to the domestic sphere.

Few families can claim the outer trappings of heteronormativity as clearly as the Cleavers of *Leave It to Beaver*, a program that reigns in the American consciousness as emblematic of 1950s innocence. Yet time itself is rendered queer in the program's construction of its backstory and of its narrative present, with further queerness anticipated in its future reception in syndication. Chapter 1, "The Queer Times of *Leave It to Beaver*: Beaver's Present, Ward's Past, and June's Future," questions the assumptions of chrononormative television criticism that attempts to pin programs down as representatives of their eras. Instead, this chapter posits the queer possibilities inherent in Beaver's troubled assumption of masculine adolescence, in Ward's traumatic childhood of abuse and its lingering aftereffects, and in June's iconic domesticity that actress Barbara Billingsley subsequently transmuted into an ironic acknowledgment of the era's feminine discontents. The Cleavers' latent queerness dismantles viewers' understanding of the past and its supposed innocence, for innocence stands as a cultural marker invariably undone by time's inevitable contradictions.

Moving from the Cleavers to the Bradys, chapter 2, "Queer Innocence and Kitsch Nostalgia in *The Brady Bunch*," ponders the impossibility of eternal innocence in depicting the Child, even the Brady children. *The Brady Bunch* is often seen as television's last gasp of innocence before the 1970s ushered in an era of frank portrayals of sexuality and other controversial topics, yet it cannot free itself from the temporal culture in which it is set. In this light, *The Brady Bunch*'s innocence is rendered queer, for in its production and reception it often broached the possibility of eroticism that its story lines appeared so strenuously to deny. This chapter also examines the numerous rebirths of the Brady family following the sitcom's cancellation in 1974, particularly the television movie *A Very Brady Christmas* (1988) and the dramedy *The Bradys* (1990). These efforts appeal to the sense of kitsch nostalgia that many *Brady* fans bring to this program—for it has proved remarkably resilient and enduringly popular in syndication and in its multiple relaunches—yet sexuality complicates these efforts as well, for it reestablishes the impossibility of the innocence on which the Bradys' attraction lies.

Among the myriad family sitcoms in television history, few invite such divergent readings as *The Cosby Show*, which has been both exalted as a pioneering achievement in portraying African American families and denigrated as insufficiently invested in relaying the challenges that blacks face in a land still grappling with slavery's legacy and the enduring threat of racism. In "No Sex Please, We're African American: *The Cosby Show*'s Queer Fear of Black Sexuality," my analysis turns to the ways in which critics' varying responses to the program highlight the obstacles to representing blackness on television. In this groundbreaking program, Cosby's efforts to present a new model of androgynous fatherhood clashed with concerns over depictions of teen sexuality, to the extent that patriarchal privilege reasserts itself in the sitcom's investment in the Huxtable children's virginities. These issues flared beyond the purview of their shared sitcom when Cosby and teen actress Lisa Bonet clashed over her career choices, particularly her decision to star in the racy film *Angel Heart* (1987), with this backstage drama treated in the popular press as if it were a family squabble. Moreover, the numerous allegations of rape and sexual misconduct that have dogged Cosby decades after the show's successful run demonstrate the ways in which shifts in viewers' perceptions of actors influence the reception of their programs. Cosby's progressive vision of paternity ultimately founders against both the program's insistently innocent depiction of teen sexuality and the metanarrative controversies surrounding its stars, thus demonstrating the destabilizing intersection of race and heterosexuality when innocence can no longer be maintained as an anchoring fiction.

In its stinging economic rebuttal to the homey comforts depicted in numerous family sitcoms, Roseanne Barr's *Roseanne* embraced a gritty, blue-collar ethos coupled with frank treatments of sexuality. Feminism, economics, and various sexual issues (including abortion, pornography, homosexuality, and premarital teen sex) converge in this program, and chapter 4, "Feminism, Homosexuality, and Blue-Collar Perversity in *Roseanne*," explores the ways in which Barr uses sexuality to dismantle the economic ethos of 1980s Reagan Republicanism. Television's treatments of sexuality are implicated with economics in various, often overlooked, ways, yet *Roseanne* consistently foregrounds how financial constraints compel its characters to consider the repercussions of their sexual desires. With story lines addressing Roseanne's gay friends Nancy and Leon, her mother Bev's coming out as a lesbian, and her daughters' sexual relationships with their boyfriends, as well as with Barr's decision to cast lesbian Sandra Bernhard and porn star Traci Lords in her family sitcom, *Roseanne* stresses the potential of women's sexuality to allow an escape from the moribund present of a faltering, antiunion economy. Queerness, as enacted through disruptive sexualities, thus mitigates oppressive ideological forces, allowing teen and adult women to assert their economic, as well as erotic, desires.

Chapter 5, "Allegory, Queer Authenticity, and Marketing Tween Sexuality in *Hannah Montana*," examines the adventures of dorky adolescent Miley Stewart and her alter ego, pop sensation Hannah Montana—as well as their exploits in marketing with star Miley Cyrus. The tween market has exploded since the 1990s and 2000s, with advertisers directing their pitches directly to these young consumers. The age-old advertising mantra that "sex sells" faces the complication of camouflaging sexuality in this tale of a girl-next-door pop princess, as it also seeks to glamorize her life through a steady stream of cute beaux. By stressing Miley's authenticity (despite the irony of stressing the authenticity of a character with a secret identity), *Hannah Montana* creates the character as a trustworthy marketing icon while simultaneously preparing young viewers for Cyrus's post-*Hannah* metamorphosis into a sexually provocative pop star. The duality of Miley Stewart's everyday life and of Hannah Montana's celebrity extravagance is mirrored in the duality of Cyrus's role as actress in a tween sitcom and as herself, in which the authenticity she claims in her multiple roles shields her from any repercussions for discarding her persona of childhood innocence. Emerging as an increasingly forceful advocate of queer rights, as well as a personal avatar of queer desire, Cyrus has exploited the foundational assumption of family sitcom innocence to launch new visions of herself as an eternally protean star.

In its depiction of the intersecting lives of the Pritchetts, Tucker-Pritchetts, and Dunphys, *Modern Family* introduced a gay couple to the dynamics of the family sitcom, as partners Mitch and Cam adopt Lily, a Vietnamese orphan, in the program's pilot. Many viewers have criticized the program's tame treatment of the men's relationship, and chapter 6, "Conservative Narratology, Queer Politics, and the Humor of Gay Stereotypes in *Modern Family*," explores the ramifications of this charge of an ultimately reactionary aspect of the sitcom's treatment of same-sex desire. By bending the expected protocols of sitcom moralism, *Modern Family* restages the ostensibly conservative narratology of the form precisely through its investment in stereotype-based humor. Furthermore, by repeatedly depicting the ways in which assumptions of heteronormativity founder against the intransigent stagings of anal eroticism, *Modern Family* posits the impossibility of tamping unruly and queer desires within the family unit, rendering the family an open site of queerness that earlier models of the sitcom tried so strenuously to hide.

My conclusion, "Tolstoy Was Wrong; or, On the Queer Reception of Television's Happy Families," surveys the ways in which the family sitcom is an oft-disparaged genre yet surmounts the inherent difficulty of portraying narrative happiness—in contrast to the lion's share of literary, cinematic, and television portrayals of familial conflict. Yes, most domestic sitcoms are predicated on the premise of normatively happy families, but, as *The Queer Fantasies of the American Family Sitcom* demonstrates, representing their happiness in narrative and on television requires endless negotiations about the meaning of the family unit in their sociotemporal setting and in their sexual politics. The conclusion also posits multiple reasons for the family sitcom's degraded status as an inferior genre; by theorizing from Pierre Bourdieu's critique of aesthetics, it suggests how the form creates lasting pleasures through diachronic readings, both naive and intellectual, that enable multiple and variant queer spectatorships. In constructing purportedly normative families, these programs create interpretive spaces for queer viewers and, at least potentially, create queer pleasures for ostensibly normative viewers as well. Assessing American family sitcoms as cheerily normative necessitates overlooking the contradictions at their heart, which thus highlights the utility of queerly viewing this genre throughout its history in order to recognize its aporias, gaps, and fissures.

Collectively, these chapters trace the ways in which sexuality and queerness can never be banished from family sitcoms but instead percolate throughout various story lines that attempt to quell their disruptive force. Also, as is apparent from these chapter overviews, my purpose is to examine the significance of sex in relation to a host of other ideological issues, each of which is addressed in the constituent chapters: time's queer potential and the limitations of chrononormative interpretations for *Leave It to Beaver*; the queerness of children's innocence and the threat of sexuality to nostalgia for *The Brady Bunch*; the struggle to represent American blackness and teen sexuality for *The Cosby*

Show; the blue-collar pessimism following Reaganomics and the disruptive force of female and queer desire for *Roseanne*; the power of marketing in creating an erotically innocent yet sexually invested tween audience for *Hannah Montana*; and the difficulties of representing queer normativity for *Modern Family* as gay Americans were achieving marital equality in the 2010s. I employ deep readings of these six programs—a curated collection of the genre—to exemplify profound shifts in the depiction of American domesticity, and I discuss additional programs to better contextualize their contributions to television's legacy. Through this combined focus—a particular show in depth, with insights gleaned from its contemporaries—we see through these chapters the development of the American family sitcom during milestone moments in its history and its long-standing challenges with confronting sexuality.[47]

These chapters also illustrate the complexity of sitcom criticism due to three distinct yet overlapping concerns: the interplays of these programs' surfaces (e.g., plots, story lines, characters) and their symptomologies (e.g., narrative structure, ideological blind spots, silences, and other lacunae); the interpretive ambiguity of comic texts; and the variant effects of television's inherent flow. Stephen Best and Sharon Marcus distinguish between surface and symptomatic readings, outlining their import for critical practice: "a surface is what insists upon being looked *at* rather than what we trust ourselves to see *through*," while a symptomatic reading seeks "absences, gaps, and ellipses in texts, and then ask[s] what those absences mean, what forces create them, and how they signify the questions that motivate the text, but that the text itself cannot articulate."[48] The tension between surfaces and symptoms raises challenging interpretive questions: at what point do symptoms overtake surfaces? When, if ever, should symptomatic readings be construed as misreadings rather than readings of the televisual texts at hand? No text can account for all possible story lines that might be addressed or characters that might be included; all texts must have absences, so at what point must a narrative assume responsibility for any symptomatic (mis)interpretations it generates? Successful sitcoms offer so much surface—at the low end of this study, *Hannah Montana* consists of 99 episodes, whereas *Leave It to Beaver* consists of 235—yet they also feature a recurrent symptomology of an approximately twenty-four-minute narrative dramatizing a humorous misadventure of family life, one that ultimately ends with the family unit preserved. *The Queer Fantasies of the American Family Sitcom* cannot resolve the surface-versus-symptom debate as it relates to television criticism, yet it advances the discussion by considering the tension inherent in sexuality both as surface and as symptom: sexuality frequently appears on the screen, but it is also hidden to protect the fantasy of children's innocence, so it lies within a program's queer symptomology as well.

The comedy intrinsic to family sitcoms similarly muddies interpretive clarity, with humor functioning both on the surface and within the symptomology of these narratives. To look at one such example, in Mary Tyler Moore's indelible performances as Mary Richards in *The Mary Tyler Moore Show* (1970–77), viewers can see either a breakthrough depiction of an independent, career woman or a regressive caricature of feminism's failures, one who frequently turns to her boss, Lou Grant (Ed Asner), for guidance with her trademark whimper, "Oh-h-h-h, Mr. Grant." Debates about comedy's ideological meaning teeter between celebrations of its liberatory flair and laments of its regressive force, as does the necessity of distinguishing between laughing *at* and laughing *with* various characters.[49] With a text as multifaceted as *The Mary Tyler Moore Show*, viewers can laugh at or with Mary Richards, enjoy the surface liberatory pleasures of her story lines or regret their regressive symptomology, or position themselves along a continuum privileging surface over symptom, or vice versa, or combine these pleasures complementarily. One finds repeatedly in the annals of television scholarship a critic tilting the interpretive balance in favor of a program's surface or of its symptomology to generate a convincing interpretation, or suggesting that a program's humor strips it of any deeper significance, yet a more compelling complexity arises when one views surface and symptom working in tandem, if not always in harmony, along with the comedy that the genre foregrounds.

Television's flow—its segmentation, framing, structure, scheduling, and other such shifts—further complicates the process of interpreting its narratives, for this concept challenges viewers to identify which elements of a program and of its broadcasting influence its reception. Raymond Williams famously defined television's flow: "What is being offered is not, in older terms, a programme of discrete units with particular insertions, but a planned flow, in which the true series is not the published sequence of programme items but this sequence transformed by the inclusion of another kind of sequence, so that these sequences together compose the real flow, the real 'broadcasting.'"[50] Since this term entered the critical lexicon in 1974, the experience of viewing television has changed dramatically, particularly with the explosion of networks and channels, the rise of streaming services, and various other technological innovations, such that William Uricchio argues that "the changing status of the term [*flow*], and particularly the criticism it generated, needs to be seen against the changing 'regime of representations' of television."[51] Television's flow demands that audiences recognize the difficulties of removing a particular episode or series from its paratexts and paratechnologies, for these elements inevitably affect how it is consumed. At the risk of personalizing this critical concept, I believe it is also necessary to extend television's flow to account for the periods of one's personal viewing history, for not only do television's technological iterations affect the perception of a program, but so, too, do the shifts in identity registered in the individuals consuming television programs—a likelihood given that viewers might watch the same show over several decades of their lives. Without ceding humanity to cyborg status, we are nonetheless viewing "technologies" ourselves, ones whose abilities to decode narratives are never stable. John Ellis cautions that "flow assembles disparate items, placing them within the same experience, but does not organize them to produce an overall meaning," with his words an apt reminder of the potential pitfalls in interpreting a televisual text that can never elude the currents of flow through which it is consumed.[52] *Flow* remains one of the more elliptical terms of television analysis—for some, it is "more of a critical provocation than a coherent analytical method"[53]—yet at the very least, it reminds viewers that, reminiscent of Marshall McLuhan, the medium affects the message.[54]

In gauging the play between surfaces and symptoms, between comedy and its interpretive discontents, and between stable texts and texts in flow, as further mediated through the lens of America's vexed relationship with sexuality, this book advances a critical understanding of these compelling, multifaceted texts that have helped to constitute the meaning of family for the wider American culture. The Cleavers, Bradys, Huxtables, Conners, Stewarts, and Pritchetts, Tucker-Pritchetts, and Dunphys have allowed America to see itself and to see itself changing, all the while obscuring the meaning of sexuality for families who may not yet have broached this essential yet vexed subject with their children. Quinn Miller calls for queer television criticism that "addresses the instability of common beliefs and binary logics of identity and difference," adding that "queer analysis of TV changes the way we see conventional representations in past eras and cultural history as a whole" by "illuminating unexpected challenges to straight conventions and spaces of non-conformity within norms."[55] Here, too, the distinction between surface and symptom enlightens the queer dynamics of these texts, for *Leave It to Beaver*, *The Brady Bunch*, *The Cosby Show*, and *Hannah Montana* depict a surface innocence continually undone by deeper symptomatic investments, whereas *Roseanne* and *Modern Family* forthrightly address sexuality in their story lines while infusing their symptomology with the pleasures of ostensible perversities. From these contrasting perspectives, it is evident that sex builds multiple, contradictory, and ultimately queer meanings in family sitcoms, for its disruptive force pervades even the most cheekily innocent of American families—as truly it must, if these families, fictional or factual, were ever to be conceived.

Queer readings of American family sitcoms prove the lie of domestic normativity in the past while highlighting the continuing challenges of queer representation in the present. They shift our perceptions of programs, characters, and actors shielded behind the patina of normativity and offer fresh, sometimes startling, insights into the duplicities of ideology and its blinkered presentation of identities deemed nonnormative. For many viewers, the beloved family sitcoms of their childhood continue to hold lasting appeal, often for the innocence they convey of simpler times, in the eternal nostalgic search for the Golden Age of the American Family. Denuding this fantasy as a fantasy—indeed, as the intersection of multiple fantasies of genre, marketing, and childhood itself—delivers a sharper vision of American self-construction and its discontents for a range of viewers simultaneously attracted to but alienated from these paragons of domesticity. Queering family sitcoms, in the end, allows a truer vision of the American family to emerge, one that represents, ironically and paradoxically, the many families left unrepresented.

1

The Queer Times of *Leave It to Beaver*

Beaver's Present, Ward's Past, and June's Future

Television entered mainstream American culture in the 1950s, with the queer fantasies of the family sitcom genre, family-friendly programming, and the preternaturally innocent child emerging along with it. Within the field of television studies, American family sitcoms of the 1950s and early 1960s, in their shared depictions of smiling clans populating suburban Edens, have long been viewed as sugar-coated fare divorced from the era's gendered, racial, and socioeconomic discontents. Such readings, accurate in the main, nonetheless whitewash the genre's and the era's complexity, inculcating a de facto presumption of heteronormativity that brooks little room for dissent. Time's ostensible linearity obscures its deeper meanings, with the chimerical illusion of forward progress masking history's inevitable contradictions. *Leave It to Beaver* (1957–63) exemplifies the gentle respectability of the 1950s nuclear family as portrayed on America's televisions, yet when one allows for the queerness of time in framing its characters, Beaver, Ward, and June emerge both as representatives of a 1950s suburban bubble and as characters impossible to contain within it. With the program ranging across the past of Ward's backstory, the present of Beaver's gendered misadventures, and into the future of June's role as a cultural icon, fleeting yet intriguing visions of familial queerness coalesce, collectively dismantling assumptions about the stifling sexual politics of television's early years.

Certainly, the 1950s occupy a privileged position in the American imaginary: prosperity reigned in the years following World War II as veterans returned home and built a suburban paradise, with President Dwight D. Eisenhower presiding over a nation expanding its international influence. Such are the lessons that the gospel of 1950s nostalgia preaches, and in many ways this nostalgia defines the decade, as Jean Baudrillard affirms: "The fifties were the real high spot for the US ('when things were going on'), and you can still feel the nostalgia for those years, for the ecstasy of power, when power held power."[1] Fredric Jameson, while acknowledging the decade's allure, complicates this vision by stressing how its televisual portrayals in effect created its legacy: "This is clearly, however, to shift from the realities of the 1950s to the representation of that rather different thing, the 'fifties,' a shift which obligates us in addition to underscore the cultural sources of all the attributes with which we have endowed the period, many of which seem very precisely to derive from its own television programs; in other words, its own representation of itself."[2] These images created enduring stereotypes of American families: white, comfortably (upper) middle class, and happily ensconced in the suburbs. Stephanie Coontz, concurring with Jameson's view, believes that television programs define the decade for many: "Our most powerful visions of traditional families derive from images that are still delivered to our homes in countless reruns of 1950s television sit-coms."[3] As she further demonstrates, however, this vision of the 1950s white, suburban family itself represents a historical anomaly, one that arose in response to a host of demographic factors, including younger ages for marriage and motherhood and increased fertility (and thus the advent of the baby boom generation).[4] Nostalgia defines many viewers' relationship to 1950s television, no matter the rose-colored glasses necessary to overlook the period's numerous problems, particularly the secondary status of women and racial minorities and the destructive silence enveloping GLBT people.

But as much as we may think we know the 1950s, any attempt to define a period inevitably falls to the impossibility of capturing a zeitgeist beyond its roughest contours. As several queer theorists have recently explored, time is often (mis)used to crudely construct a blanket sense of historical normativity that hides the varieties of existence within, and resistance to, a given era. Elizabeth Freeman questions the tyranny of "chrononormativity," which she eloquently defines as "the interlocking temporal schemes necessary for genealogies of descent and for the mundane workings of domestic life," and which she expands to include "the use of time to organize individual human bodies toward maximum productivity."[5] Chrononormativity presumes that humans will accede into dominant ideological regimes, particularly those of gender, sexuality, and social class, yet such a process is almost inevitably rendered queer through the contortions of identity essential for propagating normality. Recognizing history's weight and time's gossamer reach, Carolyn Dinshaw calls for "the possibility of a fuller, denser, more crowded *now* that all sorts of theorists tell us is extant but that often eludes our temporal grasp."[6] This concept of a *now* suffused with moments beyond its immediate passing subverts the facile view of time's linearity and complicates efforts to determine the meaning of narratives whose span includes the historical past from which they emerge, the contemporary present of their production, and the ensuing decades of their reception. Studies of television programs must urgently attend to the queer and queering ramifications of time, particularly because no program can be cordoned off solely to its years of production but by necessity must engage with the past (both in its creation and in its backstories) and with the future (in its always shifting reception). Dismantling simplistic assumptions of chrononormativity, television's inherent flow challenges the linearity of time through the multitudinous temporal construction perpetually in play in watching a given program.

Leave It to Beaver, in its crosscuttings of temporality, testifies both to the allure of chrononormativity and to its ultimate limitations. The program adheres to the core structures of the family sitcom: father Ward (Hugh Beaumont) and mother June (Barbara Billingsley) live comfortably and contentedly with their sons, Wally (Tony Dow) and Theodore "the Beaver" (Jerry Mathers), in a suburban hamlet where together they confront the gentle challenges of growing up. In each episode, one character errs and consequently learns an important lesson, with Beaver often, but by no means always, filling this role. During the series' six seasons, Wally and Beaver mature, with the program concluding as they respectively prepare to enter college and high school. But as Kathryn Bond Stockton so ably demonstrates, children do not "grow up"—with the implicit heteronormative assumption of "growing up straight"—as much as they "grow sideways": "'Growing sideways' suggests that the width of a person's experience or ideas, their motives or their motions, may pertain at any age, bringing 'adults' and 'children' into lateral contact of surprising sorts. This kind of growth is made especially palpable . . . by (the fiction of) the ghostly gay child—the publicly impossible child whose identity *is* a deferral (sometimes powerfully and happily so) and an act of growing sideways, by virtue of its *future retroaction* as a child."[7] Stockton focuses on the "ghostly gay child" in her analysis, yet the apparently stultifying innocence of 1950s domestic sitcoms obscures the necessity to consider the "ghostly straight child"—one who navigates an intriguingly queer journey to heterosexuality. In this regard, families that appear bastions of sexual normativity often merely camouflage their underlying queerness.

Further along these lines, *Leave It to Beaver* portrays Beaver on the edge of queerness, such that Ward frequently voices concern over his son's sexual development. Yet as much as Beaver represents the marginalized child growing sideways into heterosexuality, so, too, do Ward's clumsy efforts at child raising in the program's narrative present and the specters of parental abuse in his past frame his maturation as an ultimately queer process. While the series stresses Beaver's (and to a lesser extent, Wally's) maturation as its primary story line, its depictions of Ward hint at the possibility of his sideways growth from a battered childhood into a confused adulthood. In a similar vein, June Cleaver has been both lionized and vilified for the image of 1950s domesticity she embodies, yet Barbara Billingsley subverted June's chrononormative and nostalgic appeal in her later career by cagily and campily restaging the impossibility of this maternal ideal. As evident from these chinks in its late 1950s and early 1960s foundation of domestic respectability, *Leave It to Beaver* presents the Cleavers as an exemplary and wholesome family while tamping down the queer potential simmering underneath its suburban facade.

Chrononormativity and the 1950s Family Sitcom

Chrononormative readings of 1950s family sitcoms stress their patriarchal foundations, in which a wise, patient father and a nurturing, stay-at-home mother raise two or more cute children, with *The Adventures of Ozzie and Harriet* (1952–66), *Make Room for Daddy* (1953–65), and *Father Knows Best* (1954–60) modeling this paradigm. These programs depict family life as a harmonious ideal, with only the mildest disruptions to the family unit sparking an episode's plot. The narrative prominence of Ozzie Nelson, Danny Thomas's "Daddy" Danny Williams, and Robert Young's "Father" Jim Anderson registers in their show's titles, and, as Nina Leibman argues, various other televisual techniques maintain the spotlight on the father: "Dad's implicit power is rendered in the flow and content of familial conversation, in his omnipresence for both disciplinary and praise-giving occasions, in his frequent position at the center of the narrative, and in his visual and aural dominance."[8] Congruent with this perspective, Horace Newcomb observes that "domestic situation comedies . . . offered a soothing view of the traditional family, content with basic values of the home—warm, comforting, and designed along lines of gender authority";[9] David Halberstam posits that "the family sitcoms reflected—and reinforced—much of the social conformity of the period. There was no divorce. There was no serious sickness, particularly mental illness. Families *liked* each other, and they tolerated each other's idiosyncrasies."[10]

Leibman's, Newcomb's, and Halberstam's observations about the traditional structures of 1950s family sitcoms are realized throughout *Leave It to Beaver*: Ward benevolently rules the home from his book-lined study; June lovingly tends to her maternal duties in the kitchen; and although Beaver may angrily shout "rat, rat, rat!" at Wally during moments of pique (e.g., "Beaver's

Birthday," "Beaver's Electric Trains"), the vast majority of episodes feature the boys enjoying each other's company, despite their age difference.[11] One could quibble with Halberstam's statement that 1950s sitcoms eschew such topics as divorce and mental illness, for *Leave It to Beaver* tackles these themes in such episodes as "Beaver's House Guest" (in which Beaver's friend Chopper must deal with the emotional repercussions of his parents' divorce) and "Beaver and Andy" (in which Beaver realizes that the Cleavers' handyman suffers from alcoholism). Because the program condemns the former and sympathetically portrays those who struggle with the latter, the spirit of Halberstam's point holds, especially since both disruptions occur outside the family unit itself. Virtually every episode of *Leave It to Beaver* confirms Leibman's, Newcomb's, and Halberstam's readings of 1950s sitcoms, so it would be folly to deny the force—indeed, the accuracy—of chrononormative interpretations.

Further advancing this chrononormative perspective, the nostalgic vision of the 1950s as a time of suburban comfort and financial prosperity carries through in the period's sitcoms, imbuing them with an optimistic vision of America as a nation striving for ever greater heights. In his study of media depictions of America's suburbs, David Coon observes, "Family sitcoms from the 1950s and 1960s, such as *Leave It to Beaver* and *The Adventures of Ozzie and Harriet*, helped to develop an onscreen image of suburbia as a utopian space filled with desirable homes, happy families, and trouble-free lives,"[12] while Hal Himmelstein criticizes this utopic viewpoint: "Television's myth of the suburban middle landscape became an idealized representation of the quality of life of upwardly mobile white Americans divorced from the social infrastructure that allowed that mobility (we are inevitably upwardly mobile at another's expense)."[13] Within this 1950s celebration of the nation's wealth, *Leave It to Beaver* modestly concedes, but never trumpets, the Cleavers' financial comforts. June acknowledges the rise of the suburbs by referring to Levittown ("Larry's Club"), and one of the series' few story lines carrying over separate episodes depicts the family house-hunting for a larger residence (to which they have relocated in the third season's early episodes, with the boys curiously still sharing a bedroom). In a virtual ode to American prosperity, June soon reports that, according to a real estate agent, the Cleavers could sell their new home for a $10,000 profit ("The Spot Removers"). The program carefully maintains the Cleavers within the realm of the middle class—as Ward explains, "No, Beaver, we're not rich. We're what you might call 'comfortable'" ("Stocks and Bonds")—all the better to position them as a defining family of the era and thus to erase the divisions between America's social classes and any discontents they might foster among the program's viewers.

While many viewers appreciate *Leave It to Beaver* as a homey, happy time capsule from the 1950s, the program concomitantly announces its modernity.

Its creators present its characters not as relics of the past but as testaments to the changing times, and these themes frustrate chrononormative readings either steeped in nostalgia or lamenting the program's hidebound mores. Most significantly in this regard, despite current evaluations of Ward and June as an unrealistic and outmoded couple of the past, the program depicts their marriage and parenting as progressive and representative of the latest advances in gender relations. In her 1952 volume on child raising, Sidonie Matsner Gruenberg upholds the standard marital division of labor while also encouraging parents to share household responsibilities: "Many young couples realize that at some points the father has to be protected for his main job outside the home, but that at other times he has to protect and help the mother. When both feel responsible toward each other and to their common purpose, their cooperation is functional and flexible rather than set in a fixed pattern of sharply divided and arbitrarily assigned tasks."[14] Such sentiments were reinforced in the popular magazines of the day, such as Otis Lee Wiese's 1954 editorial in *McCall's* that trumpeted, "*Today women are not a sheltered sex*. . . . [Parents] are creating this new and warmer way of life not as women *alone* or men *alone*, isolated from one another, but as a *family* sharing a common experience."[15] So to judge Ward and June as exemplars of 1950s parenthood necessitates that one query the temporal standards on which such an evaluation rests: those of the program's present or those of today. At the very least, Ward and June's marriage appears in harmony with the progressive visions endorsed by Gruenberg and Wiese, thus encouraging viewers to see their relationship not as a regrettable relic of yesteryear but as a dynamic exemplar of shifting family responsibilities that had been even more sharply divided by gender in the past.

Throughout *Leave It to Beaver*, traditional gender roles and separate domestic spheres are maintained yet progressively expanded, as evident in the semiotic resignification of aprons. Ward often helps June wash the dishes, at times wearing an apron when doing so ("Eddie's Sweater"). From today's perspective such a concession registers as picayune to the point of meaninglessness, yet June's umbrage at the phrase "apron strings" indicates her impatience with maternal stereotypes:

> WARD: It's perfectly natural for a kid to want to get away from his mother's apron strings.
> JUNE: What do you mean—my apron strings?
> WARD: Nothing. That was a poor choice of words. ("Boarding School")

Aprons metonymically capture both the era's shifting gender roles and the crosscurrents in temporalities that undermine chrononormative readings of *Leave It to Beaver*. In this light, the program's various and contradictory episodes inevitably confirm Leibman's, Newcomb's, and Halberstam's views yet also open interpretive spaces to query rudimentary assumptions of the 1950s sitcom family's overarching normativity.

Along with shifting gender roles that laid the foundation for second-wave feminism in the 1960s, the 1950s was also a time of anxiety and excitement, particularly in regard to the Red Scare, the Space Race, and Cold War tensions with the Soviet Union. Responding to the challenges facing the nation, both Wally and Beaver announce their vocational ambitions in technology, thus establishing the boys as avatars not of yesteryear or even of the present but of the future: Wally aspires to be an electrical engineer and to work on missiles ("Beaver Becomes a Hero"), and Beaver plans his career as a "space scientist" ("Beaver the Caddy"). In another episode, Ward ironically chuckles of his son, "All right. I'll just have to settle for a nuclear scientist instead of an All-American halfback" ("Beaver the Athlete"), and June approvingly mentions the "scientific equipment" the boys have access to at school ("Lumpy Rutherford"). The Cleaver boys see their era as pushing impatiently into the future, such as when, in a promotional tag for the Boy Scouts, Wally praises the group: "They're really up to date." Beaver adds, commenting on the design of the Explorer's Handbook, "Yeah, kind of looks like a rocket ship taking off" ("The Grass Is Always Greener"). To look at *Leave It to Beaver* as a site of chrononormative nostalgia, then, is to overlook both its progressive investments in 1950s family structures and its enthusiasm for modernity and new possibilities, with this tension carrying over into its passing glances at evolving sexual mores and its anxieties over queer children.

Many chrononormative assessments of the 1950s remark on the era's presumed sexual innocence and ascribe the onset of sexual liberation to the 1960s, yet the 1950s planted the seeds of innocence's collapse and rebellion's rise. Joel Foreman, in the introduction to his volume *The Other Fifties: Interrogating Midcentury American Icons*, states his ambition to reorient views of this decade, so that "few Americans would . . . think of the 1950s as either simple, innocent, happy, unanimously supportive of a broad spectrum of beliefs, or radically separated from the 1960s by a culture of complacence."[16] During this decade, television audiences were frequently confronted with such miniscandals as Elvis Presley's hip-shaking performance on *The Ed Sullivan Show* (1948–71) and other rock-and-roll inspired exuberances, while juvenile delinquents were both denigrated as modern scourges and extolled as romantic antiheroes, particularly in the films of James Dean and Marlon Brando. Loosening the era's sexual mores, Hugh Hefner published the first issue of *Playboy* in December 1953, with its influence reverberating in contemporary sitcoms. *The Bob Cummings Show* (1955–59) stars Cummings as Bob Collins, a photographer of beautiful—if clothed—female models, with the program foregrounding his bachelor antics while contrasting his hedonism with his devoted family life, including his sister Margaret McDonald (Rosemary DeCamp) and her teen son, Chuck (Dwayne Hickman). Chuck marvels at his uncle's lifestyle and desires to emulate him, such as when, learning of Bob's absence, he pants, "His whole harem of beautiful models is unguarded!" ("Grandpa Moves West"). Hickman graduated from *The Bob Cummings Show* to the starring role in *The Many Loves of Dobie Gillis* (1959–63), in which adolescent Dobie single-mindedly pursues romance, as he explains in an opening monologue: "What bugs me is this—I like girls. What am I saying? I love girls. Love 'em! Beautiful, gorgeous, soft, round, creamy girls" ("Caper at the Bijou"). Dobie's indulgent mother and strict father alternatively encourage and hamper his exploits, yet their steady narrative presence maintains the loose structuring of a family sitcom, thus ensuring that the program does not devolve into a hedonistic ode to the emerging teen culture. With Bob Collins and Dobie Gillis, 1950s television merged the foundational premise of the family sitcom with these characters' pursuits of sexual conquests—a narrative tension that received increasing attention throughout the 1960s in a variety of family-oriented programs.

In line with the changing times and such adult- and teen-centered fare, *Leave It to Beaver* obliquely acknowledges shifting sexual standards, frequently through references to *The Many Loves of Dobie Gillis* that allow the latter's interest in teen sexuality to seep into the former's story lines. Beaver mentions Wally's attraction to actress Tuesday Weld, who played Dobie's crush Thalia Menninger ("Uncle Billy's Visit"), and Wally's dating life, with such passing romantic interests as Mary Ellen Rogers and Julie Foster, allows the program to stake its appeal to teen viewers and the rising baby boom culture. When June tells Beaver of a slang word ("keen") she used as a teenager, he snickers, "They don't even use that on *Dobie Gillis* anymore" ("One of the Boys"), with this telling swipe at a competing and higher-rated program ironically revealing producers' anxiety that *Leave It to Beaver* would lose its audience if it failed to keep up with the times. *Leave It to Beaver* also acknowledges cinema's increasingly risqué fare. Eddie Haskell asks if Wally is going to wear a homburg hat while attending a movie expressly for adults ("Wally's Glamour Girl")—a sly hint at stag films, with Eddie himself, in Darrell Hamamoto's phrasing, serving "as the necessary dramatic foil to the pure and noble sentiments of the Cleaver household."[17] When June looks in the newspaper for an appropriate film for the boys, she is surprised by the offerings at the local theater: "*Flowers of Spring*. Now that sounds like a happy picture. Oh dear . . . Adults only. Filmed in Sweden" ("Beaver's Old Buddy"). "Sweden"—virtually a synecdoche for erotic films, if not precisely for pornography—captures all that *Leave It to Beaver* cannot address yet nonetheless does, if only to reject it.

Such hints of America's shifting heterosexual mores do not necessitate that *Leave It to Beaver* would address homosexuality, and, a prevailing chrononormative assumption concerning early television asserts that homosexuality was rarely depicted onscreen. Again, while this simplistic assumption bears much merit, it erases the intriguing queer subcurrents in an array of programs, such as Milton Berle's crossdressing humor, Ernie Kovacs's mincing as Percy Dovetonsils (a telling caricature of Tennessee Williams and Truman Capote), and Liberace's own program and his frequent appearances on variety shows. Looking at the era's occluded yet surprisingly frequent depictions of gay characters and personalities, Amy Villarejo calls for a "more robust and rich sense of the queer [television] archive," citing as necessary interventions into popular culture's queer history such performers as Agnes Moorehead, Paul Lynde, and Nancy Kulp and such programs as *Private Secretary* (1953–57), *Our Miss Brooks* (radio 1948–57; television 1952–56), and even *Father Knows Best*.[18] Queer characters and queer actors played a significant role in television's history, yet one must look to the margins of their programs to find what lies hidden while standing in plain sight in order to undo the tyranny of chrononormativity.

Beaver's Queer Present

A queer archive of 1950s television, in line with Villarejo's call, should also include *Leave It to Beaver* owing to its insistent thematizing of Ward's fear of a queer Beaver, as the boy's misadventures consistently highlight his propensity for homosocial companionship to an extent that worries his father. At the very least, Stockton's formulation of the queer child "growing sideways" echoes 1950s sociologists' concern for children of the era. Sociologist Gertrude Chittenden, while not explicitly outlining the possibility of gay children, fears that American children are faltering in their sexual development: "The American adolescent may emerge an unsure, confused child confronted with many important choices, in some instances in conflict with his parents and unprepared to accept his own sex role."[19] Chittenden's words readily apply to Beaver, for he doggedly insists on his distaste for girls throughout most of the series (although hints of heteroerotic interest blossom toward the end of its run). Beaver's boyish distaste for feminine companionship does not in itself construct the character's queerness, yet it is merely one of many signs that the process of growing up into presumed heterosexuality takes numerous detours through realms feminine, antifeminine, and intensely homosocial.

Beaver's queer boyishness is juxtaposed sharply with Wally's more successful masculinity throughout the series, thus establishing both the gentle tension in their relationship and Ward's fears concerning his younger son. For example, Wally's repeated triumphs in sports overshadow Beaver's hobbies of clarinet and ice-skating, which places the boys at opposing ends of a gendered continuum. They are often costumed to accentuate their differences as well, such as in the "Beaver's Short Pants" episode, in which Beaver is humiliated by the clothes he is expected to wear, whereas Wally's costuming accentuates his normative boyhood masculinity (fig. 1.1). In a particularly effeminizing sequence, Beaver buys "Glama-Spray Miracle Mist" to tame his sheepdog hair, despite the saleswoman cautioning him against purchasing a woman's product ("Beaver, the Sheep Dog"). Child psychologists of the 1950s expressly warned parents against dance lessons for boys, lest they raise a sissy, as in Barney Katz's formulation: "But the boy who has long been and continues to be girlish, a sissy, is made that way by the handling of his parents. . . . They dress him in fancy clothes, keep his curls longs, and give him dancing lessons."[20] More than simply casting him within the effete realm of Terpsichore, Beaver's dancing lessons ironically afford him the opportunity to privilege homosocial, rather than heterosocial, pastimes. "As long as I'm going to be stuck here, I'm going to dance with another boy," he declares ("Wally's Girl Trouble"), and he tells June, in response to a question about his brother, "Well, I don't know. All I ever dance with at dancing school is other guys" ("Wally's New Suit"; cf. "Dance Contest"). Beaver tells his friend Gus, the auxiliary firehouse attendant, "If I do get married, I'm not getting married to a girl" ("The Black Eye"). Games of make-believe with his male friends similarly allow Beaver to enjoy gender's malleability, such as when his pal Richard tells him as they wait for the laundry, "You be the wife, and I'll be the husband, and then we can fight like our parents do" ("Beaver's Laundry").

FIGURE 1.1 Clothes unmake and make the man, as evident in Beaver's queer positioning in relation to Wally ("Beaver's Short Pants").

To argue that Beaver's preference for male dancing partners and other such pastimes indicates his latent homosexuality would be to extrapolate wildly from the program's obvious intentions, yet to deny this reading entirely would overlook the fact that Ward worries about his son's gender identity. On one occasion, Beaver admits to his father that he ran away from a fight, and Ward confesses to June, "It frightens me a little . . . a boy running away"—and even more effeminizing is that Beaver's nemesis Violet Rutherford gave him his black eye ("The Black Eye"). Ward similarly remarks after Beaver attends an exclusively female party: "Well, now I am confused. A boy that age going to an all-girl party and enjoying himself. That little character is beginning to worry me" ("Party Invitation").[21] Beaver surprises his family by announcing his appreciation of dancing school, and Ward frets, "When a boy his age suddenly says he likes dancing school, he's either covering up for something he's done, or he's downright abnormal!" ("Beaver's First Date"). Also, when his son is cast as a canary in a school play, Ward grumbles that the boy should play an eagle instead, while June, with words also hinting at their child's queerness, approves of his performance: "You know, Ward, he was so sweet, it almost makes up for not having a girl" ("School Play"). Beaver consistently vocalizes his distaste for girls—"Imagine anybody dumb enough to go steady with a girl"—and when Wally asks Beaver whom he would date, he doggedly replies, "I don't know, but it sure wouldn't be a girl," with the reaction shot of Ward—eyes glazed, chin and lips tense—capturing his consternation over his son's potential homosexuality ("Wally's Test"; see fig. 1.2). Most of these moments are played for the humor of a young boy's irrational dislike of girls or are based on misunderstandings among the characters, yet they concomitantly stage the queer trajectory of Beaver's maturation and the pleasure he finds in his childish rejection of the heteronormative imperative.

While *Leave It to Beaver* stages a young boy's distaste for girls and his preference for homosocial companionship, surely viewers are intended to interpret the series' overarching story line as Beaver's maturation into heteroerotic adolescence—his "growing sideways" as he "grows up." And to this end a new vision of Beaver appears in the series' final season: football champion ("Beaver, the Hero"), surfing enthusiast ("The Late Edition"), and even a junior Romeo, for which Wally chastises him: "A kid like you isn't supposed to go running around like Frank Sinatra" ("More Blessed to Give"). But these hints of incipient heteronormativity cannot undo the previous five seasons of Beaver's antieroticism; thus, the series as a whole stages the torturous paths of sexual maturation and the comic potential in resisting heteronormativity. In these persistent images of Beaver as a queer child, *Leave It to Beaver* no more endorses homosexuality than it endorses bestiality or incest, although the series comically flirts with these taboo topics as well. In the series' first season, Ward introduces in voice-over the themes of several episodes, and for one he

FIGURE 1.2 Ward's reaction shot captures his fear: more than a sissy, his son might just be gay ("Wally's Test").

warmly intones, "and the first time you fall in love, it's not always with a girl," as the camera frames Beaver gazing adoringly at, as the cut reveals, an alligator ("Captain Jack"). Also, planning his future romantic life, Beaver affirms, "But I'm not going to marry any silly girls. I'm going to marry a mother," with his words hinting at his unresolved Oedipal attachment to June ("Dance Contest"). The gaps and fissures of heteronormativity are continually revealed in Beaver's six-year narrative arc, yet even if one concedes that an ultimately conservative and chrononormative vision triumphs, Ward's story line further complicates the notion that "growing sideways" can ever result in an untroubled sense of gendered and erotic wholeness.

Ward's Queer Past

As mentioned previously, chrononormative visions of 1950s domestic sitcoms identify a benevolent *pater familias* as the privileged site of ideological authority, yet it is critical to note the fault lines in this view as well, for these programs frequently dramatize the limits of paternal governance: if father truly knew best in the 1950s, he would likely have made far fewer mistakes, which appear so regularly and in such a variety of programs that they can hardly be considered anomalies. Illustrative examples include when, in *The Adventures of Ozzie and Harriet*, Ozzie advises his son David, who frequently helps friends and neighbors in need, that "sometimes generosity and doing nice things for people can be overdone"; David agrees to rebuff such pleas in the future, yet Ozzie soon realizes his error when his son refuses to assist him with a favor for their neighbor Thorny ("The Fall Guy"). In *Father Knows Best*, Jim Anderson promises to take his elder daughter, Betty, to a football game but then reneges so that he can take an important client instead, only for his younger daughter, Kathy, to chastise him: "You must never break a promise to a child, Daddy" ("Football Tickets"). Jim's wife, Margaret (Jane Wyatt), taking Betty into her confidences, sighs, "Oh, it's not that I don't think your father has wonderful ideas. It's just that, well, they don't work" ("Live My Own Life"). After watching several episodes of *Father Knows Best*, one finds it difficult not to hear a distinct irony in the title, for this father is as likely to benefit from the episode's moral as much as, if not more than, his wife and children. Despite the widespread vision of Ward Cleaver as a faultless father of 1950s and 1960s television, he similarly embodies both patriarchal authority and men's inherent incapacity to govern their families effectively.

As Beaver matures from childhood queerness into a presumably normative adolescence, Ward, in complementary contrast, models the likely possibility of a father psychologically stunted from his boyhood. Numerous episodes characterize him more as a little boy, as yet another of June's children, than as her adult spouse. When Wally and Beaver shirk their painting job to gawk at a lumberyard fire, Ward decides he, too, must see it. "Once a boy, always a boy," June laments ("Wally's Job"), and she also calls him one of her "three babies" ("Beaver's Short Pants"). Indeed, Ward's ability to think like a child is frequently lauded as a marker of his superior parenting skills, such as when June defends the boys—"Just because they're quiet, it doesn't mean they're up to something"—yet Ward better understands the meanings of silence: "It always did when I was a boy" ("Beaver's Cat Problem"). In a plotline in which June hopes that Beaver will voluntarily surrender his pet monkey, Ward sympathizes with his son, envisioning himself as an eternal child: "I don't want to think like a father; I want to think like a kid" ("Beaver's Monkey"). In these and numerous other such scenes, Ward's strength as a father emerges from his deep recollection of his own childhood. Yet the father cannot physically be the child—some of chrononormativity's dictates are impossible to ignore—so Ward's performance of father-as-eternal-child increasingly subverts any vision of patriarchal authority he attempts to embody. Moreover, while often heralding Ward's deep understanding of childhood, *Leave It to Beaver* also ponders the undesirability of a Peter Pan vision of masculinity, such as when Ward himself states: "You know, the sad thing is there are some men my age who are still trying to be little boys" ("Beaver's Old Buddy"). Both adult father and child-as-father, Ward symbolizes the privileges of an adult masculinity that can shuffle between past and present to better raise his children, yet *Leave It to Beaver* also trips over this inherent contradiction in patriarchal authority.

This paradox of Ward's character as man and child is broached repeatedly in story lines touching on themes of domestic violence and child abuse. Recent analyses in television studies have queried long-standing views of 1950s family sitcoms as honeyed fare, with T. J. Jackson Lears arguing that "the bland surfaces of suburban normality, the way of life celebrated in *Ozzie and Harriet* and *Leave It to Beaver*, concealed an abyss of aggression"[22] and Erin Lee Mock detailing how the threat of violence bubbles up frequently in family sitcoms of the 1950s. Using Desi Arnaz's Ricky Ricardo of *I Love Lucy* (1951–57) as her prototype, Mock explores how "sitcom husbands . . . are crafted after his raging model, with varying degrees of subtlety."[23] Mock cites *Leave It to Beaver*'s first episode to include Ward among her examples: Beaver, mistakenly believing he has been expelled from school, hides from his parents up a tree. Fearing his father, Beaver refuses to leave his hideout—"I'm not coming down. You'll hit me." Ward initially appears to agree with his son about his violent proclivities ("Well, you just better—") but then testily tempers his anger: "Beaver, you know we never hit you" ("Beaver Gets 'Spelled"). In a later episode, Beaver cautions Wally about their father, "Yeah, you wouldn't want to get him in a hitting mood" ("Wally's Car").

A wider sampling of the program, however, reveals that these hints of Ward's violent parenting are more an anomaly than a trope, with the threat of corporal punishment more frequently diffused into the homes of Beaver's and Wally's friends, particularly Larry Mondello, Lumpy Rutherford, and Eddie Haskell. For example, Beaver mentions to Wally that Larry's father hits him (Larry) for misbehaving and then states of their father: "You know, Wally, I'm glad we don't have a hitting father" ("School Bus"). Beaver also asserts that Larry's father "walloped" his son for playing hooky ("Beaver Plays Hooky"), and Larry nonchalantly verifies his father's violent tendencies—"Sure he hit me" ("Borrowed Boat"). Lumpy Rutherford admits casually, "If I disappoint my daddy, smack! Right in the mouth" ("Wally's Track Meet"). While this undercurrent of child abuse should not simply be shrugged off, the majority of these scenes exaggerate the tenor of any violence. Surely *hit* registers as a synonym for *spank* on most occasions, and as Michael Kassel muses rhetorically, the children of Mayfield, while by no means represented as delinquents, repeatedly transgress their parents' dictates: "If the goal of *Leave It to Beaver* was to venerate the white middle class, why would the series allow for that environment to produce not only Eddie Haskell, but other problem children, including Clarence 'Lumpy' Rutherford, Larry Mondello, and Gilbert Bates?"[24] Furthermore, many of the children's discussions of abuse exploit this exaggeration for the comedic purpose of presenting the world through a child's vantage point (as much as more contemporary views of child abuse have muffled any humorous edges it may have held). Certainly, Ward and June do not see themselves as abusive parents. When June explains that Beaver was "naturally" embarrassed to tell them about a problem, Ward replies, "What's so natural about it? Are we monsters? Do we hit him? Do we beat him?" Ward's words indicate that they do not hit or beat their child, and June further explains, "Ward, the only guide the little fellow has is the love and approval of his parents. Now, if he thinks he's lost that, it's worse than a beating" ("The Haircut").

From this perspective, child abuse lingers in the subconscious of *Leave It to Beaver*—if the metaphor of a television program's subconscious is allowed—for more than depicting Ward as a violent father, the program shows that the specter of parental violence haunts him. Whereas the question of whether Ward has ever spanked Beaver engenders ambiguity and obfuscation, it is clear that Ward's father tormented him and his siblings with crippling corporal punishments. Ward tells June, "Dear, when I was a kid, if I had even implied to my father that I didn't have the best parents in the world, he'd have taken me right out to the woodshed and proved to me that I did" ("Beaver Gets Adopted"). The other Cleavers acknowledge the violence of Ward's upbringing, such as when Beaver consoles him, "Oh, yeah, you had a hitting dad, didn't you?" ("Beaver's Freckles"), and Ward wryly recalls his father's violence, which contributed to a cold atmosphere in their home: "My father had a very practical shortcut to child psychology: a razor strap. Sure cut down on the conversation around our house" ("Ward's Golf Clubs"). Haunted by his painful childhood, Ward nevertheless adumbrates the desirability of abusing children for its supposed efficacy. In another recollection of his childhood beatings, Ward states, "My father would take me out for a little walk to the toolshed. It's amazing how just looking at that toolshed would take all of the rebellion out of me"; while June hopes Beaver will not require such drastic punishment, Ward counters, "If it doesn't work, I'm afraid I'm going to have to fall back on that toolshed psychology" ("The Silent Treatment"). The phrase "toolshed psychology" encapsulates the program's inability to consistently advocate for a particular style of child raising, for it is torn between the supposed efficacy of violence and the modern call to understand one's children, as it is also set between the traumas of Ward's past and the domestic frustrations of his present.

As an effect of these narrative crosscurrents, Ward emblematizes the impossibility of psychic wholeness and its queer repercussions, for he is a father trapped by the patriarchal regimes in which he was raised. Certainly, psychoanalysis is itself haunted, if also inspired, by the figure of the beaten child, beginning with Sigmund Freud's foundational proposition: "It is surprising how often people who seek analytic treatment for hysteria or an obsessional neurosis confess to having indulged in the phantasy: 'A child is being beaten.'"[25] The beaten child sparks the need for psychoanalytic therapy, yet as Gilles Deleuze and Félix Guattari explore in their critique of Freudian thought, the father's paradoxical role in psychic coherency contains its own undoing: "So it is that psychoanalysis has much difficulty extracting itself from an infinite regression: the father must have been a child, but was able to be a child only in relation to a father, who was himself a child, in relation to another father."[26] Within the realms of Freudian thought and much chrononormative television criticism, Ward models the psychic wholeness of the father who has overcome the traumas of his past, yet from Deleuzian-Guattarian, antichrononormative, and queer perspectives, he simultaneously models the fracturing of consciousness implicitly structured through the repetitions of patriarchal history and the impossibility of closing this violent cycle.

So while chrononormative readings of 1950s sitcom morality stress the ways in which fathers teach their children important life lessons, Ward inverts this role on numerous episodes, for he is the abused child of *Leave It to Beaver*'s subconscious who has grown sideways into adulthood and is simply incapable of resolving many of the family's conflicts. To cite all of the episodes in which Ward learns an important lesson by the narrative's end would quickly devolve into an exhaustive plot summary of the series, so these four examples must stand as representative of his consistently faulty parenting:

- "You know, June, I think I've learned something from all this. To take our kids as they are, not wish they were something else, or try to make them like ourselves. It doesn't work." ("Part Time Genius")
- "Just got to tell them I flew off the handle and made a fool of myself," Ward realizes, to which June sympathetically replies, "Don't look so sad, dear. That's just one of the hazards of being a father." ("Beaver's Bad Day")
- "Um, well, I guess I made a mistake, Beaver. I guess I was so anxious to be right that I kind of forgot what it felt like when I was a little boy." ("Beaver Runs Away")
- "June, I made a mistake today a lot of fathers make. I put so much pressure on the Beaver about not disappointing me that all he could do was break down." ("The Tooth")

These passages reveal that much of the wisdom imparted in the program arises from Beaver himself, who allows Ward the opportunity to reassess his views of adulthood and of childhood that were seared into his psyche through his father's violence. By reversing the channels of wisdom anticipated by chrononormativity, *Leave It to Beaver* introduces a carnivalesque and comic air into its story lines, for viewers simply cannot expect adult authority to render reasonable judgments and must then turn to the child for guidance, despite Beaver's own questionable, always "sideways," maturation. Developing these themes, several episodes feature Beaver and his father making similar mistakes and facing similar comeuppances: Beaver moans, "I wish I were dead" after his bike, which he failed to register, is stolen, with Ward echoing his son's cry when June learns that Ward failed to insure it ("Beaver's Bike"). In "Beaver Takes a Drive," Beaver's antics culminate with the Cleavers in a courtroom, where the judge chastises Ward for his failure to responsibly discipline his children. The episode ends with Beaver and Ward sulking together—with their arms crossed, Beaver looking glumly ahead, Ward casting his eyes down—thus undermining Ward's performance of paternal authority and reminding viewers of the carnivalesque fantasy of a normative family (fig. 1.3).

As Ward's backstory indicates that he has traveled a tortuous path from childhood to adulthood, his performance of paternal heteronormativity affords viewers the opportunity to see the innumerable chinks in the psychological wholeness ostensibly promised by white patriarchal governance. So while many viewers assume that Beaver will mature into adolescent heterosexuality although they must also remember his queer moments of "growing sideways," Ward's prepaternal years likewise contain hints of homosociality and male pleasures divorced from the fetters of heteronormativity. When Beaver opens Ward's army chest, he finds a photograph of his father wearing a grass skirt, baring his midriff, and, because it is unclear which of the two men Beaver identifies as Ward, either leaning on his male friend or being leaned on by his male friend. Beaver cries out in disbelief: "These aren't ladies. These are guys. And one of 'em's dad!" ("Beaver's Hero"; see fig. 1.4). But of course, Ward was

FIGURE 1.3 Ward and Beaver sit dejectedly on the couch together, both father and son frustrated by the strictures of authority ("Beaver Takes a Drive").

FIGURE 1.4 Beaver finds photographic evidence that Ward "grew sideways" into heterosexuality, as evident from the homosocial and gender-bending pleasures of his past ("Beaver's Hero"). This photograph does not actually appear to be of Hugh Beaumont, and the episode's editing only allows a brief glance at it, yet Beaver identifies one of these men as his father, Ward.

not yet Beaver's father at the moment when this war photo was taken, so the boy's surprised view of his father's past disrupts the linearity of time and its chrononormative promises. Other than his childhood of paternal abuse and this homosocial romp during the war, viewers know little of Ward's history, yet the psychological fracturing evident in his simultaneous performances of father and of eternal child undo the 1950s vision of the faultless patriarch and reveal instead his queer discontents and his unresolved desires, cloaked under a mantle of suburban respectability.

June's Queer Future

Formulating an enduring chrononormative assumption of 1950s family sitcoms, scholars have long highlighted the genre's conservative gender politics that positions the husband's ultimate authority over his wife. Denouncing the conservative sexual politics of early television programs, Bonnie Dow argues that "the controlling value of patriarchal authority is evident in 1950s sitcoms like *Leave It to Beaver*. . . , in which the correct resolution of a problem inevitably follows the wisdom of the father."[27] Matthew Henry echoes this viewpoint: "Atop the nuclear family was posited a patriarchy in which the father was portrayed as knowing, correct, and superior to his wife and children, a structure that worked to reinforce the prevalent sexual stereotypes."[28] Diana Meehan taxonomizes the maternal characters of family sitcoms as the "good-wife" figure, whose "only interest was family and house, the focus of all meaningful action,"[29] and Susan Douglas excoriates the 1950s image of maternity in its endless array of "wasp-waisted, perfectly coiffed moms who never lost their temper."[30] Such observations, common to criticism of 1950s sitcoms, are both demonstrably true yet limited in their accuracy, particularly in their failure to recognize the genre's comedic and carnivalesque nature, in which the "world turned upside down" highlights the limits of masculine governance and the pleasures of feminine resistance. A father ruling his family competently affords fewer comedic moments than his failing to do so as the mother then intervenes to save the day, with this queer trope of gender reversals prevalent throughout television's early years.

In contrast to the paternal focus of such sitcoms as *Father Knows Best* and *Make Room for Daddy*, domestic sitcoms such as *The George Burns and Gracie Allen Show* (1950–58), *I Love Lucy*, and *I Married Joan* (1952–55) direct the audience's attention to the husband and wife dyad, and while the husbands typically restore order following Gracie's, Lucy's, and Joan's comic excess, the women's transgressions establish a narrative pattern of flouting patriarchal authority and insulting their husbands' masculinity. With breathless naiveté, Gracie mocks George's gender: "George, you're my husband. I don't think of you as a man" ("Chapter 2"). On another occasion a guest at the door declares, "I saw a man in the house," to which Gracie replies, "No, you didn't. That was George" ("Chapter 5"). Resisting the stifling constraints of marriage, Lucy (Lucille Ball) complains to her friend Ethel (Vivian Vance): "Ever since we said, 'I do,' there are so many things we don't" ("The Girls Want to Go to a Nightclub"). In a memorable exchange between Joan (Joan Davis) and her husband Brad (Jim Backus), Brad asserts his authority alliteratively—"And as your husband, what I have to say is positive, precise, and permanent"—but Joan simply bats away his pretensions: "And as your wife, what I have to say is pooh, pah, and poppycock. And back to pooh" ("Joan's Haircut"). The visual iconography of the show's opening credits, with Davis standing alone in her bridal gown while giving a kiss to the tiny groom figure from her wedding cake, establishes her as the program's focal point, and through Davis's energetic performances Joan proves her physical superiority over Brad, in one instance dipping him for a kiss ("Changing Houses").

Yet as much as Gracie, Lucy, and Joan undercut masculine authority, these programs concentrate on the humorous dynamics between husband and wife more than among broader families, and the father's role as domestic authority is heightened, while similarly undermined, in programs depicting a nuclear family. *The Donna Reed Show* (1958–63) illuminates these shifts, as Donna Reed, an Oscar-winning actress for *From Here to Eternity* (1954), took her cinematic star power to the small screen, playing the role of Donna Stone, wife of Dr. Alex Stone and mother of Mary and Jeff. While Reed's role is more maternal and demure than Allen's, Ball's, and Davis's, numerous episodes allow her to combat masculine prerogatives. Following a hiking trip with her son and his friends, she says of a forest ranger overly solicitous to set up her camp: "Well, he was a very obliging man . . . but he was just a little bit condescending, like some other men I know" ("The Hike"). Also, in a community playhouse performance, Donna plays the role of Nora in Henrik Ibsen's *A Doll's House.* With this allusion to a classic prefeminist text of women's need for independence, *The Donna Reed Show* encodes a critique of crippling domesticity as it simultaneously celebrates Donna's transcendence of the limitations of married life ("Pardon My Gloves"). As these cursory examples attest, the presumption of husbandly authority is both a reality and an illusion in 1950s sitcoms, continually undermined by comic women who refuse to cede their pleasures to their grumpy spouse's purported authority.

June Cleaver represents a vision of 1950s womanhood that contrasts with Gracie, Lucy, Joan, and Donna: whereas these protagonists typically direct an episode's plotline, June more often stands to the side of the narrative action and offers maternal warmth while her sons and husband confront the quotidian challenges of suburban life. Sociologists of the 1950s such as James Bossard and Eleanor Boll noted a transition in the United States from adult-centered to child-centered families, documenting "a radical change in the whole idea of the child's relative place in the family," such that "one finds a tendency, first, toward more 'child-centered' ritual, and, second, toward a change in the emphasis of the content of the family rituals which function as control or education, from one of narrowly channelizing behavior to one of liberating and guiding potentialities."[31] These sociological shifts took root in the era's sitcoms privileging children for their titular and narrative focus, in such shows as *Dennis the Menace* (1959–63) and, of course, *Leave It to Beaver.* Placing greater narrative emphasis on Beaver and Wally, and also on Ward in his authoritarian role, *Leave It to Beaver* leaves less narrative space for June, yet she has paradoxically become the program's defining figure in much of the cultural imaginary. In the strange alchemy of television reception, June Cleaver stands as a cultural icon both cherished and regretted, such as in Bonnie Mann's declaration that baby boomers "find June Cleaver etched so deeply in our collective sociosymbolic psyche that we are as haunted by her, I suspect, as by our real mothers."[32] Various studies of women and motherhood deploy June Cleaver as a cultural touchstone against which they rebel. For a scholarly audience of historians, Joanne Meyerowitz expands the vision of women's post–War World II experience in her *Not June Cleaver: Women and Gender in Postwar America, 1945–1960.*[33] Appealing to a popular readership, Deborah Werksman gleefully offers *I Killed June Cleaver: Modern Moms Shatter the Myth of Perfect*

Parenting, and Anne Dunnewold consoles overstressed parents with *Even June Cleaver Would Forget the Juice Box: Cut Yourself Some Slack (And Still Raise Great Kids) in the Age of Extreme Parenting*.[34] Beaver, Wally, and Ward, while integral members of the cast, lack June's enduring presence and legacy, in a surprising reformulation of the program's cultural meaning throughout its post-1950s reception.

June's mythic status appears largely to be an unlikely consequence of costuming choices, in the incongruity between her clothing (pearls and elegant dresses) and her domestic chores (cleaning the house and cooking meals). The excess of her attire thus serves as a metonym for the excess of the character: with apologies for the anachronistic allusion, June Cleaver is simply too much the Stepford housewife, too much the image of domestic perfection, even more so than her contemporaries. It is somewhat ironic, then, that this image of the well-dressed, pearl-bedecked housewife defines June Cleaver, for Billingsley states that these costuming decisions resulted not from the writers' vision of the character but were necessary owing to her neckline and height. Of the necklace she explains that "the pearls I wear because I have a hollow in my neck," with Jerry Mathers elaborating: "when they went to film her, the two muscles in her neck . . . caused a shadow." Billingsley further affirms that "it was very difficult to photograph. We didn't have as good of cameras, we didn't have as good of film," as she also elaborates on her character's footwear: "I used flat shoes when the kids were little, and as the durn kids grew, they put me in high heels."[35] Perhaps Billingsley and Mathers protest too much in these declarations: shadows, which the directors so strenuously resisted depicting in Billingsley's neck, appear frequently throughout the program, breaking the illusion of the show's reality. Still, to focus primarily on Billingsley's excessive costuming is to decontextualize the program's, and the era's, attention to formalities in dress, which appears in numerous scenes. June's pearls and heels are patently unrealistic, yet little more so than Wally doing pushups in pants and a button-down shirt ("The Pipe"), the family wearing formal attire to an alligator park ("Captain Jack"), or boys wearing coats and ties to a football game ("Brotherly Love").

If one looks past June's pearls, *Leave It to Beaver* stages several moments adumbrating women's frustration with sexism and the fragility of gender as a social construct, particularly following World War II and the Korean War, as these conflicts overturned traditional gender roles when so many men and fathers fought and died overseas and, consequently, so many women were needed to "man" factories and to financially support their families. As Beaver's class plans a father-son picnic, June notes pointedly that "women aren't allowed unless they're fathers," thereby disintegrating gender distinctions between parents and alluding to the necessity of single mothers (presumably widows) to serve as fathers ("Ward's Problem"). When Ward admits that his golf club prohibits women and children on Saturdays, June counters tartly, "I don't think you should belong to a golf club that takes a warped attitude like that" ("Lonesome Beaver"). She also pointedly reminds her son, "Well, Beaver, today girls can be doctors and lawyers, too, you know. They're just as ambitious as boys are" ("Beaver's I.Q."). In an exposition about gender roles and the separate spheres of men and women, Ward explains the Cleavers' labor division as it pertains to their family cookout: "Women do all right when they have all the modern conveniences. But us men are better at this rugged type of outdoor cooking. Sort of a throwback to caveman days. Hand me those asbestos gloves, would you, Wally?" The episode's canned laughter alerts home viewers to Ward's hypocrisy, as he then genially concedes his appreciation for feminized modern conveniences: "Well, there's no sense in us cavemen burning our hands" ("Beaver's Guest"). Such moments do not recast *Leave It to Beaver* as a progressive intervention into 1950s gender politics, for the separate spheres of masculine authority and feminine domesticity are underscored more frequently than they are undermined, but sufficient subversions emerge to complicate the vision of June Cleaver as the archetypal housewife of popular consciousness.

Furthermore, in focusing on June Cleaver as a regressive avatar of 1950s womanhood, critics overlook the fact that Billingsley, a twice remarried mother of two children, raised her family during an era notably hostile to working women, even earning top billing in the show's credits over Hugh Beaumont. So while June Cleaver can imagine nothing more terrifying than her son potentially dating a high-school dropout—"She might even be a divorcée!" she cries in alarm ("Box Office Attraction")—Billingsley deconstructs the 1950s vision of domesticity that she portrays. Of course, the actress is not the character she assumes, yet typecasting—the chrononormative bane of actors, which defines them as forever suitable for only one type of role—affects, even effects in a manner, the actors of family sitcoms more so than most other performers. Thus, the disjunction between Billingsley and Cleaver proves the lie of June's perfection through Billingsley's real-life flouting of gendered decorum, allowing a hint of queer tension between June's fastidious wholesomeness and Billingsley's star persona.

Typecast as June Cleaver and thus trapped in a 1950s bubble, Billingsley rebooted her career in the 1980s by alternately solidifying and shattering the gendered bonds of chrononormativity, further exploiting the queer potential submerged in her defining role. She returned to the screen as June Cleaver in the television movie *Still the Beaver* (1983) and its follow-up series *The New Leave It to Beaver* (1983–89), proving the enduring appeal of this character, as well as playing the Cleavers' starchy Aunt Martha in the feature film *Leave It to Beaver* (1997). Prior to and concurrent with these parts, Billingsley was cast in numerous roles in which June Cleaver serves as the satiric base for a character who disproves the normative facade of 1950s suburban motherhood. In her comeback role as Jive Lady in *Airplane!* (1980), Billingsley appears as a June Cleaver-esque passenger who translates African American dialect for a hapless flight attendant. "Oh, stewardess, I speak jive," she politely yet improbably volunteers, as she then becomes exasperated with the two black men she hopes to assist: "Jive ass dude don't got no brains anyhow." Several 1980s and 1990s television programs employed Billingsley in a similar manner: to subvert the illusion of white, maternal, suburban femininity she so effortlessly presents. Whether as a witch in the forgettable television movie *Bay Coven* (1987), the sugary-sweet mother of hard-charging principal Grace Musso in *Parker Lewis Can't Lose* (1990–93), or as an alcoholic psychic singing "I'm Just a Girl Who Can't Say No" in the series *Mysterious Ways* (2000–2002, "Handshake"), Billingsley's non–June Cleaver roles riff on her June Cleaver past to remind viewers of its impossibility. In fact, many of Billingsley's roles outside of *The New Leave It to Beaver* are simply credited as June Cleaver: in *Amazing Stories* (1985), *Baby Boom* (1988), and *Hi Honey, I'm Home* (1991–92). In each of these programs, the illusion of sugar-coated domesticity is questioned, if not satirized, with Billingsley's performances capitalizing on perceptions of her Cleaver roots.

In her most memorably queer return to a family sitcom, Billingsley played June Cleaver in *Roseanne*'s "All about Rosey" episode. In this extended and metanarrative dialogue with past sitcoms, Roseanne (Roseanne Barr) encounters June Cleaver and four other famous television mothers: Ruth Martin (June Lockhart) of *Lassie* (1954–74), Joan Nash (Pat Crowley) of *Please Don't Eat the Daisies* (1965–67), Louise Jefferson (Isabel Sanford) of *The Jeffersons* (1975–85), and Norma Arnold (Alley Mills) of *The Wonder Years* (1988–93).[36] Assuming the chrononormative values of their characters, the actresses voice their disdain both for *Roseanne* and for Roseanne, with "Joan Nash" speaking to the necessity of maintaining the sanctity of television's "family hour": "Oh, my. I'm glad I don't stay up past nine." "Louise Jefferson" riffs on her show's theme song of upward mobility, which tells how her family rose from a lower-class neighborhood to a "deluxe apartment in the sky," and then huffs, "We moved on up to get away from people like you." After a flashback to the episode featuring Roseanne overindulging on marijuana with her husband and sister, "Joan Nash" complains, "But that's the wrong image for a TV mom," and "June Cleaver" summarizes her distaste: "I don't like any of this. Why, girls kissing girls and foul language and teenage sex." Rebuffing their reprimands, Roseanne states, "On my show, I'm the boss, and father knows squat"—thereby rewriting the patriarchally inflected titles of the family sitcoms *Who's the Boss?* (1984–92) and *Father Knows Best*. Roseanne then admits that her sitcom tackles controversial story lines, and Barr emerges from character to focus on the economic payoffs she receives for her efforts: "Yeah, I know. That stuff's kinda bad, but you guys wanna hear how much money I make?" The women huddle together as she whispers, as they then gasp, with "June Cleaver" stating, "Why, I'd make out with a chick for that kind of dough," and "Louise Jefferson" quickly agreeing, "Anyone of you. Right now." The episode does not follow through on this proposed sitcom-mom, lesbian make-out session, yet it highlights the ways in which the actors playing these beloved TV mothers would gladly liberate themselves from the narrative conventions of the past to join Barr in her lucrative revisions to its sexual politics. As Billingsley flirts with June Cleaver's pecuniary and lesbian desires, the impossibility of 1950s chrononormativity is undone, and the queer potential of an archetypally resonant character springs to view (fig. 1.5).

After six years of Beaver's shenanigans, Ward's seesawing efforts at fatherhood, and June's immaculate housekeeping, *Leave It to Beaver* concludes with a flashback episode culminating in its final joke. Ward tells June of their sons, "They're practically grown men," as the camera cuts to the boys playing with one of Beaver's childhood toys that had long been packed away in storage ("Family Scrapbook"). This enduring image of one of television's leading families, then, posits the false allure of "growing up" and the boundless pleasure of "growing sideways," in which Beaver and Wally reject, at least in this

FIGURE 1.5 A lesbian June Cleaver? Surrounded by Roseanne Barr and other famous TV sitcom moms, Barbara Billingsley wears the pearls and other exaggerated accouterments of late 1950s domestic femininity that semiotically denote June Cleaver. In so doing, Billingsley further erodes the 1950s model of suburban maternity that defined her career, through a queer revisioning of the character's sexual politics.

moment, time's chrononormative teleology. Even though the characters' long-term heterosexual identities and familial affections are never in doubt, Beaver's present, Ward's past, and June's future allow for queer readings of a television series, both in its story lines and in much of its critical reception, that brooked little room for deviations from 1950s norms yet expands temporally outward to suggest the surprising paths taken when family members "grow sideways." These queer subtexts, evident in a program that ran during television's early and ostensibly innocent years, attest to the pervasive allure yet the concomitant impossibility of sexual normativity defining the American family, a tension ever more evident as the rebellious 1960s passed into the 1970s—even for that paragon of innocence, *The Brady Bunch*, as the following chapter demonstrates.

2

Queer Innocence and Kitsch Nostalgia in *The Brady Bunch*

Producer Sherwood Schwartz credited the origins of *The Brady Bunch* (1969–74) to a 1965 newspaper article documenting that "more than 29 percent of all marriages included a child or children from a previous marriage," as he also noted television's refusal to address such a widespread family issue: "at that time the 'D' word [divorce] wasn't an option on television."[1] Family sitcoms of the 1960s were awash with widows and widowers raising children alone,[2] and in a watershed moment in television history, America's first blended family came to the screen: widower Mike Brady (Robert Reed) married Carol Tyler Martin (Florence Henderson), thereby forming the eponymous Brady Bunch with their many children: Mike's sons Greg (Barry Williams), Peter (Christopher Knight), and Bobby (Mike Lookinland), and Carol's daughters Marcia (Maureen McCormick), Jan (Eve Plumb), and Cindy (Susan Olsen). *The Brady Bunch* enjoys one of the odder yet more enduring histories of American television, for it achieved only modest success during its five-year run. Following its cancellation, however, fans immediately clamored for more, and it was frequently reborn over the subsequent thirty years in rebooted television shows and feature films.

To a large degree the lasting appeal of *The Brady Bunch* arises from its impossible and ultimately queer innocence, which resisted the changing cultural mores of the United States during the late 1960s and early 1970s. Innocence stands as one of society's most amorphous values, for it defines so little other than a lack (of knowledge, of experience), and all that can result from childhood innocence is its inevitable loss. As James Kincaid memorably opines, "Innocence is a lot like the air in your tires: there's not a lot you can do with it but lose it."[3] A cultural value that must fall to its inherent contradictions, the fantasy of youthful innocence acts as an unsettling, queering force disruptive to the sense of All-American normality that the series sought to uphold, particularly in its depiction of the ever-chipper Brady children. Eve Kosofsky Sedgwick muses that queerness denotes "the open mesh of possibilities, gaps, overlaps, dissonances, and resonances, lapses and excesses of meaning when the constituent elements of anyone's gender, of anyone's sexuality aren't made (or *can't be* made) to signify monolithically," and such meshes expand beyond individuals to televisual narratives that appear flummoxed by how to treat issues of children's sexuality.[4] By the very definition of the genre, family sitcoms must depict children, yet depicting children inevitably raises thorny questions about the symbolic and cultural significance of these narrative constructions.

Queer theory intersects with children's narratives in their joint focus on the social meaning of the Child. As Lee Edelman argues, the figure of the Child, a powerful signifier of cultural innocence, demarcates normative behaviors and pleasures for adults: "The Child," he posits, "marks the fetishistic fixation of heteronormativity."[5] Within the entertainment industry, producers must often bend their artistic visions to those both of prevailing cultural standards and of network censors, so this figure of "the Child" powerfully influences what types of narratives can be aired on television. Given the shifting tides of sexuality and feminism during the 1970s, *The Brady Bunch*'s purported innocence, couched in its genre as a family sitcom with child-friendly story lines, clashed with issues of sexuality and their depiction throughout its 117 episodes. In this manner the program highlights the queer foundation of the cultural fantasy of children's sexual innocence, for this vision of the asexual child continually founders against children's interest in eroticism, their physical development during their teen years, and adults' negotiations of the taboo topic of children's sexuality. *The Brady Bunch* made an impossible promise of sexual innocence to its viewers, for issues of sexuality inevitably crept into its plotlines and production and thus subverted the innocence that the show purportedly endorses. In its later incarnations as rebooted television programs, television movies, and feature films, *The Brady Bunch*'s exaggerated innocence, so out of step with the 1970s zeitgeist, encouraged a kitschy nostalgia for an America that never was yet that holds lasting appeal, which explains both the repeated attempts to return this family to the screen and the ways in which adult sexualities undercut these endeavors. With a surface innocence and a queer symptomology, *The Brady Bunch* illustrates the unlikelihood of stripping sexuality even from television's most scrupulously wholesome domestic sitcoms.

Queer Innocence in the 1970s

The grueling Vietnam War, President Nixon's resignation, oil embargos, and economic stagflation—the 1970s are remembered as a time of social and economic dissatisfaction throughout the United States, when the last whiffs of 1950s optimism evaporated and the countercultural promise of the 1960s withered. A lack of faith in government further contributed to the era's dispirited sensibility, which Peter Carroll ascribes to "the failure of government to assure economic stability, to provide social justice, to fulfill a sense of national purpose."[6] Dan Berger casts the period as a "deeply ambivalent and contentious moment" in the nation's history, with the radical spirit of the 1960s, as evident in the women's, civil rights, and gay rights movements, facing entrenched opposition.[7] Still, the spirit of sexual liberation unleashed during the 1960s continued, with Morton Hunt concluding that erotic liberalism—"the spontaneous and guilt-free enjoyment of a wide range of nonpathological sexual acts with a guiding belief in the emotional significance of those acts"—had become "the emergent ideal upon which the great majority of young Americans . . . are patterning their beliefs in their behavior."[8] In sum, erotic exuberance coupled with communal malaise characterized the 1970s, an odd coupling of pleasure and discontent that found its way into America's family sitcoms. For example, reframing the bobby-soxed and poodle-skirted vision of the American 1950s with drag races, stag parties, and rock-and-roll, *Happy Days* (1974–84) pays homage to the lost innocence of the Eisenhower era while concomitantly acknowledging the shifting perceptions of sexuality endemic to the 1970s. In one such instance, Mr. Cunningham (Tom Bosley) invites his son, Richie (Ron Howard), to discuss sexuality frankly with him: "Sex is actually what a son should discuss with his father. I mean, you don't want to learn about it on some street corner," he patiently explains, in an episode concerning Richie's dashed hopes of losing his virginity ("All the Way"). Mr. Cunningham calmly accepts Richie's adolescent mistakes, including drunkenness, with a reassuring pat of "It's all part of growing up" ("Richie's Cup Runneth Over").

In contrast to *Happy Days*' more candid treatment of teen sexuality, a theme treated as well in such 1970s family sitcoms as *The Partridge Family* (1970–74), *Good Times* (1974–79), and *One Day at a Time* (1975–84), a determined innocence characterizes *The Brady Bunch*'s pilot episode: Carol and Mike marry and depart for their honeymoon, but soon after checking into their hotel, they find themselves guilt-wracked for earlier chastising their children. The newlyweds throw robes over their nightwear and rush to gather Carol's daughters and Mike's sons for an impromptu family vacation, one celebrating the union both of the parents and of their children. On returning to the hotel, Carol happily proclaims to the desk clerk, "If there's one thing better than a honeymoon for two, it's a honeymoon for eight" ("The Honeymoon").[9] Alice, the housekeeper (Ann B. Davis), then alights on the hotel's doorway, bringing with her the family pets, Fluffy and Tiger. The honeymoon for two blossoms into a celebration of and for the newly constituted family of stepparents and step-siblings. With its overwriting of the typical erotic dynamics of honeymoons, the pilot episode sends a clear message about *The Brady Bunch*'s content: this family-centered sitcom will focus on the Bradys' wholesome experiences and shield young viewers from candid discussions or depictions of sexuality.[10]

Carol and Mike's decision to privilege a family reunion over marital eroticism attempts to erase sexuality from *The Brady Bunch*, and the lion's share of its episodes contributes to the prevailing vision of it as wholly innocent fare. The series addresses such universal topics as Marcia's trepidation over her first day of high school ("Today, I Am a Freshman"), Peter's fear of confronting a bully ("A Fistful of Reasons"), and children's delight in practical jokes, which they often take too far ("Fright Night"). Story lines such as a family vacation to the Grand Canyon ("Grand Canyon or Bust"), Bobby and Cindy's attempt to set a new world record for teeter-tottering ("The Teeter-Totter Caper"), and the Bradys' backyard staging of "Snow White and the Seven Dwarfs" ("Snow White and the Seven Bradys") offer little opportunity to contemplate the meaning of childhood sexuality. In line with much family sitcom narratology, the program often concludes with pat morals, which Mike benevolently imparts. "It's your belief in yourself that counts, you know. You are what you think you are," he explains about self-confidence ("Juliet Is the Sun"), and he similarly advises about the necessity of maintaining one's integrity: "You really should never promise anything until you're sure you can deliver" ("Getting Davy Jones"). The Brady children appreciate the lessons that their parents share, as evident in the repeated catchphrase "I never thought of it that way," which Peter declares when Mike and Carol convince him that he will disappoint his cast mates if he quits the school play ("Everyone Can't Be George Washington"), as does Bobby when Mike and Carol teach him about the importance of enforcing rules ("Law and Disorder"), as does Greg when Mike queries his son on the ethics of switching football playbooks ("Quarterback Sneak"). As Ann B. Davis declared of the program's wholesome story lines in light of the changing times, "My feeling is that the show came out just about the time that television began to get so sexy."[11]

Further along these chrononormative lines of sitcom narratology and gender, Carol represents the tenacious grip of the 1950s model of sitcom motherhood—the "goodwife" figure theorized by Diana Meehan.[12] Sitcoms of the 1970s increasingly depicted women as the independent heads of their households, introducing a stronger feminist perspective to network fare. As David Marc observes of this transition, "Pure paternal verticalism, as found in pre-seventies sitcoms, has been replaced by a more lateral view of moral authority, in which women are commonly the moral equals or superiors of men, and in which children can occasionally reverse the generational flow of moral wisdom."[13] Like their predecessors from the previous decade, several single mothers of 1970s family sitcoms were widows, including Shirley Partridge (Shirley Jones) of *The Partridge Family* and Alice Hyatt (Linda Lavin) of *Alice* (1976–85), but in a dramatic shift, 1970s sitcoms also introduced divorced women to television. Katherine Lehman documents that Mary Richards of *The Mary Tyler Moore Show* (1970–77) was intended to be a divorcée until "the network warned producers that 'the public would never accept a divorced heroine,'" and the character was recast as never married.[14] *Maude* (1972–78) features a three-time divorcée in its lead role, and Bea Arthur's iconic portrayal of this firebrand feminist—"anything but tranquilizing," as the theme song proclaims—depicted a new vision of American womanhood.[15] *One Day at a Time* depicts divorced mother Ann Romano (Bonnie Franklin) embracing feminist ideals, as she reclaims her maiden name and asserts she will "have to be both mother and father" to her daughters ("Ann's Decision"). Recognizing the challenges these women face, their story lines limn feminism as a source of strength during trying domestic times. In contrast to these program's embrace of new paradigms of motherhood, *The Brady Bunch* depicts Mike as a widower, but the circumstances surrounding Carol's previous marriage are left unexplained, without mention of the possibility of divorce. According to Sherwood Schwartz, "I opted for him being a widower. And I opted to leave Mrs. Brady's past open. That might provide me an opportunity for future stories."[16]

Even on its initial airing, *The Brady Bunch* appeared out of synch with the zeitgeist owing to its insistent focus on innocence. In an April 1968 meeting with network affiliates, Elton Rule, president of ABC, promised to lure the youth market with daring new programming: "The younger minds are being courted as never before. We know why we appeal to them—because we have the ability to be more unconventional than our competitors. And we are going to become even more unconventional as we become more meaningful."[17] Rule's promise of unconventionality came to fruition with such programs as *The Mod Squad* (1968–73), *Room 222* (1969–74), and *The Young Rebels* (1970–71)—youth-oriented entertainment that tackled controversial themes and captured the social turmoil of the era. Beyond the immediate realm of television, demand for narratives challenging conventional lifestyles extended to the cinematic world, with films addressing such nonconformist themes as motorcycle subcultures (*The Wild Angels*, 1966; *Easy Rider*, 1969), drugs (*The Trip*, 1967; *Psych-Out*, 1968; *Wild in the Streets*, 1968), teen sexuality (*Last Summer*, 1969; *The Last Picture Show*, 1971), and youth protest movements (*The Strawberry Statement*, 1970). One of the more tumultuous periods of the twentieth century, the 1960s and early 1970s celebrated resistance to and subversion of the staid codes of previous eras, but *The Brady Bunch* primarily acknowledges the turbulent tides of American culture through its depiction of a stepfamily rather than through story lines confronting the era's social unrest.

Against this backdrop in which television and film sought to portray the rebellious spirit of the times, *The Brady Bunch* treads lightly, if at all, into contemporary social issues, which further testifies to its overarching innocence—as well as to the ways that such innocence cannot fully hold. The conflicts of the 1960s, including the civil rights movement and Vietnam War protests, register in the show only in whispered allusions. In its racial politics the Bradys' suburban world appears gently integrated, with African Americans playing token, usually nonspeaking, roles as the children's schoolmates and friends. The Bradys often act as genial cultural tourists, such as when they attend a Hopi rain dance ("Grand Canyon or Bust") or a Hawaiian luau ("The Tiki Caves"). While such tokenism shepherds minority characters to the show's sidelines, some transgress significant boundaries: an African American girl is counted among Peter's admirers, whom Mike calls his "harem," thus hinting at the possibility of his son's interracial dating ("The Personality Kid"). Also, a nonspeaking black girl is depicted as a member of the exclusive Boosters Club at Marcia's high school ("Today, I Am a Freshman"). When Bobby and Cindy find themselves lost in the Grand Canyon and encounter Jimmy, a Native American boy, Bobby asks, "What's the matter? Don't you like us palefaces?"; Jimmy replies tersely, "Cut out the paleface stuff," with his rebuttal acknowledging and resisting the prejudice he faces as a nonwhite American ("The Brady Braves"). In these brief scenes, *The Brady Bunch* illustrates that, however much its writers and producers attempted to overlook the relevance of the civil rights movement to their white, suburban family, one cannot remain wholly isolated from the culture at large.

In a similar vein neither Greg nor his parents express concern that he could be drafted to fight in the Vietnam War, despite many American families' very real fear for their adolescent sons about this issue. Instead of resisting governmental authority that might conscript their sons to death overseas, the Bradys contribute their efforts on behalf of a local park that the city is threatening to close. Carol proudly declares to Mike, "The Women's Club is going to show them that you *can* fight city hall," and Bobby and Cindy petition their neighbors for support. A surly man dismisses their juvenile rabble-rousing—"You radicals sure start young"—but Cindy does not even understand the intended insult. "What's a radical?" she wonders, to which Bobby gamely replies, "I guess it's somebody who likes to play in parks" ("Double Parked"). With this resignification of the word *radical*—the Black Panthers, SDS (Students for a Democratic Society), and the Weathermen as park-playing kids—*The Brady Bunch* covers all social discord under a patina of children's innocence. When Marcia sighs, "Parents just don't understand our generation" ("Going, Going . . . Steady"), she voices a common adolescent lament about the generation gap, but the irony is that those in the 1960s and 1970s likely to have expressed this sentiment were exploring hippie lifestyles, experimenting with drugs, and embracing the counterculture. These are hardly the problems that the Bradys face: Greg succumbs to peer pressure and smokes a single cigarette ("Where There's Smoke")—but never drops acid.

As these examples of race relations and generational protests exemplify, although the Bradys resemble a family from 1950s television in their happy suburban bubble, this bubble cannot be wholly recreated in the late 1960s and early 1970s. Similarly, the program's overarching innocence cannot erase sexuality, and brief exchanges in various episodes expose the ways in which erotic themes seep through the fissures of otherwise innocent story lines and expose the queer foundations of the family sitcom. The question of whether Mike has taught his sons basic lessons on human reproduction reveals sexuality to be a conflicted topic for the program. In the episode "A Clubhouse Is Not a Home," Mike suggests that the boys should help their new sisters and that their sisters will assist them in return. Bobby grumpily states, "I don't want any girl scratching my back," but Greg interjects, "Just wait a few years, shrimp." With this hint of sexuality entering the conversation, Mike interrupts—"OK, that's enough"—both to return the boys to the task at hand and to suppress any discussion of why Bobby is likely to reappraise the appeal of back-scratching in his future. This scene indicates that Mike has not yet sat down with his boys for a father-and-son discussion of the "birds and bees" variety, but a subsequent episode suggests that Mike has in fact discussed sexuality with them. This plotline revolves around which doctor will care for the new family—the boys' male doctor or the girls' female doctor—and Mike attempts to quell the boys' protest by telling them, "There's no difference between a man doctor and a woman doctor." Greg then exclaims: "But dad! You're the one who told us about the birds and the bees" ("Is There a Doctor in the House?"). Greg's words are contradicted later in the series when, sensing that Mike is going to discuss sexuality with him, he reminds his father, "We already had that talk." Greg suggests that he will get Bobby—skipping over Peter, who has apparently learned these lessons as well—but Mike responds, "Let's not rush things," indicating that his youngest son need not yet be taught this information ("The Undergraduate"). These contrasting lines from separate episodes represent little more than a slight continuity error in the series' overarching story line, yet they simultaneously reveal sexuality to be a challenging issue for its writers owing to the thorny issue of how to depict the Brady boys' sexual knowledge—especially that of Bobby, the youngest. From these scenes, it is never clear whether Mike has taught Bobby the facts of life, so they collectively demarcate sexuality as a site of ambivalence.

As "The Honeymoon" episode demonstrates, the presence of children often regulates adult sexuality by foreclosing the privacy necessary to enjoy an erotic encounter, and, to this end, many of the gently amorous scenes between Carol and Mike take place without any children present. At the same time, children's regulatory effect on adult sexuality can be manipulated to create unexpected erotic possibilities. In the closing scene of "Alice's September Song," Alice's plans for a romantic picnic with her boyfriend (and butcher), Sam, are dashed when he invites the Brady children to join them. Carol sympathizes with Alice that her date has metamorphosed into a family affair, and Alice agrees that the picnic will not be very romantic. Mike interjects, "On the contrary, it's very romantic—for us," as he picks Carol up, apparently to whisk her away to the bedroom while the children will be safely out of the house. Numerous scenes depict Carol and Mike engaging in light romantic play, such as when she grades his kiss and assigns it a "C" but offers him the opportunity to improve on his initial performance; she raises her assessment to a "B" and then declares, "Now that's an 'A,'" as Mike's efforts increase in intensity ("The Power of the Press"). An irony arises in that, whereas the Brady children do not witness their parents' frisky behavior, the program's child viewers do. On the surface this appears counter to the ways in which a family-friendly program should construct its story lines to guard young audiences from knowledge of adult sexuality, for in these instances the phantom construction of the Child receives greater protective care than child viewers themselves, which exposes the preposterous illusion of the Child as a regulating factor for the narrative content of domestic sitcoms.

The 1970s are remembered as a time of sexual experimentation and excess—key parties, ménages-a-trois, and Hefneresque hedonism—and although the Bradys do not participate in such orgiastic pastimes, neither are the series' plotlines entirely divorced from the sexual culture around them. *The Brady Bunch* depicts Greg's dating life in several episodes, and most of these moments feature such innocent scenes as him and his date watching a drive-in movie—with the most aggressive ploy in his arsenal of seductions being to drape his arm over her shoulder. When Peter asks Greg which film is playing for their double date, Greg rakishly answers, "Who cares?," indicating that he plans not on watching the film but on necking with his girlfriend. At the drive-in, however, it would appear that Greg should care which film is playing, for he spends more time watching it than engaging in any sexual play with her ("Peter and the Wolf"). In a later episode, Peter becomes convinced that his brother has snuck two girls into his attic bedroom—"Greg's got two girls up there? What an operator!" ("Getting Greg's Goat")—with the implicit suggestion that his brother aspires to the sexual conquests of a swinger. In a surprising scene with Bobby and Cindy, Alice discovers that the youngsters plan to attend a nude swimming party, which she forbids: "You are not going to swim in an X-rated swimming pool without your parents' permission" ("Goodbye, Alice, Hello"). This brief interaction generates more questions than it answers—which of the

Bradys' neighbors hosts swimsuit-optional parties for local children? Is there any reason to suppose that Carol and Mike might give their children the permission that Alice denies them?—but it is surely an incongruous moment in the series' run, in which the sexual counterculture appears to have infiltrated their neighborhood. Such moments also call to mind the fact that "innocent" children's entertainments are created by adults, some of whom enjoy the transgression of sneaking sexual scenes past the censors' eyes. In this regard producer Lloyd Schwartz recalls that, when shooting the opening sequence of "And Now a Word from Our Sponsor," the director of the scene's background action incorporated a low-level sex crime among the extras walking across a grocery-store parking lot: "In the background of a *Brady Bunch* episode, John [Lenox] subversively staged a scene of a prostitute picking up a client."[18] In the episode's final cut, one can see these characters, if not their transaction, as they walk away from the grocery store, which leaves a lingering trace of sexual transgression in a plot addressing the ethical quandary of whether the Bradys should endorse a particular brand of laundry detergent.

The 1969 Stonewall Riots in New York City heralded the advent of the modern gay rights movement, yet the repercussions of this landmark event were not likely to be felt in a family sitcom such as *The Brady Bunch*. Still, queer representations in various of the era's domestic sitcoms encouraged viewers to consider the possibility of identities and desires beyond the heteronormative. The monstrous and supernatural families of *The Addams Family* (1964–66), *The Munsters* (1964–66), *Bewitched* (1964–72), and *I Dream of Jeannie* (1965–70) today read as allegories of gay lives lived in the shadows, thereby expanding the vision of the American family to include the Other, even if these Others are exaggerated into cartoonish excess. *The Munsters* reverses the standards of attractiveness with its running gag that, in a house populated by Frankenstein-monster Herman Munster (Fred Gwynne), his vampire wife Lily (Yvonne De Carlo), their werewolf son, and Lily's vampire grandfather, the family's ugly duckling is comely human niece Marilyn. Lily says of Marilyn, "It's just one of those unfortunate things that happens. Poor dear," with these lines hinting at a queer allegory, in which one's sexual orientation results from the vagaries of birth and genetics, and some people are simply "born that way." Like the Munsters worrying over Marilyn, Morticia (Carolyn Jones) and Gomez (John Astin) of *The Addams Family* fret over the possibility that their son, Pugsley, could engage in such wholesome activities as the Boy Scouts, thus questioning the meaning of normality in the wider culture ("Morticia and the Psychiatrist"). With its plot of advertising executive Darrin Stephens hiding the secret of his supernatural wife, Samantha (Elizabeth Montgomery), *Bewitched* invites queer readings, especially given the many gay actors playing key parts: Agnes Moorehead as Endora, Dick Sargent as Darrin, and Paul Lynde as Uncle Arthur.[19] Similar to *Bewitched* in its plot of double lives, astronaut Major Anthony Nelson (Larry Hagman) hides his genie, Jeannie (Barbara Eden), from the world, so *I Dream of Jeannie* can also be read as a queer allegory, even as Eden's sex appeal and skimpy costumes—although without her navel visible—increase its heteroerotic allure.

Given these conditions in which homosexuality could only be broached allegorically in family sitcoms based on outlandish premises, it is not particularly surprising, within the quasi-realist fictions of *The Brady Bunch*, that Mike expresses his mild homophobia by telling Carol, "If my boys wanted to play in anybody's dollhouse, I'd take them to a psychiatrist" ("A Clubhouse Is Not a Home"). Mike's statement, with its offhand bigotry against deviations from normative gender roles, simply reflects contemporary beliefs about homosexuality, for the American Psychiatric Association did not declassify it as a mental illness until 1973. Still, the program does not erase homosexuality entirely, with some minor roles featuring flamboyant males coded as gay. The episode "Father of the Year" portrays the suggestively named Lance Pierce—an appellation indicative of phallic penetration—as an ascot-wearing television reporter with affected speech patterns who overdramatically bemoans the challenges of filming the Bradys. "Why me? Why do these things always happen to me?" he laments when Mike enters through the back door and disrupts his preparations for the interview. In "Mike's Horror-Scope," Carol worries that Mike might be seduced by cosmetics diva Beebe Gallini, whose effete secretary, Dwayne, minces about, often draped with or draping pink swaths of cloth. Writer Bruce Howard appears to have encoded a queer reference in a minor character's name: Gregory Gaylord. This outré photographer, who takes a Brady family portrait, mincingly declares: "Imagine! Gregory Gaylord forgetting his color plate" ("The Not-So-Rose-Colored Glasses"). These men, despite their brief appearances, disrupt the presentation of the Bradys' suburban lifestyle as an oasis from the counterculture. The line between innocence and ignorance is often slight, but within the Bradys' world, the children's innocence of homosexuality is complicated by the difficulty in maintaining their ignorance of it, for they cannot be quarantined from these gay men, even if they are relegated to the story's margins.

Whereas gay men are kept to the periphery of the Bradys' home life, the plot of "The Drummer Boy" ponders the pressures of gender conformity, ultimately endorsing laxer codes of masculinity. In this episode, Peter both plays football and sings in his school's glee club, but when his teammates discover his musical interests, they tease him with such disparaging and effeminizing terms as "songbird" and "canary." "We've got a canary on our team," one taunts, and another snipes, "Peter can be a pom-pom girl." Guest star Deacon Jones, a professional football player for the Los Angeles Rams, enlightens Peter's teammates from their archaic views when he informs them that he enjoys singing with his teammates; impressed by their idol, the boys reconsider their biases.

Along with Rosey Grier, Merlin Olsen, and Lamar Lundy, Jones was lionized as a member of the "Fearsome Foursome" for his gridiron achievements, with these men expanding their influence beyond the realm of sports to collectively challenge hegemonic concepts of masculinity throughout the 1970s. Grier openly discussed his hobbies of needlepoint and macramé, even penning *Rosey Grier's Needlepoint for Men* (1973), while Olsen later served as the spokesman for FTD Florists, appearing in numerous commercials as a gentle romantic lead. With Jones advocating greater flexibility in cultural codes of masculinity, "The Drummer Boy" challenges patriarchal voices insisting on gender conformity, and it can also be viewed as a queer allegory, in which Peter learns that he can safely "come out of the closet" about his pleasure in singing.

Although 1970s sitcoms rarely address homosexuality, with "The Drummer Boy" *The Brady Bunch* initiated a trend of treating queer story lines through sports, a theme developed in other programs when a protagonist learns that a longtime friend, formerly a professional athlete, is gay. In *All in the Family* (1971–79), bigoted Archie Bunker wisecracks, "A guy who wears glasses is a four eyes; a guy who is a fag is a queer," yet he is later stunned when his friend Steve, a former professional football player, comes out to him ("Judging Books by Covers"). *Soap* (1977–81) introduced television's first recurring gay character in Billy Crystal's role as Jodie Dallas, who is dating a closeted football player. In *Alice*, Alice divulges to her coworker Flo (Polly Holliday) that their new acquaintance, former professional footballer Jack Newhouse, is gay. Flo rejects the possibility that Newhouse could be gay until, in a masterful performance, Holliday depicts her character's gradual acceptance of the truth: "Alice, Jack Newhouse is a football player, honey. He's big and strong. Any woman'd die to take that hunk of candy home. Why, he spends half his life surrounded by big, virile men in locker rooms, in the showers, being tackled by other football players, jumping up and down and hugging each other . . . patting each other's butts . . ." As she speaks, the camera gradually zooms in; she slows her speech and her gum chewing, as she then exclaims, "That don't beat all! Jack Newhouse's gay" ("Alice Gets a Pass"). The episode also features Alice's hesitation to allow her son, Tommy (Philip McKeon), to accompany Newhouse on a fishing trip, lest the man either molest or effeminize him—but she soon realizes her prejudice and allows the trip to proceed. As to be expected, *The Brady Bunch*'s treatment of this queer theme is more muted than later 1970s fare, yet it questions the meaning of athletic masculinity as necessarily heteronormative in surprisingly similar terms.

Congruent with the program's hesitance over sexuality, issues of gender nonconformity spark deep anxieties in several episodes, revealing it, too, to be an issue of narrative ambivalence. Thus, as much as "The Drummer Boy" undermines gender's stranglehold on children, *The Brady Bunch* also portrays the humiliation that boys face when they transgress gender codes, particularly those concerning clothing and drag. "The Liberation of Marcia Brady" tackles the battle of the sexes in its plot, with Marcia joining Greg's Frontier Scouts troop to prove that she can succeed in outdoor activities that are ostensibly gendered male. Her brothers, mortified by her participation in their masculine milieu, attempt to mock her efforts by coercing Peter to enlist in her Sunflower Girl troop. Peter's assumption of successful masculinity, which is also questioned in such episodes as "The Drummer Boy" and "The Personality Kid," serves as a recurring theme in the series, and his faltering performance of adolescent masculinity experiences even greater duress when he must wear a Sunflower Girl outfit while traveling the neighborhood to sell cookies. Humiliated by his drag, Peter invites further ridicule due to the effete ambition assumed to motivate every member of the troop: to be named Blossom of the Month for selling the most cookies. At a neighbor's doorstep, he glumly recites his sales pitch, "I am a little Sunflower / Sunny, brave, and true / From tiny bud to blossom / I do good deeds for you," but he then quits the Sunflower Girls, with the social taboo against transgressing gender codes proving too strong for him to subvert. As Mimi Marinucci observes of this scene, "Peter's experience suggests that the feminine domain is the available default for anyone, male or female, who is unable to conquer the challenge of masculinity."[20]

In complementary contrast to Peter and his feminized drag, Marcia dons male clothing in this episode, with these story lines illustrating the typical prejudices accompanying gender transgressions: whereas boys who put on drag cede the cultural prerogatives of masculinity, girls who dress as boys often cannot access them fully. To the dismay of her brothers, Marcia initially triumphs in her scouting efforts, even as Greg sabotages her attempt to join the Frontier Scouts by leaving small markings on the trail she must hike. When Mike worries that she has been away from camp for too long, Marcia calms him: "Dad, you don't call Frontier Scouts 'sweetheart.' But I'm OK." Marcia's transvestism registers her successful crossing of gendered boundaries, yet she quits the Frontier Scouts in the episode's conclusion, explaining to Carol, Mike, and Greg: "I just wanted to prove to myself I could do it even though I'm a girl." She then adds to Carol: "Oh, has the new fashion magazine come in yet?" This episode is ultimately conservative in its outlook, as Marcia breaches gendered codes only to reinstate herself in the domestic sphere, as it also highlights the queer anxiety induced by individuals who transgress normative presumptions of gender, with Greg, Peter, and Bobby, in a state of veritable panic, struggling to ensure that their stepsister returns to the realm of the traditionally feminine. Still, the conservatism of this lesson is partially undone in its depiction of gender's performativity, for it stages the tenuous connection between clothing and biological sex that nonetheless carries so much cultural weight. Marcia again drags when, in her plan to recruit pop singer / television star Davy Jones of *The Monkees* (1966–68) to sing at a school dance, she disguises herself as a bellboy. This scene culminates as she blows a kiss of gratitude to Greg, thus imparting the queer joke that, although her drag is not terribly convincing, these bellboys are lovers ("Getting Davy Jones"). Alice drags as pilgrim John Carver in Greg's school movie ("The Un-underground Movie"), and she tells the Brady children that she starred as Julius Caesar in her high school play at an all-girls school ("Juliet Is the Sun"). In sum, clothes may make the man in the Bradys' world, but they also allow queer chinks in the social assumption of an unwavering correlation between dress and gender. Even for these innocent children presumably unaware of the 1970s culture surrounding them, ensconced in the generic bubble of a family sitcom, the outside world of shifting gender and sexual realms inevitably intrudes.

Framing Images of Queer Innocence

Beyond the ways in which issues of sexuality creep into *The Brady Bunch*'s family-friendly story lines, the program also portrays the child actors as objects of desire, thereby further dismantling its innocent facade. As numerous commentators have noted, cameras frame actors' attractiveness through close-ups, pans, and other such strategies, particularly for the purpose of idealizing female beauty. In her groundbreaking study of cinematic scopophilia, Laura Mulvey exposes its sexist bent: "In a world ordered by sexual imbalance, pleasure in looking has been split between active/male and passive/female. The determining male gaze projects its fantasy onto the female figure, which is styled accordingly."[21] Helen Haste agrees, arguing that "women are objectified through the role they play in presentation; or as objects of men's (the voyeur's) gaze."[22] Their analysis applies to the camera techniques of *The Brady Bunch*, particularly because, as producer Lloyd Schwartz explains, the program required many close-ups: "*The Brady Bunch* was filmed as a one-camera show, which means it was shot movie style. Most of the comedies today are shot on tape or film in front of live audiences, but our shows had many small scenes and had lots of close-ups. If you study the episodes, you'll notice many more close-ups of the kids in the first years of filming. The reason? The kids weren't accomplished actors and we could always work with them in close-ups until they got the line 'right.'"[23] To frame children in close-ups does not necessitate that their characters be construed as objects of desire, yet when story lines focus on their physical attractiveness, such eroticized images cannot be entirely discounted. As Helen Wheatley avers, television frequently piques scopophilic viewings under conditions that she terms "accidental erotic spectacle," an apt phrasing for the potential to frame child actors in such a manner.[24]

In this regard Maureen McCormick models the desirability of a young teen's body in her performances as Marcia. Her character is frequently shot preening in front of a mirror, such as when she plays with her facial features because, as she explains, she is "just trying to see how I look with Faye Dunaway's nose" ("Eenie Meenie Mommy Daddy"; see also the episode "Juliet Is the Sun" and fig. 2.1). Characters frequently comment on her popularity with boys, such as when Greg states at the dinner table, "You have to have a computer to keep up with her boyfriends" ("The Not-So-Ugly Duckling"). More than merely complimenting her attractiveness, various characters pay attention to her developing body and breasts. When Cindy and Marcia discuss their clothes and mutual need for closet space, Cindy tells her sister, "Mommy says you fill out, not up" ("A Clubhouse Is Not a Home"). In another scene, Marcia hopes to inherit some of Carol's sweaters as hand-me-downs, to which her mother replies, "After you've filled out a bit" ("Every Boy Does It Once"). Marcia often asserts her maturity over her younger siblings, such as when she declares to Peter and Bobby, "I no longer play kids' games"; Jan, however, reminds her of her relative youth by obliquely pointing out that her breasts have not yet developed: "You're only thirteen. You're not old enough yet to have a posture" ("Going, Going . . . Steady"). With characters commenting on Marcia's beauty and maturing body, she is established as an object of desire for the show's audience, regardless of the age-appropriateness of the connection between viewer and viewed.

FIGURE 2.1 In a pink room holding a pink hairbrush, Marcia models in front of the mirror, contemplating her beauty while inviting viewers to appreciate it as well. Her mother, Carol, enters the scene and, with furrowed features, appears worried about her daughter's potential narcissism ("Juliet Is the Sun").

Mulvey and Haste are correct to note that cameras more often frame female rather than male attractiveness, yet Greg, too, is constructed as an object of desire in *The Brady Bunch*, particularly in the series' later episodes that present him as an aspiring singer/songwriter. Talent scout Tammy Cutler sets Greg on a sure path to stardom in the persona of teen heartthrob Johnny Bravo, and during his audition she unexpectedly calls out, "Do your thing, girls," as a shrieking mob swarms him and rips his shirt open ("Adios, Johnny Bravo"). (Further heightening the episode's sexual tension, Claudia Jennings, who achieved fame as *Playboy*'s 1970 Playmate of the Year, undertook the role of Tammy Cutler—an unlikely casting decision for a family-friendly program.) Of course, one could rightly point out that, even within the staging of a sitcom, this scene is doubly staged, for Greg's desirability is undermined when he learns that the producers chose him not for his singing talent but simply because he fit the garish, and undoubtedly expensive, costume that was to define Johnny Bravo's persona for public adulation. Still, while Greg's singing talent is unnecessary for the part of Johnny Bravo, his physical attractiveness builds on previous episodes stressing his appeal, such as his shirtless surfing scenes in the Hawaii episodes. Indeed, counterbalancing Marcia's preening in front of the mirror, numerous story lines depict Greg lifting weights to enhance his masculine physique ("Eenie Meenie Mommy Daddy," "The Dropout," and "Greg's Triangle"). After successfully hefting some barbells, he self-approvingly declares to his brothers, "It takes real muscles to do that," testifying to his continued attention to his body and its desirability ("The Possible Dream").

Even young Cindy, who mugs with a face of apparently perpetual innocence, is framed in a manner to accentuate her irresistibility. As James Kincaid argues in his analysis of eroticized depictions of children and childhood, cute kids pique adult dreams: "This adorable child is both the center of and the best excuse for our wish-fulfillment fantasies about our own being, our memories, our longings, our losses, and our arousal. According to this tradition, the child is not simply radiant but disarmingly cunning, unexpected—in a word cute."[25] Along these lines, plots of *The Brady Bunch* stage how older men find Cindy irresistible. When Carol loses her voice and fears she cannot sing in her church's Christmas service, Cindy pleads with the man playing Santa Claus at their local department store, "I want my mommy to get her voice back." "Santa" attempts to redirect her wishes to toys but eventually succumbs to her desires and promises to fulfill her request. Mike then confronts "Santa," who defends himself: "That little kid is hard to resist. When she looks at you with those big baby blues, you just want to give her everything" ("The Voice of Christmas"). In a similar scene emphasizing Cindy's irresistibility, Carol takes the girls to redeem the trading stamps they won in a family competition, but the store has closed. The exhausted clerk, after initially refusing their pleas, opens the door when Cindy begs, "Oh, please, Mister," as the camera focuses on her in a close-up ("54–40 and Fight"; see fig. 2.2). Cindy's cuteness melts these men's hearts, and while it would surely exaggerate the tenor of these sequences to label them as pedophilic, they stage Cindy's desirability through her physical appearance—the adorable pigtail curls tied with blue ribbon, the pouty lips and button nose, the distraught, widened, blue eyes—that cannot be resisted.

Further troubling the show's purported innocence beyond its story lines, many viewers expected the siblings closest to each other in age—Marcia and Greg, Jan and Peter, Cindy and Bobby—to be narratively, and possibly romantically, paired. Hal Erickson describes "the latent kinkiness of the show's premise—a widow with three daughters marries a man with three sons, all of whom live under the same roof as brothers and sisters even though the proximities in the kids' ages could very well lead to relationships of a more delicate sort."[26] Thus, whereas Mike chides Greg, "Those aren't girls! Those are your sisters!" ("The Undergraduate"), and Greg reminds Peter, "Cindy doesn't date her own brothers!" ("Cindy Brady, Lady"), familial prohibitions against step-incest cannot halt the child actors' erotic interests in one another, nor can such desires be entirely erased from the series. In the program's pilot, Carol's mother says of Bobby and Cindy, "Don't they look cute together?" ("The Honeymoon"), thus encouraging viewers to see the young characters

FIGURE 2.2 This close-up of Cindy implies that no man—no matter his age, no matter her youth—can resist her cuteness ("54–40 and Fight").

as paired. The Brady kids frequently enter one another's bedrooms and their shared bathroom without knocking on the door, such as when Bobby walks in and takes a candid photo of Jan and Cindy ("Click"). In another episode, Marcia upbraids Bobby—"You're supposed to knock before you come in" ("Dough Re Mi")—and Greg enters Marcia's room while she undresses ("To Move or Not to Move"). Such scenes repeatedly stage the impossible image of children's innocence, for their interruptions of one another's privacy reflect the directors' and writers' preordained determination that the children will not discover one another undressed, while the dialogue reiterates this possibility.

The likelihood that two Brady children might find each other sexually attractive is most fully, if elliptically, explored in "Two Petes in a Pod," in which Peter becomes friends with Arthur Owens, a classmate and virtual twin. The boys trick Peter's family about their respective identities, and Arthur quickly develops a crush on Jan. Christopher Knight plays both roles, so in the scenes depicting Arthur's attraction to Jan, viewers understand that his desires do not transgress familial codes against step-incest. The image is nonetheless jarring, as Knight stages his hunger for his apparent stepsister, looking longingly at her (fig. 2.3). The episode also tacitly raises the question of why Peter would not find his stepsibling sexually attractive, just as his apparent twin does.

FIGURE 2.3 Christopher Knight (Peter) ogles Eve Plumb (Jan). In this scene Knight plays Arthur Owens, not Peter Brady, but the image invites viewers to contemplate sexual attraction between stepsiblings ("Two Petes in a Pod").

In looking for desires simmering beneath the show's surface, viewers simply discovered the behind-the-scenes hormonal excitement that the producers attempted to quell. Lloyd Schwartz recalls his efforts to dampen attractions between cast members—"Along with my script, I carried a metaphorical bucket of water to try to cool down libidos"[27]—for he realized that any attraction between cast members should not be caught on camera. He also mentions that "The Room of the Top" episode was shot during the "height of the sexual tension between Barry and Maureen. When Barry sat down on the bed and started to talk to his TV sister, it became romantic, even steamy."[28] In the resulting scene the chemistry between the two is dampened yet still flickers, especially in moments when Greg/Barry Williams briefly casts down his eyes, as if stifling the attraction he feels for Marcia/Maureen McCormick. In "My Sister, Benedict Arnold," sexual tension appears to flare between the two when Marcia dates Warren Mulaney, Greg's nemesis, who beat him for a position on the first-string basketball team. Greg warns Marcia, "You better not go out with Warren Mulaney again," as he then takes revenge by dating Kathy Lawrence, who edged out Marcia for a position on the cheerleading squad. Their prohibitions against each other's dating life, while couched in terms of sibling rivalry, also take on the air of former lovers jealous of being supplanted by new romantic interests.

In their many interviews following the show's run, cast members have freely confessed their past attractions for one another, which further imbues *The Brady Bunch* with a patina of submerged adolescent eroticism. Susan Olsen discusses how Maureen McCormick "married" her to Mike Lookinland during the filming of a camping sequence, mentioning that she "considered this to be our honeymoon." Of this episode's climactic tent-collapsing scene, Barry Williams states, "I think that's the first time I actually tackled Marcia, and it started something in me." As part of his post-*Brady* shtick cagily designed to prolong his time in the limelight, Williams has repeatedly trumpeted his attraction to his onscreen mother. "God, she's hot," he assesses lustily of Florence Henderson while reminiscing over the shooting of a scene featuring her ("A-Camping We Will Go" Commentary Track). In his autobiography *Growing Up Brady: I Was a Teenage Greg*, Williams recounts a date with Henderson and quotes her recollections of the event: "We went from liking each other to having a crush on each other and you were *always* on the make with me. I had to worry about that. You were really cute, and I was tempted a few times. I think we're lucky Carol never slept with Greg, but . . . uh . . . it coulda been, coulda been."[29] In her autobiography, however, Henderson sterilizes their relationship from any sexual residue: "What is very true is that Barry did have a serious crush on me, which I understood and helped him get past. Let us just say that if he had entertained a roll in the hay with me, I would never have done that."[30] Part of *The Brady Bunch*'s legacy entails continued interest in the sex lives of its stars, and these titillating tidbits invite new viewings of the program, those more deeply attuned to the difficulty of masking adolescent desire in a resolutely innocent family sitcom.

After the series concluded, its stars found themselves typecast in their family-friendly roles, and some sought challenging, provocative parts that would distance them from *The Brady Bunch*'s wholesomeness. Eve Plumb starred in *Dawn: Picture of a Teenage Runaway* (1976), in which the title character escapes her troubled home life only to turn to prostitution. Robert Reed guest-starred on *Medical Center* (1969–76) in a 1975 episode entitled "The Fourth Sex," playing the role of Pat Caddison, a doctor seeking a sex-change surgery.[31] Following his death in 1992, Reed's obituary revealed that he had contracted HIV, which his doctor cited as a contributing factor to his death from colon cancer.[32] With Reed posthumously outed as gay, his performance as Mike Brady casts *The Brady Bunch* in a new light, as it assumes the allegorical coloring of a 1970s family with a closeted father. Commenting on Reed's homosexuality, Sherwood Schwartz stated, "During the entire run of the series and subsequent TV movies, Lloyd and I always guarded his 'secret.'"[33] Of course they did: admitting Reed's homosexuality during the program's run in the early 1970s, or even during its rebootings in the 1980s and 1990s, would have created a major scandal, threatening the franchise's future and its financial profits. Now that today's viewers see a gay man playing the father of one of America's most scrupulously innocent television households, it exposes the lie of familial heteronormativity throughout the 1970s. Jan need not have run away from home for life as a prostitute, and Mike need not have been homosexual, for the actors' subsequent roles and revelations to highlight further the impossible innocence of the Bradys' world.

In the end the queer innocence of *The Brady Bunch* reveals the paradox of the promise of children's asexuality. Family-friendly sitcoms may cloak or otherwise marginalize story lines addressing sexuality, but sexuality, so central a part of the human experience, cannot be so readily constrained. And while the vast majority of *The Brady Bunch* maintains its illusion of innocence, the episode "Miss Popularity" rewrites the antieroticism that "The Honeymoon" established as the program's foundational premise. In this story, Carol and Mike plan their second honeymoon—during which their children are to remain at home—but Carol still laments, "It sure is going to be strange without the kids." Because they have repeatedly cancelled their vacation plans owing to unexpected scheduling conflicts, Alice brings Carol and Mike a "Do Not Disturb" sign to hang on their bedroom door. Carol frets, "What will the children think?" But Alice deadpans in reply, "Who do you think made the sign?" When did the Brady kids learn of their parents' pleasures behind closed doors? *The Brady Bunch* never answers this question, yet somehow these innocent children learned of human sexuality, thereby demonstrating the innocuousness and symptomology of sexual knowledge that the show tried so strenuously to hide from its surfaces, as well as the impossibility of stripping eroticism from a 1970s culture steeped in sexual liberation.

Kitsch Nostalgia and the Queer Afterlives of *The Brady Bunch*

In a snarky epitaph for *The Brady Bunch*, Robert Pegg mocks its ethos: "The show was the last of a vanishing breed of domestic sitcoms about the family life of unnaturally wholesome middle-class white people."[34] While easy to flippantly dismiss, these "unnaturally wholesome middle-class white people" have nonetheless proved enduringly popular since their 1974 cancellation, and *The Brady Bunch*'s unique contribution to American television is connected to its sustained legacy following its demise, which is virtually unparalleled. Quite simply, as easy as it may be to deride *The Brady Bunch* for its syrupy domesticity and the fantasy it creates of American suburban life, many young viewers delighted in its pleasures and refused to repudiate them as they aged, primarily children born in the 1960s who watched it during its initial run and children born in the 1970s who watched it as an after-school treat during its successful syndication both on local television channels and nationally on TBS. Self-proclaimed "Bradyologist" Lisa Sutton describes how she became attached to the Brady phenomenon: "Clearly it's from watching *The Brady Bunch* over and over again. It has the perfect balance of generic plotline and unchallenging sweetness with moments of arcane humor that everyone can relate to, no matter how trite or corny. It was a part of a time and place where things were truly kinder and gentler. It was our last gasp of innocence."[35] Countless viewers share Sutton's appreciation for *The Brady Bunch*'s innocence, for, following its 1974 cancellation, numerous reincarnations welcomed the family back to the American public: in addition to *The Brady Kids* (1972–73), an animated program running concurrently with the series, the Brady characters returned in such reboots as *The Brady Bunch Variety Hour* (1976); *The Brady Brides* (1981), a short-lived sitcom; *A Very Brady Christmas* (1988), a television movie; and *The Bradys* (1990), a dramedy. In the 1990s two theatrically released satirical films starring Shelley Long and Gary Cole as Carol and Mike Brady followed—*The Brady Bunch Movie* (1995) and *A Very Brady Sequel* (1996)—with *The Brady Bunch in the White House* (2002) returning the sitcom family to television.[36] It seems as if from the moment of the show's cancellation nostalgia demanded its immediate return, despite the fact that most of these revivals flopped in the ratings or at the box office—with the notable exceptions of *A Very Brady Christmas* and *The Brady Bunch Movie*. Following its cancellation, *The Brady Bunch* has resonated throughout popular culture, and this nostalgia reveals a deeper meaning of the original show's relationship to its audience—one that is tied to its conservative yet queer vision of the innocent American family and the intransigent allure of domestic sitcoms.

Nostalgia wields its inexorable pull as individuals recoat their yesteryears with patinas of affection and loss, not simply remembering events of their youth but imbuing them with a warm, hazy glow, as well as regret for their passing. As Søren Kierkegaard muses: "To live in recollection is the most perfect life imaginable; recollection is more richly satisfying than all actuality, and it has a security that no actuality possesses. A recollected life has already passed into eternity and has no temporal interest anymore."[37] The past becomes a longed-for paradise, one with its disappointments erased from view. With a dash of cynicism, Ralph Harper proposes that "nostalgia is neither illusion nor repetition; it is a return to something we have never had. And yet the very force of it is just that in it the lost is recognized, is familiar. Through nostalgia we know not only what we hold most dear, but the quality of experiencing that we deny ourselves habitually."[38] Nostalgia, then, does not simply entail a remembrance of things past but a celebration of a fantasy of that past. Furthermore, in sugar-coating one's history, nostalgia threatens to dull one's critical sensibilities, as Charles Maier suggests through his memorable analogy: "Nostalgia is to memory as kitsch is to art."[39] Few art forms are as easily mocked as kitsch, which has long been denigrated as art's antithesis, as in Clement Greenberg's classic formulation: "Kitsch is mechanical and operates by formulas. Kitsch is vicarious experience and faked sensations.... Kitsch is the epitome of all that is spurious."[40] Although some critics might desire the erasure of kitsch, deriding this cultural form has not muted its continued appeal, and nostalgia's kitschy edge invites an ironic sensibility to infiltrate one's relationship to the past, in the awareness that, although one's childhood entertainments lacked sophistication and depth, they maintain their power to please in the present as a result of the retrospective allure of their insistent simplicity.[41]

While not as rarefied as Proust's madeleines in *In Search of Lost Time*, television serves a central role for adults remembering their lost childhoods, and producers, writers, and marketers understand nostalgia's power for selling new versions of old narratives. Concerning television's ambivalent temporal positioning vis-à-vis past, present, and future, Jonathan Gray suggests: "On one hand, [television] programs can show us new ways to be, think, look, and feel ... that move us away from more ingrained identity markers such as gender, ethnicity, religion, or nationality.... On the other hand, fan texts ... can encourage us to hole up in our past."[42] This dynamic is particularly relevant for family sitcoms that viewers voraciously consumed during their childhood and then return to for nostalgic pleasures during their adulthood. For many *Brady Bunch* viewers, a kitschy sense of nostalgia is doubly refracted because many perceive the program's impossibly innocent foundations, outmoded even during its airing in the early 1970s, while also recognizing their childhood enjoyment of its guileless narratives. A given individual's viewing history shifts through time and with the flow of a given program's dissemination, as of course it must, yet the pleasures of kitsch nostalgia for *The Brady Bunch* involve insisting on one's present enjoyment of televisual narratives that one cannot help but see, with the passing of years, as serving up a vision of America endearingly and ridiculously passé in its outlook.

Cognizant of the profound nostalgia their sitcom generated among its viewers, and also of the concomitant desire to experience its pleasures anew, in the 1980s Sherwood and Lloyd Schwartz built their script for *A Very Brady Christmas* to deliver to audiences the same formula as the series, unchanged despite the passing of years. *A Very Brady Christmas* promises an excess of nostalgia, with the simple adverb *very* hinting at a kitschy revamping of the recipe enjoyed during the early 1970s. Turning the family's name into an adjective—the title announces through its semantic play both a depiction of the Brady family's Christmas and the experience of "Bradyhood" during the yuletide season—Schwartz and Schwartz amplify the cultural meaning of yesteryear through their appeal to kitsch nostalgia.

The plot of *A Very Brady Christmas* is simple to the point of simplistic: Carol and Mike, after a mix-up in which they each plan a holiday vacation without consulting the other, decide to use their travel funds to bring Greg, Marcia, Peter, Jan, Bobby, and Cindy home for Christmas. Within this framework each Brady child propels a subplot related to a minor crisis in his or her life, with these subplots registering as well that the children are now adults facing adult challenges. Greg disagrees with his wife, Nora, over whether they should spend the holidays with his family or with hers; Marcia's husband, Wally, has lost his job; Peter feels emasculated because his girlfriend, Valerie, is also his boss; Jan and her husband, Phillip, are experiencing marital difficulties; Bobby has dropped out of business school to pursue his dream of race-car driving; and Cindy worries that she will never be treated as an adult. (She is right to complain: for Christmas dinner she is seated at the children's table with her nephews and niece.) Problems quickly dissolve, virtually as soon as they are aired. Although Greg arrives without Nora, she unexpectedly follows him; Wally finds a job while joining Mike on a jaunt through the neighborhood; Peter and Valerie propose simultaneously, proving the equality of their relationship; Jan and Phillip reconcile after talking through their problems as Carol silently observes; Bobby confesses his career switch, and although Mike and Carol are upset, Mike admits, "I didn't always do what my parents wanted me to do"; and Carol invites Cindy to join the adults ("Cindy, would you like to come over now and sit with us at the big table?"), although she declines.

The simple stasis of the family sitcom is achieved anew, as viewers knew it would be.

Alongside these numerous plot arcs, the emotional highlights of *A Very Brady Christmas* hinge on its kitschiest and most sentimental moments, further stressing that this television movie seeks to enhance the experience of Bradyism through an excess of emotionality. For example, as Mike, Greg, Peter, and Bobby enter the family home with a Christmas tree in tow, they sing "Deck the Halls"; Carol, Marcia, Jan, Cindy, and Alice then enter from the kitchen, bringing with them refreshments and singing along. Soon the entire family gathers around the tree to sing "Jingle Bells." On the show's nostalgic level, this simple moment captures the emotional allure of the Brady family—singing together in perfect family harmony. This ideal stasis and kitschy nostalgia of *A Very Brady Christmas* further registers in its use of flashbacks to classic *Brady Bunch* episodes. As Carol and Mike reminisce over shared family moments from the past, the film segues into the camping trip depicted in the "A-Camping We Will Go" episode—thereby inviting viewers to relive their treasured memories of the Bradys as well. The climax of *A Very Brady Christmas* merges nostalgia with honeyed sentimentality: a building collapses because the owner did not heed Mike's architectural specifications, and although the family fears the worst, Carol's singing of "O Come All Ye Faithful" presages a holiday miracle, as Mike escapes from the construction site unharmed. This moment echoes the seasonal wonders of years past, when Carol sang the same melody for the Christmas service after Cindy's miraculous request for Santa Claus to restore her mother's voice in "The Voice of Christmas" episode. Such emotionally kitschy moments multiply as *A Very Brady Christmas* concludes: lest viewers miss the allusion, the news reporter covering the building collapse points to the street sign marking its location, celebrating "another miracle on 34th Street" in homage to sentimentalist yuletide films of the past. Sam the butcher, who has left Alice for another woman, returns to her, pleading, "Do you have it in your heart to take me back?" thus providing a happy ending for all. The movie concludes as the Bradys sing "We Wish You a Merry Christmas"—with the direct address of the song's title breaking the barrier between television program and television viewers. With its plot predicated on kitsch nostalgia, *A Very Brady Christmas* proved a ratings smash, as Lloyd Schwartz documents: "*A Very Brady Christmas* had the highest ratings of any TV movie over the last two years."[43] And while it is easy for critics to scoff at kitsch, its appeal endures, and not merely for unsophisticated viewers lacking any critical sensibility but for those pleasurably aware of their appreciation of nostalgia tweaked to its rarefied essence.

At the same time, *A Very Brady Christmas* showcases the ways in which sexuality queerly undermines the promise of kitsch nostalgia—as it also presaged the disastrous fate of the Brady Bunch's next incarnation in *The Bradys*—for the impossible innocence of its sitcom roots, as tenuous as they were in the series itself, could simply no longer hold in the 1980s. *A Very Brady Christmas* begins by obfuscating sex, in line with *The Brady Bunch*'s pilot episode. Carol flirts suggestively—"Remember, we don't have any kids at home anymore. . . . So, I thought maybe you and I could do some business together here"—but Mike responds as if the children still regulated their household. "You tempt me. You really do," he claims before leaving for work. Soon, however, sexually suggestive story lines trouble the innocent foundations on which *The Brady Bunch* relies. When viewers learn that Sam left Alice for another woman, he explains in the note that leaves her in tears: "I met a younger woman. At first we just traded meatloaf recipes; then one night she asked me over to season her rump roast." This double entendre hints at more candid treatments of eroticism, and the sexual obfuscation of *The Brady Bunch* soon cedes to images of the Brady children indulging in their amorous pleasures. As Greg passionately embraces Nora, who works as his nurse, another nurse interrupts them, and so he jokes, "It's OK. I'm just teaching this nurse mouth-to-mouth resuscitation." Wally and Marcia kiss a bit too hungrily at the dinner table for typical Christmas celebrations, and after Valerie comforts Peter—"I can't help it if I'm your boss, Peter. And that only bothers me because it bothers you, and it shouldn't, sweetheart"—they embrace, with the film's otherwise chipper score now accentuating the seductive growls of a saxophone. When Jan and Phillip reconcile after their dispute, they kiss, and Jan interrupts their rising passion to tell Carol, "Thanks, mom, for bringing us back together," as her mother acknowledges the likelihood that they will now consummate their reconciliation: "You can be late for breakfast." Such candor about Greg's, Marcia's, Peter's, and Jan's sex lives is counterbalanced by Bobby's and Cindy's eternal innocence, with little hint of any romantic story lines yet developing for the youngest offspring, yet kitsch nostalgia evokes desire for the stasis of the past, not for maturity in the present.

These hints of sexuality in *A Very Brady Christmas* escalated in the family's next incarnation in *The Bradys* during the early 1990s, which bombed in the ratings and was quickly cancelled, for kitschy nostalgia evoking a queerly innocent past clashed with the characters' sexually active present. *The Bradys* sought to update the program's family sitcom foundations by infusing dramatic elements, resulting in an hour-long comic drama, or "dramedy." The genre of dramedy, as Judith Lancioni attests, "fosters the weaving together of comic and dramatic elements across storylines, thus creating a highly complex text,"[44] yet drama and comedy have proved notoriously challenging for television to combine successfully. Foundational dramedies such as *Frank's Place* (1987–88), *Hooperman* (1987–89), and *The Days and Nights of Molly Dodd* (1987–91) struggled to find audiences; *Moonlighting* (1985–89) initially succeeded yet soon lost its comic edge—notably after Maddie (Cybill Shepherd) and David (Bruce Willis) consummated their relationship, demonstrating that romance can be the deathblow for comedy based on repartee's witty antagonism.[45] Later dramedies such as *Desperate Housewives* (2004–12), *Ugly Betty* (2006–10), and *Orange Is the New Black* (2013–) are perhaps more accurately described as soap operas reveling in story lines so overdramatic that they verge on the self-parodic. Notably, few dramedies attract child viewers, so the transition of *The Brady Bunch* into *The Bradys* conjured a vast array of narrative disjunctions.

Riffing on *The Brady Bunch*'s famous opening credit sequence and theme song, with its jaunty explanation of how the families joined together, Florence Henderson sings *The Bradys'* theme, with its lyrics alerting viewers to the program's new perspective: "When our kids were small, their problems all were smaller. As they changed, so did their point of view." By stressing the roots of *The Bradys* in its sitcom past, this theme song situates the program's appeal in kitsch nostalgia, and to this end *The Bradys* maintains many plot points from its earlier incarnations, even down to Bobby's good-luck charm that he carries with him in his racing career, with its nod to *The Brady Bunch*'s Hawaii episodes. When Bobby marries his fiancée, Tracy, Dabbs Greer returns to play the minister—the same actor who presided over Carol and Mike's nuptials more than twenty years earlier. This character then reminisces about a farcical wedding he presided over that ended with a dog chasing a cat and the bride and groom covered in wedding cake, as he is then reminded that it was Carol and Mike's. Bobby and Tracy's wedding involves similar mayhem, as her sister goes into labor during the ceremony and Greg delivers the baby upstairs, as Bobby, paralyzed from a racing accident, then rises from his wheelchair and stands for his vows. With its mixture of nostalgic homage and contemporary struggles, *The Bradys* attempts to deliver the pleasures of the past while recognizing the necessity of adult story lines for adult actors.

Whereas family sitcoms typically seek viewers of all ages, dramedies face the challenge of juggling comic antics with their serious dramatic ambitions. In one such mishmash scene the family awaits Bobby's return from the hospital after the devastating accident that left him paralyzed, with Carol hinting at the painful emotions she struggles to hide: "I'm going to try not to cry when I see Bobby in that wheelchair." Heartfelt drama segues into a cheap comedy sequence as the family mistakes a parade of guests—Alice, Peter, an insurance agent offering Marcia's husband Wally a job, and Bobby's physical therapist—for Bobby. At last, when he enters his childhood home, the camera pans as everybody tears up. Yet from this somber moment of emotional connection spring numerous scenes of slapstick humor inspired by Bobby's wheelchair. Alice sits in it for a test run but loses control and rolls down a ramp, and when Tracy accepts Bobby's marriage proposal, it rolls backward and then off-camera as they fall into a lake. Such scenes create a jarring effect, one that ultimately undercuts both the humor of the program's sitcom roots and the emotionality of its dramatic aspirations.

The Bradys ran for a mere six episodes, addressing as well such story lines as Marcia's descent into alcoholism and Mike's foray into politics, so viewers conditioned to see the Bradys resolving their problems in each episode were inevitably disappointed by nostalgia's failure. And for a program founded on innocence and asexuality—no matter the absurdity of this view—there is something jarring about seeing the Brady children pursuing their desires so openly. Having watched these characters in their youth, and having been encouraged to identify with the Brady siblings who match them in age and sex, longtime Brady fans were further confronted with the ways in which sexuality disrupts the sitcom's foundational promise of eternal innocence.[46] In one such instance, Jan and Phillip are depicted in bed together watching Bobby's car race on television; Jan says, "Bobby is making his move," and Phillip huskily adds, "So am I." Later Jan, mentioning their upcoming cruise, purrs over "three fun-filled days, three very fun-filled nights," and their marital intimacy includes household chores in dishabille (figs. 2.4 and 2.5). Likewise, Peter, who has broken up with his boss, Valerie, resumes his life as a Romeo: a coworker invites him to dinner at her place although he already has plans with another. "I hope you like your food spicy," she murmurs tantalizingly, to which he responds, "The hotter, the better"—as a saxophone wails seductively on the score. For fans of *The Brady Bunch* who grew up alongside it, such scenes break the formula of kitsch nostalgia, for it is a bit like thinking of one's siblings' sex lives: rationally, we know they are sexual beings, but musing over their erotic pastimes is a bit discomfiting and leaves one grateful for the incest taboo. Ironically, *The Brady Bunch* prospered in the early 1970s prior to the institution of family-hour protocols, yet *The Bradys* died by the family hour in the 1990s—beaten in the ratings by ABC's family-friendly TGIF lineup (standing both for "Thank God It's Friday" and, a bit more cozily, "Thank Goodness It's Funny") beginning with *Full House* (1987–95) and *Family Matters* (1989–98). The genre of dramedy mixed with Brady children's sexuality disrupted the winning formula of innocence reborn through kitsch nostalgia, and from these narrative problems *The Bradys* died while a series of cinematic parodies was born.

The Brady Bunch depicted an anachronistic and queerly innocent vision of the wholesome American family during its initial run in the early 1970s, and the failure of *The Bradys* testifies to the narrative limits of these themes against the passage of time. By the 1990s *The Brady Bunch* had become a symbol against which other family sitcoms openly revolted. In an unprecedented coincidence, three programs—*All-American Girl* (1994–95), *That '70s Show* (1998–2006), and *Family Guy* (1999–)—mocked *The Brady Bunch* in their

FIGURES 2.4 AND 2.5 Jan is no longer an innocent child, and thus no longer part of a profitable franchise, with these images capturing her in bed with her husband, Phillip, and attending to household chores while wearing lingerie. Frequent depictions of adult sexuality in *The Bradys* unsettle the pleasures of kitsch nostalgia, demanding that viewers see these characters as adults when their appeal lies in their impossible innocence.

pilot episodes, announcing their satiric disdain for this epitome of yesteryear's wholesome sitcoms. *All-American Girl*'s Margaret (Margaret Cho) tells her mother, "Mom, this is how they used to fight on *The Brady Bunch*. We can do better" ("Mom, Dad, This Is Kyle"), and *That '70s Show* portrays Eric (Topher Grace) and Donna (Laura Prepon) satirically reenacting the Bradys' "oh, my nose" plotline, in which Greg accidentally throws a football into Marcia's face ("The Subject Was Noses"). *That '70s Show*'s pilot alerts viewers to its anti-*Brady* ethos with pot smoking, beer drinking, a subplot about a gay auto mechanic, and mother Kitty Forman's admonition: "A car is not a bedroom on wheels" ("Pilot"). *Family Guy*, which packs so many allusions to television history and popular culture that its plots often fade into the background, launches its opening sequence with the Griffin family watching an outlandishly satiric version of *The Brady Bunch*: Jan tattles on Greg for smoking, and they are then respectively punished in the family's snake pit and chamber of fire ("Death Has a Shadow"). Collectively, then, this anti-*Brady* sentiment of the 1990s exposes a frustration with simple moralism, even as most of these shows similarly end with the family unit restored to its mutual, loving baseline—snarky Bradys, but Bradys nonetheless, who appeal to this program of the past through allusions both mocking and celebrating its kitsch appeal.

Excoriated by critics during its years of production, *The Brady Bunch* succeeded with a five-season run and then became a cultural touchstone over the ensuing decades, as it built a lasting legacy from an appealing suburban bubble that invites multiple and contradictory readings both celebrating its wholesome values and delighting in its kitschy underbelly. With an improbable innocence as its defining virtue, *The Brady Bunch* shunned sex in the 1970s yet could never entirely sever sexuality from its story lines, for which many of its viewers both appreciated and ridiculed its sentimental appeal. In the series' original run, Cousin Oliver (Robbie Rist) says to Cindy, "I think your mother has a problem about discussing sex" ("The Hairbrained Scheme"), yet these problems with discussing sex were key to the series' endearingly queer innocence, which created a pop-culture phenomenon of never-ending nostalgia for a past that never was. A family sitcom, even with the Bradys as its protagonists, inevitably summons the paradox of innocence and experience, thereby undermining and exposing the queer fantasies on which it is founded. And while the Bradys' innocence appeared out of step with the countercultural ethos of the 1970s, similar strands of erotic naiveté in family sitcoms continued unabated, with, as the next chapter details, the Huxtables of *The Cosby Show* illustrating in the 1980s and early 1990s the ways in which issues of race complicate the family sitcom's queer paradigms of innocence.

3

No Sex Please, We're African American

The Cosby Show's Queer Fear of Black Sexuality

Seven years prior to *The Cosby Show*'s 1984 debut, the United States Commission on Civil Rights released its study *Window Dressing on the Set: Women and Minorities in Television*, documenting the abysmal state of television's portrayals of African Americans and other minorities. Among its findings—unsurprising to most—the committee noted the overrepresentation of white males, the typecasting of minority actors, and the patent tokenism of occasional nonwhite roles in otherwise all-white casts.[1] "Whiteness frames television," Beretta Smith-Shomade succinctly states, with the medium's historical whiteness marginalizing a vast variety of minority and ethnic voices, which gives the false appearance that issues of race affect only people of color.[2] To resolve this issue, the commission advocated that "production companies and network programming executives should incorporate more minorities and women into television drama," particularly by "develop[ing] series which portray minorities and women playing a variety of roles comparable in diversity and prestige to those played by white males."[3] Heeding the commission's call, star Bill Cosby and producers Marcy Carsey and Tom Werner chose to depict an affluent black family in *The Cosby Show*, thus recalibrating prevailing cultural images of African Americans as almost uniformly poor in such 1970s programs as *Sanford and Son* (1972–77), *Good Times* (1974–79), and *What's*

Happening!! (1976–79). While breaking new ground in television's representations of African Americans, *The Cosby Show* also sparked heated debates about the cultural messages that this landmark program disseminated about race in America. Viewers and critics approached the program with conflicting assumptions about how a wealthy black family should be represented in a domestic sitcom, with their various premises reflecting as well their understanding of the queer fantasies of genre, family-friendly programming, and, in this instance, the erotic innocence of black children.

With Cosby as protagonist Dr. Heathcliff Huxtable and Phylicia Ayers-Allen Rashad as his wife, Clair, *The Cosby Show* details the daily comic misadventures of their family of five children: Sondra (Sabrina Le Beauf), Denise (Lisa Bonet), Theo (Malcolm-Jamal Warner), Vanessa (Tempestt Bledsoe), and Rudy (Keshia Knight Pulliam). Sondra marries Elvin Tibideaux (Geoffrey Owens) and bears twins Winnie and Nelson, and the series' sixth season begins with the surprise announcement that Denise, on a trip to Africa, has married Lieutenant Martin Kendall (Joseph C. Phillips), the father of a young daughter, Olivia (Raven-Symoné). The seventh, penultimate season introduces cousin Pam Tucker (Erika Alexander), who joins the Huxtable clan after her mother travels to California to tend to a sick relative and also introduces her friends Charmaine (Karen Malina White) and Lance (Allen Payne). This multigenerational family includes Cliff's parents, Russell (Earle Hyman) and Anna (Clarice Taylor), among numerous other relatives and in-laws—and in one episode even the Huxtable children's great-grandaunt, Gramtee ("The Story Teller"). The family members' abiding affection for one another imbues the program with a sentimental sensibility, albeit with a sharp edge: as Kelefa Sanneh trenchantly observes, "In Cosby's comedy, he returns endlessly, even obsessively, to this basic plot: the struggle of a man against the woman he has chosen and the children he hasn't."[4] With Cliff as an obstetrician/gynecologist and Clair as an attorney, the Huxtables enjoy a level of financial prosperity few Americans attain, yet this affluence affords a key line of critique: that *The Cosby Show* overlooks the ways in which racism undercuts many African Americans' lives and economic possibilities.

At their core such critiques posit that, in depicting a rich black family within the structures of a sitcom, *The Cosby Show* pardoned the United States' history of slavery and—with pun intended—whitewashed racial injustice by refusing to represent it. Given television's long-standing marginalization of black characters, as well as America's troubled history of race relations, numerous critics believed that the program should have directly confronted issues of racism, discrimination, and economic injustice—as the first section of this chapter details. My argument then turns to the ways in which the inherent conservatism that some see in the program is undercut by its rewriting of parenthood as an androgynous role, as Cliff acts primarily as an authoritative, not authoritarian, father who cooperates with Clair in raising their children.[5] In regendering the contours of an African American family, however, *The Cosby Show* faced the ultimately queer challenge of depicting black children's sexuality, especially in light of contemporary cultural images of black teen promiscuity and a purported pregnancy epidemic. Thus, Cliff's androgynous fatherhood—and Cosby's performance of it—is complicated by his determination to police his children's sexuality, particularly his daughters' virginity. *The Cosby Show*'s vigorous presentation of African American sexual innocence concomitantly reinstates the model of patriarchal masculinity it otherwise rejects, exemplifying the challenges of promoting egalitarian gender ideals when the children of the United States' defining black family begin dating, particularly in light of Cosby's respect for the thematic constraints of family-friendly programming. The chapter concludes by examining the ways in which metatextual issues concerning Lisa Bonet's and Bill Cosby's erotic lives influenced (and, indeed, continue to influence) *The Cosby Show*'s reception. With the popular press addressing the program's cast as if they were truly a family, issues concerning the representation of African American sexuality exploded when Lisa Bonet pursued acting opportunities beyond the family-friendly fare of her sitcom, demonstrating the utility of sexuality for a young star's career and the difficulty of maintaining one foot in a family sitcom while taking on more provocative roles, when her "father" disapproves. More than twenty years after the show's conclusion in 1992, allegations against Cosby for sexually assaulting numerous women have further complicated his sitcom's reception by demolishing the facade of familial innocence the show so earnestly projected. In seeking to portray the Huxtables as untainted by sexuality, *The Cosby Show* ironically exposes the queer anxieties perpetually latent in such repression.

The Politics of Black Representation in Family Sitcoms

As *The Cosby Show*'s critical reception illustrates, television's depictions of African Americans have historically been caught between a rock and a hard place: the rock of the demands of televisual fiction, of creating characters and story lines that national audiences will watch week after week; the hard place of doing so while recognizing the legacy of slavery as it continues into the present day, of acknowledging racism's pernicious effects on black identity. This problem is exacerbated by the television industry's primarily white power structures, as it is often white producers who greenlight African American shows—for *The Cosby Show*, Carsey and Werner—and who then often hire white writers and directors to transmit the "truth" of the African American experience. Many notable programs throughout television history bear the marks of this controversy, including *Julia* (1968–71), *Sanford and Son*, *Good Times*, and *What's Happening!!*, with questions inevitably arising about the truthfulness of their characters' lives in a nation still grappling with the devastating consequences of racism. As Diahann Carroll declared of her starring (and groundbreaking) role in *Julia*, "For a hundred years we have been prevented from seeing accurate images of ourselves and we're all overconcerned and overreacting. The needs of the white writer go to the superhuman being. At the moment, we're presenting the white Negro. And he has very little Negro-ness."[6] Hal Kanter, *Julia*'s lead writer, added as well, "This is not a civil rights show. . . . What we're driving at is escapist entertainment, not sociological document," and Mort Werner, NBC's vice president in charge of program and talent, agreed: "This is not the documentary arm of NBC—it's *en-ter-tain-ment*."[7] Redd Foxx's litany of complaints against *Sanford and Son*'s production included its creation of "white versions of black humor," as he advocated instead for episodes penned and directed by black talent.[8] John Amos, who played the father James Evans in *Good Times*, left the show after three seasons, disappointed in its emphasis on the flamboyant antics of his television son J.J. (Jimmie Walker). As Eric Monte, the program's creator, recalled, "[Amos] made it known in no uncertain terms that he was NOT going to play a degraded Black man!" And Amos stated diplomatically: "The truth is we reached a point where we were at an impasse that we could no longer dialogue civilly about the character."[9] In *What's Happening!!* the family's absent father appears after years of separation and cannot recognize his children, Raj (Ernest Thomas) and Dee (Danielle Spencer). This episode pathologizes black paternity, with this man musing regretfully—"Does seem a shame a father doesn't know his own kids, huh?"—as he then proceeds with his con ("When Daddy Comes Marching Home"). Throughout the 1960s and 1970s and into the 1980s, issues concerning black representation on television inevitably arose owing to fears of misrepresentation: that such programs denigrated African Americans by reducing them to stereotypes and homogenizing the diversity of black culture to a uniform vision of lives mired in poverty and struggle.

Much criticism of *The Cosby Show* evinces a similar concern that the program misrepresents black culture, warning that viewers may be lulled into complacency by taking this sitcom family as proof of America's successful resolution of racial conflicts. Certainly, the program's airing during the Reagan era complicated its racial politics. Herman Gray notes that characters such as Cliff Huxtable "were seen by conservatives as possessing the requisite moral character, individual responsibility and personal determination to succeed in spite of residual social impediments" such that they served as "model minorities" whom conservatives then deployed "to counter the dependence of the underclass and to affirm their commitment to racial equality."[10] Leslie Innis and Joe Feagin, in their sociological analysis of middle-class African American viewers' responses to *The Cosby Show*, conclude: "Generally, then, the opportunity cost of having Black television characters seems to be a lessening of the concern with the Black condition and a fostering of hope that things can get better. This is perhaps the dilemma that fosters the ambivalence in Black middle-class responses to *The Cosby Show*."[11] In another study examining audience reactions, Sut Jhally and Justin Lewis contend that *The Cosby Show* allows white viewers to overlook the ways in which unfettered capitalism and racism collude in the oppression of black Americans: "*The Cosby Show*, and others like it, divert attention from the class-based causes of racial inequality. More than this, the series throws a veil of confusion over black people who are trying to comprehend the inequities of modern racism. It derails dissatisfaction with the system and converts it, almost miraculously, into acceptance of its values. In a culture where white people now refuse to acknowledge the existence of unequal opportunities, the political consequences of this acceptance are, for black people, disastrous."[12] Jhally and Lewis's powerful argument, which takes into account numerous discussions with *Cosby Show* viewers, convincingly demonstrates television's numbing force and how its anodyne themes comfort viewers, both white and black, about the state of American race relations. It is critical to realize, however, that interpretations of this vein mostly arise not from detailed readings of the show's 197 plotlines but from theorizations of the meaning of its lacunae—holding it accountable for what it does not address on its surface and focusing instead primarily on the symptomology of its silences.[13]

With a pointed critique of the Huxtables' comfortable lives, Ella Taylor condemns their apparent indifference to the struggling community living beyond their doors: "The Huxtables have friends who drift in and out of their lives but no discernible community, indeed no public life to speak of aside from their jobs, which seem to run on automatic pilot."[14] In a similar vein, Henry Louis Gates Jr. alleges that *The Cosby Show* "reassuringly [throws] the blame for black poverty onto the impoverished."[15] Such readings extrapolate from the program's story lines to its supposed symptomology, and the argument that the Huxtables lack any sort of commitment to their community is patently incorrect, as they volunteer frequently at their local community center. The episode "Mr. Quiet" depicts Cliff presenting nutritional information to local pregnant women, and Theo donates his basketball to the center.[16] When Vanessa's ex-boyfriend Robert tells Cliff that he and Clair should donate money to charity and their medical and legal services to the community, Cliff offers to show him the many receipts proving their generosity ("It's Not Easy Being Green"). Further testifying to the program's concern for the Huxtables' wider community and their economically disadvantaged neighbors, the administrator at Cliff's hospital states that their facility "serves many low-income patients, and when our funds get cut, we have to do whatever we can to ensure that these

his basketball and pinochle skills, yet Clair beats him in both of these pastimes ("It's a Boy" and "Adventures in Babysitting"). One can point to rare moments of gender policing in the series, such as when Clair stops a hairdresser from adorning her grandson Nelson with feminine accouterments—"Oh, no, wait a minute now. This is a boy. You cannot put that ribbon in his hair" ("Day of the Locusts")—but the lion's share of the program dismantles crude distinctions between the sexes. Also, although Clair forbids ribbons from her grandson's locks, Cliff sports bows in his hair after playing with Olivia ("Clair's Reunion"; fig. 3.1), and Cliff's and Clair's bedclothes often reverse the standard gendered dichotomy of blue for men and pink for women ("The Dentist"). Quite simply, a heterosexual man in the 1980s who is sufficiently comfortable with his masculinity to wear pink pajamas and hair bows does not appear overly concerned with maintaining traditional gender roles.

Cosby's deconstruction of Reagan-era masculinity contrasts sharply with the many 1980s sitcom fathers inhabiting hypermasculine roles, including Alex Karras's retired pro-football player in *Webster* (1983–89), Bill Kirchenbauer's high-school gym coach in *Just the Ten of Us* (1988–90), Gerald McRaney's marine major in *Major Dad* (1989–93), and Craig T. Nelson's university football coach in *Coach* (1989–97). These characters represent the grouchy yet ultimately cuddly Arnold Schwarzeneggers and Sylvester Stallones of the

FIGURE 3.1 With red and green ribbons in his hair and a slightly wearied yet patient expression on his face, Cosby/Cliff demonstrates his comfort in challenging yesteryear's conceptions of gender ("Clair's Reunion").

home front, and even they must confront the changes to American gender roles wrought during the 1960s and 1970s. For example, *Coach*'s Hayden Fox struggles with his new relationship with his college-age daughter, Kelly, and in one episode Kelly's boyfriend tells Hayden that he is "more in touch with his female side" and that he believes all people "have male and female sides," positing as well that "women are only 51 percent female and 49 percent male." Hayden defends himself against this ostensible aspersion against his masculinity, saying that his reading on such a scale would be "in the high 90s" ("I'm in Love with a Boy Named Stuart"). Much of the focus of these series is on men adjusting to changing definitions of masculinity, such as when Hayden confesses to his assistant coach, Luther (Jerry van Dyke), about the difficulties of communicating with Kelly: "Boy, I tell you, this being-a-parent stuff, it's just a mess. You're in the dark all the time. You never know where you're going" ("Kelly and the Professor"). In contrast to these white fathers grappling with shifting gender roles, Cosby's Cliff Huxtable comfortably endorses a more equitable view of masculinity and femininity.

In its rewriting of cultural scripts of paternal masculinity, *The Cosby Show* portrays an androgynous ideal of fatherhood that exorcises strict gender roles from the family unit. As Poussaint explains, "A new movement has spawned that has been pushing American men and women closer to the acceptance of androgynous fatherhood—men who take a significant share of nurturing responsibilities for children and the home, tasks that were previously assigned exclusively to women."[24] Certainly, *The Cosby Show* rejects sexism and patriarchal attitudes, notably in casting Cosby as an obstetrician who apprises new fathers of the changing times. One patient's husband bloviates to Cliff, "There's nothing like having a pregnant wife to really prove your manhood" and announces his intention to rule as his family's boss; Cliff replies sardonically, "Mr. Lee, I used to think that I was going to be the boss. I don't know how I lost it, I don't know where I lost it, I don't think I ever had it."[25] He explains further: "You've got to understand that the days of being the boss, the barefoot and pregnant—that's thirty years ago. The old-fashioned man is out. There's more to this relationship than being boss. You're not the boss; she won't be the boss. The boss will be that baby" ("Father's Day").

Phylicia Rashad's performance of Clair Huxtable's androgynous motherhood—as an authoritative nurturer rather than as boundless maternal benevolence—complements Cliff's androgynous fatherhood, yet as with so many other elements of *The Cosby Show*, Clair, too, serves as a Rorschach test for critics. She has been celebrated for her trailblazing portrayal of a successful, professional, loving mother, and pilloried for the ostensible fantasy of this view. Donald Bogle praises the new vision of black maternity that Rashad brought to the screen: "Always maintaining her sexuality and her femininity, she could never be described as 'brassy' or 'sassy,' the terms usually associated with forceful black women in TV series of the past. Here television moved away entirely from that longtime staple of black sitcoms: the mother as hefty, desexed mammy type."[26] Esther Rolle in *Good Times*, Mabel King in *What's Happening!!*, and Nell Carter in *Gimme a Break!* (1981–87) infused their maternal roles with warmth and good humor, with their bodies conforming to the "mammy" stereotype long established as the ideal for black women to play—often in white households, as for Carter. In contrast to these characters, Rashad's Clair modeled a distinctly new vision of black motherhood, one in line with 1980s family sitcoms depicting white professional women: architect Elyse Keaton (Meredith Baxter) of *Family Ties* (1982–89), advertising executive Angela Bower (Judith Light) of *Who's the Boss?* (1984–92), and journalist Maggie Seaver (Joanna Kerns) of *Growing Pains* (1985–92).

Rebutting Bogle's praise, John Fiske derides Clair Huxtable as the height of fantasy: "She has a full-time profession, is raising five children, does all the cooking and household management, all without any hired help or child-care workers, and, to cap it all, she never has a hair out of place and rarely shows any signs of strain."[27] While many family sitcoms evoke the illusion of a self-cleaning home, Fiske both exaggerates the demands that Clair faces and overlooks the ways in which *The Cosby Show* repeatedly emphasizes the stress in her life. First, Clair can hardly be described as "raising five children" when Sondra is studying at Princeton and is, for all intents and purposes, an independent woman at the series' beginning, and Denise leaves for college at the second season's end. It is true that the family does not employ child-care workers, but criticisms in this vein overlook a central plank of the program's premise, congruent with its view of androgynous fatherhood: Cliff's office is located in their home so that he can tend to the children as necessary throughout the day. Theo and Vanessa are sufficiently mature to look after themselves, and Vanessa, in particular, is often tasked with watching Rudy. Furthermore, the program frequently refers to the time demands Clair must negotiate, such as when she sighs, "What it is is a life that's so crowded I don't have time to figure out what it is 'cause I'm going to be late for work" ("You're Not a Mother Night"), or laments, "I had a hard day," which she describes in detail ("Lost Weekend"). Viewers see her working on Saturday ("You Only Hurt the One You Love") and past midnight ("Calling Dr. Huxtable"). Cliff assists her in household management, such as when she mentions that she has been coming home late because of a case, and he demonstrates his support: "You've got a lovely dinner waiting for you in the kitchen" ("Clair's Case").

Much as *The Cosby Show* frames its treatment of race by constructing its audience as knowledgeable of America's history of race relations, the program frames its treatment of gender and feminism as an assumed part of the fabric of American lives, as it also highlights the necessity of women's networks to resist outdated views of male privilege. When Theo and his friend Walter (a.k.a. "Cockroach") define the term *burger* as a good-looking girl, Denise is offended, castigating their slang as "one of the most sexist, degrading remarks I've ever heard." Denise then asks Vanessa if she understands what *burger* denotes. Initially, Vanessa thinks the term is "cute," but after her sister decodes the metaphor of a burger as a piece of meat, she changes her mind: "You guys are disgusting" ("Theo and Cockroach"). A running gag throughout the series depicts young Rudy facing archaically sexist attitudes from her friend Kenny, as in the following exchange:

> RUDY: Well, Sondra says a woman can do anything.
> KENNY: No. A woman will do what a man says.
> RUDY: Not me. . . . A woman can have any job she wants.
> KENNY: No, she can't. ("Cliff in Charge")

As this exchange documents, Rudy relies on Sondra's lessons about women's equality to counter the sexism she faces, and while in this instance Kenny contributes the final words to their quarrel, it would be unwise to think that Rudy is vanquished, for she frequently employs the simple strategy of renaming Kenny as "Bud" to dismiss his antiquated views: "You're no man. You're Bud" ("The Visit"). Like Rudy, Kenny has learned his views of gender from an older sibling, yet his brother, although never depicted onscreen, becomes key to the series' demolition of outmoded masculinity. Clair pointedly tells Kenny, "Your brother has poisoned your mind about women. And one of these days, you're going to quote your brother to some woman who is a little less civilized than I. And she's going to grab you by the ankles and twirl you around in the air till those cavemen ideas come swirling out of your ears." Moreover, as much as Kenny may parrot his brother's lessons, he states admiringly to Theo of Rudy, "No man will ever tame her" ("57 Varieties"). As the years pass, Kenny begins to see his brother with new eyes, realizing that his hero does not measure up to the stature he assumed in his youth. "I guess this explains why my brother is always in his room . . . crying," he muses ("Thanksgiving at the Huxtables"). Within the Cosbys' world, traditional gender roles must be discarded in favor of a more androgynous ideal, yet this ideal cannot withstand the challenges of representing teen sexuality without simultaneously buckling to the queering repercussions of portraying innocence.

Family-Friendly Programming, Teen Sexuality, and the Limits of Androgynous Fatherhood

Cliff's androgynous fatherhood and egalitarian marriage fall comfortably within the parameters of a family sitcom scheduled during the so-called family hour—one that anchored NBC's Thursday lineup throughout the program's run—but the issue of his children's sexuality disrupts these dynamics and queerly subverts the show's heteronormative foundations, for in these story lines Cliff reasserts a patriarchal mode of masculinity to monitor his children's sex lives. Certainly, Cosby forcefully advocated for family-friendly programming as an important tradition and lamented its demise, as he wrote with Poussaint: "Too many programs—where do we begin—use sex as a way to capture an audience. Today, even during the so-called family hour, TV shows are so loaded with sexual innuendos, suggestive situations, and foul language you'd think you were watching the adult after-hours channel. Few of these shows say one word about love."[28] Avoiding sexuality in deference to family-friendly protocols only reinforces its significance when it does appear, rendering *The Cosby Show* a conflicted site in regard to its sexual themes.

In line with Cosby's endorsement of anodyne programming, *The Cosby Show* endorses the fantasy of the family hour, so its reticence to forthrightly address issues of sexuality is encoded into its narrative structure. The program stresses its family-friendly content in several moments of metadiscourse, such as when, in introducing the episode "The Dentist," Rudy announces in voice-over: "Hi! I'm Rudy. Tonight's show stars Mr. Danny Kaye. It's for all us kids, but you grown-ups should watch, too." Similarly, "Cliff's Nightmare" concludes with Wallace Shawn, a recurring guest star as neighbor Jeffrey Engels, intoning, "Good night, boys and girls. Eat the right things, and sleep tight," thereby constructing this episode's audience as primarily children. In one of television history's most famous network battles, FOX scheduled its ode to familial dysfunctionality, *The Simpsons* (1989–), against *The Cosby Show*, which set up a direct confrontation over the family hour's meaning for audiences. Cosby acknowledged this competition when Olivia, wearing a Bart Simpson mask, approaches Cliff, who says, "Now, cut that out" ("Same Time, Next Year")—both batting away the competition and, at least tacitly, arguing for the inappropriateness of *The Simpsons* in the family hour.[29]

The Cosby Show's head-to-head battle with *The Simpsons* foregrounded its insistently innocent treatment of sexuality, yet this contrast between the program and a culture increasingly frank about eroticism had long been apparent. Many 1980s child characters of family sitcoms were well versed in human sexuality, with programs satirizing the sexual mores of yesteryear. In this exchange from *Who's the Boss?* youngsters Jonathan and Samantha decipher their parents' euphemism-ridden discussion of sex:

JONATHAN: What was that all about?
SAMANTHA: Sex.
JONATHAN: That's what I thought. ("Pilot")

Further along these lines, many 1980s programs ridicule adults' reticence to discuss sexuality, such as when Julie of *Gimme a Break!*, studying human reproduction, reads aloud her textbook's outdated lessons: "To make a baby, a man releases a substance made of thousands of tiny, little pollywogs. . . . These pollywogs wiggle their way to a special part of a woman. This is called the oven" ("Katie the Crook"). As its peer programs cast off the fantasy of sexless story lines and tackled more challenging themes, *The Cosby Show* instead concentrated on its young characters' sexual naiveté.

The show's primary narrative strategy for preserving the innocence of the family hour is to curtail any amorous behavior between Cliff and Clair following their children's interruptions. As Cosby writes, "Children who drop in at night are a means of birth control that is one hundred percent effective. In fact, for years in my house, the meaning of coitus interruptus was coitus interrupted by someone other than the participants."[30] The series' pilot inaugurates this tradition, as Cliff kisses Clair in bed but she cautions him: "Let's just remember this is how we got the children in the first place." Cliff turns off the light and embraces her, but Rudy and Vanessa interrupt because Rudy worries that a wolf-man is growling in the closet, so Clair permits them into the bed ("Theo's Economic Lesson"). In another such moment, Vanessa confesses to Cliff that she snuck into a horror movie and now finds herself too frightened to sleep. Cliff allows her into the sanctity of the parental bed—"Would it be better if you slept with us tonight?"—yet soon regrets his act of kindness, for Vanessa appears to kick him in her sleep ("Bad Dreams"). While Clair and Cliff's relationship simmers with affectionate energy and they often snuggle amorously, intercourse even within the bounds of marriage is broached so delicately as to be virtually inscrutable. When Cliff proposes a romantic bon voyage party for a planned vacation, a murky euphemism obscures the contemplated act. Cliff purrs, "I'll be the ocean liner, and you'll be the tugboat," and Clair agrees, "OK, then we'll dock together" ("Trust Me"). Unlike the clear erotic imagery of a train in a tunnel, a hotdog in a bun, or a rocket through a cloud, an ocean liner and a tugboat docked together obfuscates rather than communicates the idea of intercourse.

Given the program's investment in repudiating hypersexualized images of African Americans, the limits of androgynous fatherhood become apparent when Cliff assumes the role of defender of his daughters' chastity. Throughout the 1980s, many media treatments of black teen sexuality fomented anxiety over a perceived pregnancy epidemic, one that exploited the worst cultural stereotypes about the dysfunctionality of black kinship. Elaine Kaplan summarizes these allegations circulating throughout the decade in a variety of outlets: "Black teen mothers' children grow up in fatherless households with mothers who have few moral values and little control over their offspring. The boys join gangs; the girls stand a good chance of becoming teen mothers themselves."[31] Sweeping away these arguments, Rickie Solinger documents the construction of this racist fantasy: "President Ronald Reagan and others began to name teenage pregnancy (and its association with welfare and 'welfare queens'), along with the crack cocaine epidemic and inner-city violence, as the chief causes of poverty and other social ills in the United States. Despite the fact that black rates of teenage pregnancy continued to fall in relation to white rates in the 1980s, New Right politicians and political commentators boldly defined teenage pregnancy as a black problem at this time."[32] With these demeaning images sharply etched in the public consciousness, *The Cosby Show* stringently avoids any potential suggestion of a Huxtable daughter's promiscuity, and Sondra, Denise, and Vanessa readily submit to their father's strict policing of their sex lives. In one instance when Denise prepares for a date, Cliff informs her: "Not in those pants. Blood cannot get up to your brain from your legs. And besides, this is a school night." After changing her clothes, Denise seeks her father's approval: "New outfit for you, Daddy. Happy?" ("Theo's Economic Lesson"). Vanessa requests Cliff's guidance about dancing with boys, and as they practice together, he cautions: "You don't mash your body up against any boy. I don't care who he is. You understand? You're not going to mash your body. Now step back—twelve inches" ("Back to the Track, Jack"; figs. 3.2 and 3.3). In another episode Clair reminisces, "I remember when she wouldn't even let a boy get next to her," as Cliff chimes in, "That's right, and now that's my job" ("Halloween").

Throughout much of the series, Vanessa is characterized as "boy-crazy," but her girlish infatuations paradoxically reinforce the efficacy of her parents' lessons. After sneaking away with her boyfriend Jeremy, she teeters between conflicting desires to follow her passions or her parents' admonitions:

VANESSA: I think we should stop.
JEREMY: Why? Aren't you enjoying it?
VANESSA: Yeah—too much. That's why I stopped.
JEREMY: You don't have to stop. (they kiss again)
VANESSA: Jeremy, I can't. What would my parents say if they knew I was up here? ("Truth or Consequences")

After Cliff and Clair learn of Vanessa's illicit escapade, Cliff talks with Jeremy in the kitchen, and with a clear nod to the story of Adam and Eve's Fall, uses apples to represent Vanessa and Jeremy in his antierotic lesson. The narrative arc of the episode, then, is less between Vanessa and her boyfriend than between Cliff and teen sexuality, with the father reclaiming authority over his

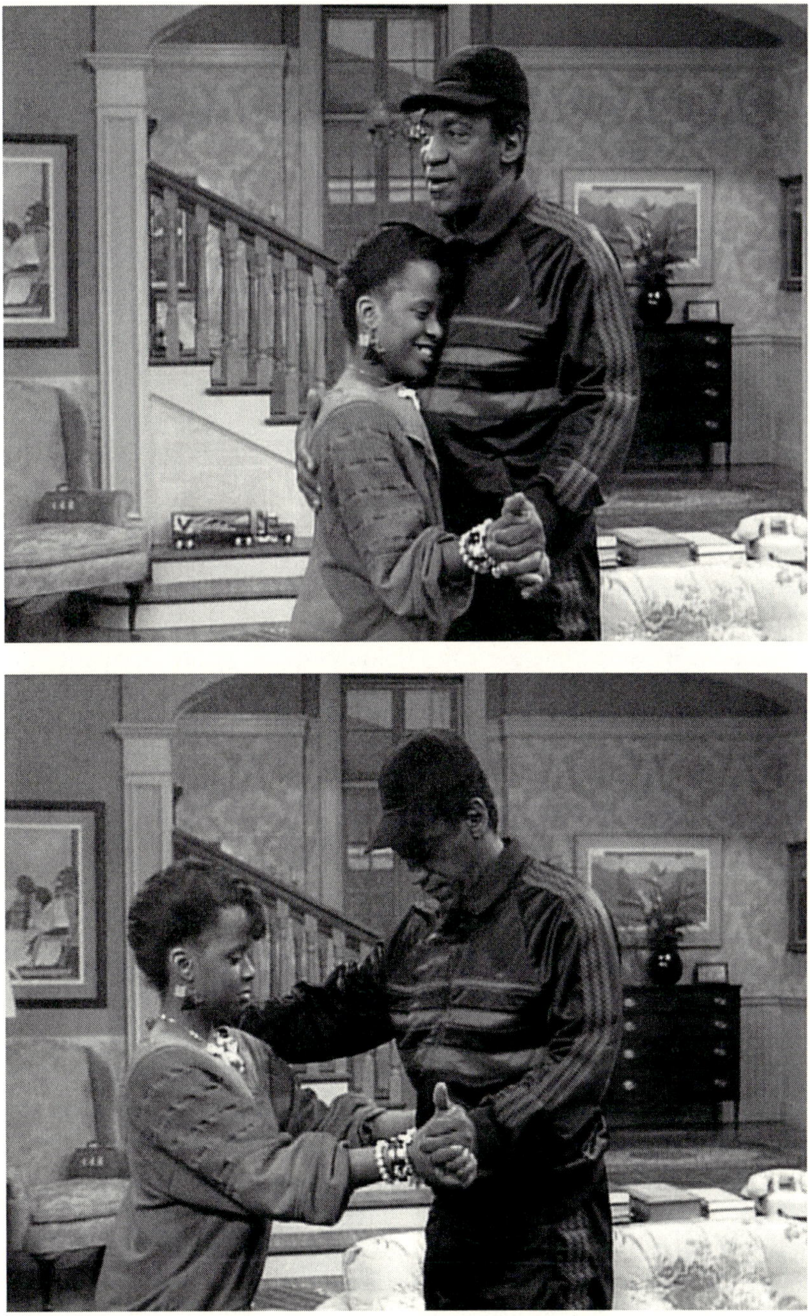

FIGURES 3.2 AND 3.3 Vanessa assumes she will dance closely with boys, but in accordance with her father's dating precepts, she should remain at a proper distance from them ("Back to the Track, Jack").

daughter. Even after Vanessa leaves for college, her father scares off potential boyfriends, as she reminds him: "You took Jeremy into that kitchen, took two apples, put 'em on top of each other, said that was us, took one of the apples, skinned it, and said that was him. I haven't heard from him since." Cliff replies, "And when you went out with him, he didn't put his hands on you, did he?" ("It's All in the Game").

At the same time that *The Cosby Show* celebrates children's asexuality as a preeminent virtue, and does so by clouding hints of illicit desire, it also seeks to reform cultural conversations about sexual development by treating them with refreshing candor. Further developing the concept of androgynous fatherhood as espoused in Cosby's show, Poussaint explains: "Children ask many questions at elementary-school age, including questions about sex. The old practice of fathers referring these questions to mothers is no longer acceptable."[33] Notably in this regard, *The Cosby Show* features fairly frank discussions about sexual development, if not about sexual intercourse. As Rudy grows older, she worries that her breasts are not maturing, and her father comforts her: "Some girls develop them later than others." Rudy's fears evaporate as she realizes the truth of her parents' words: "It's like what mom said—'You get what you get when you get it'—and a lot of us haven't gotten it yet" ("Same Time, Next Year"). Rudy experiences her first period in "The Infantry Has Landed," and Clair begins menopause in "Clair's Liberation," with both story lines disabusing viewers about long-standing hokum concerning female biology. Clair is determined that Rudy learn the facts of menstruation so that she won't fall prey to misogynistic folklore (e.g., women menstruating at the beach attract sharks), and it is apparent that Rudy needs this parental guidance, as she repeats another ridiculous superstition learned from her schoolmates: "Five beets a day keeps the transfusion away." Brushing away these canards, Clair tells her daughter, "Rudy, in biological terms, you are a woman. And if you want to be a mother someday, this has to happen." In complementary contrast, Clair melodramatically overacts to the symptoms of menopause, sticking her head in the freezer to fight off hot flashes and bursting into tears in a display of hyperemotionality when Theo offers her corn instead of carrots, yet she does so with ironic and humorous intent, for the explicit purpose of modeling the utter normality of the female body throughout its stages of development.

Such candor about human sexual development is counterbalanced by the program's evasive treatment of sexuality for its child characters, which underscores the queerness of children's sexuality as unimaginable within the program's fictions yet nonetheless a source of deep anxiety. Cliff hears Rudy singing along to her radio, "You can do it to me all night long, uh huh, baby, do it to me all night long." Shocked by the words coming from his daughter's mouth, he inquires:

CLIFF: What does "it" mean?
RUDY: Daddy, you know what "it" means.
CLIFF: Yes, I do. But I want to know if you know what "it" means.
RUDY: "It" means holding hands and kissing.
CLIFF: Holding hands and kissing? Yes, but that's not all that "it" means.
RUDY: What else does "it" mean?
CLIFF: "It" means homework. Baby, do my homework all night long. ("How Do You Get to Carnegie Hall?")

Here viewers do not see Cliff teaching his daughter about sexuality but rather resignifying "it" into schoolwork and obfuscating rather than clarifying "its" meaning. In this episode's other story line, Vanessa and her friends Janet and Kara form their singing group The Lipsticks. Cliff and Clair are shocked by the girls' low-cut and suggestive outfits emphasizing their breasts, and Clair pulls out the tissues stuffed in Vanessa's bra (fig. 3.4). The episode reads as an indictment of the lax morality promoted by popular culture, from which *The Cosby Show* distances itself, yet it is also significant for establishing the boundaries of Cliff's lessons in sex for his children and for children in his audience: in this instance not to say what "it" is but to condemn children's natural interest in sexuality.

It is further clear that Cliff's paternal interest in his daughters' sex lives revolves around maintaining their virginity until their wedding nights. Before Sondra and Elvin marry, Cliff worries that they are sleeping together after

FIGURE 3.4 Modeling the crass sexuality of popular culture, Vanessa forms the singing group The Lipsticks—and meets with her parents' stern disapproval ("How Do You Get to Carnegie Hall?").

he hears an offhand reference to a shared breakfast, but Elvin clarifies that he did not sleep over at Sondra's residence before this meal ("Monster Man Huxtable"). In an awkward, extended conversation between Cliff and his son-in-law Martin, the two men discuss Denise's virginity:

> CLIFF: You knew my daughter only two weeks, and then you got married. Now in the course of that two weeks, did, um . . .
>
> MARTIN: Oh! (laughs) Oh, boy. I don't know if I should be sharing that with you, Dr. Huxtable.
>
> CLIFF: Yes, you should.
>
> MARTIN: When I first met Denise, I was very attracted to her, because she is . . . hot. I mean, no disrespect intended.
>
> CLIFF: It's all right, it's just—watch your mouth.
>
> MARTIN: Okay. All right, anyway, uh, I can't believe I'm telling you this, but, uh . . .
>
> CLIFF: You should.
>
> MARTIN: I really wanted to, uh . . .
>
> CLIFF: Yeah, yeah, be careful.
>
> MARTIN: Express myself physically with her. Can I say that?
>
> CLIFF: Yeah, but you're borderline.
>
> MARTIN: Okay. But you'll be happy to know that Denise was having none of that.
>
> CLIFF: Really?
>
> MARTIN: On our wedding night, I discovered that, of the two of us, only one of us had had prior experience, and as you know, I'm the one with the daughter.
>
> CLIFF: So, you're telling me that my daughter . . .
>
> MARTIN: Yup. ("Getting to Know You")

Obviously delighted by the preservation of his daughter's hymen until marriage, Cliff beams and dances happily. Martin's delicate euphemisms ("express myself physically") and Cliff's steady pursuit of information about his daughter's virginity reinstate masculine prerogatives over women's bodies. And when Vanessa announces her engagement to Dabnis, who is approximately ten years her senior, she tells her parents, "I have never had experience with another man, and you guys don't think I know what I'm doing" ("The Iceman Bricketh"). The confused interplay of these statements—invoking both her virginity and her parents' assumption of her naiveté precisely because she has preserved her virginity—displays the confused site of this black woman's body, with her parents exerting their authority through the status of her hymen.[34]

Within the plotlines of *The Cosby Show*, serious sexual transgressions do not occur within the household unit but disrupt it from outside. In the episode "Denise's Friend"—which marks this young woman as unnamed, virtually unknowable—Denise tells her father that a friend needs assistance with a gynecological concern. At the community center, Cliff asks this friend if she is pregnant; she replies that she is not. He then asks if she has discussed her concerns with her parents, but she states elliptically, "If I do, then they'll know I'm not what they think I am." Cliff observes, "You don't want your parents to know you're sexually active," and she states, "Believe me, Dr. Huxtable. They would not understand." Even the specters of teen pregnancy and venereal disease are dispelled by the episode's end, as Cliff reports that this young woman suffered from a mild bladder infection. She agrees to talk to her parents because Cliff tells her he would want to know about his children's problems, yet when Cliff convenes a family meeting to discuss the necessity for honesty between parents and children, Rudy is conveniently absent—apparently too young for a frank discussion of human sexuality (with the paradox that child viewers hear the conversation that she cannot). Later in the series, when Pam's boyfriend, Slide, pressures her to sleep with him, Charmaine counsels abstinence. "What I have may not be precious to the world, but it is precious to me. You understand what I'm saying? What I got ain't no knick-knacks," she avers, and Lance agrees that he and Charmaine share an intimate relationship, yet intimacy does not require physical consummation: "See 'intimate' means that our minds have met, our souls have touched, and our spirits have sat together." Complementing this story line of sexual restraint, Cliff's duties as an obstetrician call him to tend to an adolescent girl at the hospital, as he explains to Clair: "There you go. Good example. Got a sixteen-year-old girl ready to deliver sometime tonight. Parents say, 'We want to have nothing to do with you.' The boy that did it says, 'It's not mine, I told you to protect yourself.' All she's going to do is have a baby" ("Just Thinking about It"). The specter of black teen pregnancy haunts *The Cosby Show*'s treatment of adolescent sexuality, and while Pam mentions the possibility of birth control while contemplating intercourse with Slide, no Huxtable child turns to their obstetrician father for similar assistance, for doing so would reveal the sexuality the show so strenuously cloaks. In notable contrast, Natalie of *The Facts of Life* (1979–88), a white teen on a concurrent sitcom, lost her virginity to her boyfriend, Snake ("The First Time"), demonstrating both the potential innocuousness of such a story line and the ways in which whiteness rarely faces such cultural duress as blackness.

In Theo's maturation from boy to man, his father and other mentors steer him away from the "player" model of hypersexualized black masculinity, prevalent in 1970s blaxploitation films such as *Shaft* (1971) and *Super Fly* (1972). This stereotype of African American masculinity, with its flamboyant exaggerations of machismo and bravado, nevertheless lurks in the background of his character (fig. 3.5). In one such scene, he and Cockroach share with Denise

FIGURE 3.5 With his shirt open and a gold chain dangling around his neck, Theo models a sexually libidinous vision of black masculinity from which he soon matures ("Theo and the Older Woman").

their plans for the future, envisioning a bachelor pad resplendent in its excess. "We're gonna fill the place with things that women love—like bearskin rugs," Theo jauntily avows, as his sister sarcastically rebuffs his view: "Oh, yeah, we love those things. You know what else we love? Curtains that open and close by remote control" ("Bring 'Em Back Alive"). Whereas many teen boys in the 1980s hid issues of *Playboy*, *Penthouse*, or *Hustler* in their bedrooms, Theo prefers scantily clad women posing with cars over more hardcore fare. Clair discovers this illicit stash and upbraids her son—"This magazine is demeaning to women"—but Theo feebly defends himself with the language of female liberation: "No, mom, it's not. This magazine makes women look great. And it shows that they can be mechanically inclined" ("Pentaque"). As this encounter demonstrates, Theo's nascent sense of sexual desire is staged as innocently as possible, with gazing at semiclad, not naked, women his most significant youthful transgression. In his efforts to win his girlfriend Tonya's affections, he buys her a "diamondoid" ring for $19.95, but his more effective technique in seduction arises from his knowledge of African American literature, as he shares Ralph Ellison's *Invisible Man* with her. "Theo, I love the way you read," she intones, and soon they kiss. This scene models black masculinity based on the courtship rituals of yesteryear, for Cliff and Theo report to his grandfather Russell that they had "the talk":

RUSSELL: Did he mention the part about being a gentleman?

THEO: Several times.

CLIFF: I gave him the same talk that you gave me, and your father gave you.

RUSSELL: Did you listen?

THEO: Yes, Grandpa. ("The Card Game")

For much of the series, Theo imposes chastity upon himself, refusing to see women's sexual attractiveness and concentrating instead on their personalities. When Denise teases him about his beautiful date, he becomes upset and claims, "I'm attracted to her inner beauty." Denise suggests that her brother must find this young woman at least somewhat physically desirable, to which he responds, "I try not to let that part mess with my mind" ("Home for the Weekend").

Yet during his maturation it is strongly suggested, yet never conclusively so, that Theo loses his virginity. Cliff and Clair express their disappointment over his decision, yet the sexual double standard that privileges male sexual conquest undercuts the program's otherwise progressive stances toward gender and parenting. Cliff finds a bra mixed in with Theo's laundry, so he and Clair deduce that their son has been living with his girlfriend, Justine. Clair chastises Theo for his decision: "Now I'm not saying that these people have taken a wrong turn in life and are going downhill and will never amount to anything. But we do have our own point of view on this subject, if that's all right with you" ("Theo's Dirty Laundry"). Because Theo has lied to them about his living situation, Cliff and Clair expel him from their home. The episode ends with the potential fracturing of the Huxtable household, but this family tempest has calmed by the subsequent episode, in which Theo comes and goes as he pleases in his parents' residence ("What's It All About?"). For a program so invested in dismantling gender paradigms, the issue of children's sexuality undermines its egalitarian vision, with these story lines reasserting the Huxtable daughters' virginity as an arena of narrative and parental control, whereas, while Cliff and Clair register their disappointment over Theo's sexual activity, the issue quickly recedes from view.

In a further instance of *The Cosby Show*'s discomfort with sexuality, no gay or lesbian characters enter its heteronormative world, one that brooks little possibility of queer sexuality but also little overt homophobia (other than such passing moments as Clair's concern over ribbons in her grandson's hair, as mentioned earlier). Still, in presiding over his daughters' sexual maturations, Cliff finds himself engaged in homosocial friendships that create slight chinks in the program's uniform heteronormativity by positioning him as the predominant avatar of the program's repressed queerness. When Sondra and Elvin break up temporarily, she dates Darrell, who models Cliff's brand of forward-thinking masculinity: Darrell endorses women working outside the home, cooks for himself and others, and, in a nod to Cliff as a role model, attends medical school. Cliff prefers him over Elvin and invites Darrell to dinner after his date with Sondra, although Cliff must soon admit to him that Elvin will accompany her back to Princeton. Given Sondra's obvious preference for Elvin, Darrell wonders why Cliff invited him, and Cliff answers, "Because you're the fellow I like." He plaintively adds, "You like me, don't you?" ("Cliff in Love"). Also, the episode in which Vanessa and Dabnis break off their engagement is titled "Cliff Gets Jilted," pointing to his investment in his daughters' romantic interests and his disappointments when his homosocial bonds must be broken as a result of their decisions. Cliff pesters Dabnis about the breakup so much that Dabnis finally rebuts, "Vanessa is annoying. Are you happy?" in an exasperated attempt to end the conversation. A few episodes later, Cliff tries to ward off Vanessa's possible interest in a Senegalese exchange student, telling this young man, "Her fiancé's name was Dabnis, and I liked him" ("Clair's Reunion"). As Gail Rubin and Eve Kosofsky Sedgwick have demonstrated in their pioneering studies of men's traffic in women and of male homosociality, men often negotiate their relationships through women, and despite Cliff's commitment to androgynous fatherhood, he succumbs to archaic modes of gender policing that ironically expose the homosocial underbelly of his desire to preserve his daughters' virginity.[35]

Metadramatic Black Sexualities: Cosby, Bonet, and the Queer Legacy of *The Cosby Show*

Despite *The Cosby Show*'s rigorous policing of black eroticism, metadramatic controversies concerning Cosby and Bonet proved the impossibility of quarantining sexuality from the program and thus demonstrate the queer potential of sexuality to subvert plotlines from which it has mostly been erased. Bill Cosby is not Cliff Huxtable, and Lisa Bonet is not Cosby's daughter, yet their public disagreements concerning her non-*Cosby* roles were frequently painted in terms of a family feud. Furthermore, decades-old allegations that Cosby fathered an illegitimate child and that he drugged and raped dozens of women over his career have now affected the reception of *The Cosby Show*, demonstrating the difficulty for many viewers in jettisoning the alluring fantasies both of the Huxtables' world and of the actors who created it.

During the show's run in the 1980s, Bonet sought to elude the typecasting that hounds so many child stars by appearing in Alan Parker's sexually provocative *Angel Heart* (1987), a film that required sustained editing to avoid an X rating. Cosby presented himself as above the fray, stating, "I did not want to read the script. She has a mother and father,"[36] as he dismissed the film's premise: "that film doesn't offer my appetite anything."[37] By denying his position *in loco parentis*, Cosby implies as well his ultimate authority—that he could have chosen to read the script and, at the very least, attempted to veto Bonet's participation in a film of which he did not approve. Bonet's performance as Epiphany Proudfoot fractured her good-girl image as a member of America's preeminent television family, particularly because this supernatural thriller indulges in numerous stereotypes about African American spirituality and sexuality—notably in a sequence in which Proudfoot dances in a voodoo ritual, sacrifices a chicken, and drenches herself in its blood while exposing her breasts (see fig. 3.6). For the most part the film presents its racist characters as unsympathetic and unlikable, yet audiences must still endure the ugly stereotypes that are central to its story. Proudfoot, as another character describes her, is a "a mambo priestess, like her mom. Has been since she was thirteen," and the protagonist, Harold Angel (Mickey Rourke), pursues her to learn the whereabouts of the missing Johnny Favorite—despite a policeman's warning that in Louisiana "down here we don't mix with the jigaboos." The film concludes as Angel realizes that, not only has he slept with his daughter, Proudfoot, but he has murdered her as well. Bonet received praise for her performance, with Roger Ebert opining that "she was probably right to take this controversial role as her movie debut; it's such a stretch from the Cosby character that it establishes her as a plausible movie actress."[38] Nonetheless, because her performance clashed with her *Cosby* persona and the sitcom's premise of innocence, the character of Denise was increasingly shunted to the margins.

Rebutting Bonet's and the film's lurid depiction of African American sexuality, *The Cosby Show* rewrote the horrific sex quest of *Angel Heart* in its "Dead End Kids Meet Dr. Lotus" episode, which ridicules voodoo when Theo

FIGURE 3.6 In this sensual image from *Angel Heart*, Bonet plays on her sex appeal, despite her television father's disapproval. Nighttime shots of her character sacrificing chickens with her breasts exposed were too dark for reproduction.

visits Dr. Lotus, "a specialist in the spiritual sciences," for assistance in ridding him of his amatory competition for Justine. Providing an alternative to black magic, Cliff fakes a ritual of his own, pouring oil on Theo and banging pots, as he teaches him the only magic needed: "I will pay more attention to my woman." *Angel Heart* and this episode share the same basic narrative—a man consults a voodoo shaman in his quest—with *The Cosby Show* lambasting the film for disrupting the familial ethos of the former and therefore recasting the story line of the latter into one of gentlemanly romance.

Following the controversies of *Angel Heart*, Bonet married rock star Lenny Kravitz in 1987 and gave birth to their daughter, Zoë, in 1988, which created numerous filming difficulties for *The Cosby Show* and its spin-off *A Different World* (1987–93). Behind-the-scenes accounts detailed skirmishes and Bonet's unprofessional behavior on set, notably in late arrivals and lack of preparation. Regarding Bonet's pregnancy, Susan Fales-Hill, a producer and writer of *A Different World*, recalls: "We had a lot of intense discussions about whether to incorporate the pregnancy into the show. We ultimately came to the conclusion as a group—and firmly guided by Mr. Cosby—that with the problem of teenage pregnancy, it was a little dangerous to send out an [unwed mother] message."[39] The entertainment media yet again cast these creative differences between two professional actors as a family drama. The title of a *Jet* article—"Lisa Bonet: How Bill Cosby Will Handle Return of His Prodigal Daughter"—confuses the actors with their roles, as it further blurs the borders between fiction and reality: "like the Biblical father . . . Cosby allowed his prodigal daughter to return to his show, salvaging her acting career while she deals, in real life, with her marriage and pregnancy."[40] Bonet recalled that her disputes with Cosby and the show's producers arose because they did not allow her to voice her sense of the character. "They took on, like, a heavy parental-control thing. . . . Instead of allowing me to stay true to myself, they tried to put a clamp on my spirit and my character," apparently confusing the relevance of her personal spirit to a fictional character.[41]

Of Bonet's replacements in the series, and of her screen time being redirected to newcomers Erika Alexander, Karen Malina White, and Allen Payne, Cosby took the tone of a schoolmaster distributing rewards to his honors students, saying that her story lines "will be taken up by the new kids on the show who are working hard, studying so hard, and really deserve a shot during what will be our final year."[42] He further explained of his screen daughter's arrested development: "There was nothing challenging for her. . . . I blame myself for that—creating a character who simply never developed. Denise never grew up—and it's not fun to have someone 21 acting like she's still about 12."[43] Of course, Denise's character could have evolved, and her lack of evolution as a Huxtable child reflects a decision on the part of the show's creative talent. On the contrary, Cosby acknowledged the similarities between his personal difficulties with one of his daughters and her Huxtable counterpart Denise: "There are so many things to play with. So many things that you could do with it. . . . I have a daughter that I am so in love with now because she's turned around. . . . I love her to death now because she turned around. She came back."[44] Almost a decade after *The Cosby Show* ended production, entertainment reporters still treated Bonet and Cosby as estranged kin: "Bonet's feelings toward Bill Cosby are as complicated as those between a daughter and a once-beloved but now estranged father: an unsteady combination of gratitude, respect, disappointment, and resentment," wrote Josh Rottenberg for *Us Weekly*, summarizing Bonet and Cosby's disagreements over her portrayals of African American sexuality and her life following her young marriage.[45] Bonet disappeared from *The Cosby Show*, and in its final episode Denise calls home to report her pregnancy, but viewers neither see nor hear Bonet imparting this information. Denise can be redeemed through the joys of motherhood in marriage, yet Bonet could not return to the fold.

The Cosby Show's treatment of Denise/Bonet highlights the hypocrisy of sexual policing, for Cosby's own sexual affairs were far more controversial, if occluded from public view for much longer. As Cathy Cohen observes of Cosby's extramarital affair with Shawn Berkes Thompson and the paternity allegations of her daughter, Autumn Jackson, which came to light in the late 1990s, "The case was disturbing on many levels, but it serves as a reminder that even those who struggle very publicly with their own moral challenges jump at the chance to reprimand the black poor and black youth for their 'deviant' culture and self-destructive behavior."[46] Further complicating *The Cosby Show*'s current reception, dozens of women have accused Cosby of sexual abuse and rape over the decades of his career, further eroding the innocent image of black sexuality he sought to portray, in the determinedly thin lines between his star persona, his roles, and his life.[47] These controversies led to the cancellation of his latest pilot, in which he was to return to television as the patriarch of an extended family, in an obvious homage to *The Cosby Show* and its phenomenal run. In a blow to its legacy, *The Cosby Show* has been pulled from TV Land syndication and from Black Entertainment Television's Centric Network.[48]

On one hand, such a response is little short of ridiculous: Heathcliff Huxtable is a fictional character, and if viewers demanded that all actors live morally blameless lives, very few shows would reach the air. (No such similar outcry demanded that the *Little Rascals* be shelved when star Robert Blake was accused of murder, and Woody Allen's films still garner international acclaim despite persistent allegations of child sexual abuse.) On the other hand, many family sitcoms purposefully obscure any distinctions between their stars and these actors' star personas—perhaps most obviously in *The Adventures of Ozzie and Harriet*, in which the characters of the Nelson family were played by the members of the Nelson family. As a result of these dynamics, many viewers, no matter their sophistication, can no longer see Heathcliff Huxtable as meaningfully distinct from Bill Cosby but instead as a queered husk of the black sexual normativity that he so strenuously projected for himself and his TV family. The show's star has fallen, and only time will tell if, after the taint of these rape allegations and the damage they have inflicted on his image of paternal beneficence, future generations will again appreciate *The Cosby Show* for the fantasy of its impossible innocence.

In the final analysis, television's pressures in representing African Americans and African American sexuality did not prohibit Bill Cosby and the artistic talents behind *The Cosby Show* from creating one of the most enduring and popular programs in television history, yet issues surrounding these representations dogged its critical reception over the question of how truly this family could represent black America. Of course, no single family can represent all of black America, and no family's experiences with sexuality can represent the nation's, yet such concerns coincided with rigorously sterile depictions of teen sexuality in *The Cosby Show* that queerly undercut its endorsement of androgynous parenthood through the reinstatement of patriarchal prerogatives. America's premier television father of the 1980s, otherwise progressive about gender roles and female autonomy, Cliff Huxtable had to protect his daughters from losing their virginity, for all of America was watching, and the meaning of blackness was on the line. The queerness of *The Cosby Show* attests to a troubled spirit of sexual repression that inevitably seeped out into the open—a situation sharply contrasting with Roseanne Barr's *Roseanne*, which, as discussed in the next chapter, tossed the family sitcom's chaste superego out in favor of its erotic id and the queer power of erotic representation.

4

Feminism, Homosexuality, and Blue-Collar Perversity in *Roseanne*

When Lecy Goranson auditioned to play the eldest child in a new family sitcom starring stand-up comedian Roseanne Barr, she thought she knew what to expect: "I pictured Roseanne as a Meredith Baxter-Birney type, so when I saw her in all her glory with no make-up and her sweatpants . . . I was pretty shocked," as she then diplomatically added, "but pleasantly shocked" ("Lecy Goranson Interview: I Was a Teenage Becky").[1] On *Roseanne*'s debut in 1988, much of the United States shared Goranson's surprise, for Barr demolished the "Meredith Baxter-Birney" image of television motherhood that reigned during the 1980s, with its antecedents dating back several decades.[2] In planning her transition from stand-up comedian to television sitcom mom, Barr threw down a gauntlet against a genre that frequently relegated women to the margins of its plotlines, thereby initiating a new vision of domestic relations: "In *my* show, the Woman is no longer a victim, but in control of her own mind. I wanted to make family sitcoms as we know them obsolete" (*ML* 234).[3]

With its Rust Belt setting in the fictional town of Lanford, Illinois, *Roseanne* portrays the lives of working-class Americans and the economic challenges they faced following Ronald Reagan's presidency, and the program consistently infuses its blue-collar sensibility with issues related to gender and sexuality, including women's reproductive rights, pornography, homosexuality, and children's sexual autonomy. Recasting the prevailing middle- to upper-middle-class ethos of most family sitcoms, Barr depicted feminism and sexuality as blue-collar issues that upend various cultural ideologies, filtering her humor through a dual perspective of economic and gender politics to recalibrate the mores of American culture and of sitcom narratology.[4] By highlighting *Roseanne*'s fictionality through repeated allusions and homages to past family sitcoms and their archaic sexual politics, Barr eroded the genre's governing principle of evasion when considering the erotic lives of family members in favor of a protean and proleptic queerness. Furthermore, in contrast to what we might term the symptomatic queerness of *Leave It to Beaver*, *The Brady Bunch*, and *The Cosby Show*, *Roseanne* modeled the emergent possibility throughout the 1990s for surface depictions of homosexuality to unsettle the trifold cultural fantasies of the family sitcom, of "family-friendly" television protocols, and of innocent children.

Roseanne features Barr as the eponymous matriarch of the extended Conner clan—wife of Dan (John Goodman), sister of Jackie (Laurie Metcalf), and mother of Becky (Lecy Goranson and Sarah Chalke), Darlene (Sara Gilbert), D.J. (Michael Fishman), and, in the final two seasons, her infant son, Jerry.[5] Becky's boyfriend-then-husband, Mark (Glenn Quinn), and Darlene's boyfriend-then-husband, David (Johnny Galecki), join the family as the years progress, and Roseanne's relationships with her stuffy mother, Bev (Estelle Parsons), and freethinking grandmother, Nana Mary (Shelley Winters), showcase the challenges and joys of intergenerational relationships. The primary cast of characters includes as well Roseanne's friend Crystal (Natalie West), who marries her father-in-law, Ed (Ned Beatty); family friend Arnie, as played by Barr's boyfriend/husband/ex-husband Tom Arnold; and her coworkers Leon (Martin Mull) and Nancy (Sandra Bernhard). *Roseanne* fictionalizes and allegorizes various aspects of Barr's life, including her roots in working-class America, her relationships with her sister and children, and, in the series' final season, her transition to a life of incredible wealth.[6]

Whereas popular domestic sitcoms of the 1980s typically featured upper-middle-class families, such as the Keatons of *Family Ties* (1982–89), the Huxtables of *The Cosby Show* (1984–92), and the Seavers of *Growing Pains* (1985–92), *Roseanne*'s Conner family, along with the Bundys of *Married with Children* (1987–97) and the Simpsons of *The Simpsons* (1989–), demolished the genre's decorum with their gleeful odes to dysfunction, crashing into the genre like pit bulls at a poodle show. Barr proclaimed of her success and her sensibility, "I liked and respected Bill Cosby, but business is business, and my ring-around-the-blue-collar family knocked his show out of the top ratings spot with a thud heard around the world of showbiz" (*R* 149). Defiantly queer in its treatment of economics, sexuality, and their numerous points of intersection, *Roseanne* rewrote the scripts of the family sitcom by casting ostensibly perverse pleasures as newly normative and in shifting the contours of blue-collar sexualities and of parent-child relationships in times of economic scarcity. Also, in showcasing the pleasures of resisting conservative politics and patriarchal narrative traditions, *Roseanne* heralded a groundbreaking, openly queer model of the family sitcom by reveling in the Conners' dysfunction, which then ironically highlighted the true dysfunction of the wider economic system.

Barr's Blue-Collar Feminism: Women's Sexuality, Abortion, and Pornography

Against the backdrop of 1960s and 1970s second-wave feminism, which achieved remarkable advances for women's rights in the economic, educational, and domestic realms, Barr surged to the top of the stand-up comedy circuit in the mid-1980s, developing, in her words, "a whole new kind of comedy called 'funny womanness,'" through which she molded the stereotypical figure of the American housewife into a "domestic goddess."[7] As Rosemarie Tong asserts of feminism's historical trajectory, third-wave feminists in the late 1980s began criticizing the movement's earlier orientation toward white, middle- to upper-class women: "Like multicultural, postcolonial, and global feminists, third-wave feminists stress that women and feminists come in many colors, ethnicities, nationalities, religions, and cultural backgrounds."[8] Third-wave feminist theory advocates a wider consideration of women's positions in culture and an awareness of the intersectional nodes of identity. The practice of third-wave feminist media theory, as conceived by Merri Lisa Johnson, entails "adopting a differential consciousness that allows us to move around inside our responses, between what we like and what we critique, balancing on the shifting grounds between hegemony and agency in which every text is 'an inevitable site of ideological struggle.'"[9] All programs bear ideology's imprint, particularly in Hollywood's profit-driven economy, so Barr's challenge was to create a uniquely feminist character within this system.

Barr's realization that second-wave feminism overlooked social class as a constitutive factor of a woman's identity sparked her revolutionary contribution to feminist humor, and she describes her working-class roots as key to her identity and to her comedic style: "I had found my voice. No longer wishing to speak in academic language, or even in a feminist language, because it all seemed dead to me, I began to speak as a working-class woman who is a mother, a woman who no longer believed in change, progress, growth, or hope. This was the language that all the women on the street spoke" (*MLW* 161). In a memorable swipe at bourgeois ideology, she taunts, "Hey, class is for schmucks who take life as a spectator sport anyway, so who needs it?" (*ML* 152–53). Owing to their tendency to erase class as a formative aspect of their characters' identities, presuming instead a universal upper-middle-class norm—which, of course, is not the norm—many family sitcoms promote the United States' capitalistic status quo through their refusal to consider the possibility of lives lived under socioeconomic distress. Furthermore, analyzing class elicits numerous taxonomic challenges, for even commonly employed terms—*low class, middle class, upper class*—are ambiguous in their meanings and at their margins. As Diana Kendall observes in her study of media depictions of social class, "Even sociologists who have spent years studying the U.S. class structure do not agree about what constitutes the middle class or whether such a class actually exists (some assert that there are only two classes: the upper class and the working class)."[10]

With class as an overarching theme, *Roseanne* eschews the agnostic political stances of most television programs and forthrightly condemns Reagan Republicanism, skewering in particular its antagonism toward unionized labor. In his January 1981 inaugural speech, Ronald Reagan famously proclaimed, "In this present crisis, government is not the solution to our problem; government is the problem," thus signaling his intention to rewrite the civic contract between the American government and its people.[11] The ensuing decade witnessed the ascendancy of conservatism in a range of spheres and, as Michael Schaller argues, a corresponding loss of influence for such liberal organizations as the Democratic Party, trade unions, the American Civil Liberties Union, and the National Organization for Women.[12] As Walter Galenson observes, the Reagan presidency marked "the beginning of the most difficult period for organized labor since the early 1930s," to the extent that the "concept of a 'union-free environment' gained currency," with this hostility most evident in the crushing of the air traffic controllers' strike of 1981.[13]

In contrast to *Roseanne*'s defiant liberalism and further highlighting Barr's iconoclastic and ultimately queer ethos, Reaganite conservatism pervades numerous 1980s sitcoms, with Alex P. Keaton (Michael J. Fox) of *Family Ties* serving as the era's defining avatar of Reagan Republicanism. In this show's pilot, after father Steven Keaton (Michael Gross) escorts Alex home from a whites-only country club, viewers might reasonably expect that Alex will realize his shortsightedness in abandoning his family's commitment to racial justice. Instead, both father and son admit their failings, with Steven apologizing for meddling in his son's affairs and admitting the rashness of his actions: "We're both getting older. One of us is bound to grow up sooner or later" ("Pilot"). Even young Kevin Arnold (Fred Savage) of *The Wonder Years* (1988–93), aged twelve in 1968, rejects the youthful, rebellious spirit of the 1960s on numerous occasions, primarily through Daniel Stern's voice-over narration that details his present-day understanding of his childhood. Rather than praising the era's defiant sensibility, he defends white, middle-class suburban bubbles against aspersions concerning the "anonymity of the suburbs, or the mindlessness of the TV generation" and extols it as a setting where "there were people with stories, there were families bound together in the pain and struggle of love" ("Pilot"). In an encounter dramatizing the conflict between liberalism and conservatism, Kevin's father, Jack, and his sister Karen's boyfriend argue over the Vietnam War, with Jack defending U.S. intervention against communism and the boyfriend attacking the military industrial complex and asserting his unwillingness to sacrifice his life for it. Even years later, Kevin cannot determine his moral position on the issue: "Who was right and who was wrong? Well, I'm supposed to be an adult now, and I still can't completely figure that one out" ("Angel"). Still, Jack's stance, as well as his occupational affiliation with the military industrial complex ("My Father's Office"), appears validated when Karen breaks up with this boyfriend at the episode's end, as his free-love sensibility proves his unworthiness as a suitor. With 1980s sitcom conservatism, even the Vietnam War could be redeemed as a worthy expenditure, in a spirit of resurgent patriotism reflective of Reagan's call for "morning in America."

With a sharply different tone from such Reaganite programming, Roseanne's blue-collar feminism is evident when, at the first season's conclusion, she leads a walkout from the Wellman plastics factory that employs her, Jackie, and Crystal ("Let's Call It Quits"), thus momentarily merging the program's comic sensibility with the gritty realism of such pro-union productions as *Norma Rae* (1979). In a grand irony of casting that retroactively enhances the episode's anti-Republican themes, Reagan acolyte Fred Dalton Thompson, a leading Republican politician in the 1990s and 2000s, who served as U.S. senator from Tennessee (1994–2003) and ran for the Republican presidential nomination in 2008, plays the role of the manager dismissive of his workers' concerns. The necessity of unions for blue-collar households is staged again when the Conners' state representative, Mike Summers, comes to their door, declaring that he wants to encourage businesses to relocate to Lanford by offering tax breaks as an incentive. Roseanne demands, "Who's gonna pay the taxes they ain't paying?" Summers replies, "You will . . . but you'll be working good steady employment." Roseanne barks, "Union wages?" as she steamrolls past him: "So, they're gonna dump the unions so they can come here and hire us at scab wages and then, for that privilege, we get to pay their taxes." Summers, in a futile attempt to recast economics and politics as a sphere of masculine discussion, evasively inquires, "Is your husband home?"—yet viewers realize that Roseanne's political authority cannot be evaded simply by appealing to Dan ("Aliens").

More than incidental moments establishing the Conners' socioeconomic status, such scenes contribute to the series' narrative arc, which stresses the detrimental effects of conservative politics on union households. As Barr summarizes: "The whole nine years of the show is about the union leaving Lanford. I was pretty much following what was happening in America" ("Lanford Daze" Commentary Track). While many viewers see the series' last season as the one that proverbially "jumps the shark," as the Conners win $108 million in a lottery and then cavort around Martha's Vineyard before returning home, it features as well Roseanne and Jackie cooperating with Edgar Wellman (James Brolin) so that their former coworkers can purchase ownership rights to the plastics factory, thus emancipating them from a rapacious form of capitalism.[14] Roseanne's visceral distaste for Republicanism is depicted when she tells Darlene that she should find other ways to annoy her parents than experimenting with drugs, and Darlene wisecracks, "Well, there is a young Republican I'm interested in" ("Snoop Davey Dave"). Likewise, when Roseanne records a video time capsule for Jerry, she states her fear of her children becoming Republicans ("Direct to Video"). Most family sitcoms either eschew politics altogether or serve as "equal-opportunity offenders," taking comedic potshots at both parties, with *Roseanne*'s divergence from this tradition a striking reflection of its feminist worldview.[15]

Within *Roseanne*'s allegorical consideration of blue-collar life without unions, her struggles to provide for her family showcase a mother's tribulations in times of economic duress, with Barr's body, through her defiant presentation of fatness, metonymically capturing the program's ethos. As Julie Bettie states, "In *Roseanne*, the socially 'low' is marked by Roseanne and Dan Conner's large bodies, in striking contrast to the thin and normatively beautiful characters of middle-class sitcoms";[16] in a similar vein Kathleen Rowe explains, "By being fat, loud, and ever willing to 'do offensive things,' the star persona 'Roseanne Arnold' displays, above all, a supreme ease with her body—an ease which triggers much of the unease surrounding her because it diminishes the power of others to control her."[17] The program's overarching tension, then, is between a feminist who asserts herself and her authority within her home and workplace yet who is caught within an economic system that undermines her autonomy. To this end the precariousness of the Conners' finances receives extensive narrative attention, such as when Becky takes some groceries for a food drive, but Roseanne counters that the food should be given to them ("Life and Stuff"). Similarly, when the power company turns off their electricity because they have not paid their bills, Roseanne deadpans, "Well, middle class was fun" ("The Dark Ages").

Further in this regard, *Roseanne* continually underscores the thin line between blue-collar respectability and white-trash degradation, with Roseanne striving to maintain her family's precarious social position. The program's set design accentuates the aesthetic gray area between these social castes. Matt Williams, the show's creator, sought an authentic aura for its sets—"Worn and lived in. Nothing should look new"—and Nikke Finke documents that he "sent the set designer to his grandmother's house in order to model *Roseanne*'s kitchen after hers, down to the louvered windows above the sink. And the couch and chairs in the living room were bought out of the Sears catalogue."[18]

The Conners' bad taste is often played for jokes, as evident in the Godzilla statuette perched on a bureau behind the family's afghan-draped sofa, with this tchotchke emblematizing Roseanne's character stomping through life's challenges. In Dan's ironic words, it is "the crown jewel of our collection" ("Millions from Heaven"). Contributing further to the set's bourgeois aesthetics, the iconic symbol of white-trash decorating—pink flamingoes—adorns their shower curtain, and they display in their living room the notoriously déclassé artwork of dogs playing billiards. But their taste, as is explained in numerous episodes, reflects the exigencies of their economic situation, in which they must take what they find to decorate their home—such as when they mistakenly purchase items from thieves robbing their neighbors ("Tolerate Thy Neighbor"). The decrepitude of the Conners' home serves as fodder for the program's gallows humor, as it also imparts the reality of the family's economic situation in that, quite simply, their financial circumstances are unlikely to change as they pass from job to job. Roseanne frequently comments on the family's precarious social position, and after Dan is arrested for attacking Jackie's abusive boyfriend, she sighs, "Everyone's been saying it for years, but with Dan going to jail, we are officially poor white trash" ("War and Peace"). While humor leavens these lines, when Becky and Mark move into a trailer park, Roseanne is dismayed that her daughter's socioeconomic trajectory appears to be moving downward ("Happy Trailers").

But as Reagan-era union-busting catalyzes the economic troubles that entrap the Conners, Barr's feminism and promotion of women's sexual autonomy allow a modicum of queer resistance to ideological structures that otherwise brook little hope for change. As Barr proclaims of her feminist ideals, "The *Roseanne* show is . . . about American's unwashed unconscious. Every episode sprouts at least a seed of something banal turned on its ass, something so pointedly 'incorrect,' filtered through a working class language that claims every MALE-defined thing from family to economics, to God, as belonging, rightfully, and at last, to the realm of women" (*ML* 235). Within the patriarchal economic system in which its eponymous protagonist must struggle, *Roseanne* stresses the primacy of female desire in numerous ways, even rewriting the voyeuristic tropes of scopophilia that privilege men gazing at beautiful women.[19] Instead, women wield the gaze in *Roseanne*, such as when Crystal asks Roseanne why she fell in love with Dan. She replies, "his sense of humor . . . that and the way his jeans kept falling off the back of his butt" ("Here's to Good Friends"). Whereas many family sitcoms depict husband and wife chastely relaxing in bed together, or at most mildly canoodling, Roseanne and Dan do not "make love"; simply stated, they fuck, and they do so with abandon. Their exertions tumble them back and forth over the mattress, such as when their heads appear at their bed's foot, with the blankets crumpled behind them ("Canoga Time"; fig. 4.1). On another

FIGURE 4.1 In "Canoga Time," after a raging fight, Roseanne and Dan forgive each other through their rough-and-tumble lovemaking.

occasion Dan retrieves a condom from the bedside table—"You want to be ribbed or tickled tonight?"—as, eagerly anticipating intercourse, he pants like a dog ("Two Down, One to Go"; fig. 4.2). In portraying Roseanne and Dan's efforts to conceive their fourth child, the camera frames Roseanne lying in bed with her legs sticking straight in the air: "I'm directing your sperms where to go," she explains ("Be My Baby"; fig. 4.3). It is also implied that Roseanne and Dan engage in public sex, such as when she hints that she will masturbate him at the movie theatre: "We can do that trick with the popcorn box," she wheedles ("Somebody Stole My Gal"). When they begin necking in their truck, Roseanne agrees despite her initial hesitation, but urges her husband to preserve a modicum of modesty: "OK, but try to keep your butt below the window" ("Be My Baby").

Like Roseanne, her sister Jackie faces a life of economic hardship as she moves through an array of mostly unsatisfying occupations after the plastics factory: police officer, perfume spritzer, truck driver, and other blue-collar positions. The sitcom contrasts Roseanne's monogamy with Jackie's promiscuity but primarily to enjoy the humor of this contrast rather than to judge her for her active sex life. Dan says to Becky of her aunt's wedding plans, "I don't know, babe. I think Aunt Jackie's body might reject a white dress" ("To Tell the Truth"), and viewers also learn that her sexual precociousness began

FIGURE 4.2 “Two Down, One to Go” depicts Dan “begging” for intercourse.

FIGURE 4.3 The staging of this postcoital scene in “Be My Baby” visually informs viewers that Dan has recently ejaculated in Roseanne’s vagina.

during early adolescence. Roseanne reminds Jackie that she dated a forty-year-old man in eighth grade, and Jackie declares that she "taught him more than he taught me" ("Dear Mom and Dad"). Reminiscing over her date for her first school dance, Jackie recalls his name was Marshall Gordon, but Roseanne clarifies, "That wasn't his first name. That was his job. He got kicked off the force 'cause of you" ("The Blaming of the Shrew"). When Jackie and her boyfriend Fred (Michael O'Keefe) discuss their sexual histories, he states that he has slept with three women, and she replies that she has slept with, on average, three men a year: "What's to discuss? I slept with sixty men—most of them separately" ("Past Imperfect"). By depicting Roseanne as a sexually satisfied wife and by refusing to depict Jackie within the standard story line of the "fallen woman," *Roseanne* demolishes the social construction of a woman's identity as configured through her sexuality.

Given the program's investment in women's sex lives, it is not surprising that multiple characters become pregnant: widowed mother Crystal has a young adolescent son, Lonnie, yet finds herself distraught when, after marrying Ed, she bears two children in quick succession. Jackie becomes pregnant after what she presumed to be a one-night stand with Fred. Roseanne and Dan, when pondering whether to have a fourth child, consider both their ages and their economic status as reasons not to proceed with their plans. After Roseanne misses her period, Jackie suggests that she could avail herself of an abortion. The discussion proceeds with Crystal interjecting that some people believe abortion is murder, Jackie disagreeing, and Roseanne stating definitively that "some people call it a choice" ("The Test"). In these story lines the inevitability of considering abortion arises in conjunction with women's economic distress, forthrightly thematizing their reproductive rights as an essential feature of the modern family and of the modern economy and thereby highlighting the hypocrisy of right-wing politicians who oppose women's reproductive freedom while showing little concern for the economic duress women face in providing for their families. While Crystal, Jackie, and Roseanne do not abort their pregnancies, Becky wonders aloud what she would have done if she had become pregnant in high school without legal access to an abortion, and Nana Mary divulges that she underwent two abortions in her youth ("Thanksgiving 1994"). Nana Mary shares neither the circumstances requiring these terminations nor her methods for procuring them prior to the 1973 *Roe v. Wade* decision, so the contrast between Becky's present and Nana Mary's past asks viewers to consider the necessity for women to attend to their reproductive decisions by themselves, particularly within an environment with limited financial resources.

Within this world of blue-collar feminism the male characters incarnate varying models of masculinity and sexuality: Dan is the devoted yet gruff husband and father; Fred is the sensitive and emotional 1990s man; Mark is the bad boy maturing into responsibility. Regardless of their individual characteristics, these men continually cede to women's authority, for the program simply dismisses most pretensions of patriarchal prowess as a shallow vestige of yesteryear. The phallus wields little authority in *Roseanne*, and its ineffectiveness is highlighted in scenes depicting the anxieties accompanying male performance, particularly in the story line of David's sexual maturation. Desperate to consummate his relationship with Darlene, he retires with her to a motel room after prom but finds himself impotent. Darlene comforts him: "I'm sorry David. I know how much you wanted this to happen." He then pleads, "Darlene, just please stop talking. If you say anything else, it might disappear altogether" ("Promises, Promises"). In this world where female desires dominate, the phallic promise of the penis as a signifier of male puissance fails to stand up for itself, and, tacitly acknowledging these circumstances, the male characters accept their secondary role in this blue-collar matriarchy. Certainly, they do not contest women's primacy regarding pregnancy decisions, such as when Fred declares to Jackie: "It's your body, it's your decision. There's nothing that I can do about it" ("Be My Baby"). Roseanne argues about paternal rights with Dan and Mark, pointing out to them that "Jackie has so far put in, what, eight months into this baby, and Fred, he put in—what do you think?—three minutes, and I'm being very generous here. And so you think they're equal partners in the deal?" ("Don't Make Room for Daddy"). Further advancing its feminist treatment of women's reproductive themes, the series ridicules men's discomfort with lactation. Dan is obviously taken aback when Crystal breastfeeds at the breakfast table, but Roseanne brusquely reminds him, "Oh, Dan, it's not like you've never seen a breast before" ("A Bitter Pill to Swallow"). After her son Andy's birth, Jackie leaks on her wedding dress, and in the episode's tag, she nurses Andy while she and Fred exchange vows ("Altar Egos").[20] By breastfeeding Jerry, Roseanne scares away the policeman who approaches her and Jackie in their car after the trucker whom they insulted crashes into a utility pole ("The Getaway, Almost"). Unable to control the phallus and fearful of lactating breasts, the men of *Roseanne* collectively depict the relative impotency and fragility of the male gender, presenting a queered vision of 1990s masculinity bereft of its privileges.

In light of its blue-collar feminist ethos, *Roseanne*'s interest in pornography further encodes sexuality as a woman's provenance and queries the ideological binary distinguishing between sexual normality and perversity. Numerous prominent feminists have denigrated pornography as derogatory to women, yet in the 1970s and 1980s a countervailing opinion arose, one that lauded it as a valuable narrative strategy for reassessing Western culture's long-standing debasement of female desire. As Carolyn Bronstein documents, feminists including Susan Brownmiller, Gloria Steinem, Robin Morgan, Shere Hite, and others formed an antipornography action group in the 1970s, yet their efforts sparked a pushback from prosex feminists who "accused anti-pornography [advocates] of promoting conservative views that supported women's sexual oppression and argued that efforts to protect girls and women from sexuality would create a repressive climate that would interfere with every woman's right to seek sexual liberation on her own terms."[21] Barr recalls her years in the feminist movement: "Later we changed our name to WAP, Women Against Pornography, which used a traveling slide show to raise funds to help smash patriarchy" (*R* 105). In contrast to these earlier views, Barr's sitcom often treats pornography approvingly, as in a fantasy sequence in which Roseanne thanks guest star Hugh Hefner, publisher of *Playboy* and iconic libertine since the 1950s, for loosening the United States' puritanical values ("What a Day for a Daydream"). With the advent of videocassette recorders, pornography entered mainstream American homes in the 1980s, and frequent allusions to it stress its relative banality within the Conner household.[22] The episode "House of Grown-Ups" portrays the Conners' excitement over purchasing a VCR, and it is implied that Dan's rental choice is pornographic, for Roseanne seems titillated by the prospect of viewing it together. In a similar vein, Roseanne watches a wrestling match with Dan and wisecracks, "This is like all-male porno except they're wearing bathing suits" ("Lovers' Lane"). Surely viewers are not meant to construe that Roseanne bases this opinion on her extensive consumption of gay erotica, yet her joke acknowledges that pornography depicts a range of queer desires and acts beyond the heteronormative.

Rather than simply criticizing pornography as degrading to women, *Roseanne* questions its masculinist bias and compares masculine and feminine erotica. The plotline of "Isn't It Romantic?" portrays Dan planning an idyllic evening for his wife—but one featuring a porn video entitled "Romancing the Bone." Roseanne objects, "This is nothing but disgusting pornographic filth," as Dan feebly defends himself: "It's got 'romance' in the title." Roseanne continues her attack on the ways in which much pornography speaks exclusively to heteroerotic male desire: "It's just some sick old male fantasy that only appeals to other sick old males." For Roseanne, then, the problem appears not to be pornography as much as men's pornography, leaving the possibility open for erotic narratives catering to women's experiences of desire. Developing this theme, the episode "Sweet Dreams" depicts Roseanne's fantasy life, which features shirtless hunks tending to her every whim, as she also imagines a life free from the daily commotion of her family. In this sequence a woman's desires receive the narrative's attention, while also refusing to depict Roseanne as the self-abnegating mother who puts the needs of her husband and children before her own.

In casting former porn star Traci Lords as Stacy, the bus person at Roseanne and Jackie's diner, Barr bridged the show's thematic interest in pornography as relatively banal with her objective to challenge Hollywood's mores—and its economic payoffs. Fighting the entertainment industry's antifeminist bias with a porn star may appear a counterintuitive move, yet in so doing, Barr underscored that women's sexual experiences should not preclude them from the popular-culture sphere—even within the family-sitcom genre. Lords recalls the beginnings of her acquaintanceship with Barr: "Roseanne introduced herself, generously saying she had a lot of respect for me. She said Hollywood was a tough place, especially for a woman with a past."[23] At the same time that Barr granted Lords the opportunity to continue her transition to mainstream acting roles, her performance as Stacy relies on her obvious sex appeal, which allows the program to deconstruct other prevailing visions of female sexuality. In a porn parody entitled "Lunch Box Girls"—which serves as the tag to the episode introducing Stacy—Barr, Metcalf, and Lords play hypersexualized waitresses pouting the standard lines of pornographic narratives, such as Metcalf's "I've always been a nice girl. I wish someone could teach me to be bad." A man enters the restaurant, and they proceed with their seductions, but instead of depicting the ensuing hard-core sexcapades—an impossibility for any prime-time network television show, and particularly one broadcast during the "family hour"—the camera depicts the viewer of this video fast-forwarding to its conclusion of the women smoking cigarettes as the man cleans up the kitchen ("Follow the Son"). By interpellating *Roseanne*'s audience in the place of this fictional viewer bored by the standard plotlines of porn and fast-forwarding not to the money shot but to the pleasures of male labor in the kitchen, the program's most extended rescripting of pornographic pleasure depicts for male viewers a comic vision of what blue-collar working women desire when watching X-rated fare. Women's desires, sexual or otherwise, drive *Roseanne*'s plots, thereby demonstrating the humorous pleasures derived from women's sexual autonomy in a socioeconomic environment affording them few opportunities for financial advancement.

Homosexuality, Heterosexuality, and Blue-Collar Queerness

Sexual intercourse and sexual orientation transcend social class, and in *Roseanne* the variability of sexual desire speaks to the queer pleasures available to economically strapped characters, as well as to the universality of eroticism. The 1990s heralded breakthroughs in network depictions of gay life, most notably with Ellen DeGeneres's Ellen Morgan coming out of the closet in *Ellen* (1994–98) and with *Will & Grace* (1998–2006) detailing the lives of gay urbanites Will Truman (Eric McCormack) and Jack McFarland (Sean Hayes). Notably, however, neither *Ellen* nor *Will & Grace* fall within the purview of family sitcoms, which for the most part remained uncomfortable with gay story lines and were more likely to express mildly homophobic sentiments. For instance, a running gag of *Everybody Loves Raymond* (1996–2005) paints grandfather Frank (Peter Boyle) as suspicious of his infant grandson's sexuality. Ray (Ray Romano) tells his wife, Debra (Patricia Heaton), that Frank fears "little Matthew has homosexual tendencies" ("Pilot"), and later, when the child appears fascinated by a vaginal sculpture created by his grandmother Marie (Doris Roberts), Ray voices his relief: "My father was concerned about him in that department" ("Marie's Sculpture"). For the most part, queers were still banished from the family sitcoms of the era.

In contrast to such reticence over homosexuality, Barr has cited several motivating factors for depicting gay characters in her program. On a personal note she mentions that it was "an important thing to do for me because I have a gay brother and a gay sister" ("Ladies' Choice" Video Commentary), and in a quip she celebrates her friendships with gay men: "Thank God for gay guys—without 'em, us fat women wouldn't have anyone to dance with."[24] She also credits her early success in comedy to lesbian audiences: "They made me popular in Denver, they made it safe for me there, too, in comedy. Now you know why I try accurately and respectfully to have lesbians portrayed on all my shows" (*ML* 49). She also notes that such portrayals of gay life were groundbreaking in television's history: "We wanted to do a woman gay character because that had not been done." In casting Sandra Bernhard as Nancy, *Roseanne* allowed a queer actor to play a queer role, as Barr recalls: "Sandra Bernhard was the first actor ever who was gay and who played gay, years and years ahead of Ellen [DeGeneres] and Rosie [O'Donnell] . . . and I still tell her no one has ever been that brave since" (*R* 148). On the intersection of sexuality and Hollywood economics, it is instructive to contrast Barr's praise of Bernhard with her sharp criticism of Jodie Foster, who remained closeted until the 2012 Golden Globes: "I hate everything she stands for, and everyone gathered around her to help her stand for it. It's a big fuckin' lie. Let's not be who we are. Let's hide behind our art. . . . In her fuckin' Armanis with her tits hangin' out. And constantly rewarded and rewarded. And by who? The power structure that she totally speaks for."[25] Here Barr identifies the financial payoffs available to closeted stars who cloaked their sexual orientation, thus tacitly endorsing the Hollywood system that required the denial of their very selves. In contrast, by casting Bernhard in a continuing role in a hit family sitcom spanning nine years, Barr created financial incentives for gay actors to proclaim their sexualities as a core feature of their humanity.

Throughout its run, *Roseanne* grew bolder in its depiction of queer lives and desires, in many ways mimicking the transition out of the closet that gay people undertake, while also repudiating the "guppie" (gay urban professional) stereotype by casting gay men and women as blue-collar workers, facing the same economic challenges as their straight peers.[26] Viewers first learn of Leon's sexual orientation when he refuses his female supervisor's advances, and Roseanne meets his "friend" Jerry at the episode's conclusion, with their sexual relationship implied when Leon states he was looking for the blue shirt Jerry is wearing ("Dances with Darlene"). Leon comes out to Dan and his poker buddies, who are fantasizing over famous actresses, by declaring himself uninterested in sleeping with Melanie Griffith, with the audience's applause signifying their approval of the character's honesty ("Why Jackie Becomes a Trucker"). *Roseanne* acknowledges the homophobia confronting gay people, such as when Roseanne defends Leon to their employer, believing he will be fired for his homosexuality: "You're trying to scrounge up some dirt on Leon just because he's gay. Well, I ought to call the ACLU 'cause this is totally un-American. And I'm not going to give you any help on your little witch-hunt. No crappy job is worth that" ("Lies"). Roseanne's tirade is misdirected—ironically, her interviewer did not know of Leon's homosexuality until she outed him—but her concern that he could lose his job bespeaks her awareness that homophobia bears dire consequences for gay people in the workforce.

Upending the sexual conservatism of most family sitcoms, *Roseanne*'s story lines about gay characters register their core normativity—and conversely, the perversity inherent in heterosexuality. With Nancy and Leon, the program incorporates gay characters into the fabric of the Conners' lives, but more so, these characters challenge the chimerical vision of sexual normativity as ostensibly embodied in heterosexuality. Viewers first meet Nancy in her role as Arnie's girlfriend and then wife, but Nancy suggests that heteroerotic desires can be queer as well, telling Roseanne that she and Arnie met when he worked for the water company and, while checking her meter, he peeped through her window. "It was so perverted," Bernhard intones disgustedly, as she then chirps after a pause, "and then we started dating" ("Vegas"). After Nancy and Arnie separate, Roseanne and Jackie inquire about her dating prospects, and she confides her nascent sense of her shifting sexual desires: "Her name is Marla. I'm seeing a woman." They laugh, but Nancy continues: "I'm serious. I'm gay." By casting Morgan Fairchild, the glamorous star of prime-time soap opera *Flamingo Road* (1980–82), as Marla, *Roseanne* refuses the stereotype of the butch lesbian, even as Roseanne appears to endorse this stereotype when she sarcastically says to Jackie of Marla, "Well, she doesn't look like a lesbian, you know. I mean, lesbians are big ole truck drivers who wear flannel shirts and faded jeans" ("Ladies' Choice"). Jackie laughs at Roseanne's riff but then recalls her occupation and looks down at her clothes. As she realizes the match between this stereotypical portrait of lesbians and herself, the episode dissolves any distinctions between heterosexuality and homosexuality as based on a person's exterior appearance—with Metcalf's performance capturing Jackie's discovery that, although she thought she was laughing at Marla, she was really laughing at herself.

As the contrast between Marla's lesbian chic and Jackie's heterosexual frumpiness evinces, viewers cannot distinguish between gay and straight characters by costume alone, and *Roseanne* further stages debates about sexual identity in the 1990s by refusing to enforce a rigid sense of sexual orientation on its characters. Viewers learn that Leon was previously married, and when Roseanne points out to Nancy that her date Roger (Tim Curry) is an "outie" (i.e., has a penis) but Nancy now prefers "innies," Nancy replies, "Please don't label me. I am a people person," to which Jackie wryly moans, "Now I'm losing men to lesbians" ("Promises, Promises"). Nancy later expands on this theme, stating, "Sexuality isn't all black and white; there's a whole gray area," and Roseanne acknowledges her personal sense of sexual fluidity: "I am not afraid of any small percentage of my gayness inside." Furthermore, Roseanne sarcastically reverses the standard poles of discrimination when she says that Nancy has not introduced them to her gay friends because "You've never been able to accept our alternate lifestyle. It isn't a choice, you know" ("Don't Ask, Don't Tell").

Along with evacuating any meaningful distinctions between heterosexuality and homosexuality, *Roseanne* demystifies gay sex through jokes about anal and other eroticisms, for their inclusion assumes that viewers of this family sitcom will understand and appreciate this humor, as it also sets up the possibility that parents might need to explain such jokes to their young offspring. While chatting at a bowling alley, Nancy complains to Roseanne, "Arnie's on my back to have a baby"; Roseanne replies sardonically, "Well, maybe one of these days he'll get it right" ("The Bowling Show"). At a beauty parlor Roseanne and Jackie meet an effeminate man who plays softball with Fred; Roseanne asks pointedly with the euphemistic metaphors of sodomy, "Was Fred pitching or catching?" ("Skeleton in the Closet"). Roseanne's antagonistic relationship with Leon brooks little sentimentality, so when she encounters him at an Alcoholics Anonymous meeting and says, "I guess you'd have to be pretty drunk to do what you do in bed" ("My Name Is Bev"), the joke's surface homophobia is balanced by her long-standing friendship with him. Humor about homosexuality functions similarly to humor about heterosexuality in *Roseanne*, with the program's sharply antisentimental sensibility demonstrating respect for gay characters by subjecting them to the same mistreatment meted out to the Conners while also refusing to censor such jokes in deference to any young viewers in its audience or to the phantom construction of the Child.

Beyond its portrayal of gay characters and gay humor, *Roseanne* challenged the U.S. culture's prevailing consensus against gay marriage, which surged to national attention in 1991 with Hawaii's *Baehr v. Miike* case. The ensuing legal battles resulted in passage of the 1996 U.S. Defense of Marriage Act, which prohibited federal recognition of same-sex marriages.[27] Countering this vilification of gay marriage, *Roseanne* stages Leon's wedding to his fiancé Scott (Fred Willard) with Liza Minnelli impersonators, male strippers, and drag queens. Leon rages, "This isn't a wedding; it's a circus. You have somehow managed to take every gay stereotype and roll them up into one gigantic, offensive, Roseanne-iacal ball of wrong." The scene's excesses soon give way to a tartly sentimental exchange of vows with Scott professing his eternal affection: "I love you in a way that is mystical, and eternal, and illegal in twenty states." This episode, entitled "December Bride," highlighted the inevitable controversies accompanying depictions of gay life in family sitcoms, for when it aired on 12 December 1995, ABC moved *Roseanne*'s scheduled broadcast time from 8:00 p.m. (the "family hour") to 9:30 p.m., while denying that the switch was due to the episode's subject matter. In ABC spokeswoman Janice Gretemeyer's words: "After all, the program has often had gay humor. We just felt the adult humor in this episode was more appropriate for the later time period."[28] Here the fantasies of family-friendly programming and of the family hour reemerge, and again the boundaries of this elastic, imaginary construction are protected while any such controversy inevitably generates greater media interest and higher ratings. In depicting Leon and Scott's wedding, *Roseanne* pushed the boundaries of network and familial propriety, yet only a little more than a month later, on 18 January 1996, *Friends* (1994–2004) aired the episode "The One with the Lesbian Wedding," in which Ross's ex-wife marries her long-term partner. As Ron Becker argues, the lesson that networks drew from the portrayal of same-sex story lines was that "Gay material, especially same-sex kissing, could arouse controversy and network nerves, but it and the scandal it might create could also draw huge ratings without serious economic consequences."[29]

Roseanne delineates the frustrations of a closeted life in the story arc of Bev, Roseanne and Jackie's mother, with whom they share a rocky relationship. Bev is primarily characterized as a starchy prude, yet she earns the nickname "Craftmatic adjustable Bev" when she breaks her hip after having sex with her boyfriend, Jake (Red Buttons). Roseanne soon wonders if Bev ever enjoyed sex, and her mother replies, "Your father was good, in the sense that he never took longer than the commercials." In the episode's tag, Jake and Bev discuss their sex life offscreen, as she, clad in a leather dominatrix outfit and carrying a whip, enters the living room to retrieve a pair of handcuffs before returning to the bedroom ("Body by Jake"; fig. 4.4). Bev's sexual evolution reaches its climax when, as she becomes so frustrated describing her joyless marriage, she confesses that she could tolerate sex only if she read *Playboy* beforehand. Darlene deadpans, "Well, I think Grandma just outed herself," and Roseanne adds, "My right-wing, conservative, Republican mother is a great big old lesbo" ("Home Is Where the Afghan Is"). Bev then enjoys a remarkable transformation, as she finds companionship with the local chanteuse, Joyce (Ruta Lee). In the series' final episode, Roseanne explains in voice-over the meaning of this transition: "My mom came from a generation where women were supposed to be submissive about everything. I never bought into that, and I wish mom

FIGURE 4.4 Bev's sexual desires are staged for humor in this scene ("Body by Jake"), yet her sexual evolution into lesbianism during her twilight years highlights the necessity for women to pursue their true sexual desires.

hadn't either. I wish she had made different choices, so I think that's why I made her gay. I wanted her to have some sense of herself as a woman" ("Into That Good Night, Part 2"). Seeing her mother as economically trapped in a life of erotic malaise, and depicting her socially conservative Republicanism as a denial of her innermost, repressed desires, *Roseanne* views lesbianism as a narrative solution to the erasure of women's economic and individual autonomy. With Bev as a lesbian, the series suggests, she can also simply be a woman.

Whereas Roseanne's interactions with gay characters emphasize her progressive outlook, Dan evinces discomfort with homosexuality in several episodes and thus appears to represent the program's conservative viewers needing enlightenment about their prejudices. Foremost, he frets over any incipient sign of D.J.'s effeminacy: "Two daughters isn't enough for you?" he demands of Roseanne when his son dresses as a witch for Halloween ("Trick or Treat"). When Nancy and Marla lean in to kiss under the holiday mistletoe, the camera cuts away to Dan jabbering nervously on the phone. He also asks Nancy and Marla, "Could you guys cool it with 'giving each other presents' in front of the kid?"—fearing that he will need to decode for his offspring this apparently queer euphemism—but Nancy responds she is simply referring to a sweater. Nancy later tells Dan, "At some point I think Marla and I could get pregnant and have a baby." He asks how they could accomplish this feat but requests that she impart this information "without getting too specific." Nancy nonchalantly shrugs, "you just get some sperm," but the staging of the scene—Dan is basting the Thanksgiving turkey as the discussion unfolds—implies that his willful ignorance merely protects him from what he already knows ("It's No Place Like Home for the Holidays"). Like Dan, as *Roseanne* indicates, viewers at home might know more about homosexuality than they otherwise admit—including its core normativity.

Despite the visibility that Nancy, Leon, and Bev receive, their sex lives are implied rather than depicted, with any same-sex eroticism, even kisses, transpiring offscreen—in contrast to the series' candid depictions of heterosexual eroticism. Because networks censored even saccharine depictions of same-sex affections in the 1990s, Roseanne herself must serve as the privileged site of homoerotic presence. Although viewers never see Nancy kiss Marla, Sharon (Mariel Hemingway) kisses Roseanne at a gay bar ("Don't Ask, Don't Tell"). On another occasion Roseanne dresses in drag and finds herself menaced by the belligerent patrons at a local bar, and Dan must rescue her from a fight with an aggressive boor. This man asks, "What's it to you?" to which Dan declares, "He's my husband" ("Trick or Treat"). Dan and Roseanne kiss while she remains in drag, so the series' two onscreen homoerotic kisses involve its heterosexual protagonist. *Roseanne* revolutionized the structures of the family sitcom by integrating gay characters and plotlines into its story lines, and in undermining the very concept of heteronormativity through a television mom's gender-bending, same-sex kissing, and transvestism, it further collapsed the prevailing invisibility of same-sex desire within the family sitcom—proving simultaneously the perversity of heterosexuality and the fundamental normativity of homosexuality, as much as possible within the protocols of network television and its ostensible family hour.

Children's Queer Sexual Autonomy

While *Roseanne*, for the most part, candidly portrays the sexual development of the Conner children, traces of the cultural fantasy of the innocent child remain, thereby acknowledging its appeal to parents unready to discuss their youngsters' budding understanding of eroticism. In this light, children's sexuality, even their heterosexuality, often registers as queer, for it fractures the fantasy of innocence so many adults cherish. Confronted with evidence of Becky's sexual activity, Dan turns to Roseanne for guidance, and as he lays his head in her lap, she tells him a fairy-tale allegory of a princess who, with her royal parents, decides "to live happily ever after in a totally sex-free world"; Dan claps and pleads, "Tell it again" ("A Bitter Pill to Swallow"). Furthermore, when working with child actors, many adults express their concern for the children cast in provocative story lines, as evident in John Goodman's concern for Michael Fishman: "I was worried if we were going to warp his life because he was hanging out with these foul, vulgar people all day, and he's this little kid" ("John Goodman: A Candid Interview"). Despite Dan's desire not to learn of his children's sexuality, and despite Goodman's concern over exposing Fishman to crudity, *Roseanne* primarily showcases the Conner children as sexually aware. When Dan makes a double entendre about a pair in poker and Roseanne's breasts, Darlene responds, "You guys think we don't get your corny little sex jokes" ("Dear Mom and Dad"), thus highlighting the precocious knowledge of children who correctly interpret the sexual discussions surrounding them.

Even in the show's early episodes, Becky's and Darlene's sexual maturation receives detailed attention, primarily to question the necessity of parental intervention in matters of teen sexuality. The mise-en-scène of their shared bedroom features stuffed animals and a poster of shirtless men, a muddled statement of desires both infantile and pubescent. Sexual development sparks competition between the two, such as when Becky tells her sister: "Shut up, Darlene. You're just jealous because I'm dating, and you're flat" ("Dan's Birthday Bash"). Only eleven, Darlene experiences her first period in the episode "Nightmare on Oak Street," with this title alluding to the purported horror of female menstruation (as evident in Stephen King's *Carrie* and other such works that construe female sexuality as terrifying). While Darlene appreciates Roseanne's guidance in this episode, learning that she can remain a tomboy even as she matures into adolescence, more often *Roseanne* rewrites the sitcom tropes of benevolent parental authority, for quite simply, the Conner parents concede their inability to influence their children's decisions—sexual or otherwise. When Becky finds herself in trouble at school for "flipping the bird" in her class photograph, Roseanne explains to the school's principal: "Because no matter how much we try to control what our kids do, at some point they're just going to do what they're going to do. They're like people that way" ("Bird Is the Word"). In a similar moment Becky and Mark take Dan's motorcycle without permission. He is furious but does not punish her because, as he angrily explains, "You're just going to do whatever the hell you want anyway" ("Her Boyfriend's Back"). Such scenes reject the standard telos of many family sitcoms, in which pat moralizing solves children's problems and reasserts parental authority.

As much as *Roseanne* demolishes the myth of the "Father Knows Best" sitcom, the program does not simply replace paternal wisdom with maternal wisdom, concentrating instead on the necessity for children to seek their own understanding of their sexual and emotional maturation. Rarely at a loss for words, Roseanne finds herself flustered when discussing sex with her daughters, who dominate the conversation:

DARLENE: What you're trying to say is that we're far too young to go all the way.
BECKY: Well, both your body and your mind have to reach a certain level of maturity.
ROSEANNE: Yeah.
DARLENE: And you don't want to regret it later . . .
BECKY: And, hey, you have to love the guy . . .
ROSEANNE: Yeah, and you know, you would like to make sure . . .
DARLENE: That you respect him.
BECKY: Or it's meaningless. ("Like a Virgin")

Roseanne can only chime in approvingly to the lesson her daughters teach her. When Dan says "we can't just let this happen" in reaction to Becky's request for birth control, Roseanne responds, "Well, I don't want it to happen either, but, I mean, it is going to happen. I don't want our daughters getting birth control out of the men's room of the Chevron station like we used to" ("A Bitter Pill to Swallow"). Becky and Mark later marry despite Roseanne and Dan's misgivings; Dan wants to intervene, but Roseanne stops him. "That's your plan? We do nothing?" Dan demands, but Roseanne counters, "You do something stupid, we lose her" ("Terms of Estrangement, Part 2").

Just as Roseanne and Dan cannot control their daughters' dating decisions, Mark and David, their respective boyfriends and then husbands, cannot rewrite the tropes of female autonomy that their mother-in-law embodies. Roseanne and Dan are disappointed when Becky begins waitressing in a skimpy outfit at Bunz—a nod to the Hooters chain—and Dan chides Mark for allowing her to work there. Mark defends himself: "What do you mean, let her? I don't make my wife's decisions." He also tells Dan that he tried to forbid Becky from this job but that she refused to obey his wishes ("White Trash Christmas"). Darlene's control of David is virtually inviolate, as he laments to her: "You have all the power in this relationship and I have nothing" ("Pretty in Black"). Roseanne reminds Dan of Darlene's power over her boyfriend—"Have you seen the control she has over David? . . . David isn't even his real name. She just made that up" ("Everyone Comes to Jackie's")—with her lines alluding to the fact that David was first introduced as Kevin ("The Bowling Show"), with the program never explaining his name change. In sum, parental and masculine control of adolescent female sexuality is repeatedly shown to be a collective fantasy of the family unit, which the Conner women reject even during their early dating experiences. Indeed, when Dan recalls how he seduced Roseanne following her argument with her mother, she reveals to him, "I just set the whole thing up so you would be able to take advantage of me in my time of need." She adds, "Face it, Dan. I seduced you. And Darlene may very well have seduced David. . . . Darlene had sex because she wanted to have sex" ("Everyone Comes to Jackie's").

Within the Conners' blue-collar world, Becky's and Darlene's sexual autonomy registers as a necessary component in their quest to improve their financial prospects. Again, sexuality intersects with Reaganite economics, for Roseanne's concern over her daughters' boyfriends reflects her concern for their financial well-being. After Roseanne commandeers Darlene's home-economics class, Darlene tells her mother—in one of the few moments when she respects maternal authority—"Well, I just wanted to tell you that I learned something kinda important today. Your job is important, and it's tough, so I'm going to make a lot of money, or marry a rich guy, so I don't have to do any of it"; Roseanne ironically replies, "Ah, the student surpasses the teacher, Grasshopper" ("Home-Ec"). Notably, the series indicates that both Darlene and Becky will succeed in their vocational endeavors, and they will likely do so without their husbands' assistance. Dan and Roseanne are shocked and impressed when Darlene tells them that she has been offered a job paying $30,000 annually but that she refused it to finish college; they worry that Darlene will become "one of them"—the rich people who scorn blue-collar workers ("The White Sheep of the Family"). In moving into a trailer park with Mark, Becky appears to have given up hope of upward financial mobility, yet the episode "Becky Howser, M.D."—a titular nod to Neil Patrick Harris's starring role as a child doctor in *Doogie Howser, M.D.* (1989–93)—depicts her decision to return to college, with hopes of eventually becoming a doctor. Again, the prospect of financial success troubles the family—Mark worries that Becky will leave him, pointing out that few doctors are married to mechanics—yet his trepidation further underscores the fact that, for Darlene and Becky, their sexual autonomy correlates with their economic potential. They have found men whom they love, yet they do not tie themselves down to futures of financial duress.

As the youngest of the Conner children until his brother Jerry's birth, D.J. undertakes a journey from innocence to experience that highlights the potentially transgressive nature of sexuality to the family unit, for a darkly comic theme hints that his psychosexual development may be taking a pathological turn. Viewers learn that he tied squirrels together in a bizarre act of animal cruelty ("Do You Know Where Your Parents Are?"), and Becky and Darlene are jittery when they find his box of severed doll heads ("Good-bye Mr. Right"). Crystal tells Roseanne that D.J. frightens her son Lonnie ("The Courtship of Eddie, Dan's Father"), and Darlene calls him a "little perv" for spying on their neighbor Molly and threatens him with jail, "where peepers like you get their eyelids sewn shut so they can never peep again" ("Looking for Loans in All the Wrong Places"). Surmising that her brother has begun masturbating, Darlene states that D.J. hides himself in the bathroom for an hour at a time—"Either he's really, really good at it, or he's really, really bad at it"—but Roseanne fears that her son's psychosexual development could go awry, instructing

Darlene: "Well, I don't want you to give him any grief about this, 'cause you could traumatize him, turn him into a serial killer" ("Homeward Bound"). As D.J. begins dating, it is apparent that he follows in his father's footsteps and seeks independent girls unafraid to speak their minds—and who will, one assumes, prevent him from succumbing to any potential psychosis. Lisa, his date for his first school dance, calls him Doofus, whereas he refers to her by her name. Roseanne soon coaches Lisa on the proper way to manage a boyfriend, advising her protégée, "You don't want to take all the fight out of your guy. You want him to still be able to bark at strangers" ("The Blaming of the Shrew"). Later, based on their mutual interest in movies and filmmaking, D.J. begins dating Heather (Heather Matarazzo), and the relationship progresses to the point that they contemplate consummating their affections. D.J. searches madly for condoms, but after he rifles through his parents' bedroom, Heather tells him she has birth control in her backpack, following her mother's advice ("Roseanne-Feld"). D.J. and Heather do not have sex on this occasion, but through the staging of this scene—D.J.'s confusion, Heather's calm—it is clear that she will determine the pace of their burgeoning romance, and the episode never moralizes over their relative youth of approximately fourteen or fifteen years.

And while Becky, Darlene, and D.J. pursue heteroerotic desires, *Roseanne* hints strongly that the extended Conner clan already includes a gay child: Jackie and Fred's son, Andy. Fred worries that Jackie dresses Andy like a girl, and in the tag to the episode "Maybe Baby," the program jumps fifteen years into the future, when Andy, obviously played by a young woman, leads his/her school's cheerleading squad.[30] Jackie later tells Roseanne that she enjoys her newfound freedom without Fred, including the pleasure of "put[ting] pretty clothes on Andy, and if he turns out gay, we don't care because I'll march in one of those parades with him," as she coos over her son ("Husbands and Wives"). While recording a video diary for Jerry prior to his birth, Roseanne says that his cousin Andy is likely growing up to be a "little flamer," but she adds that gay people are just like everyone else and considers the possibility that her unborn child could be gay, stating that there is nothing the child could be that they would not love ("Direct to Video"). Contemplating her unborn child's sexual desires, Roseanne demolishes the myth of the innocent and asexual child, foregrounding instead the possibility that, as with Becky, Darlene, and D.J., children need to forge their own paths through their sexual development, rather than following the social codes of yesteryear or the patriarchal paradigms of sexuality that for too long foreclosed women's and gay people's erotic autonomy.

Sitcom Morality and Feminist Metatextuality

In filtering the standard protocols of family sitcoms through a lens of blue-collar feminism and queer sexuality, *Roseanne* eschews the facile morals that conclude many such programs and thus recodes the genre's prevailing normative structures. In a notable exception to this pattern during the series' first season, when Barr was still battling with creator Matt Williams for control of its story lines, Roseanne tells the children, after Dan comes in fourth place in a songwriting contest with four entrants, "We didn't really lose. The only people who lose are the people who don't try. At least we tried" ("Radio Days"). In another moment of such moralizing, Roseanne tells Becky, who is worried that she will receive a C in her biology class if she refuses to dissect a frog, that she will only be angry if she does something she knows is wrong ("The Monday thru Friday Show"). Such homiletic endings reinforce the structures of sitcom narratology that *Roseanne* otherwise rejects; more common is its flouting of the genre's didacticism. When Roseanne begins a diet, loses some weight, and finds that her pants fit her again, viewers might expect that she has learned a lesson in self-control, but she then decides that the winter cold prohibits her from walking the two-and-a-half miles to her job as a sign of commitment to her new healthy lifestyle ("I'm Hungry"). Roseanne, Dan, and Jackie react in horror when they think David is smoking marijuana, but they later steal from this stash and relive their youthful indiscretions. As they recover from their binge, David emphatically denies that the drugs were his: "It's really important what you guys think of me. And I'm not stupid enough to do drugs. Yeah, I tried it when I was younger, but I'm much too mature and smart now to do anything that stupid." The camera then pans from Dan to Jackie to Roseanne, who, while looking a bit worse for wear, also provoked the episode's outrageous humor, thereby overriding any pat moral against recreational drug use ("A Stash from the Past").[31]

Overtly mocking the simplistic morality and gender politics of sitcoms past, *Roseanne* simultaneously pays affectionate homage to its forebears. The episode "Call Waiting" depicts Barr assuming the lead roles in Marlo Thomas's *That Girl* (1966–71), Barbara Eden's *I Dream of Jeannie* (1965–70), and Mary Tyler Moore's *The Mary Tyler Moore Show* (1970–77), thereby parodying their depictions of femininity in the 1960s and 1970s through her richly satiric performances. When Roseanne asks Dan what he would do if she had died in a tornado that struck Lanford, he replies, "Probably go out and look for Florence Henderson" ("Toto, We're Not in Kansas Anymore"), and Henderson guest-stars as an overprotective mother in a send-up of her *Brady Bunch* persona ("Suck Up or Shut Up"). *Leave It to Beaver* (1957–63) appears to haunt the program's collective subconscious: Jackie hums its theme song as she cooks breakfast for the children, and it plays extradiegetically when she sends them off to school ("An Officer and a Gentleman"). Dan calls a family meeting to discuss Roseanne's overtime hours, to which she deadpans, "Oh, god, this ain't the Ward Cleaver speech" ("Workin' Overtime"). In a proud moment of parenting, Dan says to Roseanne, "What can I say? I'm a model dad"; she responds by calling him "Ward" ("Fathers and Daughters"). While these examples cannot cover the vast range of *Roseanne*'s allusions to yesteryear's sitcoms, they collectively pillory the genre's constructions of the normative nuclear family and its exaggerated deference to patriarchal privilege, as well as contrasting these families' middle-class comforts to the Conners' straitened circumstances.

Roseanne concludes its run as the television sitcom equivalent of a künstlerroman, with the final shots capturing Roseanne writing the story that audiences have watched over the past nine years. Barr states, "The whole series is that she was writing a book" ("Season 9: Breaking the Sitcom Mold"). Viewers learn that Roseanne aspires to be a writer in the series' third episode ("D-I-V-O-R-C-E"); for a birthday present to her, Dan refits the downstairs basement as a writing room ("Happy Birthday"), although viewers never see her pursuing this vocation, and the basement became a bedroom for the children as they matured. The final vision of *Roseanne* asks viewers to ponder the meaning of a woman who finally found a room of her own to write in and the seismic effects of her representations of social class and queer sexualities for blue-collar America and beyond. Contemplating her show and her feminist commitments, Barr proclaimed, "Television and truth are enemies," and she expounded further that "any time any woman gets on TV and tells the truth about anything, that's a big breakthrough, and I did it" ("Roseanne: Working Class Actress"). Speaking for the necessity of women's economic and sexual autonomy, Barr turned the cute feminism of Marlo Thomas and Mary Tyler Moore into a roar, forever changing the ways in which women's, gay men's and lesbians', and children's sexualities are depicted onscreen.

And beyond the ways in which *Roseanne* represented in its narratives a woman's struggle to survive economically challenging times, the production of the show testifies to Barr's determination not to cede her vision to the Hollywood forces attempting to rewrite the character she created. As Metcalf remembered of her first days on set, "I knew it was [Barr's] show because she held the reins on everything" ("Laurie Metcalf Interview: The Sister That Never Leaves"). Goranson likewise stated admiringly, "She knew what she wanted from the show, and she was ruthless about it" ("Interview with Lecy Goranson and Michael Fishman"). Recalling her guest-starring appearance as Roseanne's cousin, Joan Collins observed that "Roseanne was definitely the boss and, except for Sandra Bernhard and a couple of the other actors, everyone was frankly terrified of her. Understandably. Three of the sycophantic sniggering writers had already been fired, and as Roseanne demanded slicker, better dialogue, the remainder were on tenterhooks."[32] Tabloid fodder for numerous years because of her behavior on set, perceived by many as imperious and autocratic, Barr endured endless criticism, yet the sexism inherent in such discussions was noted in *Penthouse*—hardly a citadel of feminist thought—in an article by Nanette Varian: "Never mind that Bill Cosby jettisoned a few longtime writers with nary a peep from the press. Or that *In the Heat of the Night* star Carroll O'Connor marked his return by announcing his intention to 'get rid of everyone' who defied his creative authority. When Roseanne Barr fires, it's a federal offense."[33] Film critic Peter Rainer asserted Barr's determination to ensure that her program adhered to her vision: "She has the reputation of being very forthright. She's unpredictable and tells it like it is. Many of the male stars like Brando and Nicholson have the same thing, but it's very hard for a woman to get away with. Jessica Lange has a reputation for being difficult, but she's a beauty."[34] The story behind *Roseanne*'s production, then, is the story of Barr's refusal to conform to Hollywood's expectations for women—particularly for fat women intent on rewriting the industry's normative scripts.

Yet it is difficult to imagine *Roseanne*'s success without Barr's control. Matt Williams originally envisioned the show as a sitcom featuring three blue-collar women—a married woman with children, a divorced woman with a child, and a single woman—working in a factory in Indiana. The program was to be called *Life and Stuff*—with this title surviving as that of *Roseanne*'s pilot episode—and its general format is realized in the characters of Roseanne, Crystal, and Jackie and their employment at Wellman Plastics.[35] As Barr recalls, Matt Williams told her bluntly, "I just didn't think people would like you as the main character," as Roseanne defended the integrity of her vision: "Then I quit. I'm not gonna give away my character after it took my whole goddamn life to build it" (*ML* 4).[36] She further explained that Williams "didn't get it that I wanted a totally *female-driven show*" (*ML* 5). Backstage fracases aside, what is perhaps most important to remember about these production scuffles is Williams's concessions: "I lay no claim to her character. That is the character she developed in her stand-up routines," and he also admitted, "What Roseanne brought to the mix that I didn't was the strong feminist point of view."[37] Without its strong feminist point of view, *Roseanne* would likely have resulted in a moralistic family sitcom similar to those of the past and of its present (e.g., *Family Matters* [1989–98] or *Home Improvement* [1991–99]), and as Barr describes, "They were eviscerating my show, goddammit, they were Osterizing it into the pastel purée that had been spread over the networks for too long now, the same unsatisfying, tasteless, colorless (forget odorless—it stunk) polenta of sitcoms that I couldn't stomach" (*ML* 92). Rescuing her program from others who did not share her vision, Barr created a uniquely feminist, queer, and sex-positive vision of the American family, with all of its ostensible perversities—from pornography to homosexuality, abortion to sexually active teens—exposed for Reagan Republicans and their children to see. Still, as much as *Roseanne* subverted the prevailing fantasies of the family sitcom, its long-standing tropes have proved strikingly resilient, a phenomenon evident in the popularity of the tween family sitcom subgenre in the 2000s and notably embodied in pop-princess everywoman Hannah Montana—to whom the next chapter turns.

5

Allegory, Queer Authenticity, and Marketing Tween Sexuality in *Hannah Montana*

Any advertiser—or consumer of advertising—knows the hoary but time-tested adage of the field: sex sells. Sparking consumers' erotic desires encourages them to open their wallets, but it would appear that preteen children, who may have only vague ideas about human sexuality, would prove the exception to this axiom. Most children's television simply avoids the topic of sexuality altogether,[1] yet, within the subfield of tween sitcoms, many programs depict their protagonists taking initial steps in courtship: first dates and first kisses—but rarely first experiences with intercourse. Marketing tween programs also necessitates appealing to children's parents, who may or may not watch these shows with their children yet who will determine whether family funds are spent on related merchandise.[2] As a subgenre of the family sitcom, tween sitcoms must negotiate between dual audiences of young viewers and their parents, as they must also negotiate the need to address their protagonists' dating lives without tackling topics of teen sexuality too graphically, lest they prompt a parental backlash. Confronting the inherently queer fantasies of genre, family-friendly programming, and children's innocence, these programs mask sexuality on their surface yet must inevitably confront the ways in which it seeps through into their story lines, even if only allegorically.

Among the many tween programs of the early twenty-first century, *Hannah Montana* (2006–11) achieved phenomenal popular success and a financial windfall for the corporations backing it: It's a Laugh Productions, Michael Poryes Productions, and Disney Channel Original Productions.[3] This family sitcom stars Miley Cyrus in the role of Miley Stewart, a self-admittedly dorky teen living in all respects a normal life—except for her secret alter-identity as international pop-sensation Hannah Montana.[4] Miley's family includes her father, Robby Ray (Billy Ray Cyrus), who also serves as her manager; her brother, Jackson (Jason Earles), with whom she shares an antagonistic yet affectionate relationship; and her deceased mother (Brooke Shields), who appears in several dream and fantasy sequences to guide her daughter's path. The series' first episodes depict Miley sharing her secret with friends Lilly Truscott (Emily Osment) and Oliver Oken (Mitchel Musso), who then assume the alter-identities of Lola Luftnagle and Mike Stanley III so that they may join Hannah on her glamorous escapades. Miley's misadventures begin in middle school, as she suffers the unwarranted antagonisms of mean girls Ashley and Amber, as well as her dating tribulations with a stream of cute beaux, including movie star Jake Ryan and brooding bad-boy rocker Jesse. Most episodes feature a subplot focusing on Jackson and his "frenemy" relationship with Rico (Moises Arias), his boss's son at the beachside stand where he works. The series ends as Miley and Lilly enroll at "Standford University"—having learned many valuable lessons about life, family, and friendship along the way. Featuring vivacious Miley Stewart as its lead character, *Hannah Montana* creates an appealing heroine who follows a long tradition of television's plucky teens. Bill Osgerby discerns the cultural popularity of a "teen girl TV tradition whose accent on freedom and fun *always* gestured towards a femininity that was independent and active," with Miley embodying this archetypal character.[5]

Hannah Montana evokes the presumed innocence of the tween sitcom genre on its surface level of narration, yet the program concomitantly allegorizes Cyrus's controversial transition into a sexual provocateur, thus preparing young viewers to accompany the protagonist/actor as she segues out of the show and into her career as a solo artist. The program asserts its interest in duality in its theme song "Best of Both Worlds," which explains the foundational premise that Miley Stewart doubles as superstar Hannah Montana. This celebrity duality extends to her friends, who accompany her in her jet-set lifestyle, and to her brother, who begins dating bikini model Siena in the series' later episodes, thereby proving the availability of sexually desirable romantic partners to everyday schlubs. The presumed innocence of tween sexuality establishes another level of duality within the program's marketing and narratology: through the core value of Cyrus's personal authenticity, *Hannah Montana* hides sexuality from parental view and depicts its protagonist as an age-appropriate role model, thus paradoxically marketing an absence of sexuality that merges seamlessly into Cyrus's marketing of herself as a queer advocate and icon. In this light, Cyrus's post-*Hannah* declaration of her pansexuality encodes another queer meaning to her sitcom, encouraging an allegorical reading of Miley's "coming out" as Hannah Montana as equivalent to Cyrus's revelations of her adult erotic interests.[6]

Family Sitcoms and the Rise of the Tweens

Many popular family sitcoms of the legacy and broadcast networks in the 1990s and 2000s adhered to the time-tested strategy of depicting characters of various ages to appeal to audience members of various ages—a tendency evident in a bounteous array of the era's successful programs, including *The Fresh Prince of Bel-Air* (1990–96), *Step by Step* (1991–98), *Home Improvement* (1991–99), *The Nanny* (1993–99), *Malcolm in the Middle* (2000–2006), *According to Jim* (2001–9), *Reba* (2001–7), *The Bernie Mac Show* (2001–6), *8 Simple Rules* (2002–5), *George Lopez* (2002–7), *Everybody Hates Chris* (2005–9), and *The Middle* (2009–). Many of these programs also loosely followed the dysfunctional model of the family sitcom as inaugurated by *Married with Children* (1987–97), *Roseanne* (1988–97), and *The Simpsons* (1989–), although this form had mellowed over the years. A tart domestic disharmony reigns in these programs' households, yet a sugar-coating of sentimentalism ensures viewers that, as much as these family members claim their distaste for one another, affection lies just below the surface, with *Malcolm in the Middle* exemplifying this trend. This program tells the story of a dysfunctional family from their genius son's point of view: "I want a better family!" Malcolm (Frankie Muniz) shouts in the series pilot, which features such comic grotesque moments as his mother giving his father a full-body shave. Yet even he realizes the centrality of his parents and siblings to his life: "See? That's what I'm talking about. This family may be rude, loud, and gross, and have no shame whatsoever . . . anyway, with them, you know where you stand. And when I have a problem, they're always there" ("Malcolm Babysits"). Mom Frankie of *The Middle* describes herself as "just a cranky, tired mom with nothing to lose" ("The Block Party"), but viewers readily understand that her voice-over conveys her true feelings for her family: "That's the thing about family. Oh, sure, they eat your food and wreck your face, you gotta save them a thousand times a day from God knows what, but every now and then, they save you" ("Pilot").

For the 2000s, then, familial dysfunction creates a slight ironic edge to domestic sitcoms yet so slight that both characters and viewers understand the primacy of the family unit. Also during this period, cable and premium channels were challenging the hegemony of the legacy networks, with many attracting their audiences through provocative programming, including family sitcoms verging on dramedies, pitched to niche demographics, such as *Weeds*

(2005–12), *United States of Tara* (2009–11), and *Nurse Jackie* (2009–15). Freed from the constraints of network standards, these programs embraced daring story lines, going where few network families could follow: in *Weeds*, financially strapped Nancy Botwin (Mary-Louise Parker) begins selling marijuana and ensnares her family in the murderous affairs of a Mexican drug cartel; in *United States of Tara*, Tara Gregson (Toni Collette) struggles with multiple-personality disorder and seeks to understand its roots in her traumatic childhood; and in *Nurse Jackie*, Jackie Peyton (Edie Falco) juggles her professional and domestic responsibilities while hiding her drug addiction.

Increasingly throughout this era, the subgenres of teen and tween sitcoms flooded the television screen, with their foundations reaching back to the late 1950s and early 1960s with *The Many Loves of Dobie Gillis* (1959–63), *Gidget* (1965–66), and *The Patty Duke Show* (1963–66). Tween innocence confronts adolescent sexuality in these programs, which generally alternate in treating these themes straightforwardly in some instances, euphemistically in others. *Blossom* (1990–95) dramatizes these tensions as its eponymous protagonist (Mayim Bialik) discusses her physical maturation with her father. "I'm a woman now," she tells him, as he ironically invokes the familiar fantasy of the sexless child: "Couple years after you're married, you'll want to have sex for the first time. But hopefully by then I'll be blind, deaf, and in a home in New Jersey" ("Blossom Blossoms"). The definitive tween romance of the 1990s belongs to Cory Matthews (Ben Savage) and Topanga Lawrence (Danielle Fishel) in *Boy Meets World* (1993–2000), yet Cory nervously hesitates during many moments of their burgeoning relationship. Cory's teacher Mr. Feeny (William Daniels), attempting to inspire an appreciation of Shakespeare's *Romeo and Juliet* in his students, waxes eloquently, "It's about the all-consuming power of love, and the inevitability of its influence on each of our lives," to which Cory replies in a panic: "Are you aware that I'm only eleven years old?" ("Pilot"). In these and many other such instances, sexual innocence defines the tween, with sexual angst defining his or her parents.

Against the 1990s backdrop of shifting audiences, multiplying channels, and new images of the American family, numerous films and television programs, especially those airing on the Disney Channel and Nickelodeon, were targeting specifically the female tween market. Many of these channels' sitcoms tweak the basic formula of the family sitcom by casting young adolescents as their stars while maintaining siblings and parents in subsidiary roles. This subgenre of family sitcoms, disparagingly referred to as "zitcoms," includes such titles as *Lizzie McGuire* (2001–4), *The Suite Life of Zack and Cody* (2005–8), *Zoey 101* (2005–8), *Wizards of Waverly Place* (2007–12), *iCarly* (2007–12), and *Big Time Rush* (2009–13). For the most part these programs handle teen sexuality gingerly, acknowledging burgeoning attractions but eschewing visual depictions beyond light kisses. A shared theme of this genre encourages teens to be true to their authentic selves, and, for female characters, this story line portrays them breaking free from the bonds of traditional femininity. After beating a boy at arm wrestling, Lizzie McGuire learns from her gym coach, "There are people that think being strong is a boy thing, but that's because they're severely lacking in brains" ("One of the Guys"). While it is difficult to think of anything less authentic than a record label's prepackaged boy band, the teens of *Big Time Rush* insist on their authenticity. When their studio wants to hire a "bad boy" for their group owing to this stock character's demographic appeal, lead singer Kendall (Kendall Schmidt) insists, "We just don't want anything fake about our band" ("Big Time Bad Boy"). Thematically teaching (pre)adolescents to believe in themselves, tween sitcoms position their youthful protagonists as role models guiding viewers to their unique truths.

The entertainment industry has long been governed by a masculinist bias in its offerings, yet studio executives began perceiving that girls—half of the youth population—constitute a powerful market in themselves, with tween sitcoms proving the power of this demographic. Jane Startz, the producer of such family-friendly sitcoms and films as *Charles in Charge* (1984–90) and *Ella Enchanted* (2004), outlines Hollywood's previous reasoning and its realization of the depth of the female tween market: "The time I was growing up in this industry, the conventional wisdom was girls will watch something that has a boy [as the lead character], but the boys won't watch something that has a girl. That may or may not be true. But I think what people are realizing is it really doesn't matter that much if the boys are going to come or not because there is such a faithful following for some of these girl projects."[7] Within the cinematic world, Anne Hathaway found her path to stardom in a string of hit movies marketed to tween girls, including *The Princess Diaries* (2001), its sequel *The Princess Diaries 2: Royal Engagement* (2004), and *Ella Enchanted*, as did Lindsay Lohan with *Freaky Friday* (2003), *Mean Girls* (2004), and *Confessions of a Teenage Drama Queen* (2004). For many young female actors a Disney Channel or Nickelodeon tween vehicle initiates their path to stardom (and a singing career): Hilary Duff in *Lizzie McGuire*, Raven-Symoné in *That's So Raven* (2003–7), Selena Gomez in *Wizards of Waverly Place*, Miranda Cosgrove in *iCarly*, and Demi Lovato in *Sunny with a Chance* (2009–11). As Belinda Luscombe explains of the rise of Gomez, Lovato, and Cyrus, "Each of these youngsters was given a TV show—the so-called zitcom—followed usually by a recording contract with Disney-owned Hollywood Records, songs in heavy rotation on Radio Disney and on Disney-movie sound tracks, a concert tour with Disney-owned Buena Vista Concerts and tie-in merchandise throughout the Disney stores. Miley & Co. are like modern Mouseketeers, but instead of M-I-C-K-E-Y, they spell C-A-S-H."[8]

As the above programs illustrate, tween sitcoms stand as a recognizable subset of family sitcoms, with young actors in their starring roles and young viewers solicited as their foremost audience, yet they stake their further appeal to other family members, including siblings of both sexes and parents. For marketing purposes, while many tweens spend significant amounts of cash, their parents must be pitched to as well because they control the family's purse strings; thus arises the utility of casting tween programs under the overarching framework of a family sitcom. *Hannah Montana* emphasizes this narrative imperative in a moment of metadramatic staging, when Jackson and Rico sing of their boyish preference for a narrative "a little bit more gory" before conceding that their desires will not be met because "they said we had to tell a family story" ("He Could Be the One").[9] This "they"—presumably the show's producers and Disney executives—insists on the family nature of the program, for the tween herself can stand in as the primary, but not the sole, point of focalization.

To this end, *Hannah Montana* creates an appealing, bubbly, and wholesome vision of American family life. Although Miley and Jackson squabble frequently, their affection for each other is never in doubt, and in a show based on a celebrity fantasy, this bickering captures a realistic and humorous aspect of sibling rivalry. One memorable such scene occurs when Jackson mocks Miley's hair extensions, and they subsequently mimic each other by repeating "hair extensions, hair extensions"; Robby Ray, driving and driven to distraction, mutters to himself "Almost home, almost home" ("I Am Mamaw, Hear Me Roar!"). Parents, it would seem, should be able to relate to such moments, as they would also likely enjoy decoding the program's numerous references to sitcoms past, particularly those from their childhoods.[10] In further framing its appeal to various family members, *Hannah Montana* serves up frequent doses of light scatological humor appealing to young children yet not so vulgar as to alienate parents. Robby Ray's ode to toilet training—"I like to sing, I like to dance, but I can't do it with poopy in my pants"—is unlikely to offend ("Lilly, Do You Want to Know a Secret?"). When Jackson, Hannah, and Lilly eat prune butter and then flee to the bathroom for immediate release, the scatology is implied rather than depicted ("Lilly's Mom Has Got It Goin' On"). Summing up *Hannah Montana*'s appeal, Jason Earles declares, "I think the thing that we're most proud of is the fact that we came up with a show that the whole family will sit there and watch together. I think it's really gonna end up being the show for this generation" ("From Auditions to Wrap: The Cast Looks Back," *Hannah Montana: The Final Season*). Thus, despite *Hannah Montana*'s primary orientation to a female tween audience, its solicitation of parental and sibling viewers results in a program that these family members, while perhaps not their first choice, are likely to watch along with their sisters and daughters. And once viewers begin watching the show, its marketing efforts that rely both on the program's surface treatment of children's innocence and on its occluded treatment of sexuality can begin in earnest, demonstrating further the elasticity of the queer fantasies on which family sitcoms rely.

Marketing *Hannah Montana* to Tweens: Queer Authenticity and Merchandising

The entertainment and advertising industries see tweens as a lucrative fan base, as evident in the title of David Siegel, Timothy Coffey, and Gregory Livingston's marketing guide to this demographic: *The Great Tween Buying Machine*. Tweens form a somewhat indeterminate amalgamation for marketing purposes, with the term shifting for the particular advertising objective of a given project. After reviewing potential age demarcations for tweens, whether from seven to fourteen, eight to twelve, or ten to sixteen, Siegel, Coffey, and Livingston define the group in terms of its purchasing power: "all of these definitions are right if the basis for choosing them is to identify a sizable, definable market that represents an opportunity for the marketer's business."[11] Tween culture is adaptive and reactive, as Claudia Mitchell and Jacqueline Reid-Walsh argue, noting that it "seems to be moving progressively downward in age to touch upon even the lower age limits of girlhood and expanding outward to include boys."[12] The maxim that children "are growing older younger" captures the controversial nature of tween marketing, in the fear that children are barraged with consumerist messages that they do not yet have the mental or emotional capacity to digest. Notwithstanding these valid concerns, it is also worth remembering that tweens are not sheep. Dan Freeman and Stewart Shapiro characterize this demographic as "skeptical beyond their years" and warn marketers that "as tweens become more skeptical of the truthfulness of promotional messages, they are more likely to avoid the message or transfer their dislike of the message onto the brand."[13] Also, the consumerist trend of children's increased buying power comes with the corollary of infantilizing the adult market, and Benjamin Barber documents marketers' efforts to "induc[e] puerility in adults and preserv[e] what is childish in children trying to grow up, even as children are 'empowered' to consume."[14]

Various cultural commentators, expressing concern for the child viewers involved, have decried the fact that television is a commercial enterprise, particularly in regard to the reputedly family-friendly cable channels. Ruth-ann Mayes-Elma, on reading Disney's 2008 Annual Report, is dismayed that it "discusses kids, from birth to teenagers, as mere consumers—there is no indication of interest in the health and well-being of Disney constituents," as she then compares the corporation to a pimp: "In the case of *Hannah Montana*,

Disney is selling a sixteen-year-old girl, a form of pop cultural prostitution."[15] With more restrained terms, Tyler Bickford notes the "unapologetically commercial entertainment" offered "from large corporations such as Disney"—hinting that corporations should indeed apologize for creating commercial entertainment.[16] It is tempting to compare cultural critics disparaging the commercial nature of the entertainment industry to Renault in *Casablanca* ("I am shocked—shocked!—to find that gambling is going on in here!") because, for the most part, television's commercialism does not warrant moralizing as much as analysis for the constraints it places on artistic creation and for its framing of cultural ideologies. The profit motive is a precondition of the medium, one that enables the free dissemination of programs through the airwaves on network television, thus providing entertainment to the masses at no cost beyond the purchase of a television set, and with consumers opting to pay more for the bounties of cable channels.[17]

Precisely because of its commercialism and its hybrid status as a jointly financial and artistic endeavor, television has long been derided as an inferior art form, and throughout its history it has frequently interwoven marketing into its narratives—demonstrating clearly that *Hannah Montana* is no outlier in this regard. From the early days of television, *The George Burns and Gracie Allen Show* (1950–58) incorporated Carnation evaporated milk into its plotlines. Gracie advises her friend Blanche, "Always use Carnation evaporated milk in your coffee. Men love it," and the program's announcer, Bill Goodwin, demonstrates to George and Gracie's houseguest that "the best shortcake is made with Carnation evaporated milk" ("Episode 1"). In the first episode of *Hazel* (1961–66) shot in color, Hazel and the Baxters buy color televisions, in an unsubtle hint to viewers to upgrade their sets ("What'll We Watch Tonight"). The theme song of *The Beverly Hillbillies* (1962–71) originally included lyrics dedicated to its sponsor Winston cigarettes ("Winston tastes good like a cigarette should," in "Getting Settled"). Various family sitcoms have increased their profits through merchandising tie-ins: *Leave It to Beaver* (1957–63) lunchboxes, *I Dream of Jeannie* (1965–70) board games, even *Happy Days* (1974–84) slot machines. Sometimes objects in a program—such as Buffy's Mrs. Beasley doll from *Family Affair* (1966–71)—spark a lucrative fad. *Hannah Montana* adheres to and amplifies the standard protocols of television marketing, offering an array of products inspired by the show—from clothes to alarm clocks, school supplies to jewelry—as it also markets a celebrity lifestyle that both avows and disavows consumerist consumption. Through this duality—Miley as a nonconsumerist consumer—*Hannah Montana* acknowledges criticisms of tween marketing while proceeding apace with its presentation of Cyrus and Hannah as authentic role models for young viewers.

A guiding trope of contemporary celebrity is founded on the presumption of a star's authenticity and, as a corollary to this authenticity, her relatability.

As Jo Littler proposes, stars such as Jennifer Lopez proclaim their authenticity by rewriting the Cinderella myth, in which they revel in glamour while highlighting their impoverished roots: "Instead of merely luxuriating in her palatial excess, Cinderella now has to show that she can still remember that she started out in the kitchen. This knowledge or awareness structures her character; it stops her 'getting above herself,' it keeps her 'real.'"[18] Such stars appear to be not just rich and famous (and thus distanced from their fans) but also grounded and authentic; they consequently remain relatable to their audiences, despite vast disparities in income and lifestyle. For *Hannah Montana* the tween viewer should be able to identify equally with Miley Cyrus, Miley Stewart, and Hannah Montana, with the actor and her character's dual identity facilitating this process. Melanie Kennedy outlines how *Hannah Montana* modulates between celebrity and tween culture, fusing a hybrid reality cognizant of the myriad and contradictory ideologies related to tweendom: "*Hannah Montana*, and the broader tween media landscape, should be understood as products of the contemporary postfeminist, neoliberal, pop-cultural moment, highly invested in celebrity as well as the attendant discourses of the self, the real, and the authentic."[19] Authenticity is key to the narrative adventures of *Hannah Montana* in creating an appealing character for tween viewers, one who strives to maintain her genuine, grounded self as she juggles her everyday and superstar lives, as it is also key to marketing related merchandise to the demographic she represents.

To enhance their appeal, family sitcoms have long exploited the thin line between their stars and their protagonists. With such characters as Lucille Ball's Lucy Ricardo, Andy Griffith's Andy Taylor, Bill Cosby's Heathcliff Huxtable, and Roseanne Barr's Roseanne Conner, the actors collapse the distance between themselves and their roles, thus appearing as authentic and relatable people rather than as celebrities. Will Smith in *The Fresh Prince of Bel-Air* and George Lopez in *George Lopez* share their real-life names with their characters—merging actor with role to the point that they are virtually indistinguishable. In a similar manner, *Hannah Montana* blurs the distinction between fiction and reality in numerous ways, most obviously in the razor-thin line between star Miley Cyrus and protagonist Miley Stewart, with both actor and character hailing from Tennessee and achieving international acclaim as a pop star. Cyrus's father, Billy Ray, a country singer best known for his hit single "Achy Breaky Heart," plays Miley's father, with this character similarly experiencing a successful singing career in his past and now writing songs for his daughter. Even Miley's horse correlates with Cyrus's childhood pet—a connection acknowledged in an episode's dedication to "Roam-Man (1988–2009)" ("Love That Lets Go"). The marketing of Miley/Cyrus/Hannah consistently obfuscates the borders between them, such as in the "Back Home Again with Miley" minidocumentary, which follows Cyrus and her father on a journey to their Tennessee residence. A caption reads, "Even though it's across the country from their Hollywood home, this farm is the heart of the Cyrus family," and Miley's return to Tennessee provides the plot for *Hannah Montana: The Movie*.

Further enhancing the fictional authenticity of *Hannah Montana*, many guest stars play thinly disguised versions of themselves or simply themselves. In a recurring role, country superstar Dolly Parton plays Aunt Dolly, a famous singer, and Vicki Lawrence riffs on her character Thelma Harper (from *The Carol Burnett Show* [1967–78] and *Mama's Family* [1983–90]), appearing as Miley's Mamaw. When Angus T. Jones of *Two and a Half Men* (2003–15) guest-stars as the Stewarts' new neighbor, his character's name is T. J.—taken from his initials ("Sweet Home Hannah Montana"). Celebrities who play themselves include the Jonas Brothers ("Me and Mr. Jonas and Mr. Jonas and Mr. Jonas"), Sheryl Crow ("It's the End of the Jake as We Know It"), David Archuleta ("Promma Mia"), and Ray Romano ("We're All on This Date Together"). When Miley confesses her true identity to the world, she does so to Jay Leno, host of *The Tonight Show* ("I'll Always Remember You"), and she follows this revelation with interviews with Robin Roberts, cohost of *Good Morning America* ("Can You See the Real Me?"), and Kelly Ripa of *Live! with Regis and Kelly* ("I Am Mamaw, Hear Me Roar!"). Cyrus asserts of the overlap between herself and her character: "Most people know me as Hannah Montana, but Hannah is a television character. She's fiction. Sure, I've put a lot of myself in her. I've tried to make her come to life. But that doesn't make her real, and it doesn't make her *me*" (*MG* 5–6).[20] This duality between Miley's and Cyrus's lives is key to the marketing endeavors behind *Hannah Montana*, for it builds levels of discourse and metadiscourse that both obfuscate and escalate the program's treatment of sexuality. In the ensuing play between virginal innocence and sexual maturation, the character and the celebrity are both rendered relatably "authentic" while denuding this authenticity of its purported value.

Certainly, the executives, marketers, and writers of *Hannah Montana* consistently foreground Miley's need to maintain her authenticity, as they concomitantly trumpet her relatability to the program's tween viewers. As the program's sell sheet declares, "It is about everyday girls with secret, superstar lives both real and imagined. . . . All girls can relate to girl next door Miley Stewart, but they want to be like her alter ego, Hannah Montana."[21] Rich Ross, the Disney executive who greenlit *Hannah Montana*, agrees: "It's not just that she's a rock star; . . . it's that she's relatable, too. She's someone you want to be friends with. And she's working to balance what she has in her intense life."[22] Miley's authenticity and relatability deepen her appeal for parental viewers as well, as the *New York Post* proposes: "Her young fans relate to episodes about crushing on a boy at school, fighting with a sibling, or sneaking out to a movie with friends, only to get caught and grounded. Yet the subtext—lessons on friendship, loyalty, and respect—pleases parents as well, making Cyrus an utterly safe and ultrapopular choice for both generations."[23] Relatable to her teen viewers while demonstrating her appropriate values to adults, Miley models an authenticity attractive to disparate strands of her audience yet one that must ultimately collapse beneath its inherent paradox and reveal the queer fissures in her character.

For Cyrus/Miley to assert herself as a moral authority, she must remain true to her authentic self, a theme introduced in the series' first episode through the lyrics of "This Is the Life," in which she sings "I'm going to take my time, I'm still getting it right." Given this credo, Miley's mistakes become the means for viewers to learn alongside her, and her authenticity is evident in the fact that she is disarmingly candid with friends and family, often blurting out a version of her "say what" catchphrase when another character states something unexpected.[24] Also key to the character's relatability and authenticity is her outsider status in her everyday life as Miley Stewart. The program frequently stresses Miley's southern roots, establishing a red state / blue state dichotomy that she bridges effortlessly: southern in her upbringing and values ("I can't. I'm from Tennessee. We don't do that," Miley pleads to Lilly), yet Californian in her celebrity subculture ("Well, you're in California now, and we do do that," Lilly replies ["I Can't Make You Love Hannah If You Don't"]). Her authenticity is further encoded in her relationships with her peers, as she teaches her boyfriend, Jake, an actor who revels in the perks of his celebrity, "Being normal is not stupid. It lets me have real friends, and it reminds me that I'm just like everybody else" ("Achy Jakey Heart, Part 2"). To stress Miley's credibility as an average teen, she and Lilly are victims of school mean girls Ashley and Amber, with the former mocking her, "Could you be any more of a hillbilly?" ("Ooh, Ooh Itchy Woman"). They also place her and Lilly, along with recurring character Dandruff Danny, last on their "cool list" ("The Idol Side of Me"). School bully Henrietta Laverne, more menacingly known as "the Cracker," targets Miley for torment ("Schooly Bully"). As in fiction, so in life, and Cyrus recalls in her autobiography her sixth-grade struggles with friends and foes, thereby establishing her relatability to her tween audience in their joint struggles for acceptance among classmates: "The cool people find each other. The smart people find each other. Me and all the other in-between artsy people realize we'd better join forces and make the best of it" (*MG* 13).

Ironically, even Hannah's and Cyrus's assumptions of their diva personas deepen their core authenticity and thus foreshadow its queer fissures. This evolution occurs in *Hannah Montana: The Movie*, in which Robby Ray takes Miley to Tennessee to "detox" her from her Hollywood airs, after she fights with supermodel Tyra Banks over a pair of shoes and ruins Lilly's sweet-sixteen birthday by arriving as Hannah—and consequently causing a media hullaballoo—rather than as Miley. As her grandmother (Margo Martindale) tells Miley after she sulkily arrives in Tennessee, "Look, missy. You may be Hannah Montana back home, but here we're britches and boots. And if that ain't good enough for you, maybe you should just pack up and git." With life again conscripted to imitate art, Cyrus mentions in her autobiography that at one point she "was being a brat. Stardom had changed me. I wasn't Miley anymore. I was Hollywood. Something *had* to shift" (*MG* 172). Hollywood transforms Miley and Cyrus into glamorous narcissists, yet both the character and the actor, reminded of their core values, shift back to their authentic selves—all the while maintaining their Hollywood lifestyles of celebrity excess.

Miley's authenticity is directly tied to *Hannah Montana*'s merchandising, which is not solely a lucrative revenue stream but key to the program itself, as it dramatizes Hannah's appeal both as a likable character and as a successful marketing icon. With disarming candor, Cyrus writes in her autobiography, "The show had proven so successful that Hannah Montana had gone from being a character to being a brand" (*MG* 164). Carissa Rosenberg, *Seventeen* magazine's entertainment director, echoes this sentiment yet switches the actor for the character: "Miley Cyrus herself is a brand, not just Hannah Montana."[25] The program's theme song, "Best of Both Worlds," begins as an ode to celebrity culture and shopping: "You got the limo out front, / Hottest styles, every shoe, every color." Developing this consumerist motif, *Hannah Montana* stages numerous scenes emphasizing Hannah's appeal in marketing products. As her publicist, Vita (Vanessa Williams), tells her: "Do you know what a well-placed photo of you shopping is worth? You're a star, an icon. You look at it, touch it, wear it, and the whole world has to have it" (*Hannah Montana: The Movie*). The Disney Channel positions Hannah Montana as the ultimate endorsement available through its crossover marketing of multiple programs. In *That's So Suite Life of Hannah Montana* the characters of *That's So Raven*, *The Suite Life of Zack and Cody*, and *Hannah Montana* encounter one another, with Hannah endorsing Raven's fashion designs: "Well, I want a Raven original." Raven then exults that "London Tipton and Hannah Montana are having a catfight over my dress," knowing that Hannah's endorsement will increase her viability as a designer, as the scene also enhances the desirability of products marketed to *Hannah Montana*'s viewers.

Several episodes of *Hannah Montana* portray young fans eagerly purchasing merchandise endorsed by their icon, such as the young girl who buys a scarf that Hannah promotes while standing underneath a mannequin of herself ("It's a Mannequin's World"). Lilly reads Hannah's email aloud to her, which includes a fan's determination to emulate her pop idol: "Dear Hannah, I love, love, love that scarf you wore at the video awards. Where, where, where can I get one?" ("Oops! I Meddled Again"). The show refrains from providing the answer—Walmart—yet this bifurcation of worlds—down-home simplicity and celebrity glamour—extends to Cyrus's description of the fashions in her two closets: "Both are stuffed with more clothes than I could wear in a year. Half of the stuff is clothes I bought at Forever 21 and Walmart, and half is gifts from designers like Chanel, Gucci, and Prada that I began to get as the show took off" (*MG* 112). While few celebrities would admit to hanging Walmart fashions in their wardrobes, this corporation sells the Hannah Montana line of clothing, with Cyrus describing its creation: "We look at what I wear, and then we try to make it for $16."[26] Beyond the merchandise marketing in the program, many *Hannah Montana* products promote other such products, such as the *Hannah Montana in the Mix* Book and Magnetic Set. The booklet first admonishes, "Every girl should have her own personal style," and then encourages young readers simply to emulate Hannah: "Take this quiz and find out which Hannah Montana style is right for you!"[27] In the series, Hannah endorses the skin cream Magic Glow, which further enhances her credibility as a pitchperson: the episode dramatizes her embarrassment over a pimple caught in the advertising photograph, which accentuates her relatability to her tween viewers through their shared problems ("You're So Vain, You Probably Think This Zit Is about You"). In marketing terms such scenes create the series' and Cyrus's "brandscape," which Nicholas Carah defines as "an experiential social space where marketers engage consumers in the co-creation of brand meaning."[28]

Yet at the same time that Hannah is depicted as part of the marketing industry behind her success, the authenticity that is core to the Miley/Hannah dyad often emerges to trouble her image as a celebrity pitchperson—and, consequently, to strengthen it. For example, the sitcom mocks the Hollywood publicity machine when Hannah and her love interest, Jake, are hosting the Teen Scene Awards, and Hannah errs by reading from the teleprompter both the scripted dialogue and the stage directions she should omit. Jake delivers his lines correctly, but she follows with, "Oh, Jake, I bet you say that to all your co-stars. Push Jake. I mean . . ." as she belatedly pushes him. Too authentic to understand the scripted banter she should perform, Hannah repeats her error when she reads aloud "Hold for laughter" ("People Who Use People"). The episode "Smells Like Teen Sellout" extends Hannah's credibility to the commercial realm, with its title alerting young fans to the possibility that their icon could exploit her celebrity by endorsing products that she does not use. While shooting a commercial for "Eau Wow" perfume, Hannah discovers, to her dismay, that it smells like raspberries, as she then recalls winning a raspberry-pie-eating contest and vomiting on the governor of Tennessee. Colin Lassiter, a recurring character in the role of a Larry King–style interviewer, declares, "I'm glad you're not one of those celebrities who goes out and pushes something she doesn't believe in." Hannah realizes she cannot sabotage her integrity by endorsing Eau Wow, even though the company gave her a car in appreciation of her marketing appeal; she tells Robby Ray, "The truth is always the best thing. Even though sometimes it hurts." Within the standard narratology of a family sitcom, such moralizing indicates that the protagonist has learned a valuable lesson, with viewers at home learning one as well: that Hannah Montana—and Miley Cyrus—are trusted voices within the commercial milieu.

Along with establishing Hannah's credibility as a pitchperson, *Hannah Montana* depicts Miley decrying the consumerism that her alter ego endorses. This aspect of her character, while surprising given the sitcom's investment in commercialism, cements Cyrus's ethos for her fans because, as Catherine Driscoll explains, the tension between consumer conformity and resistance to consumer conformity are deeply intertwined in tween culture: "The girl market has always utilized nonconformity and, in particular, relations between conformity and nonconformity. But the opposition between pleasure in consumption figured as conformity and pleasure against the grain of such conformity does not provide a useful model for considering girl culture, where resistance is often just another form of conformity and conformity may be compatible with other resistances."[29] In an episode illustrating her slavish devotion but then resistance to consumerism, Miley goes to outlandish lengths to purchase a new cellphone, which involves a harebrained scheme to sell photographs of actor Dwayne "The Rock" Johnson, dressed in drag, to a sleazy tabloid. When her plan unravels, she confesses to Johnson, "I guess I just got so caught up in having the next new thing." He patiently explains, "You know, Miley, there's always going to be something new coming around the corner." Lilly chimes in as well, realizing that she has heard Johnson's lesson before: "Hey, that's what my mom says" ("Don't Stop 'til You Get the Phone"). Having learned her lesson about rampant consumerism, Miley now stands as a stronger moral authority. She will not endorse products she does not believe in, and she recognizes the dangers of untamed consumerism, with the implicit message that when Hannah/Cyrus endorses a product, it meets her standards of excellence and necessity.

In contrast to the fantasy world of Hannah Montana's glamorous success, Miley Stewart's everyday life affords her only a modest allowance that leaves her with little disposable income—again enhancing her relatability to her fans—until Robby Ray dispenses $5,000 of her fortune into a checking account. After this windfall, Miley initially resists consumerism, telling Lilly while shopping: "You want to know something else? It feels good not to buy anything. To no longer be one of those weak spineless consumers that these malls prey on." Yet the plot twists when she spies a product she desires: "But it's Pearls by Henri. The finest makeup in the world." The episode's physical comedy involves Miley tripping into a display clamshell filled with makeup, but the episode's moral resignifies her economic follies into a lesson in believing in oneself. As Robby Ray explains, "The only reason that you couldn't handle this money is because you didn't trust yourself as much as I trust you." He then adds: "The problem is, you have to remember that sometime it's OK to say yes. Unless you're talking about boys, then the answer is always no" ("You Never Give Me Money"). With these nuggets of paternal wisdom, Robby Ray advocates self-validation through consumerism while discouraging sexuality, thus encouraging viewers at home to promote adolescent chastity through adolescent consumerism. Consumerism takes precedence over sexual maturation in a girl's evolution into womanhood, as Miley muses in voice-over: "My very first credit card. Today, I am a woman." In a sitcom trope famous from *Sex and the City* (1998–2004), with Carrie Bradshaw's penchant for Jimmy Choo, Manolo Blahnik, and other high-end designer shoes, Miley likewise chirps, "I have to have these shoes"—although she finds hers at a flea market ("Debt It Be"). Buying shoes announces a girl's womanhood in the world of *Hannah Montana*, yet the intersection of adolescence and sexuality complicates efforts to market Cyrus as a superstar to the tween masses, many of whose parents frowned on the young woman's metamorphosis into a sexual provocateur, with her relatability and moral authority thus assuming ever queerer aspects.

Marketing the Queer Tween in *Hannah Montana*

Many parents and child-rearing authorities worry that children will find television's candid depictions of sexuality confusing and upsetting and so seek out "family-friendly programming"—that emptiest of television signifiers—to shield their children from sexually mature themes. Diane Levin cautions that "today's children are bombarded with large doses of graphic sexual content that they cannot process and that are often frightening. While children struggle to make sense of mature sexual content, they are robbed of valuable time for age-appropriate developmental tasks."[30] On its surface, *Hannah Montana* shies away from candid depictions of eroticism, with its most blatant references to sexuality appearing in episode titles alluding to more risqué pop-music fare: "She's a Super Sneak" points to Rick James's "Super Freak," "Oops! I Meddled Again" to Britney Spears's "Oops! . . . I Did It Again," "Lilly's Mom Has Got It Goin' On" to Fountains of Wayne's ode to attractive mothers, "Stacy's Mom," among many others. Even double entendres are rare within the overarching innocence of *Hannah Montana*. When Jackson falls while filming his outdoor adventuring, he tells Oliver that he "landed right on the coconuts"—with a pun on testicles stressed by the "nuts" he holds in his hands ("Smells Like Teen Sellout"). In a pique, Miley snaps at Lilly, "You're in love with Orlando Bloom, and he doesn't even know you exist," with Lilly countering, "Yet. But he will. And then you will watch the Lilly bloom" ("The Test of My Love"). Lilly's suggestive words hint at an erotic flowering, but its tame timbre masks sexuality more than uncovers it.

Within *Hannah Montana*'s tween world, girls' interests are divided between shopping and boys, with these twin desires dramatized when Lilly suggests that "the mall has cute clothes," but Miley replies that "the beach has cute boys"—and in this instance, the beach wins ("It's My Party and I'll Lie If I Want To"). Many similar story lines dramatize Miley's crushes and dating relationships with boys, yet these hints of adolescent sexuality rarely disrupt the series' vigilant innocence. Even though much of the series is set on the strip of Malibu beach outside the Stewarts' home, the female characters are modestly attired, and the male characters keep their shirts on. The program acknowledges girls' desires to see boys shirtless, such as when Miley points out that Lilly can watch Orlando Bloom movies for some scopophilic pleasure, and she sighs over her idol's attractiveness, "And in the shirtless scenes, slo-mo" ("The Test of My Love"). Hoping to catch a glimpse of Jake's chest as he changes into swimwear, Lilly groans, "Oh, man, I missed his muscles. His zombie-slaying muscles" ("More Than a Zombie to Me"). At the same time, the program cannot entirely overlook the actors' maturing bodies, which are recognized through light jokes. Miley calls Jackson "Captain Hormone" when he daydreams of pillow fights with the daughter of Robby Ray's date ("She's a Super Sneak"), and Oliver complains, after Miley roughhouses with him for accidentally giving Jake the video camera containing her confession of love, "You ripped out my only chest hair" ("Good Golly, Miss Dolly").

When the possibility of light eroticism for these adolescent characters becomes too real, *Hannah Montana* often slips into fantasy, such as when Miley kisses a cookie jar while thinking of Jesse ("He Could Be the One"; fig. 5.1) or when Jackson declares, "Prepare to be kissed, as you've never been kissed before"—with the camera revealing that he is addressing Miley's toy pig ("California Screamin'"; fig. 5.2). Even within Hannah's wider celebrity culture, the "Teen Scene Award for Best Kiss" goes to "Frankie Muniz and his pillow in *The Lonely Sophomore*" ("People Who Use People"). This joke satirizes the MTV Movie Award for Best Kiss, with this category repeatedly won during the years of *Hannah Montana*'s production by Kristen Stewart and Robert Pattinson for the *Twilight* series (2009–12). Here even *Twilight*'s PG-13 sexuality is scrubbed away in the vision of young Muniz necking—or, one assumes, practicing necking—with a pillow.

Cookie jars, stuffed animals, and pillows aside, *Hannah Montana* must confront the likelihood of teens kissing, yet it does so gently, and camera cuts and other evasive editing techniques consistently delay depicting Miley's sexual maturation. Hannah thinks that she will kiss her crush, Jake, as they shoot a film in which she plays Zaronda, Princess of the Undead, and he a zombie slayer, with Jake advising her how to stage their embrace: "Just close your eyes, and count to sixty. It'll be over before you know it." Intimidated by the possibility of a kiss lasting so long, Hannah replies in shock, "Sixty?"

FIGURES 5.1 AND 5.2 Hannah kisses a cookie jar, and Jackson flirts with a stuffed animal, displaying the series' predilection for obfuscating depictions of teen sexuality.

Even this staged embrace is never seen, for the director stops filming at the moment before their lips meet ("More Than a Zombie to Me"). This strategy is repeated in the episode "Good Golly, Miss Dolly": as Miley fantasizes about a kiss with Jake, the camera cuts away when their lips almost touch.

Robby Ray assumes the role of the father hopeful his daughter will never mature into teen—or even adult—sexuality. When she moons over her cute classmate Johnny Collins (Corbin Bleu), Robby Ray reminds her of her recent interests, "Honey, at your age, there's only two things that are cute—squirrels and little puppy dogs" ("Lilly, Do You Want to Know a Secret?"), and he sighs to Jackson: "You realize how much easier life was when she believed boys still had cooties?" ("I Can't Make You Love Hannah If You Don't"). As Miley's dating life blossoms, he frequently shatters the mood for romance. On one occasion, Hannah apologizes to Jake because they were forced to leave a movie early because of a mob of fans. Jake readily forgives her because, as he suggestively leans in for a kiss, "it gives us more time to . . ."; Robby Ray interrupts to offer lemonade, as Jake continues his sentence in an unexpected direction: "say hi to your dad!" Robby Ray genially warns his daughter's suitor away: "Yes, sir. Sweet lemonade. Refreshing and as close to puckering as anybody's gonna get around here." In addition to evacuating these hints of teen eroticism, and throughout her on-again-off-again romances, Miley realizes the primacy of familial bonds over romantic attractions, concluding that her father's love is more enduring: "At least I know one big handsome guy who will always love me" ("Achy Jakey Heart, Part 2").

In a similar vein, as much as Robby Ray wards off her suitors' affections, Miley strategizes against competitors who threaten the primacy of the father/daughter bond. Fearing that any parental eroticism would subvert the sanctity of the family unit, she sabotages Robby Ray's dating life as she also demands, "Explain how you could ever think there's someone out there who could ever replace my mom" ("She's a Super Sneak"). In "Me and Mr. Jonas and Mr. Jonas and Mr. Jonas," with this episode's title riffing on Billy Paul's soulful tribute to adulterous love "Me and Mrs. Jones," Miley, jealous of the Jonas Brothers' collaboration with Robby Ray, disparages them as "Stupid, cute Jonas Brothers"—with her words revealing both her envy of them and her attraction to them. More so, as Miley explains to Lilly, the possibility of homosocial bonding between her father and these young men undermines her preeminent status in Robby Ray's world, particularly in the professional venue of music recording: "I'm sorry, but they're guys, and he's a guy, and what if he figures out that he likes writing for guys more than he likes writing for Hannah?" She laments, "He's having a Jo-bro-mance." The episode ends with the family reunited, as Robby Ray gently admonishes Miley, "You can't seriously be jealous of me spending time with the Jonas Brothers." Such jealousy borders on the ridiculous, even within the humorous and child-friendly story lines of a tween sitcom, yet it reinforces the primacy of the family against outside intrusions—whether adolescent amorousness, professional obligations, or the homosocial pleasure of a "Jo-bro-mance."

Developing these profamily themes and their antierotic undertones, Miley learns that parents should take precedence over their children's dating and light erotic pleasures. Enjoying a picnic with Jesse after repeatedly cancelling plans with Robby Ray, Miley finds herself tormented by her conscience, which speaks in his voice. "Get out of my head, old man!" she snaps, as she then clarifies to Jesse: "I'm with you." The inner/outer dialogue continues with Robby Ray's voice complaining, "And not me," as she then says to Jesse: "On this beautiful day, having a lovely picnic." Concentrating on Jesse, who leans in for a kiss, Miley appears to have vanquished her father's claims for attention in favor of romance, yet Jesse's father interrupts their burgeoning romance by calling on his cell phone. Miley expects Jesse to dismiss his father quickly, as she has done repeatedly to Robby Ray, but Jesse greets his father warmly, "Hey. No, now's a great time." She attempts to redirect his attention to her—"Hello! Losing the hoo-ah over here"—but he responds, "I'm sorry. It's kind of important" ("Been Here All Along"). After learning that Jesse's father serves in the military and is stationed in Afghanistan, Hannah gives a tribute concert for the families of armed forces members, thus again transforming the insistently chaste pleasures of teen dating into a celebration of the family unit.

The camera's cutting away from teen amorousness eventually becomes little more than a joke in the series, with filming strategies hinting at deeper passions than those depicted onscreen. *Hannah Montana: The Movie* features Miley kissing Travis Brody (Lucas Till), but instead of a cut, the camera pans away slowly, thus implying that their kiss continues longer than viewers are allowed to see. In *Hannah Montana*'s final episode, as Lilly and Oliver declare their love for each other at the airport, some fellow travelers park their luggage in front of them—shielding young viewers from their kiss yet implying a long and heartfelt embrace after the bags are finally moved. This setup is repeated with the same travelers and the same luggage when Miley and Jesse kiss goodbye, as Miley virtually breaks into metadiscourse by telling these travelers, "Excuse me. Take your time"—thus letting viewers know that the kiss they cannot see is more passionate than standard tween television fare ("Wherever I Go"; fig. 5.3). Eroticism is absent yet present, maintaining Miley's innocence at the same moment it can no longer narratively hold.

Given *Hannah Montana*'s hesitation to depict teen sexuality beyond brief kisses, parents of tween viewers know they need not be concerned about escalating depictions of eroticism. Even the slightest possibility that Miley/Hannah could lose her virginity—which, of course, would never be allowed to happen—is rendered impossible by the many layers of surveillance to which she is subjected. The paparazzi hound her to the extent that she must pretend

FIGURE 5.3 Luggage conveniently obfuscates teen passion—even in *Hannah Montana*'s final episode ("Wherever I Go").

to date her brother ("My Boyfriend's Jackson and There's Gonna Be Trouble"), and her bodyguard Roxy repeatedly drops her catchphrase, "I got my eyes on you," with her zealous prosecution of her duties necessitating that she impersonate a middle-school student to protect Miley throughout the day ("Schooly Bully"). One of the many security personnel who guards Hannah says, "It's my job to keep that southern belle from getting dinged" ("Double Crossed," of *Wizards on Deck with Hannah Montana*)—with the double entendre of "getting dinged" suggestive of the intercourse that cannot occur within the program's fictions. Thus, within Miley/Hannah's world, little attention is paid to issues of teen sexuality such as unplanned pregnancies. Miley approaches the school nurse, Lori (Christine Taylor), saying, "I need to talk to you about something a little awkward and potentially embarrassing," and Lori's comforting reply stresses her awareness of teens' problems: "Miley, relax. I'm a nurse. I've seen it all." While "seen it all" might imply pregnancy, venereal disease, and drug addiction, Lori snaps on a rubber glove to examine Miley's head for lice ("California Screamin'"). Within the construction of her celebrity persona that complements her screen character, Cyrus affirms her commitment to maintaining her virginity: "When I got old enough and there were boys in the picture, I asked if it was time for me to get my own [purity] ring. My mom gave me one that has a circle on it, to represent the circle of marriage" (*MG* 241). Within both its discourse and metadiscourse, *Hannah Montana* treats teen sexuality so lightly and endorses virginity so earnestly that many parents would likely applaud its Disneyfication of sexuality for young viewers.

In line with this ethos of innocence, *Hannah Montana* flirts with issues of tween sexuality only obliquely, yet in casting Brooke Shields as Miley's deceased mother, it encodes a queer layer of sexual transgression and commercialism that it concomitantly purifies. Shields burst into the limelight in a string of provocative films, including *Alice Sweet Alice* (1976) and *King of the Gypsies* (1978) but more notoriously *The Blue Lagoon* (1980) and *Endless Love* (1981), which featured frank depictions of teen eroticism. Additional controversy accompanied her commercials for Calvin Klein jeans, including one in which she purred, "Do you know what comes between me and my Calvins? Nothing." *Hannah Montana* reminds its parental audience of this connection when they learn the name of Miley's horse: Blue Jeans. The risqué blue jeans of Shields's past are resignified into a reminder of Miley's simpler life in Tennessee, washing away the lingering aura of pedophilia that many viewers found so unsettling in Shields's adolescent commercial career. With the specters of her past behind her and now donning a maternal image, Shields imparts loving wisdom to Miley from beyond the grave, such as in her comforting declaration, "You were loved before you were Hannah Montana, and you'll be loved long after Hannah's on one of those 'Where are they now?' shows" ("I Am Hannah, Hear Me Croak"; fig. 5.4). Child viewers are unlikely to know of Shields's career highlights from the early 1980s, yet in recoding her sexually charged past through the wholesome image of Miley's deceased mother, *Hannah Montana* also rewrites the scripts of Cyrus's sexually incendiary stunts, suggesting it is a phase that she will grow out of, just as her television mother did. From this vantage point, Miley's determined innocence reveals its queer

FIGURE 5.4 Brooke Shields, as a sexually suggestive tween in her youth and as Miley's mother in *Hannah Montana*, models the recuperation of the sexualized youth in adulthood.

subtext, for viewers realize that, just like her fictional mother, a provocative sense of adolescent sexuality is hiding beneath her plucky exterior.

Allegory and Marketing Cyrus's Queer Evolution in *Hannah Montana*

Whereas *Hannah Montana* disavows teen sexuality throughout its story lines, its cagey thematizing of marketing and of Miley's and Cyrus's authenticity prepares its young audience to accompany Cyrus through her post-Hannah metamorphosis into a titillating and openly queer pop star. This transition into a sexual provocateur, as well as her later coming out as pansexual, coincides with, and becomes allegorized into, Hannah's quest for authenticity as an artist. The litany of Cyrus's sexually titillating, headline-grabbing acts during and following her years as Hannah Montana bespeaks her continuous efforts to align her celebrity with her changing age and audience. Midway through the show's run, she posed for a June 2008 *Vanity Fair* photo shoot with Annie Leibovitz that portrayed her draped in bed sheets, her bare back suggesting nudity. An additional photo with her father, Billy Ray—with her bare midriff, his bare shoulders, she leaning into his lap as they hold hands—struck some readers as disturbingly incestuous and pedophilic. The manufactured controversy worked as intended, as Camille Paglia sardonically pointed out: "They knew perfectly well it would cause a storm. . . . I'm so tired of Annie Leibovitz."[31] Cyrus dutifully apologized for the ensuing firestorm: "I took part in a photo shoot that was supposed to be 'artistic' and now, seeing the photographs and reading the story, I feel so embarrassed. . . . I never intended for any of this to happen and I apologize to my fans who I care so deeply about."[32] Gary Marsh, the president of entertainment for Disney Channel Worldwide, chided his star, warning her to maintain her all-American image: "For Miley Cyrus to be a 'good girl' is now a business decision for her. Parents have invested in her a godliness. If she violates that trust, she won't get it back."[33]

Negotiating among children's innocence, adolescent maturation, and adult provocation, Cyrus detailed her muddled understanding of her status as a children's role model: "My job is to be a role model, and that's what I want to do, but my job isn't to be a parent. . . . My job isn't to tell your kids how to act or how not to act, because I'm still figuring that out for myself. So to take that away from me is a bit selfish. Your kids are going to make mistakes whether I do or not. That's just life."[34] Cyrus's jumbled words bespeak the difficulty of pinning down a coherent celebrity identity for her throughout her many personas. She claims her responsibility to be a role model—presumably one of whom parents would approve—but then asserts for herself the right to be a typical adolescent who will make frequent mistakes—thus distancing herself from the position of role model that she has previously claimed. Many public appearances continued to shock some fans, including her August 2009 performance at the Teen Choice Awards, in which she spun around a stripper pole while singing "Party in the USA." Anticipating the conclusion of *Hannah Montana*, the June 2010 release of her "Can't Be Tamed" single, with the lyrics "I go through guys like money flyin' out the hands" and a video with risqué costuming, announced a striking shift in her celebrity persona. Perhaps the incident that generated the most controversy was her August 2013 performance at MTV's Video Music Awards, in which she twerked—a dance move symbolic of anal sex—with Robin Thicke. The backlash included such comments as news host Mika Brzezinski's pointed criticism: "There's pushing the envelope and there's porn—there's raunchy porn that's disgusting and disturbing."[35] Various other incidents extensively covered in the entertainment media—penis birthday cakes, daring haircuts, selfies in various stages of dishabille with her surprisingly nimble tongue in exaggerated display—testify to Cyrus's strategic marketing of herself to a public always eager to learn of her latest escapades. Unsurprisingly, many children and their parents were taken aback by this new image, castigating her for her actions, particularly while she still inhabited the tween-friendly role of Hannah Montana.

Yet because the lines between Cyrus, Miley, and Hannah are drawn with such cagey ambiguity, parents who would discourage their children from following the post–*Hannah Montana* version of Cyrus are cast as, in effect, stifling their children's psychosexual development—at least within the moral universe of the program, which frequently emphasizes the need to let children assume responsibility for themselves. When Robby Ray is injured and cannot fly with Miley to Florida, she tricks her bodyguard, Roxy, into accompanying her. Furious at Miley's disobedience, Robby Ray ultimately learns that he is inhibiting his daughter's maturation, as Jackson points out to him: "I mean, you raised us to believe we could do anything we set our minds to. And the whole time we were growing up, you told us, 'I know you can do it. So get ready, get set, go.' Why aren't you saying that now?" Robby Ray realizes that Miley is mature enough to travel across the country without him and sings "Ready, Set, Don't Go"—an ode to the difficulties parents face in letting their children establish their independence. He then tells her, "No daddy wants to see his little girl grow up, every dad knows some day she has to" ("I Want You to Want Me . . . To Go to Florida"). The episode's implicit lesson for adult viewers is that they, too, must let their children blaze new paths, even those that they are not yet ready to let them embark on.

Two contrasting episodes—"Yet Another Side of Me" and "Hannah's Gonna Get This"—dramatize the quandary Hannah faces in developing as an artist: whether to remain true to her musical roots and to her current fans or to experiment with new genres and risk alienating these fans, with these story lines allegorically framing the question of her sexual maturation. In "Yet

Another Side of Me," Hannah encounters Isis, the long-standing queen of pop obviously modeled on Madonna. (The writers allude to Madonna's hits in Isis's repertoire—"Material Girl" becomes "Immaterial Girl," "Express Yourself" becomes "Impress Yourself.") Intimidated by Isis's career longevity and convinced by her advice to be perpetually preparing her next incarnation, Miley abandons her musical roots for a thrash metal sound, singing about her former days as a "nice girl"—one who obeyed her parents but now finds herself bored by such youthful innocence. By this episode's end, after Hannah has a nightmare of tween girls rioting to her song at a wholesome Sunshine Girls event, she seeks Robby Ray's guidance. "There's got to be a way to keep them interested and still be me," she laments, with her father advising authenticity as the solution to her dilemma: "As long as you're true to yourself, your fans will always be there." Hannah rejects the sexually suggestive aspects of this new persona, telling her costume designer, Dahli, "I won't be needing the torn fishnets, the combat boots, or the bullwhip," with these accessories hinting at a sadomasochistic, dominatrix outfit. The episode ends as Hannah discovers that Isis has fashioned herself into a Hannah Montana clone for her latest reincarnation, so Hannah's authenticity contrasts with Isis's inauthenticity, proving the superiority of the adolescent who knows herself and, in this instance, rejects a hypersexualized persona in favor of continued innocence.

While it is easy to mock Madonna, it is not so easy to enjoy her striking career longevity in a pop-culture arena where the vast majority of performers—even those who experience great success—maintain their fame for only a few years. So as much as Hannah refuses to change her act in "Yet Another Side of Me," she updates her sound and image in "Hannah's Gonna Get This." Further testifying to the sitcom's interest in the marketing of pop stars, pop songs, and pop merchandise, her producer hires a focus group of young fans to discuss their reactions to her new release "This Boy, That Girl." This song pulses to a techno beat that metonymically represents sexuality—in contrast to the innocent, bubble-gum pop of traditional Hannah fare. Of the focus group member who appreciates her artistic evolution, Hannah declares, "See, somebody's not afraid to let an artist grow. I mean, clearly my audience is wise beyond their years." The balloting is close, however, so Hannah encourages the children who voted against her new sound to embrace change: "Now, look, I know change can be scary, but it's a part of growing up. It's how we find out who we are and who we're gonna be. Change is exciting, and it's fun, just like this song, and that's why I love it, and you guys should love it, too." One little girl whimpers, "I don't want you to change. I love you just the way you are." With Hannah caught in the double bind of pleasing some fans and displeasing others, Robby Ray again advises her to pursue authenticity as her primary goal: "Any time an artist tries to grow, there's always gonna be people who don't like it. You just gotta ask yourself, are you gonna listen to the naysayers, or are you gonna listen to your heart?" Miley offers an unenthusiastic rebuttal—"Well, when the naysayers are crying seven year olds, your heart kinda gets torn"—but the evolution that the sitcom has evaded in its surface treatment of sexuality now approaches, as Robby Ray again encourages her to be true to herself: "Well, I'm proud of you, honey, for trying to make all your fans happy, but since you can't do that, the one that you really need to make happy is you."

With Hannah maintaining her authenticity as an artist and moving in a new musical direction, she sparks a controversy when she publically confesses her alter ego of Miley Stewart, which parallels Cyrus's assumption of her risqué and increasingly queer celebrity persona. These "coming out" episodes function on the narrative level as the climax of the series' story arc, yet they concomitantly assume queer inflections within the metadiscourse concerning Cyrus's celebrity persona. On Colin Lassiter's interview program, adults phone in to voice their outrage over Miley's revelation. One tells her, "You ought to be ashamed of yourself," to which Miley responds: "What? All I did was tell the truth." The parent angrily replies, "A little late for that now! How am I supposed to teach my kid to be honest when her hero is nothing but a liar?" and hangs up. Cyrus's sexually provocative stunts are resignified into the "truth" of Hannah's confession of her identity, which thus becomes defendable as the "truth" of Cyrus's identity as an artist. The episode continues as Miley defends herself to Lassiter, declaring "I was just trying to do what felt right for me," and he consoles her, "Well, don't worry, sweetheart. Some parents are just a little overprotective." Lassiter then adds, "It's not as if she's a licensed child psychologist," apparently disqualifying the caller's comments as uninformed. In a comic twist, he reverses course by introducing the next caller—licensed child psychologist Dr. Mark Lynch. Lynch emphasizes the disastrous consequences of Hannah's confession:

LYNCH: Miley, I think you've done a wonderful thing for yourself.
MILEY: Thank you, doctor.
LYNCH: Unfortunately, it may prove catastrophic for children everywhere.
MILEY: Huh?
LYNCH: Hannah Montana was real for children, and well, how do I say this in a way you'll understand? You killed her.
LASSITER: Wow! People hate you. ("Kiss It Goodbye")

Given Lynch's hyperbolic argument—that Hannah Montana, like Santa Claus and the Tooth Fairy, is a beloved children's fantasy that must be preserved—Miley's position of honesty is ironically validated. And so within the sitcom's allegorical metadiscourse, Cyrus's sexualized performances are naturalized as part of her growth as an artist. As the analogy implies, just as parents cannot preserve their children in the eternal stasis of believing in Santa Claus and the Tooth Fairy, they must allow their children to enjoy Hannah's artistic metamorphosis to better appreciate Cyrus's queer transition into adult stardom.

As the father both of Hannah Montana and of the divisive pop star, Robby Ray/Billy Ray Cyrus defends his daughter. On the program, Robby Ray disparages the parents who object to her revelation: "Most of those people who called in are a bunch of stopped-up adults who probably don't have enough fiber in their diets." *Hannah Montana* then depicts Miley moving past these criticisms to perform again, as Aunt Dolly, hosting a musical special, introduces Hannah to the audience: "Well, I want to introduce somebody to you now that's been getting a lot of criticism lately, but she is not gonna let that stop her from doing what she loves to do, and that is singing for you." The children in the audience cry out "We love you, Miley," proving her endurable appeal as she sings "Kiss It Goodbye," a song of personal transformation that includes the lyric "I'm a different girl" ("Kiss It Goodbye"). With real life again echoing the program, Parton defended Cyrus's controversial transition. Guy Trebay documents that "when asked whether she was shocked by Ms. Cyrus's rapid shift from . . . a 'wholesome teenager' to a 'raunchy performer,' Ms. Parton said, 'Well, yeah, but in a good way.'"[36] For Cyrus's star to continue rising, she must convince tween viewers to accept her "coming out" as a different girl, with her show promoting this sexual evolution within the muted tones of a family sitcom reticent to address teen sexuality.

Even light kisses rarely appear on *Hannah Montana*, yet Miley/Hannah effectively lays the groundwork for Cyrus's sexual and celebrity metamorphosis through the power of marketing. In constructing the character's authenticity, her outsider status, her relatability to her fans, and her ethical values as a spokesperson, Miley wins over tween viewers and their parents through her surface authenticity that allows queer countercurrents to overcome tween innocence. And as Cyrus's career has flourished in the years since *Hannah Montana*'s conclusion, she has continually shifted her erotic image while maintaining the pseudo-authenticity key to her enduring success, particularly in her advocacy for homeless queer youth. The *New York Times* praised her as "a natural avatar for a post-gender generation,"[37] and she recently declared her ecumenical erotic interests: "I'm very open about my sexuality—I am pansexual."[38] She also proclaims of herself, "Everything I've ever done has been true to me at that minute," a statement of eternal authenticity that bedazzles with its chameleon play of time, image, and truth, in its collapsing of tween innocence and provocative queerness.[39] As *Hannah Montana* proceeded from its tween roots and its star began emphasizing her sexuality and her desire to evolve as an artist, the show demonstrates that, even when children's sexual innocence is used as a primary marketing tool, it is simply preparing young consumers for the moment when they can be treated to the flip side of Miley's winsome wholesomeness. Sex sells, even, paradoxically, when tween marketing is predicated on its absence and an accompanying sub-rosa allegory of an erotic evolution. The long-standing fantasies of the domestic sitcom imbue *Hanna Montana* with much of its appeal and its queer subversions of this appeal, but in refusing to address sexuality candidly, the program resisted contemporary efforts to present the American family in a new and forthright erotic perspective finally freed from the sitcom mores of yesteryear—a dynamic that was concurrently pursued in *Modern Family* (2009–), as the following chapter investigates.

6

Conservative Narratology, Queer Politics, and the Humor of Gay Stereotypes in *Modern Family*

With its terse yet instructive title, *Modern Family* (2009–) articulates the provocative claim that television will, at long last, depict a clan reflective of contemporary mores rather than the hidebound traditions of the 1950s.[1] Sitcoms are often accused of an inherent conservatism in their plotlines and structure, so *Modern Family* allows viewers to gauge the tension between a program progressive in its ambitions and the narratological structures that might bend it to an ultimately conservative arc. Many viewers have criticized aspects of this purportedly modern family that they deem regressive, notably the program's depiction of gay couple Mitch and Cam, who, in their flamboyant excess, may appear to represent denigrating caricatures of gay life; this apparent embrace of stereotypes becomes a key reason for dismissing the program's sexual politics as superficial. Yet by conforming to while tweaking the traditional parameters of sitcom narratology, *Modern Family* proves the queer potential latent in the sitcom genre, which invites numerous thematic and structural subversions of the sexual status quo. Deploying yet defanging the satirical edge of stereotype-based humor, the program dismantles the ideological weight of culturally inflected humor, particularly in relation to the long-standing assumption of queer liberalism. Furthermore, in its encoding of anal eroticism as a staple of this modern family's sexual imagination, the program disproves the likelihood of heteronormativity curtailing the erotic interests of its members; it also demonstrates the humorous potential that arises in resignifying certain erotic desires, hitherto rendered abject by rigid codes of sexual policing, into a source of liberation.

Modern Family tells the story of the extended clan of the Pritchetts, the Tucker-Pritchetts, and the Dunphys. Divorced from his children's mother, Dede (Shelley Long, in a recurring role), wealthy closet manufacturer Jay Pritchett (Ed O'Neill) has married Gloria Delgado (Sofia Vergara), a Colombian bombshell and the mother of mooning romantic Manny (Rico Rodriguez); the fourth season dramatizes the birth of their son Joe. In the series pilot, Jay's gay son, Mitchell (Jesse Tyler Ferguson), and his partner, Cameron Tucker (Eric Stonestreet), adopt a Vietnamese daughter, Lily (Aubrey Anderson-Emmons). Jay's straight and straight-laced daughter, Claire (Julie Bowen), is married to Phil Dunphy (Ty Burrell), a realtor, trampoline enthusiast, and former college cheerleader, with whom she is raising their three children: Haley (Sarah Highland) is popular and pretty yet struggles academically; Alex (Ariel Winter) excels academically yet struggles socially; and Luke (Nolan Gould) wanders goofily throughout his school and home life. Most episodes consist of interweaving story lines that climax as the three families come together for a dinner, party, or other such event, where escalating tensions dissolve into domestic harmony and mutual affection.

With Claire and Phil's family representing the upper-middle-class, white, suburban, nuclear norm typical of many family sitcoms, it falls to Jay's interethnic marriage to Gloria and, more so, to Mitch's same-sex relationship with Cam to define the program's clan as "modern." Homosexuality is thus necessary to advance *Modern Family*'s titular premise, despite the fact that visual depictions of Mitch and Cam's romance are mostly occluded from view. Railing against network television's hesitancy to depict same-sex relationships candidly, some viewers have therefore decried *Modern Family* as ultimately reactionary. Yet the matter is more complicated than simple representation, as Lynne Joyrich presciently cautioned of queer television depictions: "in formulating a politics of representation, we need not—indeed, should not—simply ask for more (more disclosure, more true-to-life drama, more explicit imagery)," noting further that "the explicit revelation of sexuality on commercial television need not explode the logic of the closet."[2] Truly, a queer couple onscreen need afford little revolutionary potential in itself. Nonetheless, *Modern Family*, through its portrayal of queer lives and through its restaging of the protocols of sitcom narratology, creates a narrative space to challenge heteronormative paradigms while also subverting assumptions about the assumed political sensibilities of sitcoms, whether progressive or regressive. With its queer sensibility demolishing ready referents to liberal or conservative politics,

Modern Family casts a new light on an entertainment genre that many malign as staunchly regressive, and it questions as well the prevailing stereotype of modern-day homosexuality as necessarily politically progressive. More so, if homosexuality alone were insufficient to unsettle *Modern Family*'s treatment of ideological normativity, the ways in which anal and other desires float through its story lines testify to the unruly and carnivalesque spirit of eroticism that quickly deflates the queer fantasies of the family sitcom, even within the protocols of network television and its celebration of the family and children's innocence.

The Conservative Narratology of Sitcoms

"The sitcom is, literally, child's play," declares Jane Feuer, in a provocative statement that she immediately deconstructs, as she acknowledges the simplistic accusation of the genre's ostensible conservatism and then broadens the contours of her analysis. Of the foundations of the conservative view of sitcoms, she observes, "such an argument is based on the fact that the nuclear family is considered an ideologically conservative social unit that supports the status quo of 'family values.' Therefore, to base a sitcom on a nuclear family is to affirm rather than question the status quo."[3] Certainly, a steady stream of sitcom criticism argues for an inherent conservatism to the genre, such as Gerard Jones's assessment that "it's a very conservative form," one that "is an expression of the underlying assumptions of the corporate culture that has come to dominate American society."[4] David Grote posits that the situation comedy rejects the revolutionary potential of other comedic forms because "the principal fundamental situation of the situation comedy is that things do not change. No new society occurs at the end."[5] Without cultural rebirth, as Grote opines, a soporific, if not deadening, effect is achieved, with any revolutionary flair to the comic form quelled. Saul Austerlitz sees in sitcoms "a profound aesthetic conservatism," although he grants as well its "ingrained desire to shock."[6] Even in programs whose premises challenge the prevailing status quo, such as *Julia* (1968–71), *The Mary Tyler Moore Show* (1970–77), and *Ellen* (1994–98), critics often see countervailing conservative threads that undercut their progressive aims.[7] To label an entire narratological structure—rather than particular narratives within that overarching structure—as conservative, however, is to encode political meaning into an empty form that may be adapted in accord with a vast range of desires. Those opposing this perspective would likely argue that form is formative, that structures are structuring, yet I would reply that narratological genres retain an inherent plasticity allowing them to be redeployed in surprising ways irrespective of a clear political affiliation. Even that old shibboleth of the cultural right—"family values"—shifts remarkably in its meaning if it is allowed to signify the multiplicity of America's families, including its queer ones, rather than a staid vision of the "right" way to be a family (pun intended).

At the outset of this argument, I concede that a tension arises between *Modern Family*'s genre and any progressive vision it may advance. This dynamic is evident in the fact that, although the program's title proclaims its modernity, several of its story lines, and thus its ethos, are linked to the honeyed moralism of sitcoms past, particularly to *The Brady Bunch* (1969–74). Like the Bradys, the Pritchetts, Tucker-Pritchetts, and Dunphys travel to Hawaii ("Hawaii") and enjoy a Western vacation ("Dude Ranch"). Phil buys his family a recreational vehicle ("Games People Play"), just as Mike did for the Bradys' trip to the Grand Canyon. Even the mise-en-scène of the Dunphys' living room mirrors the Bradys', with the staircase a focal point for each family. Claire hopes for a portrait to be taken of "the whole extended family . . . in a single-file line down the staircase" ("Family Portrait")—an image that would echo the iconic promotional photographs of the Bradys.[8] Aligning *Modern Family* with the saccharine *Brady Bunch* would appear to undercut the depiction of modernity promised in *Modern Family*'s title—for doing so exhibits a nostalgic yearning for sitcoms of an earlier, ostensibly simpler era—yet the program's homage to the past coexists with a narratology updated for the new millennium.

For it must be noted that the sitcom's basic structure enables its play with numerous discourses, social movements, and historical moments, and Feuer observes as well that "it has been the *ideological flexibility* of the sitcom that has accounted for its longevity."[9] She adds to this point elsewhere by affirming that even "if the episodic series sitcom was static at the level of situation, it was not so at the level of character."[10] While much narratological theory presumes that characters serve a structural function but that their individual depictions matter little, the critical conversation has turned of late to acknowledge that characters shape form—or at least that they alter the deployment of forms for new purposes. As Susan Lanser explains of much narratology, "the sex and gender (let alone the sexuality) of textual personae have not been graciously welcomed as elements of narratology; they have been relegated to the sphere of 'interpretation,' which is often considered a 'temptation' into which narratology must be careful not to 'fall.'"[11] Yet these personae are central to television narration and the story lines framed to accommodate them. Thus, the introduction of a married, gay couple to the standard format of an American television sitcom would at least potentially alter its prevailing rhythms and structures, although this potential would need to be further realized through the characters' shifting of the genre's protocols.

Critical to its innovative narrative structure, *Modern Family* belongs to the pseudo-verité, mockumentary style of sitcom, which traces its cinematic roots to Woody Allen's *Take the Money and Run* (1969) and Rob Reiner's *This Is*

Spinal Tap (1984) and became a television fixture in the 2000s with *The Bernie Mac Show* (2001–6), *Reno 911!* (2003–9), *The Office* (2005–13), and *Parks and Recreation* (2009–15). Mockumentaries intermix their unfolding plots with character interviews, as well as subtle indications that the characters realize they are being filmed during narrative scenes, such as raised eyebrows in the camera's direction. Producer Christopher Lloyd declares of *Modern Family*'s mockumentary style, "The interviews are a chance to have characters more honestly express things than they might openly do in a scene with someone. So we get a laugh from the contrast between what they're feeling and what they were willing to admit they were feeling in the scene."[12] Given this filming strategy, much of the humor of *Modern Family* emerges in the duplicity of domestic life: family members know they must proceed cautiously when dealing with one another's feelings yet unburden themselves to the camera as confessor. Also, this strategy mitigates conflict among characters, with the audience realizing that although deeper tensions bubble beneath the surface, not every disagreement must then come to a boil.

Congruent with *Modern Family*'s minimization of conflict, the structure of most family sitcoms involves only a slight disruption to the status quo and then a comfortable return to normality after a character learns a valuable lesson. *Seinfeld* (1989–98) famously rejected these traditional parameters of sitcom narratology with its production maxim of "No hugging, no learning"—a disavowal of the premises of affection and education that the genre as a whole endorses.[13] Yet the repeated moralism of most sitcoms bears within it the seeds of its own critique, for the very necessity for characters to continually relearn these little life lessons episode after episode suggests the impossibility of their emotional maturation. If morals fail to cohere within the family unit supposedly learning them, how valuable are they to characters and viewers alike? To label the sitcom genre as inherently conservative thus opens the postmodern paradox of morals unmoored from meaning—which would undermine the conservatism ostensibly at the genre's core.

Certainly, many *Modern Family* episodes end with overt moralizing, as a character speaks in voice-over to apprise viewers of the lessons learned over the preceding twenty-two minutes. Further enhancing the apparent conservatism of this narrative strategy, Jay, in his role as family patriarch, often speaks these voice-overs, such as in the conclusion to "Earthquake," in which he calmly assesses the episode's meaning: "There's nothing mystical about an earthquake. Pressure builds, and it's released. And you just hope there's not too much damage. But it makes you realize what matters. And for me, that's my family." With his touching endorsement of the importance of family, Jay affirms life's value in kinship over all other considerations—a moral appropriate to a family sitcom's ethos, whether of the 1950s or of today. Likewise, "Fears" portrays various characters overcoming their phobias—Manny's and Jay's fear of roller coasters, Haley's fear of failing her driver's test, Alex's fear of not being asked to the school dance. The episode concludes as Phil intones reassuringly: "Everybody's afraid of something, right? Heights, clowns, tight spaces. . . . Those are things you get over. But then there's our children. Will they fit in? Will they be safe? Those are fears you never get past. So, sometimes all you can do is take a deep breath, pull 'em close, and hope for the best. I mean, things don't always work out, but you gotta love it when they do." As Phil concludes his moral, the episode's narrative action depicts Mitch and Cam, deeply hurt when Lily's first word was "mama," realizing that she is merely mimicking her talking doll. They then quickly recover from the trauma that Mitch described as "every gay father's worst nightmare" ("Fears"). Domestic unity is restored in all homes, and the episode cruises to its tidy ending.

Yet it would be unwise to assume that this concluding narrative strategy, or any homages to *The Brady Bunch*, reinstates a simplistic moralism to *Modern Family*, for many times what appears to be an extradiegetic homily unexpectedly continues the show's plotlines in new directions. The series' pilot inaugurates this tradition, as Jay appears to speak directly to the audience: "We're from different worlds, yet we somehow fit together. Love is what binds us through fair or stormy weather." Given the episode's emotionally charged arguments, including the firestorm that erupted when Jay said of Mitch and Cam's adoption of Lily—"Well, kids need a mother. I mean if you two guys are bored, get a dog"—it appears that he realizes his error and will redouble his efforts to respect his son's family. The program then leaves its voice-over and returns to the narrative present, and viewers see that Jay is reading aloud the poem that Manny wrote for his crush, Brenda ("Pilot"). Thus, to assume that Jay learns a deeper lesson about family depends on the applicability of his words to his plotline, but his words, it is now evident, belong to Manny. This type of "bait-and-switch" moralism, in which the audience is tricked into believing an episode is divulging its didactic lesson only then to see that the moral does not cohere with the narrative action, undoes the assumed connection between words and visuals that television, in most cases, seeks to preserve.

In another instance of an episode's moralism losing its meaning, Mitch, fatigued by Jay's history of homophobia, hesitates to invite his father to join him and his friends for drinks when they unexpectedly encounter him at a bar. As the episode concludes, Mitch apparently voices the episode's moral: "People can surprise you. You get used to thinking of them one way, stuck in their roles. They are what they are. And then they do something that shows you there's all this depth and dimension that you never knew existed" ("Boys' Night"). Cam, however, does not acknowledge the relevance of Mitch's words to recent family events and instead inquires if his partner is talking about Rob Lowe, whose career trajectory went from bad-boy heartthrob in 1980s cinema (*St. Elmo's Fire* [1985], *About Last Night . . .* [1986]) to television roles of surprising depth (*The West Wing* [1999–2006], *Brothers and Sisters* [2006–11]) and comic charm (*Parks and Recreation*) in the 1990s and 2000s. Another episode concludes with Jay's voice-over apparently informing viewers of the episode's deeper meaning: "There are certain queer times and occasions in this strange mixed affair we call life when a man takes this whole universe for a vast practical joke, though the wit thereof he but dimly discerns, and more than suspects that the joke is at nobody's expense but his own." These words apply well to the episode's intersecting plotlines, particularly the one of Mitch defeating Lily's bullying classmate at handball in order to teach him the necessity of sharing, but then viewers see that Jay is reading aloud a passage from *Moby-Dick* ("The Wow Factor").[14] The segue from Melville's Ahab and his mad quest for vengeance against a white whale to Mitch's exploits on his daughter's playground bespeaks a comic devolution of plotlines, yet it further dismantles the assumed connection between the episode's moral and the possibility that the characters have progressed in their understanding. With lessons that continually founder at the moment of their enunciation, *Modern Family* delivers the type of Aesopian conclusions standard to family sitcoms yet then tweaks them into meaninglessness. As with the show's purported conservatism, its morals can be used to accuse it of ultimately reactionary values, yet viewers must then confront its postmodern questioning of axiomatic truths.

Furthermore, to see in sitcom narratology an intrinsic impulse toward political conservatism contradicts the apolitical stances many programs foster so as not to alienate potential viewers. Political readings of family sitcoms, whether they seek to expose a conservative or liberal bias to their story lines, must confront the largely agnostic stances of the genre's producers, many of whom do not want to risk alienating large segments of their potential audience and therefore prefer to avoid politics altogether—aside from such notable exceptions as Norman Lear, with programs like *All in the Family* (1971–79) and *Maude* (1972–78), and Linda Bloodworth-Thomason, with *Designing Women* (1986–93), among others. As Rob Long, a writer for *Cheers* (1982–93), argues, integrating politically didactic viewpoints within the framework of a sitcom threatens to overburden the format with rhetoric rather than humor: "Using an essentially trivial format to convert the audience to a particular political view is not only condescending and arrogant, it's also impossible to do and still be funny."[15] Janet Leahy, whose credits include *The Cosby Show* (1984–92), *Roseanne* (1988–97), and *Gilmore Girls* (2000–2007), outlines the necessity of averting moral lessons: "Because just at the moment where it looks like you're going to preach to people, or take yourself too seriously, you cut out of there with something funny."[16] This is not to obscure the necessary point that even an apparently apolitical stance might cloak a political stance; that is to say, the decision to stage a family sitcom ostensibly removed from the realm of conservative versus liberal politics occludes various other spheres (racial politics, sexual politics, the economy) that pierce the suburban bubble of many family sitcoms. Despite this essential caveat, within the political divide of conservative and progressive, many sitcoms eschew direct involvement with issues that could cost them countless viewers.

Congruent with this point, programs that engage with explicitly political issues and figures tend to take the role of "equal opportunity offenders," skewering sacred cows of the right and left. For example, in *Family Guy* (1999–) Lois warns Peter about Bill Clinton—"That former President Clinton is nothing but a bad influence. I forbid you to hang out with him any more"—as Clinton proceeds to sleep with Lois and then Peter ("Bill and Peter's Bogus Journey"). The Griffins later travel to Texas and encounter George W. Bush, where they see evidence of his alliance with Osama bin Laden and Satan, as well as his cocaine paraphernalia ("Boys Do Cry"). *Family Guy* travesties presidents of the left and right, aiming for laughs rather than political persuasion. As this issue relates to *Modern Family*, writer and producer Abraham Higginbotham, addressing the issue of Mitch and Cam's marital status, affirms *Modern Family*'s apoliticism, despite the controversial nature of gay marriage in contemporary America: "We wanted to deal with, what is Mitch and Cam's relationship to gay marriage—to marriage, in general—without having to be a political episode because I think what's best about this show is we rarely deal with hot topic social issues" ("*Modern Family* Writers"). Of course, the fact that writers eschew political engagement does not entail that their programs fail to encode political readings, primarily because of the tension between surface and symptom that generates multiple, contradictory readings of the texts at hand, yet it also stresses the ambivalence in these moves, in which they tread lightly on issues about which they may care deeply. A key question, then, in regard to sitcom narratology and its ostensible conservative bent arises in this tension: at what point might the surface of given episodes transcend the symptomology of narrative structure to escape the purported conservatism endemic to this form? And a concomitant paradox emerges as well, as acknowledged previously: form cannot be transcended because it is integral to any given narrative. While acknowledging these complex interrelationships of surface and symptom, I argue that assumptions about the politically conservative meaning of form should not then trump the possibility of meaningful surface transgressions that trigger symptomatic restructuring as well.

As many family sitcoms avoid tackling controversial political issues, many also avoid topical references, for they potentially undermine the genre's unstated premise of timelessness, as well as threaten future profits in syndication. On this subject Phil Rosenthal, producer of *Everybody Loves Raymond* (1996–2005), warns: "Nothing dates a show sooner than a line about Monica Lewinsky," as he also recalls his ambition for his program's longevity: "The show was for CBS, but in the back of my mind, it was for *Nick at Nite*."[17] Topical jokes might succeed during a program's initial run, but as the years pass and future generations join its audience, they bear the potential both to become stale for older viewers and to be incomprehensible to younger viewers—with the program's syndication value plummeting. Iconic moments of sitcoms past illustrate the lasting appeal of humor unbound from temporality: Lucy Ricardo in *I Love Lucy* (1951–57) stuffing chocolates in her mouth as the conveyor belt speeds up ("Job Switching") or getting drunk while pitching *Vitametavegamin ("Lucy Does a TV Commercial")* remain defining moments in the history of television humor, with this comedy unhitched from its 1950s sociotemporal setting. For the most part *Modern Family* adheres to this formula of timelessness, as the vast majority of its story lines unfold in the present but not a present specifically tied to its years of production. The events of "Door to Door" include Manny selling wrapping paper for a fund-raiser and Cam and Gloria searching for Jay's lost dog, Stella—plotlines that could have occurred just as easily in the 1950s as in the 2010s.

Modern Family's writers, however, tossed aside such atemporal chronology to address the issue of gay marriage: the fifth season's first episode "Suddenly, Last Summer"—its title riffing on Tennessee Williams's Grand-Guignol play of cannibalism and homosexuality—announces a specific date for its narrative action: June 26, 2013, the day of the U.S. Supreme Court's *Hollingsworth v. Perry* decision, which, by refusing to take up a previously appealed decision, granted gay people the legal right to marry in California. This date also marks the *United States v. Windsor* decision, which struck down the 1996 Defense of Marriage Act and entitled married gay couples to federal benefits. One of the milestone dates of the modern gay rights movement, June 26, 2013, interjects *Modern Family* into a historical moment that subverts its promise of timelessness. By beginning on this day and concluding with Mitch and Cam's marriage, the fifth season casts aside any pretense of apoliticism to join in the celebration of gay rights. Sitcom moralism and timelessness may contribute to the overarching conservatism of the genre as a whole, but *Modern Family* demonstrates the elasticity of generic frameworks in treating modern lives, as it also, through its cheery Brady allegiance, asks viewers to ponder the ways in which earlier sitcoms resisted generic conformity as well.

Gay Stereotypes and Representational Debates

Given *Modern Family*'s narratological investment in recoding moralism and timelessness in its promotion of gay marriage, its repudiation by some queer viewers raises questions about the ethics of representing minorities in popular culture. Television's representation of racial minorities frequently sparks widely divergent and impassioned responses, as evident in the critical histories of such programs as *Julia*, *The Cosby Show*, and *All-American Girl* (1994–95); so, too, has its representation of gay men and lesbians. Brett Mills explains the frequency of these debates: "If the ways in which representation takes place matter, it's only because there is seen to be some disparity between the ways media characterises people and how they 'really' are. In most cases, problems occur because it's felt that media portrayals conform to limiting and outdated assumptions about people, based on such characteristics as race, age, gender, nationality, and sexuality."[18] Owing to this erasure in much mainstream media, members of minority communities hunger to see ourselves onscreen, yet owing to the scarcity of these images, each is imbued with a deeper responsibility, warranted or not, to depict the "truth" of our collective lives.

Depictions of homosexuality in recent Western media have rightly received much criticism, such as Sarah Schulman's excoriating argument that many such portrayals formulate a "fake public homosexuality [that] has been constructed to facilitate a double marketing strategy: selling products to gay consumers that address their emotional need to be accepted while selling a palatable image of homosexuality to heterosexual consumers that meets their need to have their dominance obscured."[19] Ron Becker concludes his authoritative study *Gay TV and Straight America* by noting the need to situate "contemporary gay-themed programming . . . within the broader history of America's straight panic," for so many network depictions of homosexuality offer a truer depiction of straight America's discomfort with gay people than of gay people ourselves.[20] Even *Will & Grace* (1998–2006), with its breakout success in the 1990s attesting to America's eagerness for queer story lines, generated a backlash, as evident in Thomas Linneman's assertion that "*Will & Grace* consistently feminized the gay men on the show, often in potentially harmful ways."[21] From the early days of television when homosexuality was occluded from view, to the 1970s when Billy Crystal starred as Jodie Dallas on *Soap* (1977–81), to the 1990s with *Will & Grace* and Ellen DeGeneres's *Ellen*, and to the present with *Modern Family*, the history of gay television representation inevitably has prompted both celebration and disappointment over each milestone: celebration that queer lives are represented onscreen yet disappointment that many of these depictions seem trapped by tired preconceptions of queer lives.

Along these lines, *Modern Family* has engendered controversy over its depiction of Mitch and Cam. During its early seasons, some viewers registered their disappointment over the apparent chastity of their relationship, in that they were rarely depicted as physically affectionate. Such criticism took the writers and cast by surprise, as evident in Eric Stonestreet's reaction: "While I appreciated that fans care about our characters . . . I never understood why people put their focus on *Modern Family*, a show that introduced a loving, grounded gay couple on television who adopted a baby, and accused it of being homophobic."[22] The critiques nonetheless poured in: Arianna Reiche endorses the program's portrayal of "gay main characters who are authentic, sympathetic, universally loved among viewers, and who only very occasionally delve into worn stereotypes" but concludes that "it seems like these 'progressive aspects' of the show are qualifiers to regressive, gender-bizarre messages."[23] Observing the shared core values of *Modern Family* and yesteryear's sitcoms such as *Leave It to Beaver* (1957–63) and *The Cosby Show*, Bruce Feiler observes, "Perhaps that's why a study last year listed *Modern Family* as the third-most popular show among Republicans. In its fundamentally conservative vision *Modern Family* turns out to be not so modern after all."[24] Out actor Tuc Watkins, known for his roles in *One Life to Live* (1968–2013) and *Desperate Housewives* (2004–12), harshly criticized Cam and Mitch's depiction. "It feels a little bit like the gay equivalent of 'blackface,'"[25] he alleged, although later softening his words: "What's happening over at *Modern Family* is not 'blackface.' 'Blackface' is hateful. However, I do believe a stereotype is being perpetuated that can be harmful."[26] Christina LaVecchia summarizes such criticisms: "In the end, *Modern Family* delivers a non-normative family that still functions with normative family dynamics. While its conservative play on the family sitcom genre has led to the show's commercial and critical success, it has hindered *Modern Family*'s ability to say 'Sayonara!' to conventional gender and familial roles: the show works because, in actuality, its 'modern' families largely function in ways that ultimately reinforce the status quo."[27] For these viewers and critics, *Modern Family* fails to realize the promise of its title, thus faltering in its progressive commitment to present America with a new, queer-friendly vision of itself because of the inherent conservatism of its genre.

Such criticisms are predicated on a rather telling assumption: that sexual modernity, as reflected in the program's portrayal of Cam and Mitch's relationship, and stereotypes conflict. And truly, the history of homosexuality in the United States, writ large, can be seen as the history of gay people's struggles against social and sexual conservatism that wields regressive stereotypes as a particularly toxic rhetorical weapon. Resisting the tyranny of stereotypes, progressive proponents of sexual and gender equality argue instead that sexualities and genders represent hierarchical cultural constructions rather than intrinsic truths, which are then deployed to ascribe social privilege to straight people, particularly men, and to denigrate gay people and women as socially inferior.[28] In contrast, conservative political and religious institutions bolster the ideological power accorded to those who adhere to the prevailing norms of sexuality and gender, and they often endorse enduring cultural views about proper enactments of masculinity and femininity. Given these poles of the debate, the very possibility of conservatism coexisting with homosexuality has long been treated as virtually a self-negating paradox of political identity—despite the fact that a significant portion of gay men and lesbians describe themselves as politically conservative.[29] Stereotypes, for the most part, identify one's stance in these debates: those who tear them down fight for queer equality; those who employ them do not.

But if queer theory has been built on the foundation of questioning cultural constructions of social and sexual normativity, and if homosexuality is increasingly seen as within the realm of the culturally normative, the conservatism that some viewers see in the show could also reflect the shifting mores around marriage and queer culture generally. That is to say, as sitcom criticism often hinges on a binary view aligning conservatism with normativity and progressivism with antinormativity, and also identifies the roots of the genre in 1950s patriarchalism, it overlooks the subversions of the form in the past and the reimagining of the form in the present. Moreover, with gays winning the right to marriage, some theorists are questioning the rise and repercussions of "homonormativity," fearing that the queer rights movement will be conservatively co-opted through the perceived threat of coupledom and marriage registries.[30] Homonormativity productively complicates the very meaning of normativity, as it upsets any semantic assumption that homosexuality and cultural norms are unequivocally at odds with each other.

Notwithstanding these recent shifts, the gay rights movement—and thus the population of gay people as well—has historically been linked to leftist and progressive politics. As Paul Robinson documents, "Gay Liberation was the third major social eruption, after the civil rights and women's movements, to emerge out of the dissident political culture of the 1960s. Throughout the following two decades, as gays developed national organizations, the movement continued to be tied to the left. . . . Like blacks and feminists, gays were natural Democrats."[31] Robinson accurately assesses the historical link between gay people and the Democratic Party, but his words do raise a question: what is a "natural Democrat"? Any such essentialist assumption denies gay people the autonomy of political affiliation, as it enforces a rigid preconception of philosophical identity tied to the biology of one's sexual partners. While the right's harsh resistance to gay rights surely explains much of the affiliation of gays with the Democratic Party, it is also worth remembering the many surprising anomalies that have arisen over the years, such as Dick Cheney endorsing gay marriage before Barack Obama. As most sitcoms reside in a zone of political neutrality—I have no idea whether Carol Brady of *The Brady Bunch* voted for Richard Nixon or George McGovern in the 1972 presidential election because the show was completely uninterested in dramatizing this information—so, too, is it mostly unsurprising that Cam and Mitch inhabit a political gray area. One might suspect that they would have voted for Barack Obama over Mitt Romney in the 2012 presidential election, but it would be idle speculation at best, for the program endorses gay marriage without endorsing the Democrats who fought for it, or condemning the Republicans who fought against it, or acknowledging the countless examples of those who transgressed their party's platforms.

In many ways, then, *Modern Family* upends the type of political binary operative in so much critical analysis, resulting in a queer vision both of homosexuality and of gender—that is, queer precisely because it allows the infiltration of supposedly conservative elements rather than adhering to the stereotype that would depict Cam and Mitch as "natural Democrats." Thus, to see a conservative backlash against gay and ethnic characters in *Modern Family* misses the ways in which comic stereotypes function queerly, for it accords a prejudicial valence to identities untethered from political discourse and performing in humorous modes. Of course, this is not to defend stereotypes as a positive force within the wider culture—they are not—but to theorize instead how they work in comic forms and how they register shifting codes of humor. Certainly, some would persuasively argue that stereotypes cannot be emancipated from political discourse, for they function within an ideological system in which one deployment of a stereotype could never be divorced from its wider cultural force. Yet many television programs, in employing humor based on stereotypes, attempt to achieve just this feat. For example, blackface is likely the most odious tradition in the history of American humor, one that has been abhorred for decades and that usually generates a controversy when it emerges, yet *30 Rock* (2006–13) employed this trope in its story lines (e.g., "Believe in the Stars," "Christmas Attack Zone"), with little outcry ensuing. The show's treatment of blackface, within its wider context of intelligently probing the state of race relations in America and dismantling racial stereotypes in numerous other instances, attests to the ways in which stereotypical humor, despite its painful history and ideological repercussions, can be carefully recuperated.

Within this recuperative play with stereotypes it is essential to note that *Modern Family* invites gay and Hispanic viewers to enjoy the comic exploits of gay and Hispanic characters, thus observing the distinction between laughing *at* and laughing *with* a minority, or perhaps more accurately, blurring the categories of "laughing at" and "laughing with" so that a sharp distinction no longer holds.[32] Still, even if stereotypes are being reformulated, it is undoubtedly true that comic uses of cultural stereotypes register more strongly for minorities than for those in the majority, a phenomenon also evident in bigoted epithets. White people do not feel a similar sting from *honkey* as black people do from the "N-word," nor must straight people confront their fears of discrimination based on sexual orientation if the term *breeders* is applied to them, as queer people must confront our quite rational fears when we hear *fag*, *dyke*, or *tranny*. As it is simply more difficult to insult straight, white people with epithets, it is also more difficult to apply cultural stereotypes to them for humorous purposes. Still, Jay's grumpy-old-man crustiness, Phil's perpetual dorkiness, and Claire's pins-and-needles maternal irritability push these characters to the point of caricature. Indeed, a recurring humorous trope hints at Claire's alcoholism to paint her as the stereotype of the alienated suburban mother. Phil tells Claire that he and Dede "had a long talk last night after you and I 'split' that bottle of wine and you 'fell asleep' on the stairs," employing scare-quote fingers around "split" and "fell asleep" to suggest that she drank the entire bottle and passed out. When Gloria says that Claire, who has chipped her tooth, sounds drunk on her Election Day radio interview, Haley counters, "That's not her drunk voice"—which suggests that she has heard her mother's drunk voice numerous times before. Later, after losing the election, Claire says, "I don't know about you, but I could use a glass of wine," to which Luke replies, "Now you're gonna hear her drunk voice" ("Election Day"). The humor of Claire's suburban alcoholism, which never threatens her children or her marriage, depends on a stereotype of the emotionally unsatisfied, suburban housewife—a Stepford wife who drinks away the pain of her existence.

Beyond its treatment of Mitch and Cam's romance, *Modern Family*'s depiction of Gloria also raises hackles among some viewers, particularly because both she and Claire are initially depicted as stay-at-home mothers. As James Parker ponders, "The gays are so gay, and Gloria so Hispanic-bosomatic—surely *Modern Family* is simply a reactionary caricature?"[33] Michelle Haimoff laments, "I love *Modern Family*. I want to simply enjoy it. But in 2012, I can't get behind a 'modern family' where a woman's place is only in the home."[34] For those who choose to view Gloria as a stereotype, ample evidence abounds, particularly in her accounts of life in Colombia, her birth country. The nation's troubled history with drug cartels inspires black humor, such as her declaration, "I'm Colombian. I know a fake crime scene when I see one" ("Truth Be Told"). In an interview, she endorses the stereotype of the fiery Latina: "And yes, people are allowed their private thoughts, and I shouldn't be so angry. But I am Latin, so I get to feel whatever I want" ("iSpy"). Alongside these lines played for humor, *Modern Family* depicts other characters learning valuable lessons in multiculturalism from her. Jay, realizing his cultural myopia, apologizes to Gloria: "If you said as much about America as I said about Colombia, I'd be plenty ticked off." He then gives her plane tickets to Colombia and declares, "I want to see your village, learn your culture. I love you. I'm sure I'm gonna love where you come from" ("Unplugged"). In sum, *Modern Family* exaggerates ethnic stereotypes—and thus the concern over its ostensibly reactionary bent—yet it does so to stage their simultaneous transcendence. And certainly, Gloria avails herself of stereotypes when they suit her desires, as in the following conversation with Claire:

GLORIA: In my country, it is tradition. When the men are out seeking vengeance, the women stay home and they drink.
CLAIRE: Sometimes I think you just make this stuff up.
GLORIA: Do you want a drink or not? ("Hit and Run")

Gloria's ethnicity thus becomes a means for her to advance her ambitions in a primarily Anglo community ignorant of the truth of Colombian customs. For Gloria the dangers of stereotyping are counterbalanced by her wily play with them, as she pursues her desires through the creation of a Colombian heritage unmoored from its reality.

Along these lines, it is certainly true that Mitch and Cam enact certain queer stereotypes, yet even if viewers see them as regressive caricatures of fussy queens, nonstereotypical traits balance out their excess. In an early interview, Cam introduces himself to viewers: "I collect antique fountain pens. I'm quite adept at Japanese flower arrangement—ikebana—and I was a starting offensive lineman at the University of Illinois. Surprise!" ("Coal Digger"). Both effeminate in his passion for flower arranging and masculine in his football playing (and subsequent coaching), Cam simultaneously reinforces and shatters stereotypes about gay men. Moreover, the program explicitly tackles the tendency of straight America to treat gay men not merely as effeminate but as women:

CAMERON: There's nothing gays hate more than when people . . .
MITCHELL: (joining in) treat us like women.
CAMERON: We're not. We don't want to go to your baby shower. We don't have a time of the month. We don't love pink.
MITCHELL: You love pink.
CAMERON: No, pink loves me. ("Mother's Day")

Performing various and conflicting gradations of masculinity, Mitch and Cam leave gendered binaries collapsed in their wake. As Jacques Rothmann argues, "One need only consider the androgynous performances of Cameron and Mitchell . . . as subtle commentary on the fallibility of binary logic."[35] One might quibble with Rothmann's description of their gender performance as androgynous and posit instead a continual oscillation between gendered poles; nonetheless, it is clear that these characters surpass the gendered binary and create a vision of homosexuality that seems uniquely true to them rather than to a preconceived vision of gay lives—whether regressive or progressive in its political sensibility. And certainly, one could note as well Mitch and Cam's blanket use of the word *gays* to refer exclusively to gay men rather than to gay people, as they apparently assume their experiences can be universalized to all others. Many queer women might find this scene exasperatingly true to life, as Mitch and Cam remain blithely ignorant of their privilege (a charge often levied against conservatives) while debunking long-standing assumptions about gay men (in a mostly progressive scene).

Congruent with this perspective, *Modern Family* depicts Mitch and Cam espousing viewpoints that could be construed as conservative, such as when they discuss their decision that Cam will remain at home to raise Lily:

> MITCH: We just felt that it was really important that one of us stayed home to raise her, so . . .
>
> CAM: Yeah, and that's not a judgment on other people's choices. It's just that we happen to be a very traditional family. ("Travels with Scout")

Such scenes, with their tacit endorsement of homonormativity, lead Alexander Doty to lament that "these characters are 'good' gays who keep their 'place at the table' by striving to be just like their straight middle class counterparts, living in a monogamous relationship and building up a (mildly dysfunctional) family with children, a stay-at-home 'mom,' and a working 'dad.'"[36] LaVecchia sees in this decision the reinstatement of outmoded gender roles: "Through such portrayals, the show implies that a 'modern' gay family must still identify with and embrace gender-normative roles of breadwinner and caregiver."[37] Yet in Mitch and Cam's claim to traditional values, *Modern Family* dismantles the type of binary reasoning that would pigeonhole one type of child-raising as conservative and another as progressive, for despite the 1950s norm of the working father and stay-at-home mother, its sense of modernity refuses to cede privilege to yesteryear's gendered paradigms. Today a parent's decision to remain home with his or her children may reflect conservatism—e.g., in adhering to patriarchal religious and social codes—as it may also reflect a progressive vision of parenthood that enables either parent to step in and out of multiple roles, whether professional or domestic. Mitch comments ironically on Cam's statement of their traditional values: "Mm-hmm. Yes, that's what the disabled lesbian shaman who blessed Lily's room said, too" ("Travels with Scout"). Moreover, Cam later returns to work, admitting that he finds his domestic duties frustrating—which again undoes any consistency with the domestic vision that some viewers find troubling.

Modern Family's treatment of homophobia is similarly ambivalent, for it looms within its imaginary primarily for its humorous potential rather than for presenting the brute force of prejudice against gay people. In light of this theme, many of Mitch's assumptions of homophobia rebound on him and demonstrate instead his heterophobia, for he frequently overreacts to perceived acts of discrimination that do not reflect any antigay intent. When bringing Lily from Vietnam to their California home, Mitch believes his fellow airline passengers are mocking him and his family when one says, "Look at that baby with those creampuffs." He self-righteously hectors them about the true meaning of family: "Love knows no race, creed, or gender. And shame on you, you small-minded, ignorant few." His words trail off as Cam points out that their daughter is, in fact, holding the creampuffs purchased for her snack ("Pilot"; fig. 6.1). Also, when Lily begins daycare, Mitch expects to face discrimination, telling Cam, "We're going to be judged enough as the gay parents there. I don't want to be the late ones, too," as they then discover straight parents warmly welcoming another gay couple ("The Bicycle Thief"). Such scenes could be taken as evidence of *Modern Family*'s disinclination to depict homophobia as a core condition of gay people's lives, but in line with its apolitical leanings, the crude binary between homophobia and heterophobia lies fractured, with individuals instead learning to grapple with the miscommunications on which humor depends.

Still, even if one views Mitch's and Cam's characterizations, actions, and plotlines as simultaneously bolstering and undercutting tired stereotypes about homosexuality, it is certainly true that, as numerous fans have complained, gay desire is visually absent from the screen, for the two men rarely kiss or display physical affection for each other. To explain this absence, the series pilot informs viewers that Jay does not want to see evidence of the men's

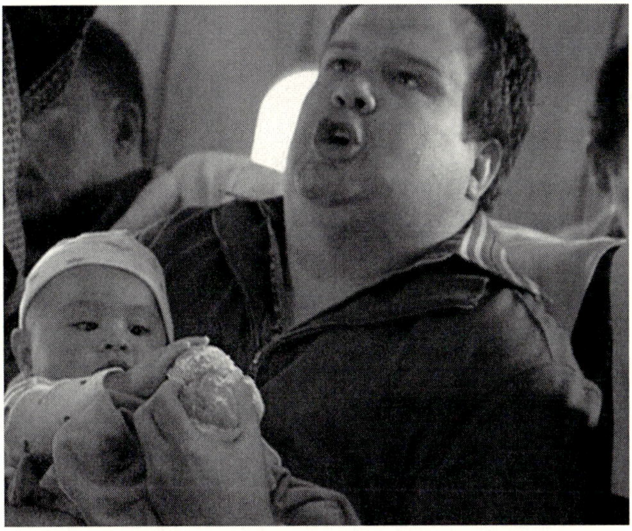

FIGURE 6.1 Mitch interprets homophobia in a woman's remark about "that baby with those creampuffs," while viewers see the humor based on the disjunction between the words' literal meaning and their antigay connotations.

affections, as Mitch explains in an interview: "Uh, my dad still isn't completely comfortable with this"—he indicates Cam and continues—"He still does this thing . . . where he announces himself before walking into any room we're in—just to make sure he doesn't have to ever see us kiss" ("Pilot"). In one of the program's sharpest ironies, Jay's profession as a manufacturer of high-end closets contrasts with his son's need to "come out of the closet" as a gay man, contrapuntally highlighting the ways in which a childhood under outdated modes of masculinity necessitates that the father and son refashion their relationship. In this light, because the series rarely depicts Mitch and Cam's affection for each other, it aligns its audience members with Jay—in their ostensible desire not to see men kissing, despite the express desire of many viewers to see precisely that.

Responding to these criticisms, the episode "The Kiss" dramatizes Mitch's reticence to kiss Cam in public. While shopping for clothes, Cam moves to embrace his partner, but Mitch ducks, and Cam soon confronts him: "You won't kiss me in front of other people because you're ashamed of who you are." Mitch attempts to appease Cam, telling him, "I'm not the most demonstrative guy around. But . . . I'm, I'm working on it." At a family get-together, Cam again approaches Mitch for a kiss, yet again he dodges, and Cam announces to the family: "Mitchell is embarrassed to kiss me in front of other people" ("The Kiss"). Discussion ensues, with Gloria contributing, "Jay doesn't like the lovey-dovey in public either," as she berates her spouse: "It's because of you that your son cannot kiss his own lover." Cam and Mitch reject the hypersexualization of their relationship—"Don't say 'lover,'" Cam interjects, and Mitch agrees, "We don't like 'lover'"—because this word would imply the primacy of erotic pleasure over emotional intimacy in their relationship. The conflict is resolved when Jay hugs Claire in the shot's foreground, with Mitch and Cam giving each other a quick kiss in its background. With a father and daughter's chaste affection visually privileged in this image, homoerotic affection remains marginalized yet present—and in the staging of this scene, Jay still does not have to see his son kiss Cam (fig. 6.2).

These issues raise the question of how graphically *Modern Family* must depict Mitch and Cam's sex lives for the program to register as progressive—and to escape the accusation of homophobia—for some viewers, which is further complicated by the purposeful conservatism of their romance. Of the episode "Best Men," in which Mitch and Cam's friend Sal (Elizabeth Banks) marries her fiancé after making out with a bartender on the way to the altar, producer Higginbotham avows: "We wanted to turn on its head the conversation where Mitch and Cam are the conservative couple who have to deal with this wild crazy party girl who can have a meltdown an hour before the wedding" ("*Modern Family* Writers"). Thus, with its agnostic political leanings

FIGURE 6.2 "The Kiss" episode shows Cam and Mitch kissing and cuddling together, yet even now Jay does not witness their affection.

and its casting of Mitch and Cam as an instructively conservative, long-term gay couple, *Modern Family* presents a comforting vision of homosexuality for its audiences, one that, in many respects, takes the heterosexual paradigm of marriage as the respected norm. But the confused conflation of marriage with conservatism functions in much the same way as blanket accusations of sitcom conservatism: a genre, I have been arguing, is neither conservative nor progressive but a structural foundation for a story, one that can then be capaciously reimagined for endless permutations, much like the ways in which a marriage represents little more than an agreement between two consenting adults, one that reveals precious little of their political beliefs or any of their amatory practices.

Extending this issue, one could also posit Mitch and Cam's monogamy as indicative of a conservative stance toward sexuality, albeit while expanding the purview of sexual conservatism to include homosexuality. Certainly, along with their distaste for the word *lover*, Mitch and Cam repeatedly stress the monogamous nature of their relationship. When in Palm Springs for New Year's Eve, they follow a man into a gay bar but quickly rush back out, embarrassed by what they witnessed inside. Cam states, "Okay, no judgment. Perfectly acceptable lifestyle," with Mitch chiming in, "Just not for us" ("New Year's Eve"). During a trip to Las Vegas, and following a series of miscommunications, Mitch and Cam find their friend Langham in their hotel bathtub. Langham gamely inquires, "Both of you? Well, OK," to which Mitch replies, "No, no. No, not okay. What are you doing here?" ("Las Vegas").[38] Yet by raising the possibility that Mitch and Cam could engage in a threesome yet choose not to, *Modern Family* alerts its audience to a wide range of sexual possibilities beyond the realm of hetero- or homonormativity.

Does the series' play with Mitch and Cam's child-rearing, marital monogamy, and other such potentially "homonormative" and conservative viewpoints thus construct them as reactionary? For numerous critics, such as Doty and LaVecchia, the answer would appear to be a firm yes, yet in the end it would be rather limiting to foreclose the possibility that these fictional characters could be revolutionarily conservative rather than conventionally liberal. In these and other such scenes, *Modern Family* dismantles the presumption that gay characters should represent exclusively progressive practices, which could in effect be more radical for exploding the binary equivalencies uniting homosexuality with liberalism, despite their historic tethering throughout the decades before and after Stonewall. And while it is certainly true that many of us queers are quite liberal in our politics, to seek a doctrinaire liberalism for queer television characters would ironically bleach them of the individuality and quirkiness necessary for their longevity and appeal.

For Higginbotham the power of Mitch and Cam's relationship arises in its apolitical applicability to heterosexuals as a paradigm to follow: "Straight couples all over this country often identify with and enjoy the neurotic relationship bullshit Cam and Mitch endure together. I love when people approach me with, 'My dad and mom are so Mitch and Cam.' Every time it happens, the broken, freaked-out teenager in me heals a little bit more."[39] Within Higginbotham's therapeutic assessment of the characters and their social function, the possibility that straight people will see themselves in gay characters, and thus offer greater acceptance to young gay people, accords a revolutionary power to gay characters who could nonetheless be construed as stereotypically gay and unthreateningly conservative. If conservatism merges comfortably with queerness in these instances, if queerness includes conservatism within its purview, then conservatism is not the monolithically patriarchal force that it once was, and the meaning of gay stereotypes has forever changed. In the end, *Modern Family* proves the radical oversimplicity of much television scholarship and viewer response, for it shreds the poles of conservatism and liberalism on which so much analysis is staked for an oscillating, vibrant, yet rather staid queerness, one awash in clichés and stereotypes that are simultaneously transcended through the reinvention of one of television's oldest and most enduring genres.

Modern Family and the Anal Imaginary

Even if one cedes merit to the allegations of *Modern Family*'s conservative bent, it would be remiss to overlook the program's repeated staging of anal desires to counterbalance assumptions of heterosexual normativity. As homosexuality was long designated the love that dare not speak its name, so, too, has anal eroticism long been considered beyond the purview of sexual normativity—despite the fact that one need not be gay to indulge in its pleasures. The ostensible shock of anal sexuality arises because of cultural definitions of masculinity that discount the likelihood of men—the penetrators of heterosexual intercourse—allowing themselves to be penetrated, in an erotic abdication of the hierarchical dynamics that fall within the ambit of male privilege. Within the realm of sexual politics, such reversals trigger discrimination and prejudice, resulting in unfathomable repercussions to the lives of real people, but within the realm of humor, such reversals invite ironic and comic revisions to the erotic sphere. Leo Bersani daringly posits the latent power of passive sex for reformulating cultural views of eroticism: "But what if we said, for example, not that it is wrong to think of so-called passive sex as 'demeaning,' but rather that *the value of sexuality itself is to demean the seriousness of efforts to redeem it*?" Building on the long-standing denigration of homosexuality as a moribund pursuit because it engenders no children, he further makes the point about anal sex that "if the rectum is the grave in which the masculine ideal (an ideal shared—differently—by men *and* women) of proud subjectivity is buried, then it should be celebrated for its very potential for death."[40] Bersani does not theorize the comic potential of anal sex in his argument, but his suggestive phrasings—"demean the seriousness," "celebrated"—capture the latent humor always possible when upending hierarchies of desire.

Even today the issue of gay sex appears to perplex some straight people, with countless questions about which partner does what to whom. Foremost, the sexually uninformed fret over the mechanics of two women or two men copulating, with the symmetry of same-sex bodies confounding assumptions based on the asymmetrical coupling of heterosexual intercourse. Such curiosity relies on an insistent ignorance of the answers readily available to heterosexuals as well as gay people: cunnilingus, fellatio, and anal sex (to name the most obvious possibilities). The real question, then, is not how gay people pleasure each other sexually but which partner does what to whom. With heterosexual intercourse, one knows who is the penetrator and who is the penetrated—or, at least, one might assume one knows—but with same-sex relationships this information is occluded from view.

To this end, if *Modern Family*'s audience wonders about the logistics of Mitch and Cam's sex life, they simply enact their friend Sal's long-standing curiosity. When the two men fight over Sal's wedding ring because Cam thinks her impending nuptials will mock the sanctity of marriage, Mitch struggles atop Cam, who bends over defensively. Sal approaches and declares, "Well, this is a mystery solved" ("Best Men"; fig. 6.3). Sal surely knows the myriad enactments of gay sexuality—she refers to Cam as "Big Bear" and

FIGURE 6.3 Mitch wrestles himself atop of Cam as they struggle over Sal's wedding ring. Their positioning, or so she assumes, resolves her long-standing curiosity about their sex life ("Best Men").

to Mitch as "Baby Cub," suggesting her awareness of bear culture ("Great Expectations")—yet this pivotal question of top and bottom has remained unanswered over their many years of friendship. Of course, Sal merely extrapolates the relevance of this happenstance positioning to her friends' sex lives, but her quest for knowledge testifies to the power of the anal imaginary, in that it unleashes tantalizing questions about desire that cannot be readily answered.

Notwithstanding Jay's unquestioned performance of heterosexuality and his enjoyment of its benefits, *Modern Family* repeatedly stages him in positions of anal eroticism—both acknowledged and unacknowledged in the plotlines' narrative action. Foremost, as an avatar of yesteryear's masculinity, Jay embodies the privileges of white heterosexuality, such as when, in an interview, he expresses his nostalgia for yesteryear's social codes: "Man, those were the good old days." Gloria points out to him the limitations of this era—"Yeah, unless you were a woman, black, Hispanic, or gay"—which he acknowledges: "True. But if you were a straight white guy who played football, [you] really couldn't have a bad day" ("Planes, Trains, and Cars"). Surprisingly, then, this epitome of straight male privilege finds himself in an array of homoerotic positions. He and Cam bump butts when changing in a locker room ("Moon Landing"), and when they practice passing off a football in a huddle, Jay bends over his (future) son-in-law, as Cam states, "Perfect. That one kinda hurt" ("Coal Digger"; fig. 6.4). The joke hinges on the unlikelihood of passing off a football to another man causing any pain, whereas anal sex can entail initial discomfort. At the driving range with his friend Shorty, Jay is uncomfortable as his friend

FIGURE 6.4 Jay and Cam pass off the football in "Coal Digger."

helps him with his swing, as Shorty embraces him from behind and advises him with a double entendre: "If you never relax, you're never going to get that shaft where it belongs" ("Fifteen Percent"; fig. 6.5). These repeated hints of Jay's anal eroticism complicate his performance of heterosexuality, for they stage homosexuality as a spectral desire repeatedly arising in his relationships with other men.

Numerous plotlines and scenes likewise thrust Phil into encounters brimming with homoerotic tension. After Jay throws his back out and convalesces in a hammock, Phil falls in with him and explains his apparent erection: "I keep my wallet in my front pocket, so that's what that is" ("Hawaii"). When Phil helps Cam decorate the Christmas tree, its lights spark suggestively between their crotches, as if their unspoken passion ignites ("Express Christmas"; fig. 6.6). Phil invites his new friend Dave (Matthew Broderick) over for a "man date," unaware that Dave is romantically attracted to him. Following a series of mishaps, they end up shirtless, and Phil apparently invites Dave to have sex with him: "How about we head up to the bedroom for some half-time festivities?" Dave, emotionally fragile over a recent breakup, kisses Phil and leaves ("Mistery Date"). These scenes rely on Phil's hapless naiveté and do not suggest his homosexuality, yet they concomitantly depict the precarious position of heterosexuality in *Modern Family*'s story lines. With homoerotic

FIGURE 6.5 Shorty helps Jay with his golf swing in "Fifteen Percent."

FIGURE 6.6 Phil assists Cam with the falling Christmas tree with their crotches in close proximity in "Express Christmas." In the moving video, the sparking lights symbolize an unacknowledged erotic tension.

desires percolating throughout its main and supporting characters, the attraction of homosexuality arises in its comic potential to destabilize the ubiquity of heterosexuality within both the clan and their wider culture.

While *Modern Family* stages a spectral anal eroticism for Jay and Phil, it clearly suggests that Claire and Phil enjoy an active sex life—which it visually hints could include anal intercourse. When Haley, Alex, and Luke bring their parents breakfast in bed, they discover them in *flagrante delicto*. Phil explains in the ensuing interview, "Yeah, our kids walked in on us. We were, as they say, having sex," to which Claire adds: "That's not a euphemism, Phil. It's exactly what we were doing. Having sex . . . in front of our children" ("Caught in the Act"; fig. 6.7). While the image is only onscreen for a flash, it is clear that Claire and Phil are positioned "doggy-style," which at least broaches the possibility of anal intercourse. Furthermore, in response to an interviewer's prompt of "the thing I can't believe we got away with," writer Danny Zuker offers, "The kids walking in on Phil and Claire having sex. More specifically, the position they were in when they were caught having sex. Watch the episode again. It was the funniest choice by a mile, and . . . it was definitely one of the most racy moments we ever put out there."[41] Of the myriad postures women and men can employ for sexual pleasure, Phil and Claire choose one that both disrupts the missionary position's privileged status in the normative imaginary and invites questions about the ways in which this long-married couple pursue erotic pleasures. As viewers will likely never know whether Sal is correct in her presumption about Mitch and Cam's respective positions in bed, neither will viewers likely ever know whether Phil and Claire enjoy anal

FIGURE 6.7 Like Cam and Mitch, Claire and Phil apparently partake of anal pleasures ("Caught in the Act").

sex. But in raising the question, *Modern Family* resignifies the understood telos of familial sexuality—procreation—into heterosexual pleasures deemed perverse when engaged in by gay people.[42]

As this modern family pursues erotic delights beyond the standard missionary position, they also acknowledge interfamilial desires, which range outside the committed pairs of Claire and Phil, Gloria and Jay, and Mitch and Cam. Most obviously, Phil has a crush on Gloria, as evident when she, a hairdresser before marrying Jay, offers to cut Phil's hair because she still cuts Jay's: "I guess I could. I do Jay. Why can't I do you?" Phil stammers in reply, "You—you can do me" ("Regrets Only"). Numerous scenes hint that Manny's relationship with his mother borders on the incestuous, such as when he tells his stepfather, who impatiently waits for his wife, "I think you've lost perspective, Jay. You know what I would give to wait around for a woman like that?" Jay replies, "Reel it in, creepy. That's your mother up there" ("The Late Show"). Manny's crush on Haley is apparent when he excitedly asks Jay whether she is coming over for a family sleepover, to which his stepfather replies, "You're related. I will spray you with the hose" ("Great Expectations"). Likewise, Lily's coy greeting of Manny suggests that she has a crush on him ("And One to Grown On"). Jealous over Mitch's friendship with Gloria, Claire climbs in bed with Jay in a scene that grows uncomfortably sexual, as she hypothesizes that her brother seeks Gloria's companionship as a substitute for their mother: "It'd actually be adorable if it weren't so sick." She continues, "I feel like Mitchell is a grown man, he has a child, and he's still working out some psychodrama from twenty years ago. Daddy, can I have a sip of your beer? Thanks." With Jay's beer bottle tellingly positioned at his crotch, Claire reaches for it and drinks, as she then realizes, "Mitch cozies up to Mom. I go running to Daddy" ("After the Fire"; fig. 6.8). Positing Mitch's Oedipus complex while enacting her Electra complex with her father's phallic beer bottle in hand and mouth, Claire embodies the ways in which interfamilial desires blur relationships ostensibly clearly demarcated. This is not to suggest that *Modern Family* portrays actual incestuous undertones to the family's interactions but that normative family desires involve the difficulty of defining normative family desires.

In another comic theme popping up throughout the series that testifies to its unruly anal and erotic imaginary, adult conversations assume a pedophilic register, such as when Cam discusses the musical program he is directing at Luke and Manny's middle school and declares, "Years from now, some of these kids will still be talking about the way I Sondheimized them" ("The Musical Man")—oblivious to the disturbing pun on Stephen Sondheim's name. When Manny needs assistance in flirting with his latest crush, Cam assumes the role of his Cyrano de Bergerac, coaching him over the phone while standing in line at a bakery: "You are the prettiest, smartest, funniest girl in the sixth grade. I know you're only eleven, but I can't stop thinking about you. I've loved

FIGURE 6.8 Claire sips Jay's beer in bed—with incestuous undertones humming throughout the scene.

talking to you online. I think we should become boyfriend and girlfriend." As his fellow customers look on in horror, he escalates matters by explaining, "Oh, no, it's not what you think. I'm talking to a little boy" ("The One That Got Away"). Because Cam was born on a Leap Day, he claims his fortieth birthday as his tenth, and after a small squabble, Mitch consoles him—"In fact, you're still that sexy little eight-year-old I fell in love with"—as a nearby mother shields her child and walks away ("Leap Day"). Pederastic humor is not limited to the gay characters, and when Manny and Jay go to a local courthouse to get a copy of the boy's birth certificate—on the day that gay marriage has been legalized in California—their conversation unsettles the joyous couples waiting to be wed:

MANNY: Jay, I'm scared. I'm not sure I want to go through with it.

JAY: We didn't drive all the way down here for that piece of paper for you to get cold feet at the last second. And what happened anyway? You've been looking forward to this day for months.

MANNY: I know, but maybe we should wait until next year. I'm still kind of young to be doing this.

JAY: We're not waiting. I already paid for you, and your mother signed off. This is happening. ("Suddenly, Last Summer")

Modern Family does not attempt to redeem pederasty and to position it within the realm of the sexually normative; on the contrary, the shocked reactions of the onlookers in these scenes register their abhorrence for the violations they imagine are being carried out against children. At the same time, by exploiting the comic line between normative and perverse sexualities, the writers continually foreground the elasticity of sexuality for defining familial relationships. The Pritchetts, Tucker-Pritchetts, and Dunphys pursue desires well within the realm of the normative, as the show has expanded anal eroticism into this purview, yet much of its humor depends on sexuality's ability to destabilize their visions of one another and the ways in which outsiders see this family during chance encounters. Given the wrong words at the wrong time, *Modern Family* proposes, just about anyone can look like a pervert.

"Li'l Dribblers" and the End of the Innocent Child

Despite its provocative story lines, *Modern Family* has generated few controversies concerning its depictions of familial eroticism and children's sexuality. To some degree this could be because its primary scheduled time—Wednesday at 9 p.m. on ABC—lies outside the presumed "family hour" of network programming, as well as the fact that several contemporary shows airing within the phantom construction of the family hour, such as *How I Met Your Mother* (2005–14) and *The Big Bang Theory* (2007–), feature risqué sexual humor. Moreover, even as this modern family pushes into the anal imaginary and incestuous and pedophilic humor, and even as it depicts frank discussions between parents and their children about sex, it retains the vision of the innocent child. Gloria, who at one point worries that Manny will never experience sexual pleasure—"The poncho, plus the flute, plus the stupid dance—my son will die a virgin" ("Run for Your Wife")—also worries that he is growing up too fast and has bought pornography. "Do you think he ordered some movies?" she anxiously asks Jay, who admits the likelihood that he has: "Movies, magazines. Whatever the hell." Refusing to see her son as a maturing adolescent, Gloria clings to her vision of innocence: "How dare do you say that, Jay? He's a little boy! He's just a boy" ("Go Bullfrogs!"). Similarly fearing that Luke has consumed Internet pornography, Claire plans to sabotage her son's voyeuristic pleasures—"But I am telling him that every time he looks at porn, God kills a puppy"—as she soon laments: "Is it really too much to ask that he stay a sweet, innocent kid forever?" ("Not in My House").

As mothers fret over their sons' sexual innocence, Phil likewise worries that Haley will lose her virginity and discourages her boyfriend, Dylan, from escalating their relationship, employing the hackneyed baseball metaphor of sex as they watch a game: "He's been stuck on second base forever, and I'm pretty sure he's gonna try and steal third, which is just a terrible, terrible idea. How are you and Haley doing?" ("Come Fly with Me"). In accord with Phil's wariness over Haley's sexual activity, the series suggests more than depicts her erotic maturation. In the first season, Dylan sleeps on the floor next to Haley's bed. She says her parents will think they slept together, but he replies "As if"—thereby clearly indicating that they have not consummated their relationship ("Airport 2010"). He repeatedly serenades Haley, singing to her, "I just wanna do you, do you" ("The Incident"), and after a breakup he hopes to win her back with the lyrics, "Imagine me naked, I imagine you nude" ("Bixby's Back")—words indicating that they have not yet had sex. When Phil realizes that Haley has lost her virginity, and that Claire has guarded this secret for three months, it first appears that he is angry over his wife's deception, asking her, "So this giant thing happened to our firstborn and you kept me in the dark about it for three whole months?" Claire responds, "I'm sorry. I just wasn't sure how you'd . . ." as he hugs her in gratitude ("Virgin Territory"). Writer Danny Zuker admits he expected the episode in which Claire sends Haley to college with condoms to generate a controversy—"I was utterly convinced there would be an uproar when the episode aired, but happily I was wrong"—which testifies to the overarching normality of the story line. Zuker further concedes: "Honestly, I don't think this particular show is harmed by the restrictions of network television."[43] *Modern Family* obliterates the family sitcom's queer fantasy of children's innocence yet still showcases its appeal, recognizing the simple fact that as children grow up, most become sexually active adults.

"Li'l Dribblers" is the name of Luke and Manny's basketball team ("Benched")—which apparently refers to their youth and the necessary skill of dribbling but which also encodes a slang term for ejaculations that, rather than shooting forth, ooze out. So basketball dribbling becomes a metaphor for sexual maturation, as these "Li'l Dribblers" will presumably grow into manhood and achieve more impressive sexual feats than simply dribbling. In satirizing the familial fetishization of the innocent child, *Modern Family* asks viewers to see domestic sexuality from a new and queer perspective. Whether its depictions of homosexuality are deemed conservative or progressive by viewers, whether its stereotypes are enjoyed as playful statements of a postprejudiced America or denounced as antiquated bigotries of yesteryear, *Modern Family*'s queerness demands that its viewers acknowledge the protean force of sexuality—which, since the appearance of the American family sitcom, has repeatedly restructured the codes of the genre, even when apparently absent from the screen. In myriad ways *Modern Family* envisions the potential of an audience seeking out the queer pleasures possible through the various fantasies encoded in domestic sitcoms—a theoretical possibility explored in the conclusion of this volume.

Conclusion

Tolstoy Was Wrong; or, On the Queer Reception of Television's Happy Families

Leo Tolstoy's *Anna Karenina* famously begins by identifying the narrative potential percolating in familial discord: "Happy families are all alike; every unhappy family is unhappy in its own way."[1] This opening line, one of the most renowned in literary history, relies on a dour assessment both of kinship and of narratology, assuming that only dysfunction breeds stories worth telling, whereas contentment requires little attention and would likely bore audiences. In a similar moment of familial and narrative pessimism, Lionel Shriver's protagonist Eva in *We Have to Talk about Kevin* muses over the necessity of conflict for tale telling, as she recounts the devastation wreaked by her homicidal son: "Not that happiness is dull. Only that it doesn't tell well. And one of our consuming diversions as we age is to recite, not only to others but to ourselves, our own story. I should know; I am in flight from my story every day, and it dogs me like a faithful stray. Accordingly, the one respect in which I depart from my younger self is that I now regard those people who have little or no story to tell themselves as terribly fortunate."[2] Hungry for the banal happiness of others, Eva sees both family and narrative anew, in the quotidian joy of stories without striking emotional impact but merely a gentle satisfaction. Indeed, fairy tales end at the moment of marriage and the assurance of a "happily ever after" resolution, presumably because conflict has been vanquished from the protagonists' lives, so what story is there to tell about the presumed monotony of a "happily ever after"?

As a whole, America's family sitcoms transpire during this "happily ever after" of the parents' marriage while eschewing any deep antagonism to inspire their story lines, thereby disproving the necessity of conflict for telling engrossing tales and demonstrating the limitless narrative possibilities predicated on a homey contentment and lives relatively free from adversity. Yet this innovative narrative structure—revolutionary in its reframing of conflict's necessity—has not preserved the genre from stinging critiques. As is well known, various cultural commentators have long derided television as bereft of cultural value, such as in Newton Minow's famed and blistering admonition, "Keep your eyes glued to that set until the station signs off. I can assure you that you will observe a vast wasteland."[3] Within this degraded medium, family sitcoms have long received particular opprobrium. Heather Havrilesky aptly summarizes a dismissive vision of the genre, lambasting "the old formula of goofy dad, nagging mom and adorable, supernaturally clever kids gathered around the couch," which she derides as "so tired and stale."[4] Tellingly, even David Marc's praise of literate sitcoms, or "litcoms," eschews those focusing on families, as apparent in his discussion of the genre's evolution in the 1970s and 1980s: "In the eighties, sitcom attention shifted away from single people . . . and back toward the genre's traditional center: the family. Family and 'family values' shows such as *Diff'rent Strokes*, *The Facts of Life*, *Silver Spoons*, and *Family Ties*, and later, *The Cosby Show*, *Who's the Boss?*, and *Growing Pains* defined the state of the art. Meanwhile, however, series such as *Taxi*, *Cheers*, and *Brothers* . . . continued the litcom tradition, making it into a kind of prestigious, if commercially limited, subgenre."[5] Within this tacit binary of litcom versus domestic sitcom, the family finds disfavor owing to its apparent lack of wit and sophistication, in contrast to programs liberated from the protocols of domesticity. Indeed, family sitcoms occasionally defame themselves, such as when in *Family Guy* Lois defends television to Peter, who has momentarily forsworn its pleasures: "Don't you miss TV just a little? The familiar stories, the broadly drawn characters, the convenient plot turns that bring a character around at exactly the right moment?" ("I Never Met the Dead Man"). The apparent simplicity of the form encourages an abundance of critical and metacritical derision.

Family sitcoms must endure the slings and arrows directed at this multiply maligned genre, for, in addition to their status as a comic form, they commonly feature didacticism and sentimentalism, and they belong as well to the realm of children's media. Even a brief survey of these genres' histories testifies to their denigrated aesthetic statuses. Comedy's secondary position to tragedy is long established. Few scholars mention William Shakespeare's *Twelfth Night* or *As You Like It* as his finest works, preferring instead the dark themes of his tragic masterpieces *Hamlet*, *Othello*, *King Lear*, and *Macbeth*. In film the Academy Awards repeatedly lionize drama over humor, with only a handful of comic movies named Best Picture (e.g., *It Happened One Night*, *Annie Hall*, *Shakespeare in Love*). After decades of neglect, domestic and sentimental fictions of the American nineteenth century—Fanny Fern's *Ruth Hall*, E.D.E.N. Southworth's *The Hidden Hand*, Louisa May Alcott's *A Long Fatal Love Chase*, among many others—are being appreciated anew, for their female authors, heroines, and subject matter relegated them to an aesthetically inferior caste. A similar historical shift in reception is evident in the cinematic melodramas of actors (e.g., Bette Davis, Barbara Stanwyck) and directors (notably Douglas Sirk). Didactic and children's media are denigrated simply by their generic status, with the moralism of the former and the targeted audience of the latter eliciting assumptions of their lack of sophistication. Given the confluence of maligned forms within its overarching genre, it is hardly surprising that the family sitcom, as a whole, receives scant praise.

It would be facile to end this volume with a stirring proclamation that family sitcoms are an underappreciated master form of American television, yet it is equally facile to dismiss the genre as inherently lackluster. And as discussions of criticism, aesthetics, and popular culture have repeatedly demonstrated, high-culture and low-culture artifacts erect and dissolve borders between them, as Pierre Bourdieu describes: "Intellectuals could be said to believe in the representation—literature, theatre, painting—more than in the things represented, whereas the people chiefly expect representations and the conventions which govern them to allow them to believe 'naively' in the things represented. The pure aesthetic is rooted in an ethic, or rather, an ethos of elective distance from the necessities of the natural and social world, which may take the form of moral agnosticism."[6] Bourdieu's analysis provides a key to understanding the enduring appeal of family sitcoms, in that they invite naive and intellectual readings both simultaneously and over the passage of years. Representation and reception are never static but always kaleidoscopic, and family sitcoms highlight the vagaries and pleasures of viewing over one's lifetime, as a viewer's personal biography develops alongside the families watched on television.

More so, family sitcoms, through their multiple and oscillating appeals to various family members, as well as through their surface innocence and their symptomatic subversions, invite spectators to inhabit queer positions and subjectivities in response to their pleasures. Many media theorists explore television's strategies for influencing viewers, plumbing the ways in which television "molds our vision of the outside world and informs our socialization within it."[7] Of particular relevance to family sitcoms are the effects that viewing and popular culture wield on children and their purportedly impressionable young minds. Donald Roberts's vision of children "who have clearly fallen prey to . . . negative images" echoes numerous studies cautioning against the media's effects on young viewers.[8] At the very least, as Ron Lembo details, audiences may practice a range of viewing strategies, including narrative-based viewing, critical viewing, and image-based viewing, among others.[9] As Judith Mayne theorizes of film spectatorship, in a formulation that applies equally well to television viewing, desire and pleasure pique many viewers' experience of visual narratives: "Film theory has been so bound by the heterosexual symmetry that supposedly governs Hollywood cinema that it has ignored the possibility, for instance, that one of the distinct pleasures of the cinema may well be a 'safe zone' in which homosexual as well as heterosexual desires can be fantasized and acted out. I am not speaking here of an innate capacity to 'read against the grain,' but rather of the way in which desire and pleasure in the cinema may well function to problematize the categories of heterosexual versus homosexual."[10] One may well read family sitcoms "against the grain," and find deep pleasures in so doing, yet as Mayne posits, the deconstruction of the categories of heterosexual and homosexual is inevitable virtually in their enunciation. Family sitcoms, whether they dramatize erotic normativity or its subversions, open inherently queer spaces for spectators to query the presumed limits of the American family and thus to create a praxis of spectatorship unmoored from the erotic discipline implied throughout America's history of heteronormativity. In another milestone theorization of gay spectatorship, Brett Farmer proposes that "the fantasmatic represents gay spectatorship as a processual activity in which the forms of gayness (the fantasies, desires, discourses, relations, practices, and knowledges that constitute gayness as a site of psychocultural subjectivity) figure as determinative categories but in ways that are wholly provisional."[11] As Mayne problematizes the heterosexual/homosexual dyad, Farmer locates provisional identities circulating around various ephemeral sites of desire, with both theorists dismantling narrow assumptions of identity and pleasure in viewing.

To theorize the queer viewing of family sitcoms, then, is not merely to suggest that gay, lesbian, and other queer-identified spectators can find pleasure in their homey domesticity, even when gays are absent from the screen, but that these programs cannot help but to summon such viewings and such viewers, for their problematic and provisional construction testifies to the always contingent nature of the erotic in the domestic sphere. Family sitcoms speak to the family, yet through their overlapping, conflicting, and simply numerous plotlines, they inevitably touch on that which they might aspire to avoid, including the queerness at their core. With all due respect to Tolstoy, television's happy families are all queer, and each is happy in its own, unique way, with this happiness disassembling the productions of normativity that crumble so readily.

At the very least, many viewers, queer or otherwise, proudly proclaim their long-standing allegiance to the television families of their childhood, with present-day nostalgia enhancing their affection for a program likely embraced before their critical facilities were finely tuned. Horace Newcomb proposes the importance of continuity and intimacy in the experience of viewing television, suggesting that this intimacy "creates the possibility for a much stronger sense of audience involvement, a sense of becoming a part of the lives and actions of the characters they see."[12] The longevity of popular family sitcoms enhances this connection between audience and actors, for young viewers witness a family growing up over approximately five to eight years, as they mature as well. To watch a family sitcom during one's childhood helps to formulate that very childhood, which influences how one perceives both television and family in the ensuing years. For queer child viewers, many of whom watched these programs before their adolescence and so likely did not yet grasp the meanings of queerness and its peculiar relevance to their own psychosexual development, the pleasure of family sitcoms can arise from the disjunction between representation and experience, the jouissance of difference recognized in the limitations of and personal affinities for the impossibility of the innocence depicted onscreen.

And, in turn, adults who naively loved a family sitcom during their childhood may grow to admire it intellectually for its steadfast naiveté complementing its metatextual discourses, appreciating the complexity of representing such determined innocence and its inevitably queer echoes. Also, even children who view programs naively do not uniformly submit to the messages encoded in these narratives, as various viewers respond to or resist the genre's moralism. Rob Long, channeling film director Lionel Chetwynd, mordantly points out "the irony . . . that the generation raised on the sanitized, family-values-laden sitcoms of the 1950s grew up to take LSD and riot in the streets; whereas the generation that grew up on the Maoist sitcoms of Norman Lear voted twice for Ronald Reagan and once for George Bush. So much for the transformative power of television sitcoms."[13] To posit, following Bourdieu, that family sitcoms encourage both naive and intellectual readings over the passage of time highlights the possibility that naiveté and intellectualism are not binaries but rather contemporaneous continua, with viewers shifting in their audience positions depending not necessarily on their age but on their openness to the televisual text before them and to their openness to their and its queerness, as well. Adults often revel in naive pleasures, and children can be surprisingly sophisticated in their viewing choices. In eliciting naive and intellectual responses, family sitcoms open their doors to as wide an audience as the span of their characters' ages, and then beyond, with viewers determining for themselves whether wholesome family antics reflect or distort the truth of the American experience, with this truth, as usual, lurking between the poles of realism and fantasy. Queer spectatorships are inherently elicited as well, whether from viewers who identify as gay, straight, or otherwise on the continuum of sexuality, for constructing normative visions of the family inevitably undoes the very normativity so solicited.

Looking to the recent past and present, the surface queerness of the American domestic sitcom is becoming ever more apparent. Building on the success of *Modern Family*, the short-lived *The New Normal* (2012–13) tells the story of a single mother and her daughter who move in with a gay couple when the mother decides to serve as their pregnancy surrogate. *The Goldbergs* (2013–) reframes the *Cosby*-era 1980s as a time of goofy, off-kilter, and personally humiliating moments in the life of adolescent Adam (Sean Giambrone), and *Raising Hope* (2010–14) begins with the execution of the baby's mother for multiple murders, as the remaining family soon bonds over their new infant: "Jimmy, you almost killed it, and we both threw up on it" ("Pilot"). Most significantly, *Transparent* (2014–) introduces the issue of transgender lives to the family sitcom tradition, as the Pfeffermans' matriarch, Maura (Jeffrey Tambor)—formerly its patriarch—explains to her daughter: "My whole life I've been dressing up . . . like a man" ("The Letting Go"). These programs depict with greater candor issues of human sexuality than those of yesteryear, yet they also present the intransigent and symptomatic queerness of the American family sitcom, in various moments when the fantasies of genre, family-friendly programming, and innocent children collide in their creation of unique visions of domesticity.

While these programs point to television's increasing openness about matters of human sexuality—in its surface treatment of such themes—they also ironically highlight by contrast the queer symptomology of earlier incarnations of the American family sitcom. As is apparent, the queer symptomologies of the sitcom families receiving the lion's share of attention in this study—the Cleavers, the Bradys, the Huxtables, the Conners, the Stewarts, and the Pritchetts, Tucker-Pritchetts, and Dunphys—prove the inherent dissimilarity of familial happiness, for each faced the unique challenges of representation during the era of their production. In *Leave It to Beaver*, the hints of queerness in Ward's past, in Beaver's present, and in June's future similarly speak to parents and children conscripted into gender and erotic roles that stifle their more unruly desires. Hemmed in by chrononormative assumptions circulating throughout the 1950s and early 1960s, as well as during this era's subsequent reception, the Cleavers nonetheless display queer potential undermining the homogeneity of their era. *The Brady Bunch*, as it struggled with representing children's innocence during a time of rapidly shifting social mores, clung to the past while its subtexts subversively acknowledged the changing times. Consequently, the program's impossible innocence defied the shifting social codes of the 1970s while tacitly registering them and building a kitschy sense of nostalgia for the very impossibility of its suburban utopia. In *The Cosby Show* during the 1980s and early 1990s, the Huxtables' financial comfort engendered critique for the very possibility of portraying a happy and wealthy black family. Nonetheless, in its determination to present a wholesome vision of African

American domesticity, the program could not overcome the queer tensions of erasing eroticism from its plotlines and critical reception, as it concomitantly expressed striking anxieties about the potential of sexuality to undermine its optimistic message, both within its staging and within metacritical discourses about stars Lisa Bonet and Bill Cosby. Along with the rise of the dysfunctional subgenre of the family sitcom in the late 1980s throughout the 1990s, *Roseanne* brought issues of teen sexuality and homosexuality to the surface of its story lines, theorizing queerness and blue-collar eroticism as means of resisting the financial inequities engendered by Reaganism. *Hannah Montana*, in the following decade, reinvigorated the trope of the innocent tween yet simultaneously pivoted to her queer alter ego in the creation and marketing of a teen pop sensation, with the Stewarts' adventures glorifying the teen as a preferred locus of innocence, consumerism, and allegorical sexuality in the 2000s. The Pritchetts, Tucker-Pritchetts, and Dunphys of *Modern Family* tackled the vagaries of queer representation during a period of increasing acceptance of gay marriage in the 2010s while recoding the political significance of stereotypes within a mostly apolitical genre. This program brought a gay (and ultimately married) couple to the screen, yet this family, facing criticism from progressives, testifies to the challenges of queer representation in a genre dismissed as inherently conservative yet one that, through its humor and carnivalesque spirit, infuses the family unit with a daring challenge to visions of erotic and domestic conformity.

Yes, as Tolstoy would likely agree, these are happy families, but perhaps he would concede that representing their happiness on television required endless negotiations about the meaning of kinship in their sociotemporal settings and in their sexual politics. The queer fantasies of the American family sitcom lingered in their creation and consumption, attesting to the challenges of representing domestic bliss in light of these families' shifting relationships to sexuality. In sum, America has seen itself and its changing sense of sexuality on the television screen, with queer representations both absent and depicted, both skewed and truthful, both exaggerated and recognizable, both metaphoric and realistic. The Cleavers, Bradys, Huxtables, Conners, Stewarts, and Pritchetts, Tucker-Pritchetts, and Dunphys inhabit a world removed from reality yet still true to the American experience, where sexuality builds families—even if, at times, any hints of eroticism appear to be expunged from the screen. At the same time, to see the queerness central to these various sitcom families reveals new insights into the very nature of the television archives and what lies hidden just below the surface. The paradox of sex, queerness, and family sitcoms, as with much of American culture, is that innocence coexists with experience, even when the nation's children sit watching, glued to the screen, with adults laughing right there beside them.

Acknowledgments

Chapters 2 and 6 expand on previously published essays, appearing respectively as "The Queer Innocence of *The Brady Bunch*," in the *Journal of Popular Culture* 48.4 (2015): 639–51; and "Conservative Narrativity, Queer Politics, and the Humor of Gay Stereotypes in *Modern Family*," in *Camera Obscura* 32.3 (2017): 1–31. I appreciate the editors' permission to republish these materials here.

Television Programs

$#! My Dad Says*	2010
8 Simple Rules	2002–5
30 Rock	2006–13
According to Jim	2001–9
Addams Family, The	1964–66
Adventures of Ozzie and Harriet, The	1952–66
Alice	1976–85
All-American Girl	1994–95
All in the Family	1971–79
Amazing Stories	1985–97
Andy Griffith Show, The	1960–68
Baby Boom	1988–89
Bernie Mac Show, The	2001–6
Beverly Hillbillies, The	1962–71
Bewitched	1964–72
Big Bang Theory, The	2007–
Big Time Rush	2009–13
Blossom	1990–95
Bob Cummings Show, The	1955–59
Boy Meets World	1993–2000
Brady Brides, The	1981
Brady Bunch, The	1969–74
Brady Bunch Variety Hour, The	1976
Brady Kids, The	1972–73
Bradys, The	1990
Brothers	1984–89
Brothers and Sisters	2006–11

Carol Burnett Show, The	1967–78
Charles in Charge	1984–90
Cheers	1982–93
Cher	1975–76
Coach	1989–97
Cosby Show, The	1984–92
CSI: Crime Scene Investigation	2000–2015
Days and Nights of Molly Dodd, The	1987–91
Dennis the Menace	1959–63
Designing Women	1986–93
Desperate Housewives	2004–12
Diff'rent Strokes	1978–86
Different World, A	1987–93
Donna Reed Show, The	1958–63
Doogie Howser, M.D	1989–93
Doris Day Show, The	1968–73
Ed Sullivan Show, The	1948–71
Ellen	1994–98
Everybody Hates Chris	2005–9
Everybody Loves Raymond	1996–2005
Facts of Life, The	1979–88
Family Affair	1966–71
Family Guy	1999–
Family Matters	1989–98
Family Ties	1982–89
Father Knows Best	1954–60
Flamingo Road	1980–82
Flintstones, The	1960–66
Frank's Place	1987–88
Fresh Prince of Bel-Air, The	1990–96
Friends	1994–2004
Full House	1987–95
George Burns and Gracie Allen Show, The	1950–58
George Lopez	2002–7
Gidget	1965–66
Gilligan's Island	1964–67
Gilmore Girls	2000–2007
Gimme a Break!	1981–87
Goldbergs, The	2013–
Good Times	1974–79
Growing Pains	1985–92
Hannah Montana	2006–11

Happy Days	1974–84
Hazel	1961–66
Here's Lucy	1968–74
Hi Honey, I'm Home	1991–92
Home Improvement	1991–99
Hooperman	1987–89
How I Met Your Mother	2005–14
I Dream of Jeannie	1965–70
I Love Lucy	1951–57
I Married Joan	1952–55
iCarly	2007–12
In the Heat of the Night	1988–95
Jean Arthur Show, The	1966
Jeffersons, The	1975–85
Julia	1968–71
Just the Ten of Us	1988–90
Lassie	1954–74
Laverne and Shirley	1976–83
Law & Order	1990–2010
Leave It to Beaver	1957–63
Little House on the Prairie	1974–83
Lizzie McGuire	2001–4
Lost in Space	1965–68
Lucy Show, The	1962–68
Major Dad	1989–93
Make Room for Daddy	1953–65
Malcolm in the Middle	2000–2006
Mama's Family	1983–90
Many Loves of Dobie Gillis, The	1959–63
Married with Children	1987–97
Mary Hartman, Mary Hartman	1976–77
Mary Tyler Moore Show, The	1970–77
*M*A*S*H*	1972–83
Maude	1972–78
Medical Center	1969–76
Middle, The	2009–
Modern Family	2009–
Mod Squad, The	1968–73
Monkees, The	1966–68
Moonlighting	1985–89
Mr. Belvedere	1985–90
Munsters, The	1964–66

Mysterious Ways	2000–2002
My Three Sons	1960–72
Nanny, The	1993–99
New Leave It to Beaver, The	1983–89
New Loretta Young Show, The	1962–63
New Normal, The	2012–13
Nurse Jackie	2009–15
Office, The	2005–13
One Day at a Time	1975–84
One Life to Live	1968–2013
Orange Is the New Black	2013–
Our Miss Brooks	1952–56
Parker Lewis Can't Lose	1990–93
Parks and Recreation	2009–15
Partners in Crime	1984
Partridge Family, The	1970–74
Patty Duke Show, The	1963–66
Please Don't Eat the Daisies	1965–67
Pretty Little Liars	2010–17
Prime Suspect	1991–2006
Private Secretary	1953–57
Punky Brewster	1984–88
Raising Hope	2010–14
Reba	2001–7
Reno 911!	2003–9
Room 222	1969–74
Roseanne	1988–97
Rowan and Martin's Laugh-In	1967–73
Sanford and Son	1972–77
Saved by the Bell	1989–93
Seinfeld	1989–98
Sesame Street	1969–
Sex and the City	1998–2004
Sha Na Na	1977–81
Silver Spoons	1982–87
Simpsons, The	1989–
Soap	1977–81
South Park	1997–
Spin City	1996–2002
Step by Step	1991–98
Suite Life of Zack and Cody, The	2005–8
Sunny with a Chance	2009–11

Taxi	1978–83
Teletubbies	1997–2001
That '70s Show	1998–2006
That Girl	1966–71
That's So Raven	2003–7
Transparent	2014–
Two and a Half Men	2003–15
Ugly Betty	2006–10
United States of Tara	2009–11
Webster	1983–89
Weeds	2005–12
West Wing, The	1999–2006
What's Happening!!	1976–79
Who's the Boss?	1984–92
Will & Grace	1998–2006
Wizards of Waverly Place	2007–12
Wonder Years, The	1988–93
Young Rebels, The	1970–71
Zoey 101	2005–8

Notes

Introduction

1 Kirk Cameron, with Lissa Halls Johnson, *Still Growing: An Autobiography* (Ventura, CA: Regal, 2008), 137.

2 Maria Cowell, "How *Two and a Half Men* Star Became a 'Paid Hypocrite,'" *Christianity Today*, 27 Nov. 2012.

3 Cameron, *Still Growing*, 16.

4 David Eng, Jack [Judith] Halberstam, and José Esteban Muñoz, "What's Queer about Queer Studies Now?" *Social Text* 23.3–4 (2005): 1–17, 1. Among the numerous groundbreaking studies of queer theory see Judith Butler, "Critically Queer," *GLQ: A Journal of Lesbian and Gay Studies* 1.2 (1993): 17–32; Elizabeth Grosz, "Experimental Desire: Rethinking Queer Subjectivity," *Space, Time, and Perversion: Essays on the Politics of Bodies* (New York: Routledge, 1995), 207–27; and Sara Ahmed, "Queer Feelings," *The Cultural Politics of Emotion* (New York: Routledge, 2004), 144–67.

5 Michel Foucault, *The History of Sexuality: Volume 1, An Introduction*, trans. Robert Hurley (1978; New York: Vintage, 1990), 105–6.

6 Alexander Doty, *Making Things Perfectly Queer: Interpreting Mass Culture* (Minneapolis: University of Minnesota Press, 1993), 3.

7 In addition to Doty's monograph, milestone studies in gay representations on television include Amy Villarejo, *Ethereal Queer: Television, Historicity, Desire* (Durham, NC: Duke University Press, 2014); Ron Becker, *Gay TV and Straight America* (New Brunswick, NJ: Rutgers University Press, 2006); James Keller and Leslie Stratyner, eds., *The New Queer Aesthetic on Television: Essays on Recent Programming* (Jefferson, NC: McFarland, 2006); Larry Gross, *Up from Invisibility: Lesbians, Gay Men, and the Media in America* (New York: Columbia University Press, 2001); Steven Capsuto, *Alternate Channels: The Uncensored Story of Gay and Lesbian Images on Radio and Television* (New York: Ballantine, 2000); and Suzanna Danuta Walters, *All the Rage: The Story of Gay Visibility in America* (Chicago: University of Chicago Press, 2001).

8 Lynne Joyrich, "Queer Television Studies: Currents, Flows, and (Main)streams," *Cinema Journal* 53.2 (2014): 133–39, 139. See also her "Epistemology of the Console," *Critical Inquiry* 27.3 (2001): 439–67.

9 Jason Mittell, *Genre and Television: From Cop Shows to Cartoons in American Culture* (New York: Routledge, 2004), 1. On genre as a "contractual" relationship between the creator and the audience of a given work, see Fredric Jameson, *The Political Unconscious: Narrative as a Socially Symbolic Act* (Ithaca, NY: Cornell University Press, 1981), esp. 106.

10 Richard Butsch, "Five Decades and Three Hundred Sitcoms about Class and Gender," *Thinking Outside the Box: A Contemporary Television Genre Reader*, ed. Gary Edgerton and Brian Rose (Lexington: University Press of Kentucky, 2005), 111–35, 111.

11 Paul Attallah, "The Unworthy Discourse: Situation Comedy in Television," *Critiquing the Sitcom: A Reader*, ed. Joanne Morreale (Syracuse, NY: Syracuse University Press, 2003), 91–115, 107.

12 Lawrence Mintz, "Situation Comedy," *TV Genres: A Handbook and Reference Guide*, ed. Brian Rose (Westport, CT: Greenwood, 1985), 107–29, 107.

13 Lynn Spigel, *Make Room for TV: Television and the Family Ideal in Postwar America* (Chicago: University of Chicago Press, 1992), 136.

14 Horace Newcomb, *TV: The Most Popular Art* (Garden City, NY: Anchor, 1974), 43. See also William Douglas, *Television Families: Is Something Wrong in Suburbia?* (Mahwah, NJ: Erlbaum, 2003), esp. 156–70.

15 To minimize documentation, sitcoms are cited parenthetically by episode title.

16 David Marc, *Comic Visions: Television Comedy and American Culture*, 2nd ed. (Malden, MA: Blackwell, 1997), 191.

17 Lawrence Laurent, "Commercial Television: What Are Its Educational Possibilities and Limits?" *Television's Impact on American Culture*, ed. William Elliott (East Lansing: Michigan State University Press, 1956), 125–73, 154.

18 Vance Packard, *The Hidden Persuaders* (New York: McKay, 1957), 158–59. Packard quotes several advertising executives and experts in his study; in this instance his source is Clyde Miller, author of *The Process of Persuasion*.

19 Thomas Johnson, "The Decline of Television's Family Hour," *USA Today Magazine*, Nov. 1996.

20 United States Department of Health, Education, and Welfare, "Television and Growing Up: The Impact of Televised Violence: Report to the Surgeon General, United States Public Health Service from the Surgeon General's Scientific Advisory Committee on Television and Social Behavior" (Rockville, MD: National Institute of Mental Health, 31 Dec. 1971), 127.

21 Richard Blake, "The Censoring of TV's Family Hour," *America*, 11 Dec. 1976, 415–18, 416.

22 Geoffrey Cowan, *See No Evil: The Backstage Battle over Sex and Violence on Television* (New York: Simon and Schuster, 1979), 19.

23 "TV Producers: All in the Family Hour," *Broadcasting*, 15 Sept. 1975, 29–30, 30.

24 For more on Ferguson's decision, see Cowan, *See No Evil*, 230.

25 David Hatch, "Lawmakers: Reinstate 'Family Hour,'" *Electronic Media* 16.20 (1997): 1.

26 L. Brent Bozell, "'Family Hour' Landscape Is Moral Wasteland," *Human Events* 54.18 (1998): 10.

27 Quoted in Hatch, "Lawmakers: Reinstate 'Family Hour,'" 1.

28 "The TV Parental Guidelines," tvguidelines.org.

29 "Going into November Sweeps, Members of Congress Last Week Urge Six Broadcast Networks to Bring Back the Family Hour," *Broadcasting & Cable*, 15 Nov. 1999, 113.

30 Quoted in J. Max Robins, "The Robins Report: Feeling Frisky in Early Prime Time," *TV Guide*, 9 Nov. 2002, 53–54, 53 (italics in original).

31 Quoted in Edward Wyatt, "NBC Tests Family Hour Boundaries," *New York Times*, 14 Apr. 2008.
32 Quoted in Brian Steinberg, "Swearing during Family Hour? Who Gives a S#*! CBS Has Little Concern about How Its Hottest New Sitcom Will Be Received, Despite Airing on the Early Side," *Advertising Age*, 31 May 2010, 2.
33 Nellie Andreeva, "ABC Family to Be Renamed as Freeform," *Deadline: Hollywood*, 6 Oct. 2015, deadline.com.
34 Emily Yahr, "*Pretty Little Liars*: When Will the Show Stop with Its Creepy Underage Relationships?" *Washington Post*, 10 Jun. 2014 (italics in original).
35 Quoted in Ileane Rudolph and Mike Hammer, "The Family Hour: Imagine June Cleaver in a Bustier," *TV Guide*, 31 Jul. 1996, 18–21, 19.
36 The speaker is Campbell Brown, as quoted in Valerie Strauss, "Campbell Brown Responds to Critics (Including Me)," *Washington Post*, 13 Aug. 2014. With this cry to protect the children, Brown argues against tenure and other job protections for public school teachers, eliding the central question of how an adult's professional right to due process threatens what is "good for the child."
37 Colin Heywood, *A History of Childhood: Children and Childhood in the West from Medieval to Modern Times* (Malden, MA: Polity, 2001), 9. On the historical constructions of children and childhood, see also Philippe Ariès, *Centuries of Childhood: A Social History of Family Life*, trans. Robert Baldick (New York: Knopf, 1962); and Steven Mintz, *Huck's Raft: A History of American Childhood* (Cambridge, MA: Belknap, 2004).
38 Gary Cross, *The Cute and the Cool: Wondrous Innocence and Modern American Children's Culture* (Oxford: Oxford University Press, 2004). For further discussions of the cultural fantasy of children's innocence, see Steve Bruhm and Natasha Hurley, eds., *Curiouser: On the Queerness of Children* (Minneapolis: University of Minnesota Press, 2004).
39 David Buckingham, "Introduction: The Child and the Screen," *Small Screens: Television for Children*, ed. David Buckingham (London: Leicester University Press, 2002), 1–14, 8.
40 Quoted in Kirk Cameron, *Still Growing*, 140.
41 On the McMartin case—truly a modern-day Salem Witch Trial—see Richard Beck, *We Believe the Children: A Moral Panic in the 1980s* (New York: PublicAffairs, 2015); and Paul and Shirley Eberle, *The Abuse of Innocence: The McMartin Preschool Trial* (Buffalo, NY: Prometheus, 1993).
42 Frank Bank, with Gib Twyman, *Call Me Lumpy: My "Leave It to Beaver" Days and Other Wild Hollywood Life* (Lenexa, KS: Addax, 1997).
43 Dustin Diamond, *Behind the Bell* (Montreal: Transit, 2009).
44 Marie Winn, *The Plug-In Drug: Television, Computers, and Family Life*, rev. ed. (New York: Penguin, 2002), 298. For another consideration of these issues, see Edward Palmer, *Television and America's Children: A Crisis of Neglect* (New York: Oxford University Press, 1988).
45 Brian Simpson, *Children and Television* (New York: Continuum, 2004), 4.
46 Mary Strom Larson, "Sibling Interaction in Situation Comedies over the Years," *Television and the American Family*, ed. Jennings Bryant and Alison Bryant, 2nd ed. (Mahwah, NJ: Erlbaum, 2001), 163–76, 175.
47 I selected these six programs as particularly apt specimens both of their eras and of the sexual zeitgeist of their productions, but other programs could well illustrate these shifts. For example, I can envision an alternate version of this study with

chapters addressing *The Donna Reed Show* (1958–63), *The Partridge Family*, *Good Times* (1974–79), *Home Improvement*, *Lizzie McGuire* (2001–4), and *The Middle* (2009–). In many ways *Leave It to Beaver*, *The Brady Bunch*, *The Cosby Show*, *Roseanne*, *Hannah Montana*, and *Modern Family* reflect my personal history and interests as a television viewer—a disclaimer that, I hope, does not discount the insights shared herein, despite the stance of impervious aloofness too often assumed to be required for critical endeavors.

48 Stephen Best and Sharon Marcus, "Surface Reading: An Introduction," *Representations* 108 (2009): 1–21, 9 and 3 (italics in original).

49 The carnivalesque exemplifies the challenges of interpreting comic texts, for does this comic mode subvert the prevailing ideological order, or does it merely reinstate a culture's dominant ethos after an ultimately meaningless diversion? On the carnivalesque, see Mikhail Bakhtin, *Rabelais and His World*, trans. Hélène Iswolsky (Bloomington: Indiana University Press, 1984); but also Terry Eagleton's critique: "Carnival, after all, is a *licensed* affair in every sense, a permissible rupture of hegemony, a contained popular blow-off as disturbing and relatively ineffectual as a revolutionary work of art. As Shakespeare's Olivia remarks, there is no slander in an allowed fool." Terry Eagleton, *Walter Benjamin, or Towards a Revolutionary Criticism* (London: Verso, 1981), 145–46 (Eagleton's italics).

50 Raymond Williams, *Television: Technology and Cultural Form*, ed. Ederyn Williams, 2nd ed. (1974; London: Routledge, 1990), 91.

51 William Uricchio, "Television's Next Generation: Technology / Interface Culture / Flow," *Television after TV: Essays on a Medium in Transition*, ed. Lynn Spigel and Jan Olsson (Durham, NC: Duke University Press, 2004), 163–82, 168.

52 John Ellis, *Visible Fictions: Cinema, Television, Video* (London: Routledge and Kegan Paul, 1982), 117.

53 Michael Kackman, Marnie Binfield, Matthew Thomas Payne, Allison Perlman, and Bryan Sebok, eds., *Flow TV: Television in the Age of Media Convergence* (New York: Routledge, 2011), 2. See also the online journal flowjournal.org.

54 In a provocative critical move, Gregory Waller proposes that "genre removes us from the flow and viewing strip." Gregory Waller, "Flow, Genre, and the Television Text," *In the Eye of the Beholder: Critical Perspectives in Popular Film and Television*, ed. Gary Edgerton, Michael Marsden, and Jack Nachbar (Bowling Green, OH: Popular Press, 1997), 55–66, 63. This study is invested in genre as a critical tool yet also pays attention to the influences of flow.

55 Quinn Miller, "*The Dick van Dyke Show*: Queer Meanings," *How to Watch Television*, ed. Ethan Thompson and Jason Mittell (New York: New York University Press, 2013), 112–20, 120.

Chapter 1 The Queer Times of *Leave It to Beaver*

1 Jean Baudrillard, *America*, trans. Chris Turner (London: Verso, 1986), 107.

2 Fredric Jameson, *Postmodernism, or, The Cultural Logic of Late Capitalism* (Durham, NC: Duke University Press, 1991), 281.

3 Stephanie Coontz, *The Way We Never Were: American Families and the Nostalgia Trap* (New York: Basic Books, 1992), 23; see also Coontz's *The Way We Really Are: Coming to Terms with America's Changing Families* (New York: Basic Books, 1997). On the appeal and limitations of nostalgia for the 1950s, see Arlene Skolnick, *Embattled Paradise: The American Family in an Age of Uncertainty* (New York: Basic

Books, 1991), especially for her aptly titled prologue: "Who Killed Ozzie and Harriet?" (xv–xx).

4 Coontz, *The Way We Never Were*, 25.

5 Elizabeth Freeman, *Time Binds: Queer Temporalities, Queer Histories* (Durham, NC: Duke University Press, 2010), xxii, 3.

6 Carolyn Dinshaw, *How Soon Is Now?* (Durham, NC: Duke University Press, 2012), 4.

7 Kathryn Bond Stockton, *The Queer Child, or Growing Sideways in the Twentieth Century* (Durham, NC: Duke University Press, 2009), 11 (italics in original).

8 Nina Leibman, *Living Room Lectures: The Fifties Family in Film and Television* (Austin: University of Texas Press, 1995), 118.

9 Horace Newcomb, "The Opening of America: Meaningful Difference in 1950s Television," *The Other Fifties: Interrogating Midcentury American Icons*, ed. Joel Foreman (Urbana: University of Illinois Press, 1997), 103–23, 121.

10 David Halberstam, *The Fifties* (New York: Villard, 1993), 509 (italics in original).

11 References to the program are taken from *Leave It to Beaver: The Complete Series* (1957–63; NBC Universal, 2010), DVD, and are cited by episode.

12 David Coon, *Look Closer: Suburban Narratives and American Values in Film and Television* (New Brunswick, NJ: Rutgers University Press, 2013), 2.

13 Hal Himmelstein, *Television Myth and the American Mind*, 2nd ed. (Westport, CT: Praeger, 1994), 124.

14 Sidonie Matsner Gruenberg, ed., *Our Children Today: A Guide to Their Needs from Infancy through Adolescence* (New York: Viking, 1952), 15.

15 Otis Lee Wiese, "Live the Life of *McCall's*," *McCall's*, May 1954, 27 (italics in original).

16 Joel Foreman, introduction to *The Other Fifties: Interrogating Midcentury American Icons* (Urbana: University of Illinois Press, 1997), 1–23, 1.

17 Darrell Hamamoto, *Nervous Laughter: Television Situation Comedy and Liberal Democratic Ideology* (New York: Praeger, 1989), 26.

18 Amy Villarejo, *Ethereal Queer: Television, Historicity, Desire* (Durham, NC: Duke University Press, 2014). Of *Father Knows Best*, Villarejo cites the episode "Betty, the Track Star," which David Marc proposes "might as well have been titled 'Betty Meets the Lesbians.'" David Marc, *Comic Visions: Television Comedy and American Culture*, 2nd ed. (Malden, MA: Blackwell, 1997), 50.

19 Gertrude Chittenden, *Living with Children* (1944; New York: Macmillan, 1951), 3. Chittenden compares American children to those of Samoa, as studied in Margaret Meade's classic *Coming of Age in Samoa*, and extols the greater social and sexual equanimity of Samoan youth.

20 Barney Katz, *How to Be a Better Parent: Understanding Yourself and Your Child* (New York: Ronald Press, 1953), 205.

21 In this episode, Ward's fears over his son are unfounded: Beaver enjoyed the party not because of the opportunity for exclusively female companionship but for the opportunity to engage in homosocial bonding with the host's father, who commiserates with the boy: "I know what it's like to be the only rooster in a hen party" ("Party Invitation").

22 T. J. Jackson Lears, "Making Fun of Popular Culture," *American Historical Review* 97.5 (1992): 1417–26, 1420.

23 Erin Lee Mock, "The Horror of 'Honey, I'm Home!': The Perils of Postwar Family Love in the Domestic Sitcom," *Film & History* 41.2 (2011): 29–50, 30. See also Stanley Pelkey's brilliant reading, "Music, Maturity, and the Moral Geography in *Leave*

It to Beaver (1957–1963)," *Anxiety Muted: American Film Music in a Suburban Age*, ed. Stanley Pelkey and Anthony Bushard (Oxford: Oxford University Press, 2015), 107–18.

24 Michael Kassel, "Mayfield after Midnight: Images of Youth and Parenting in *Leave It to Beaver*," *Images of Youth: Popular Culture as Educational Ideology*, ed. Michael Oliker and Walter Krolikowski (New York: Peter Lang, 2001), 112–29, 116.

25 Sigmund Freud, "'A Child Is Being Beaten': A Contribution to the Study of the Origin of Sexual Perversions," *The Standard Edition of the Complete Psychological Works of Sigmund Freud*, trans. and ed. James Strachey (London: Hogarth, 1953–74), 17.175–204, 179.

26 Gilles Deleuze and Félix Guattari, *Anti-Oedipus: Capitalism and Schizophrenia* (1977; New York: Penguin, 2009), 274.

27 Bonnie Dow, *Prime-Time Feminism: Television, Media Culture, and the Women's Movement since 1970* (Philadelphia: University of Pennsylvania Press, 1996), 149.

28 Matthew Henry, "The Triumph of Popular Culture: Situation Comedy, Postmodernism, and *The Simpsons*," *Critiquing the Sitcom: A Reader*, ed. Joanne Morreale (Syracuse, NY: Syracuse University Press, 2003), 262–73, 265.

29 Diana Meehan, *Ladies of the Evening: Women Characters of Prime-Time Television* (Metuchen, NJ: Scarecrow, 1983), 34.

30 Susan Douglas, *Where the Girls Are: Growing Up Female with the Mass Media* (New York: Random House, 1995), 26. For a rebuttal of these critiques of 1950s female characters, see Cary O'Dell, *June Cleaver Was a Feminist! Reconsidering the Female Characters of Early Television* (Jefferson, NC: McFarland, 2013).

31 James Bossard and Eleanor Boll, *Ritual in Family Living: A Contemporary Study* (Philadelphia: University of Pennsylvania Press, 1950), 24.

32 Bonnie Mann, "The Lesbian June Cleaver: Heterosexism and Lesbian Mothering," *Hypatia* 22.1 (2007): 149–65, 149.

33 Joanne Meyerowitz, ed., *Not June Cleaver: Women and Gender in Postwar America, 1945–1960* (Philadelphia: Temple University Press, 1994).

34 Deborah Werksman, ed., *I Killed June Cleaver: Modern Moms Shatter the Myth of Perfect Parenting* (Naperville, IL: Hysteria, 1999); and Anne Dunnewold, *Even June Cleaver Would Forget the Juice Box: Cut Yourself Some Slack (And Still Raise Great Kids) in the Age of Extreme Parenting* (Deerfield Beach, FL: Health Communications, 2007). Margaret Talbot, the sister of child actor Stephen Talbot, who played the role of Beaver's friend Gilbert Bates, cites Meyerowitz, Werksman, and Dunnewold to make a similar point in her *The Entertainer: Movies, Magic, and My Father's Twentieth Century* (New York: Riverhead, 2012), 379.

35 "Forever the Beaver: The Cleavers Look Back," *Leave It to Beaver: The Complete Series*.

36 Lockhart is also remembered for playing Maureen Robinson in *Lost in Space* (1965–68), another notable maternal role of her career.

Chapter 2 Queer Innocence and Kitsch Nostalgia in *The Brady Bunch*

1 Sherwood Schwartz and Lloyd J. Schwartz, *Brady Brady Brady: The Complete Story of "The Brady Bunch" as Told by the Father/Son Team Who Really Know* (Philadelphia: Running Press, 2010), 20, 28.

2 Family sitcoms of the 1960s with widows as protagonists include *The Lucy Show* (1962–68) and *Here's Lucy* (1968–74), *The New Loretta Young Show* (1962–63),

The Jean Arthur Show (1966), *The Doris Day Show* (1968–73), and *Julia* (1968–71); those with widowers include *The Andy Griffith Show* (1960–68), *My Three Sons* (1960–72), and *The Beverly Hillbillies* (1962–71).

3 James Kincaid, *Erotic Innocence: The Culture of Child Molesting* (Durham, NC: Duke University Press, 1998), 53.

4 Eve Kosofsky Sedgwick, "Queer and Now," *The Routledge Queer Studies Reader*, ed. Donald Hall and Annamarie Jagose (London: Routledge, 2013), 3–17, 8 (italics in original).

5 Lee Edelman, *No Future: Queer Theory and the Death Drive* (Durham, NC: Duke University Press, 2004), 21.

6 Peter Carroll, *It Seemed Like Nothing Happened: The Tragedy and Promise of America in the 1970s* (New York: Holt, Rinehart and Winston, 1982), 335.

7 Dan Berger, ed., *The Hidden 1970s: Histories of Radicalism* (New Brunswick, NJ: Rutgers University Press, 2010), 3.

8 Morton Hunt, *Sexual Behavior in the 1970s* (Chicago: Playboy Press, 1974), 361.

9 Citations of *The Brady Bunch* specify the episode in question, as taken from *The Brady Bunch: The Complete Series*, prod. Sherwood Schwartz, perf. Robert Reed, Florence Henderson, Ann B. Davis, et al. (1969–74; Paramount, 2007), DVD.

10 "The Honeymoon" does not erase marital sexuality entirely, for it depicts Carol and Mike's costume changes into nightwear to indicate that they have consummated their marriage. Still, the narrative directs viewers' attention to the reintegration of the family after an initial separation, not on the newlyweds' pleasureful escape from their children's prying eyes.

11 Quoted in Robert Pegg, *Comical Co-stars of Television: From Ed Norton to Kramer* (Jefferson, NC: McFarland, 2002), 92. On the 1970s sexual culture against which *The Brady Bunch* apparently inoculated itself, see Elana Levine, *Wallowing in Sex: The New Sexual Culture of 1970s American Television* (Durham, NC: Duke University Press, 2007).

12 Diana Meehan, *Ladies of the Evening: Women Characters of Prime-Time Television* (Metuchen, NJ: Scarecrow, 1983), 34. As discussed in the previous chapter, numerous episodes allow these "goodwives" to challenge patriarchal prerogatives, with this model capturing key aspects of 1950s domesticity yet overlooking its subversive potential.

13 David Marc, *Comic Visions: Television Comedy and American Culture*, 2nd ed. (Malden, MA: Blackwell, 1997), 191.

14 Katherine Lehman, *Those Girls: Single Women in Sixties and Seventies Popular Culture* (Lawrence: University Press of Kansas, 2011), 12–13.

15 Most famously, *Maude* dramatized its commitment to feminism and women's reproductive rights in a plot featuring Maude and her fourth husband, Walter (Bill Macy), opting for an abortion rather than raising a baby during their middle-aged years. Anguished by the decision, Maude turns to Walter for comfort: "For you, Maude, and for me, in the privacy of our own lives, you're doing the right thing" ("Maude's Dilemma, Part 2").

16 Schwartz and Schwartz, *Brady Brady Brady*, 29.

17 Les Brown, "Elton's Rule: Be Different: ABC-TV Prez Puts Accent on Youth," *Variety*, 3 Apr. 1968, 33, 52. See also Aniko Bodroghkozy, *Groove Tube: Sixties Television and the Youth Rebellion* (Durham, NC: Duke University Press, 2001), 199.

18 Schwartz and Schwartz, *Brady Brady Brady*, 150.

19 See Patricia White's reading of queerness in *Bewitched* in her *Uninvited: Classical Hollywood Cinema and Lesbian Representability* (Bloomington: Indiana University Press, 1999), 139–42.
20 Mimi Marinucci, "Television, Generation X, and Third Wave Feminism: A Contextual Analysis of *The Brady Bunch*," *Journal of Popular Culture* 38.3 (2005): 505–24, 514.
21 Laura Mulvey, *Visual and Other Pleasures* (Bloomington: Indiana University Press, 1989), 19.
22 Helen Haste, *The Sexual Metaphor* (Cambridge, MA: Harvard University Press, 1994), 71.
23 Schwartz and Schwartz, *Brady Brady Brady*, 106.
24 Helen Wheatley, *Spectacular Television: Exploring Televisual Pleasure* (London: I. B. Tauris, 2016), 191.
25 Kincaid, *Erotic Innocence*, 113. See also his *Child-Loving: The Erotic Child and Victorian Culture* (New York: Routledge, 1992).
26 Hal Erickson, *Television Cartoon Shows: An Illustrated Encyclopedia, 1949–1993* (Jefferson, NC: McFarland, 1995), 111.
27 Schwartz and Schwartz, *Brady Brady Brady*, 156.
28 Ibid., 182.
29 Barry Williams, with Chris Kreski, *Growing Up Brady: I Was a Teenage Greg* (New York: HarperPerennial, 1992), 74–75 (italics in original).
30 Florence Henderson, with Joel Brokaw, *Life Is Not a Stage: From Broadway Baby to Lovely Lady and Beyond* (New York: Center Street, 2011), 184.
31 Stephen Tropiano, *The Prime Time Closet: A History of Gays and Lesbians on TV* (New York: Applause Theatre, 2002), 27–30.
32 "H.I.V. Contributed to Death of Robert Reed, Doctor Says," *New York Times*, 20 May 1992.
33 Schwartz and Schwartz, *Brady Brady Brady*, 64.
34 Pegg, *Comical Co-stars of Television*, 89.
35 Ted Nichelson, Susan Olsen, and Lisa Sutton, *Love to Love You Bradys: The Bizarre Story of "The Brady Bunch Variety Hour"* (Toronto: ECW, 2009), 3.
36 For a history of *The Brady Bunch Variety Hour* see Nichelson, Olsen, and Sutton, *Love to Love You Bradys*. Because of space limitations, I do not address *The Brady Bunch Hour*, *The Brady Brides*, or the feature films in this chapter, yet they, too, exploit a brew of kitsch nostalgia in their plotlines.
37 Søren Kierkegaard, *Either/Or, Part 1*, ed. and trans. Howard Hong and Edna Hong (Princeton, NJ: Princeton University Press, 1987), 32.
38 Ralph Harper, *Nostalgia: An Existential Exploration of Longing and Fulfillment in the Modern Age* (Cleveland, OH: Press of Western Reserve University, 1966), 26–27.
39 Quoted in Svetlana Boym, *The Future of Nostalgia* (New York: Basic Books, 2001), xiv.
40 Clement Greenberg, "Avant-Garde and Kitsch," *Clement Greenberg: The Collected Essays and Criticism*, vol. 1, *Perceptions and Judgments, 1939–1944*, ed. John O'Brian (Chicago: University of Chicago Press, 1986), 5–22, 12.
41 Although I focus on nostalgia's retrospective allure and its kitsch appeal in this chapter, some scholars argue for its progressive and radical potential; see, e.g., Alastair Bonnett, *Left in the Past: Radicalism and the Politics of Nostalgia* (London: Continuum, 2010).
42 Jonathan Gray, *Television Entertainment* (New York: Routledge, 2008), 56–57. See also Amy Holdsworth, *Television, Memory, and Nostalgia* (Basingstoke, Hampshire: Palgrave Macmillan, 2011).

43 Schwartz and Schwartz, *Brady Brady Brady*, 229.

44 Judith Lancioni, "Murder and Mayhem on Wisteria Lane: A Study of Genre and Cultural Context in *Desperate Housewives*," *Reading "Desperate Housewives": Beyond the White Picket Fence*, ed. Janet McCabe and Kim Akass (London: I. B. Tauris, 2006), 129–43, 131.

45 While many television critics place the birth of the dramedy in the 1980s, others identify it in such earlier programs as *M*A*S*H* (1972–83)—and, of course, Shakespeare merged comedy and drama in many of his plays. The birth of this genre is difficult to pin down, yet the programs most relevant to *The Bradys* include these 1980s incarnations of the form.

46 Such identifications between cast and audience were key to Schwartz's plan for the series, as Florence Henderson notes: "By having nine cast members that include three children of different ages from each gender, Sherwood also insured that each viewer at home would have at least one character with whom they could identify closely" (*Life Is Not a Stage*, 181).

Chapter 3 No Sex Please, We're African American

1 United States Commission on Civil Rights, *Window Dressing on the Set: Women and Minorities in Television* (Washington, DC: Aug. 1977), 148.

2 Beretta Smith-Shomade, *Shaded Lives: African American Women and Television* (New Brunswick, NJ: Rutgers University Press, 2002), 31. See also Alan Nadel, *Television in Black-and-White America: Race and National Identity* (Lawrence: University Press of Kansas, 2005).

3 United States Commission on Civil Rights, *Window Dressing on the Set*, 150.

4 Kelefa Sanneh, "The Eternal Paternal: Bill Cosby's Never-Ending Tour," *New Yorker*, 15 Sept. 2014.

5 Joanne Carlson differentiates between authoritarian and authoritative childrearing: "Authoritarian parents . . . are more controlling and less emotionally responsive, and authoritative parents . . . are responsive and warm but also provide structure, expectations, and supervision." Joanne Carlson, *The Parent Effect: How Parenting Style Affects Adolescent Behavior and Personality Development* (Washington, DC: National Association of Social Workers Press, 2011), 104.

6 Quoted in Richard Warren Lewis, "The Importance of Being Julia," *TV Guide*, 14 Dec. 1968, 24–28, 28; repr. in Aniko Bodroghkozy, "'Is This What You Mean by Color TV?': Race, Gender, and Contested Meanings in NBC's *Julia*," *Private Screenings: Television and the Female Consumer*, ed. Lynn Spigel and Denise Mann (Minneapolis: University of Minnesota Press, 1992), 142–67, 152.

7 Both quoted in Lewis, "The Importance of Being Julia," 27.

8 Louie Robinson, "Redd Foxx," *Ebony*, Jun. 1974, 154+, 160.

9 Both quoted in Margena Christian, "The Death of James Evans, Sr.," *Jet*, 28 Jan. 2008, 36. Amos elaborated on these issues in another interview: "The writers blew right by [the story lines of other characters], not out of any ingrained sense of suppression, the necessity to suppress that imagery, but more so because it was easy for them. They were lazy. If we put J.J. in a chicken hat and have him walk into a room, we don't have to write anything for maybe another two pages." Tammy L. Brown, "An Interview with John Amos," *African Americans on Television: Race-ing for Ratings*, ed. David Leonard and Lisa Guerrero (Santa Barbara, CA: Praeger, 2013), 34–44, 39. For Jimmie Walker's defense of the show's representation of black

life, see his *Dyn-o-mite! Good Times, Bad Times, Our Times—A Memoir* (Boston: Da Capo, 2012), 134–37.

10 Herman Gray, *Watching Race: Television and the Struggle for "Blackness"* (Minneapolis: University of Minnesota Press, 1995), 19.

11 Leslie Innis and Joe Feagin, "*The Cosby Show*: The View from the Black Middle Class," *Say It Loud: African-American Audiences, Media, and Identity*, ed. Robin Coleman (New York: Routledge, 2002), 187–204, 202. See also Robin Coleman's *African American Viewers and the Black Situation Comedy: Situating Racial Humor* (New York: Garland, 2000), for her chapter on *The Cosby Show*, in which she also considers conflicted responses to the program (189–98).

12 Sut Jhally and Justin Lewis, *Enlightened Racism: "The Cosby Show," Audiences, and the Myth of the American Dream* (Boulder, CO: Westview, 1992), 129.

13 Throughout the series' run I see only one moment that could be construed as encouraging viewers to discount the necessity for political intervention in addressing America's history of racism. When Cliff is honored at his hospital's Physician of the Year Banquet, Dr. Wessler, the chief of staff and a white man, proclaims that their hospital is the best because they hire "talent the other hospitals overlook. We've got Blacks, we've got Native Americans, we've got Hispanics, we've got Asian Americans. We've even got a Texan. I don't hire those people because they are minorities; I hire them because they are talented" ("Physician of the Year"). One could interpret these lines as dismissive of affirmative-action programs, yet they appear more to condemn the racist attitudes of these other hospitals that overlook talented minority candidates.

14 Ella Taylor, *Prime-Time Families: Television Culture in Postwar America* (Berkeley: University of California Press, 1989), 162–63.

15 Henry Louis Gates Jr., "TV's Black World Turns—But Stays Unreal," *Race, Class, and Gender: An Anthology*, ed. Margaret Andersen and Patricia Hill Collins (Belmont, CA: Wadsworth, 1992), 310–17, 312.

16 Citations of *The Cosby Show* are taken from *The Cosby Show: The Complete Series* (1982–94; Mill Creek Entertainment, 2015), DVD. "Mr. Quiet" laid the foundations for a *Cosby Show* spin-off focusing on this community center (based on the Hudson Guild in Chelsea) and starring Tony Orlando as its director. On the spin-off's failure to launch, Orlando ruefully opined: "The network turned down a spin-off, and it's no wonder. I've watched it several times over the years, and even with the mellowing effect of time, my performance stunk." Tony Orlando, with Patsi Bale Cox, *Halfway to Paradise* (New York: St. Martin's, 2002), 227.

17 Michael Dyson, "Bill Cosby and the Politics of Race," *Z Magazine*, Sept. 1989, 26–30, 27 and 30.

18 *Essence* is marketed to a black female readership, so Cliff's enjoyment of it suggests his relaxed vision of black masculinity, which I discuss in the following section.

19 Dyson, "Bill Cosby and the Politics of Race," 28. In his collaborations with Cosby, Poussaint wrote the forewords and afterwords for many of his books, including *Fatherhood* (New York: Doubleday, 1986) and *Childhood* (New York: Putnam's, 1991). Cosby and Poussaint cowrote *Come On, People: On the Path from Victims to Victors* (Nashville, TN: Thomas Nelson, 2007). Poussaint's clinical expertise in child-rearing is evident in his cowritten monograph, with James Comber, *Raising Black Children* (New York: Plume, 1992).

20 June Frazer and Timothy Frazer, "*Father Knows Best* and *The Cosby Show*: Nostalgia and the Sitcom Tradition," *Journal of Popular Culture* 27.3 (1993): 163–72, 172.

21 Anthonia Kalu, "Bill Cosby, Blues, and the Reconstruction of African-American Literary Theory," *Literary Griot: International Journal of Black Expressive Cultural Studies* 4.1–2 (1992): 1–15, 6.
22 Mike Budd and Clay Steinman, "White Racism and *The Cosby Show*," *Jump Cut* 37 (1992): 5–12, 9.
23 Cosby, *Fatherhood*, 96.
24 Alvin Poussaint, introduction to *Fatherhood*, by Bill Cosby (New York: Doubleday, 1986), 9.
25 Compare these lines with Cosby's words from *Fatherhood*: "I am not the boss of my house. I don't know how I lost it and I don't know where I lost it. I probably never had it to begin with. My wife is the boss" (57).
26 Donald Bogle, *Brown Sugar: Over One Hundred Years of America's Black Female Superstars* (New York: Continuum, 2007), 255. See also his *Primetime Blues: African Americans on Network Television* (New York: Farrar, Straus and Giroux, 2001), esp. 286–303.
27 John Fiske, *Media Matters* (Minneapolis: University of Minnesota Press, 1996), 112. For another reading of Clair's professional career and family life see Barbara Villez, "Clair Huxtable, Meet Renée Raddick: How Long a Way Have You Really Come, Baby?" *Cercles: Revue pluridisciplinaire du monde Anglophone* 8 (2003): 136–47.
28 Cosby and Poussaint, *Come On, People*, 148.
29 The two programs battled to a virtual draw in the ratings. Still, as Daniel Kimmel points out, the publicity surrounding the head-to-head competition, as well as the fact that *The Simpsons* "was actually beating *Cosby* among such key demographics as teenagers and men 18–49," paid immense dividends for FOX. See Daniel Kimmel, *The Fourth Network: How FOX Broke the Rules and Reinvented Television* (Chicago: Ivan R. Dee, 2004), 96–97.
30 Cosby, *Childhood*, 42.
31 Elaine Kaplan, *Not Our Kind of Girl: Unraveling the Myths of Black Teenage Motherhood* (Berkeley: University of California Press, 1997), xviii. See also Maris Vinovskis, *An "Epidemic" of Adolescent Pregnancy? Some Historical and Policy Considerations* (New York: Oxford University Press, 1988).
32 Rickie Solinger, "Teen Pregnancy," *Girlhood in America: An Encyclopedia*, ed. Miriam Forman-Brunell, 2 vols. (Santa Barbara, CA: ABC-CLIO, 2001), 2:645–53, 650.
33 Poussaint, afterword to *Fatherhood*, by Bill Cosby (New York: Doubleday, 1986), 171.
34 Vanessa's words that she has "never had experience with another man" could be interpreted to indicate that she has had sex with Dabnis (yet not with any other of her previous boyfriends); this interpretation, while plausible, seems unlikely, given the program's overarching considerations of young black women's sexuality.
35 See Gayle Rubin, *Deviations* (Durham, NC: Duke University Press, 2011); and Eve Kosofsky Sedgwick, *Between Men: English Literature and Male Homosocial Desire* (New York: Columbia University Press, 1985).
36 "Bill Cosby Says: 'I did not read the script . . . Lisa made the decision,'" *Jet*, 23 Mar. 1987, 62.
37 Quoted in Lynn Norment, "Lisa Bonet: The Growing Pains of a Rising Star," *Ebony*, 1 Dec. 1987, 150+, 154.
38 Roger Ebert, "*Angel Heart* (1987)," 6 Mar. 1987, RogerEbert.com.
39 Quoted in Margena Christian, "*A Different World* Twenty-Five Years Later: A Look at *The Cosby Show* Spin-Off That Educated Viewers," *Ebony*, Sept. 2012, 155+, 156–57.

40 "Lisa Bonet: How Bill Cosby Will Handle Return of His Prodigal Daughter," *Jet*, 19 Sept. 1988, 56+, 56.

41 Josh Rottenberg, "Lisa Bonet Doesn't Pray Everyday [*sic*]," *Us Weekly*, 17 Apr. 2000, 74–79.

42 Quoted in "Lisa Bonet Dropped from *The Cosby Show*," *Jet*, 15 Apr. 1991, 52.

43 Ibid.

44 Quoted in "Lisa Bonet: How Bill Cosby Will Handle Return of His Prodigal Daughter," 57.

45 Rottenberg, "Lisa Bonet Doesn't Pray," 77.

46 Cathy Cohen, *Democracy Remixed* (Oxford: Oxford University Press, 2010), 50–51. For more on this scandal, see Mark Whitaker, *Cosby: His Life and Times* (New York: Simon and Schuster, 2014), esp. 257–58, 358–59.

47 For a review of these accusations, see Bill Carter, "Lawyer Defends Cosby over Assault Claims," *New York Times*, 16 Nov. 2014.

48 Bill Carter, "NBC and Netflix Shelve Projects with Bill Cosby," *New York Times*, 19 Nov. 2014; Michael Del Moro and Dan Good, "TV Land Pulls *The Cosby Show* Reruns amid Sexual Assault Allegations," *ABC News*, 20 Nov. 2014; Rachel Swarns, "Trying to Separate Bill Cosby from Cliff Huxtable," *New York Times*, 31 Jan. 2016.

Chapter 4 Feminism, Homosexuality, and Blue-Collar Perversity in *Roseanne*

1 Quotations from *Roseanne* and its stars are taken from *Roseanne: The Complete Series* (Mill Creek Entertainment and Carsey-Werner Company, 2013), which includes its entire run of 222 episodes and numerous interviews and video commentary with the cast.

2 On the "Meredith Baxter-Birney" image of television motherhood see p. 90. Baxter came out as a lesbian in 2009 and married her wife in 2013, further dismantling the image of the quintessential 1980s sitcom housewife.

3 To date Barr has written three autobiographies: Roseanne Barr, *My Life as a Woman* (New York: Harper and Row, 1989); Roseanne Arnold, *My Lives* (New York: Ballantine, 1994); and Roseanne Barr, *Roseannearchy: Dispatches from the Nut Farm* (New York: Gallery, 2011). The following abbreviations—*MLW*, *ML*, and *R*—are used in parenthetical citations. Furthermore, it should be noted that I refer to the actor as Barr, to her sitcom as *Roseanne*, and to her character as Roseanne, while acknowledging the difficulty of maintaining firm distinctions among these overlapping figures and their fictions.

4 Barbara Ehrenreich documents Barr's preference for the term *working class* over *blue collar* because, in her paraphrase of Barr's words, "it reminds us of the existence of class, a reality that Americans are all to disposed to forget." Barbara Ehrenreich, "The Wretched of the Hearth: The Undainty Feminism of Roseanne Barr," *New Republic*, 2 Apr. 1990, 28–31, 29. I use the terms interchangeably. For Ehrenreich's account of middle-class economic fears during the period roughly contemporary with *Roseanne*'s early seasons, see Barbara Ehrenreich, *Fear of Falling: The Inner Life of the Middle Class* (New York: HarperPerennial, 1990).

5 Goranson initiated the role of Becky but left *Roseanne* to attend college, with Chalke replacing her. The two alternated the role for several seasons.

6 Responding to a question about how closely her character matched her real-life identity, Barr declared, "That's me up there, but there's a deliberate choice of what to expose." Elaine Dutka, "Interview: Slightly to the Left of Normal," *Time*, 8 May

1989, 82+, 83. Her ex-husband Bill Pentland confirmed that "[Barr's sister] Geraldine would provide the basis for the character of Jackie and her love/hate friction with Rosie's husband Dan Conner," adding as well, "Although our three kids were the primary models for Becky, Darlene, and D.J., Rosie would weave real details, peccadilloes, accents, clothing, etc., from actual people she knew" (*R* xii). This is not to argue that *Roseanne* transparently depicts Barr's experiences but to point to her clarity of vision for the program, which became a point of contention during its production. I return to this issue in this chapter's final section. The principal distinction between Barr's and Roseanne's primary traits would appear to be that the former is Jewish whereas, as Janet Lee observes, the latter is apparently not; see Janet Lee, "Subversive Sitcoms: *Roseanne* as Inspiration for Feminist Resistance," *Women's Studies* 21 (1992): 87–101, 91.

7 Susan Dworkin, "Roseanne Barr: The Disgruntled Housewife as Stand-up Comedian," *Ms.*, Jul.-Aug. 1987, 92+, 205–6; see also Tracy Young, "The Return of the Housewife: Roseanne Barr, Domestic Goddess," *Vogue*, Apr. 1987, 335+.

8 Rosemarie Tong, *Feminist Thought*, 3rd ed. (Philadelphia: Westview, 2009), 285. See also Rory Dicker and Alison Piepmeier, eds., *Catching a Wave: Reclaiming Feminism for the Twenty-First Century* (Boston: Northeastern University Press, 2003), for the necessity of expanding feminism's purview.

9 Merri Lisa Johnson, "Ladies Love Your Box: The Rhetoric of Pleasure and Danger in Feminist Television Studies," *Third Wave Feminism and Television: Jane Puts It in a Box*, ed. Merri Lisa Johnson (London: I. B. Tauris, 2007), 1–27, 22. Johnson's quotation of the phrase "an inevitable site of ideological struggle" is taken from John Fiske, "British Cultural Studies," *Channels of Discourse: Television and Contemporary Criticism*, ed. Robert C. Allen (Chapel Hill: University of North Carolina Press, 1987), 254–89, 259.

10 Diana Kendall, *Framing Class: Media Representations of Wealth and Poverty in America*, 2nd ed. (Lanham, MD: Rowman and Littlefield, 2011), 165. For an overview of social class in television studies, see also Nicole Cloarec, introduction to *Social Class on British and American Screens: Essays on Cinema and Television*, ed. Nicole Cloarec, David Haigron, and Delphine Letort (Jefferson, NC: McFarland, 2016), 1–16.

11 Ronald Reagan, "Inaugural Address (20 Jan. 1981)," The American Presidency Project, www.presidency.ucsb.edu.

12 Michael Schaller, *Right Turn: American Life in the Reagan-Bush Era, 1980–1992* (New York: Oxford University Press, 2007), 27.

13 Walter Galenson, *The American Labor Movement, 1955–1995* (Westport, CT: Greenwood, 1996), 53. On the air-traffic controllers strike see Joseph McCartin, *Collision Course: Ronald Reagan, the Air Traffic Controllers, and the Strike That Changed America* (Oxford: Oxford University Press, 2011).

14 *Roseanne*'s final episode reveals that much of the ninth season has been a fantasy sequence, in which the Conners did not win the lottery, and Dan died from his heart attack at Darlene and David's wedding. But events in a fictional series need not have truly occurred on its narrative level to affect the development of its themes and political interventions. On *Roseanne* and "jumping the shark," see Jon Hein, *Jump the Shark* (New York: Dutton, 2002), 66–67.

15 For more on the political ethos of family sitcoms, see chapter 6. *Roseanne* portrays Barr's distaste for Republicans yet leaves Democrats unscathed; Barr, however, has attacked both parties, such as in her 1991 statement: "The Democratic party

[is] farther away from the people than the Republican party appears to be, and that's why George [H. W.] Bush is president. . . . I *hate* liberals. . . . The liberals are in there fudging every issue, selling out this group of people to make points with that group of people." Nanette Varian, "*Penthouse* Interview: Roseanne Barr," *Penthouse*, Jan. 1991, 81+, 177 (italics in original). Barr ran for U.S. President on the Peace and Freedom Party ticket in 2012, with peace activist Cindy Sheehan as her running mate.

16 Julie Bettie, "Class Dismissed? *Roseanne* and the Changing Face of Working-Class Iconography," *Social Text* 14.4 (1995): 125–49, 137.

17 Kathleen Rowe, *The Unruly Woman: Gender and the Genres of Laughter* (Austin: University of Texas Press, 1995), 64.

18 Nikke Finke, "The Blue-Collar Backgrounds behind a Blue-Collar Hit," *Los Angeles Times*, 26 Jan. 1989.

19 On the gendered dynamics of viewing see chapter 2.

20 Barr succinctly defines a tag as the "short scene following the final commercial break featuring the show's credits" and discusses *Roseanne*'s innovative use of tags, particularly in breaking the fourth wall between the production and its viewers ("Trick Me Up, Trick Me Down" Video Commentary). The program's tags frequently continue story lines developed in the preceding episode or metadramatically stage the program's fictionality (as when guest star Sharon Stone sighs over her unfulfilled attraction to young Michael Fishman—"There's a whole lot of man walking out that door right now" ["Happy Trailers"])—or sometimes veer into an undefined reality (such as when aliens abduct family friend Arnie ["Aliens"]).

21 Carolyn Bronstein, *Battling Pornography: The American Feminist Anti-pornography Movement, 1976–1986* (Cambridge: Cambridge University Press, 2011), 173, 244.

22 On the evolution of pornography from film to video and into its patrons' homes, see Chuck Kleinhans, "The Change from Film to Video Pornography: Implications for Analysis," *Pornography: Film and Culture*, ed. Peter Lehman (New Brunswick, NJ: Rutgers University Press, 2006), 154–67. On the gendered dynamics of VCR viewing in the 1980s, see Ann Gray, "Behind Closed Doors: Video Recorders in the Home," *Feminist Television Criticism: A Reader*, ed. Charlotte Brunsdon, Julie D'Acci, and Lynn Spigel (Oxford: Clarendon, 1997), 235–46.

23 Traci Lords, *Underneath It All* (New York: HarperEntertainment, 2003), 240.

24 Quoted in Dworkin, "Roseanne Barr," 108.

25 Quoted in John Lahr, "Dealing with Roseanne," *Life Stories: Profiles from "The New Yorker,"* ed. David Remnick (New York: Random House, 2000), 441–67, 465. This interview originally appeared in 1995.

26 *The Oxford English Dictionary* dates the earliest use of *guppie* to 1984, in *The Official British Yuppie Handbook*.

27 For an account of *Baehr v. Miike* and Hawaii's early role in the fight for gay marriage, see Evan Wolfson, "The Hawaii Marriage Case Launches the US Freedom-to-Marry Movement for Equality," *Legal Recognition of Same-Sex Partnerships: A Study of National, European, and International Law*, ed. Robert Wintemute and Mads Andenæs (Oxford: Hart, 2002), 169–75.

28 Quoted in John Carmody, "The TV Column," *Washington Post*, 11 Dec. 1995.

29 Ron Becker, *Gay TV and Straight America* (New Brunswick, NJ: Rutgers University Press, 2006), 155.

30 While one should refer to transgender characters with the pronoun with which they identify, it is unclear from this brief scene how Andy views him- or herself;

thus, I employ "his/her" as a marker of the scene's cloudy depiction of Andy's gender orientation.

31 For an instructive comparison see the similar plotline in *The Cosby Show*'s "Theo and the Joint" episode, in which viewers learn that Theo never smoked marijuana, and the young offender, a classmate of Theo's, is quickly rehabilitated.

32 Joan Collins, *Second Act* (New York: St. Martin's, 1996), 309.

33 Varian, "*Penthouse* Interview: Roseanne Barr," 82.

34 Quoted in Anne Taylor Fleming, "Roseanne's Tough Act: Is It Too Harsh?" *New York Times*, 17 Jan. 1990.

35 On the program's genesis from *Life and Stuff* to *Roseanne*, see Judine Mayerle, "*Roseanne*—How Did You Get Inside My House? A Case Study of a Hit Blue-Collar Situation Comedy," *Journal of Popular Culture* 24.4 (1991): 71–88, 72–73.

36 For another account of her conflicts with Williams, see Jim Jerome, "Roseanne Unchained," *People Weekly*, 9 Oct. 1989, 87+.

37 Finke, "The Blue-Collar Backgrounds behind a Blue-Collar Hit."

Chapter 5 Allegory, Queer Authenticity, and Marketing Tween Sexuality in *Hannah Montana*

1 Frank discussions of eroticism may be rare in children's programming, yet many shows depict unusual romantic pairings, such as Kermit the Frog and Miss Piggy of the Muppets franchise. Furthermore, some viewers express their desires—or their fears—of seeing sexuality addressed in these programs. Queer-friendly fans have urged *Sesame Street* (1969–) to "out" Ernie and Bert as a gay couple, and televangelist Jerry Falwell famously accused Tinky Winky of *Teletubbies* (1997–2001) of being gay. Such desires and fears bring up a host of perplexing questions, such as, how could a frog and a pig have sex? Should advocates of gay marriage employ the obviously dysfunctional friendship of Ernie and Bert as a model for children? Do Teletubbies have genitalia? As occurs so frequently with attempts to erase sexuality from discourse, its absence ironically solicits its queer, if spectral, presence.

2 On the rise of the tween market in the entertainment industry, see Valerie Wee, *Teen Media: Hollywood and the Youth Market* (Jefferson, NC: McFarland, 2010), esp. 166–91, in which she documents that by 2002, tweens had become the "hottest demo[graphic] in Hollywood" (166).

3 Various sources document the lucrative payoffs and popularity of *Hannah Montana* and its related merchandise. Anne Becker noted that in 2007 "*Hannah* clothes are already the No. 1 tween brand at Macy's," as well as the fact that "*Hannah* has averaged about 1 million tweens 9–14 in its primary time slot—7:30 ET on Fridays, Saturdays, and Sundays—since its premiere." Anne Becker, "*Hannah Montana* Superstar: Disney Plans International Marketing Blitz for Tween Hit," *Broadcasting and Cable*, 26 Mar. 2007, 3+, 3, 44. Bruce Handy cites Miley Cyrus's platinum albums and ticket sales, as well as a *Condé Nast Portfolio* estimate that Cyrus would personally hold a billion dollar fortune for her work—although he guesses that this "seriously overestimates her personal cut of the *Hannah Montana* pie." Bruce Handy, "Miley Knows Best," *Vanity Fair*, Jun. 2008. See also Ann Donahue, "Tween Idol: After Almost Five Years Building *Hannah Montana* on TV, in Record Stores, and on Tour, Miley Cyrus Makes a Movie—and Maybe a Dance Craze," *Billboard*, 28 Mar. 2009, 16+.

4 I use "Cyrus" to refer to star Miley Cyrus, "Miley" for her character Miley Stewart, and "Hannah" for Stewart's alter ego Hannah Montana—while acknowledging the purposeful ambiguity between the actor and her roles.

5 Bill Osgerby, "'So Who's Got Time for Adults!': Femininity, Consumption, and the Development of Teen TV—from *Gidget* to *Buffy*," *Teen TV: Genre, Consumption, Identity*, ed. Glyn Davis and Kay Dickinson (London: British Film Institute, 2004), 71–86, 83 (italics in original). See also Bill Osgerby, *Youth Media* (London: Routledge, 2004).

6 As a relatively new term in the erotic lexicon, it may be helpful to define *pansexual*. Pansexuals are erotically attracted to people of any sex or gender identity, rejecting any erotic binary based on male and female. Furthermore, pansexuality is a sexual orientation inherently supportive of the transgender community, as pansexuals affirm their potential interest in partners regardless of whether their genitalia align with their gender.

7 Quoted in Peggy Tally, "Re-imagining Girlhood: Hollywood and the Tween Girl Film Market," *Seven Going on Seventeen: Tween Studies in the Culture of Girlhood*, ed. Claudia Mitchell and Jacqueline Reid-Walsh (New York: Peter Lang, 2005), 311–29, 312–13.

8 Belinda Luscombe, "How Disney Builds Stars," *Time*, 2 Nov. 2009, 50–52, 50.

9 Quotations of *Hannah Montana* are cited by episode, as published on the following DVDs: *Hannah Montana: Life's What You Make It* (Walt Disney Studios, 2007); *Hannah Montana: Season 1* (Walt Disney Studios, 2008); *Hannah Montana: One in a Million* (Walt Disney Studios, 2008); *Hannah Montana: Keeping It Real* (Walt Disney Studios, 2009); *Hannah Montana: Miley Says Goodbye?* (Walt Disney Studios, 2010); and *Hannah Montana Forever: Final Season* (Walt Disney Studios, 2011). Additional Hannah Montana story lines include *Hannah Montana: The Movie* (Walt Disney Studios, 2009) and the crossover episodes of *That's So Suite Life of Hannah Montana* (Walt Disney Studios, 2007) and *Wizards on Deck with Hannah Montana* (Walt Disney Studios, 2009).

10 *Hannah Montana* alludes to many past sitcoms, which adult viewers are likely to recognize: Lilly/Lola's skirt features a cursive L that evokes Laverne's iconic sweater in *Laverne and Shirley* (1976–83; "It's the End of the Jake as We Know It"); Miley appropriates Gary Coleman's catchphrase from *Diff'rent Strokes*, "What you talking about, Willis?" (1978–86; "People Who Use People"); and Miley's choreographer is named Shawn Nahnah in homage to the 1950s tribute ensemble Sha Na Na and their syndicated program (1977–81; "Papa's Got a Brand New Friend")—among many other such allusions.

11 David Siegel, Timothy Coffey, and Gregory Livingston, *The Great Tween Buying Machine: Marketing to Today's Tweens* (Ithaca, NY: Paramount Market, 2001), 2.

12 Claudia Mitchell and Jacqueline Reid-Walsh, "Theorizing Tween Culture within Girlhood Studies," *Seven Going on Seventeen: Tween Studies in the Culture of Girlhood*, ed. Claudia Mitchell and Jacqueline Reid-Walsh (New York: Peter Lang, 2005), 1–21, 14. See also Kathleen Sweeney, *Maiden USA: Girl Icons Come of Age* (New York: Peter Lang, 2008), particularly her chapter "Reigning Tweens and Alternative Tweendoms," 67–91.

13 Dan Freeman and Stewart Shapiro, "Tweens' Knowledge of Marketing Tactics: Skeptical beyond Their Years," *Journal of Advertising Research* 54 (Mar. 2014): 44–55, 44.

14 Benjamin Barber, *Con$umed: How Markets Corrupt Children, Infantilize Adults, and Swallow Citizens Whole* (New York: Norton, 2007), 82.

15 Ruthann Mayes-Elma, "From Miley Merchandising to Pop Princess Peddling: The *Hannah Montana* Phenomenon," *Kinderculture: The Corporate Construction of Childhood*, ed. Shirley Steinberg (Boulder, CO: Westview, 2011), 173–86, 175.

16 Tyler Bickford, "The New 'Tween' Music Industry: The Disney Channel, Kidz Bop, and an Emerging Childhood Counterpublic," *Popular Music* 31.3 (2012): 417–36, 417.

17 In a rare defense of the industry's executives, William Deresiewicz reviews the tension between "the artists and the suits" and proposes, "When television is at its best . . . it's not because the suits capitulate. It's because they're smart enough, or confident enough, or desperate enough, to bet that creative freedom can itself conduce to profit." William Deresiewicz, "Ready for Prime Time: Why TV Got Good," *Harper's*, Nov. 2016, 82–86, 82.

18 Jo Littler, "Making Fame Ordinary: Intimacy, Reflexivity, and 'Keeping It Real,'" *Mediactive* 2 (2004): 8–25, 14.

19 Melanie Kennedy, "Hannah Montana and Miley Cyrus: 'Becoming' a Woman, 'Becoming' a Star," *Celebrity Studies* 5.3 (2014): 225–41, 227.

20 Miley Cyrus, with Hilary Liftin, *Miles to Go* (New York: Disney Hyperion, 2009). Quotations from this text are cited parenthetically, with any italics appearing in the original text.

21 Becky Ebenkamp, "Hannah and Her Boosters," *Brandweek*, 8 Sept. 2008, MO40–MO42, MO40.

22 Quoted in ibid.

23 Wayne Barrett, "America's Tween Idol Rules," *USA Today Magazine*, Mar. 2008, 78. Barrett cites the *New York Post* for this statement but does not provide any bibliographic details.

24 Memorable examples of this dialogue tic include "Melon-headed hottie say what?" ("The Test of My Love") and "Future of sleaze journalism say what?" ("Don't Stop 'til You Get the Phone").

25 Quoted in Ebenkamp, "Hannah and Her Boosters," MO40.

26 Quoted in Amy Larocca, "The Real Miley Cyrus," *Harper's Bazaar*, 6 Jan. 2010.

27 *Hannah Montana in the Mix* Book and Magnetic Set (New York: Disney Press, 2009), second unnumbered page.

28 Nicholas Carah, *Pop Brands: Branding, Popular Music, and Young People* (New York: Peter Lang, 2010), 8.

29 Catherine Driscoll, *Girls: Feminine Adolescence in Popular Culture and Cultural Theory* (New York: Columbia University Press, 2002), 269. See also Morgan Genevieve Blue, who reads *Hannah Montana*'s light feminism as a marketing strategy, in "The Best of Both Worlds? Youth, Gender, and a Post-Feminist Sensibility in Disney's *Hannah Montana*," *Feminist Media Studies* 13.4 (2013): 660–75.

30 Diane Levin, "So Sexy, So Soon: The Sexualization of Childhood," *The Sexualization of Childhood*, ed. Sharna Olfman (Westport, CT: Praeger, 2009), 75–88, 84.

31 Quoted in Teresa Wiltz, "The Latest Ingenue To-Do," *Washington Post*, 29 Apr. 2008.

32 Quoted in Alyssa Toomey, "What Happened to Miley Cyrus?! Her Biggest Controversies and Scandals," Eonline.com, 27 Aug. 2013.

33 Quoted in ibid.

34 Quoted in Larocca, "The Real Miley Cyrus."

35 Quoted in Joe Coscarelli, "Miley Cyrus on Nicki Manaj and Hosting a 'Raw' MTV Video Music Awards," *New York Times*, 27 Aug 2015.

36 Guy Trebay, "Miley Cyrus's Style: An Exuberant Sexuality," *New York Times*, 27 Aug. 2015.

37 Ibid.

38 Lena de Casparis, "The Gender Debate: Miley Cyrus Gets the Conversation Started," *Elle UK*, Oct. 2015, 236+, 240.

39 Quoted in Coscarelli, "Miley Cyrus on Nicki Manaj."

Chapter 6 Conservative Narratology, Queer Politics, and the Humor of Gay Stereotypes in *Modern Family*

1 This book has demonstrated, I hope, the simplicity of the view that 1950s sitcoms were inherently innocent, as well as the fact that many sitcoms foregrounded modern families for their moment—most notably *Roseanne* (1988–97) of the programs analyzed herein, but also such shows as *All in the Family* (1971–79) and *One Day at a Time* (1975–84), among many others. *Modern Family* establishes a historically myopic and chrononormative view of the governing ethos of American sitcoms, yet such a straw man is critical to its presentation of itself and its story lines.

2 Lynne Joyrich, "Epistemology of the Console," *Critical Inquiry* 27.3 (2001): 439–67, 467.

3 Jane Feuer, "Situation Comedy, Part 2," *The Television Genre Book*, ed. Glen Creeber, Toby Miller, and John Tulloch (London: British Film Institute, 2001), 67–70, 69.

4 Gerard Jones, *Honey, I'm Home! Sitcoms: Selling the American Dream* (New York: Grove Weidenfeld, 1992), 6, 4. See also Doyle Greene, *Politics and the American Television Comedy: A Critical Survey from "I Love Lucy" through "South Park"* (Jefferson, NC: McFarland, 2008), in which he frames the tension between avant-garde television and political conservatism; and Philip Green, *Primetime Politics: The Truth about Conservative Lies, Corporate Control, and Television Culture* (Lanham, MD: Rowman and Littlefield, 2005), in which he dissects the corporate strategies of network television and its conservative tendencies.

5 David Grote, *The End of Comedy: The Sit-Com and the Comedic Tradition* (Hamden, CT: Archon, 1983), 105.

6 Saul Austerlitz, *Sitcom: A History in Twenty-Four Episodes from "I Love Lucy" to "Community"* (Chicago: Chicago Review Press, 2014), 7.

7 Several essays in Mary Dalton and Laura Linder's *The Sitcom Reader: America Viewed and Skewed* (Albany: State University of New York Press, 2005) exemplify this analytical perspective; see, for example, Demetria Rougeaux Shabazz, "Negotiated Boundaries: Production Practices and the Making of Representation in *Julia*" (151–62); Judy Kutulas, "Liberated Women and New Sensitive Men: Reconstructing Gender in the 1970s Workplace Comedies" (217–25); and Valerie Peterson, "*Ellen*: Coming Out and Disappearing" (165–76).

8 Quotations from *Modern Family* and its producers, writers, and actors are taken from *Modern Family: The Complete Seasons 1–5* (Beverly Hills, CA: Twentieth Century Fox, 2009–14), DVD. This chapter focuses exclusively on the series' first five seasons.

9 Feuer, "Situation Comedy, Part 2," 70 (italics in original).

10 Jane Feuer, "Narrative Form in American Network Television," *High Theory / Low Culture: Analysing Popular Television and Film*, ed. Colin McCabe (Manchester: Manchester University Press, 1986), 101–14, 110.

11 Susan Lanser, "Queering Narratology," *Ambiguous Discourse: Feminist Narratology and British Women Writers*, ed. Kathy Mezei (Chapel Hill: University of North Carolina Press, 1996), 250–61, 250. Lanser writes of literary narratives in this essay, yet her point pertains to screen narrative theories as well.

12 Quoted in Bruce Feiler, "What *Modern Family* Says about Modern Families," *New York Times*, 21 Jan. 2011.

13 James Parker, "Family Portrait," *Atlantic*, Nov. 2011, 42–44, 44.

14 Herman Melville, *Moby-Dick, or The Whale*, ed. Harrison Hayford, Hershel Parker, and Thomas Tanselle (1851; Evanston, IL: Northwestern University Press, 2001), chap. 49, 226.

15 Rob Long, "Three Cheers," *National Review*, 7 Jun. 1993, 62–63, 63.

16 Christina Kallas, *Inside the Writers' Room: Conversations with American TV Writers* (Houndmills, Basingstoke: Palgrave Macmillan, 2014), 87.

17 Phil Rosenthal, *You're Lucky You're Funny: How Life Becomes a Sitcom* (New York: Viking, 2006), 101.

18 Brett Mills, *Television Sitcom* (London: British Film Institute, 2005), 103. See also his *The Sitcom* (Edinburgh: Edinburgh University Press, 2009).

19 Sarah Schulman, *Stagestruck: Theater, AIDS, and the Marketing of Gay America* (Durham, NC: Duke University Press, 1998), 146.

20 Ron Becker, *Gay TV and Straight America* (New Brunswick, NJ: Rutgers University Press, 2006), 225.

21 Thomas Linneman, "How Do You Solve a Problem Like Will Truman? The Feminization of Gay Masculinities on *Will & Grace*," *Men and Masculinities* 10.5 (2008): 583–603, 589. See also Denis Provencher, "Sealed with a Kiss: Heteronormative Narrative Strategies in NBC's *Will & Grace*," *The Sitcom Reader: America Viewed and Skewed*, ed. Mary Dalton and Laura Linder (Albany: State University of New York Press, 2005), 177–89.

22 Quoted in Feiler, "What *Modern Family* Says about Modern Families."

23 Arianna Reiche, "Does *Modern Family* Preach Blatant Sexism?" *Gawker*, 14 Apr. 2010.

24 Feiler, "What *Modern Family* Says about Modern Families."

25 Quoted in Curtis Wong, "Jesse Tyler Ferguson Responds after Tuc Watkins Deems *Modern Family* Couple the Gay Equivalent of 'Blackface,'" *Huffington Post*, 22 Dec. 2014.

26 Quoted in Greg Hernandez, "Out Actor Tuc Watkins Challenges Hollywood to Create More Diverse Gay Characters," *Gay Star News*, 31 Dec. 2014.

27 Christina LaVecchia, "Of Peerenting, Trophy Wives, and Effeminate Men: *Modern Family*'s Surprisingly Conservative Remediation of the Family Sitcom Genre," *Harlot: A Revealing Look at the Arts of Persuasion* 6 (Spring 2011): n. pag.

28 For foundational studies of these perspectives, see Michel Foucault, *The History of Sexuality: Volume 1, An Introduction* (New York: Pantheon, 1978); Judith Butler, *Gender Trouble: Feminism and the Subversion of Identity* (1990; New York: Routledge, 2006); and Judith Butler, *Bodies That Matter: On the Discursive Limits of "Sex"* (New York: Routledge, 1993).

29 Many gay people self-identify as conservative politically. Reviewing data from the 2012 presidential election, the *New York Times* states that, "Exit polls showed that 76 percent of voters who identified as gay supported Mr. Obama last week, and that 22 percent supported Mr. Romney." Micah Cohen, "Gay Vote Proved a Boon for Obama," *New York Times*, NYTimes.com, 15 Nov. 2012. In a similar analysis

of an October 2012 Gallup poll, Gary Gates and Frank Newport conclude that whereas "45% of LGBT individuals describe their political views as liberal or very liberal, one in five (20%) describe themselves as conservative or very conservative." Gary Gates and Frank Newport, "Gallup Special Report: The LGBT Vote in the 2012 Presidential Election," Williams Institute of UCLA Law School, Oct. 2012, williamsinstitute.law.ucla.edu. Moreover, in adherence with their belief in limited government, many Republicans—if not their party platform—endorse gay rights, including Theodore Olson, who with David Boies, argued the *Hollingsworth v. Perry* case before the U.S. Supreme Court, which, as discussed previously, serves as a key point in *Modern Family*'s narrative arc.

30 See, for example, D. Gilson, "'Homonormativity' and Its Discontents," *The Gay & Lesbian Review*, Jan.-Feb. 2016, 22–24.

31 Paul Robinson, *Queer Wars: The New Gay Rights and Its Critics* (Chicago: University of Chicago Press, 2005), 1.

32 For an instructive theorization of the difference between laughing *at* and laughing *with*, which posits as well the possibility of bridging cultural differences through humor based on stereotypes, see Delia Chiaro, "Laughing At or Laughing With?" *Hybrid Humour: Comedy in Transcultural Perspectives*, ed. Graeme Dunphy and Rainer Emig (Amsterdam: Rodopi, 2010), 65–83.

33 Parker, "Family Portrait," 44.

34 Michelle Haimoff, "Not So Modern Family: Top Sitcoms Make for Sexist, Inaccurate Television," *Christian Science Monitor*, 27 Jan. 2012.

35 Jacques Rothmann, "'Send in the (Gay) Clowns': *Will & Grace* and *Modern Family* as 'Sensibly Queer,'" *Acta Academica* 45.4 (2013): 40–83, 72.

36 Alexander Doty, "*Modern Family*, *Glee*, and the Limits of Television Liberalism," *FlowTV* 12.9 (24 Sept. 2010).

37 LaVecchia, "Of Peerenting, Trophy Wives, and Effeminate Men."

38 One passage in *Modern Family* could be construed as indicative of Mitch's former promiscuity. Convinced that his father's friend Shorty (Chazz Palminteri) is gay, he claims: "My gaydar is never wrong, and it is pinging like we're at a bathhouse" ("Fifteen Percent"). Still, this simile does not prove conclusively that Mitch has patronized bathhouses, just that he knows of them. Other hints of Mitch and Cam's extramarital flings are simply misdirectional humor, such as when Cam tells Jay that he and Mitch "met at an orgy" to watch Jay's pained reaction; Cam immediately reveals his joke with a pointed "Come on" ("The Old Wagon").

39 Quoted in Lacey Rose, "*Modern Family* at 100: As the Top Comedy Hits a Milestone, Creators Christopher Lloyd and Steve Levitan, along with Their Wickedly Funny Writing Staff, Reveal Their Writers Room Squabbles (Condoms!), What the Show Would Be Like on Cable, and More," *Hollywood Reporter*, 18 Oct. 2013, 62+.

40 Leo Bersani, *Is the Rectum a Grave? and Other Essays* (Chicago: University of Chicago Press, 2010), 29 (italics in original).

41 Quoted in Rose, "*Modern Family* at 100."

42 This is not to suggest that *Modern Family* rejects procreation, particularly in the story line of Jay and Gloria having their son Joe. Also, despite Phil's assertion that his planned vasectomy "will allow for a little more freestylin' in the boudoir if we're not having to worry about adding more critters," he and Claire decide to keep their reproductive options open ("Snip").

43 Quoted in Rose, "*Modern Family* at 100."

Conclusion

1 Leo Tolstoy, *Anna Karenina*, ed. Leonard Kent and Nina Berberova, trans. Constance Garnett (1877; New York: Modern Library, 1993), 3.
2 Lionel Shriver, *We Have to Talk about Kevin* (New York: Counterpoint, 2003), 17.
3 Quoted in David Bianculli, *Teleliteracy: Taking Television Seriously* (Syracuse, NY: Syracuse University Press, 2000), 72. Minow served as head of the Federal Communications Commission during John F. Kennedy's administration.
4 Heather Havrilesky, "*Parenthood* Fumbles, *Modern Family* Triumphs," Salon.com, 13 Mar. 2010.
5 David Marc, *Comic Visions: Television Comedy and American Culture*, 2nd ed. (Malden, MA: Blackwell, 1997), 166.
6 Pierre Bourdieu, *Distinction: A Social Critique of the Judgement of Taste*, trans. Richard Nice (Cambridge, MA: Harvard University Press, 1984), 5.
7 Deborah Macey, Kathleen Ryan, and Noah Springer, eds., *How Television Shapes Our Worldview: Media Representations of Social Trends and Change* (Lanham, MD: Lexington, 2014), 2.
8 Donald Roberts, "Adolescents and the Mass Media: From *Leave It to Beaver* to *Beverly Hills 90210*," *Teachers College Record* 94.3 (1993): 629–44, 629. See also George Comstock with Haejung Paik, *Television and the American Child* (San Diego, CA: Academic, 1991).
9 Ron Lembo, *Thinking through Television* (Cambridge: Cambridge University Press, 2000), 167–214.
10 Judith Mayne, *Cinema and Spectatorship* (London: Routledge, 1993), 97.
11 Brett Farmer, *Spectacular Passion: Cinema, Fantasy, Gay Male Spectatorships* (Durham, NC: Duke University Press, 2000), 66.
12 Horace Newcomb, *TV: The Most Popular Art* (Garden City, NY: Anchor, 1974), 253.
13 Rob Long, "Three Cheers," *National Review*, 7 Jun. 1993, 62–63, 62.

Works Cited

About Last Night. . . Dir. Edward Zwick. Perf. Rob Lowe and Demi Moore. 1986. Film.

Ahmed, Sara. *The Cultural Politics of Emotion*. New York: Routledge, 2004.

Airplane! Dir. Jim Abrahams, David Zucker, and Jerry Zucker. 1980. Film.

Alice Sweet Alice. Dir. Alfred Sole. Perf. Brooke Shields. 1976. Film.

Andreeva, Nellie. "ABC Family to Be Renamed as Freeform." *Deadline: Hollywood*, 6 Oct. 2015, deadline.com. Web.

Angel Heart. Dir. Alan Parker. Perf. Mickey Rourke, Lisa Bonet, and Robert De Niro. 1987. Film.

Annie Hall. Dir. Woody Allen. Perf. Woody Allen and Diane Keaton. 1977. Film.

Ariès, Philippe. *Centuries of Childhood: A Social History of Family Life*. Trans. Robert Baldick. New York: Knopf, 1962.

Arnold, Roseanne. *My Lives*. New York: Ballantine, 1994.

Attallah, Paul. "The Unworthy Discourse: Situation Comedy in Television." Morreale 91–115.

Austerlitz, Saul. *Sitcom: A History in Twenty-Four Episodes from "I Love Lucy" to "Community."* Chicago: Chicago Review Press, 2014.

Bakhtin, Mikhail. *Rabelais and His World*. Trans. Hélène Iswolsky. Bloomington: Indiana University Press, 1984.

Bank, Frank, with Gib Twyman. *Call Me Lumpy: My "Leave It to Beaver" Days and Other Wild Hollywood Life*. Lenexa, KS: Addax, 1997.

Barber, Benjamin. *Con$umed: How Markets Corrupt Children, Infantilize Adults, and Swallow Citizens Whole*. New York: Norton, 2007.

Barr, Roseanne. *My Life as a Woman*. New York: Harper and Row, 1989.

———. *Roseannearchy: Dispatches from the Nut Farm*. New York: Gallery, 2011.

Barrett, Wayne. "America's Tween Idol Rules." *USA Today Magazine*, Mar. 2008, 78.

Baudrillard, Jean. *America*. Trans. Chris Turner. London: Verso, 1986.

Bay Coven. Dir. Carl Schenkel. Perf. Barbara Billingsley and Pamela Sue Martin. 1987. TV Movie.

Beck, Richard. *We Believe the Children: A Moral Panic in the 1980s*. New York: PublicAffairs, 2015.

Becker, Anne. "*Hannah Montana* Superstar: Disney Plans International Marketing Blitz for Tween Hit." *Broadcasting & Cable*, 26 Mar. 2007, 3+.

Becker, Ron. *Gay TV and Straight America*. New Brunswick, NJ: Rutgers University Press, 2006.

Berger, Dan, ed. *The Hidden 1970s: Histories of Radicalism*. New Brunswick, NJ: Rutgers University Press, 2010.

Bersani, Leo. *Is the Rectum a Grave? and Other Essays*. Chicago: University of Chicago Press, 2010.

Best, Stephen, and Sharon Marcus. "Surface Reading: An Introduction." *Representations* 108 (2009): 1–21.

Bettie, Julie. "Class Dismissed? *Roseanne* and the Changing Face of Working-Class Iconography." *Social Text* 14.4 (1995): 125–49.

Bianculli, David. *Teleliteracy: Taking Television Seriously*. Syracuse, NY: Syracuse University Press, 2000.

Bickford, Tyler. "The New 'Tween' Music Industry: The Disney Channel, Kidz Bop, and an Emerging Childhood Counterpublic." *Popular Music* 31.3 (2012): 417–36.

"Bill Cosby Says: 'I did not read the script . . . Lisa made the decision." *Jet*, 23 Mar. 1987, 62.

Blake, Richard. "The Censoring of TV's Family Hour." *America*, 11 Dec. 1976, 415–18.

The Blue Lagoon. Dir. Randal Kleiser. Perf. Brooke Shields and Christopher Atkins. 1980. Film.

Blue, Morgan Genevieve. "The Best of Both Worlds? Youth, Gender, and a Post-Feminist Sensibility in Disney's *Hannah Montana*." *Feminist Media Studies* 13.4 (2013): 660–75.

Bodroghkozy, Aniko. *Groove Tube: Sixties Television and the Youth Rebellion*. Durham, NC: Duke University Press, 2001.

———. "'Is This What You Mean by Color TV?': Race, Gender, and Contested Meanings in NBC's *Julia*." *Private Screenings: Television and the Female Consumer*. Ed. Lynn Spigel and Denise Mann. Minneapolis: University of Minnesota Press, 1992. 142–67.

Bogle, Donald. *Brown Sugar: Over One Hundred Years of America's Black Female Superstars*. New York: Continuum, 2007.

———. *Primetime Blues: African Americans on Network Television*. New York: Farrar, Straus and Giroux, 2001.

Bonnett, Alastair. *Left in the Past: Radicalism and the Politics of Nostalgia*. London: Continuum, 2010.

Bossard, James, and Eleanor Boll. *Ritual in Family Living: A Contemporary Study*. Philadelphia: University of Pennsylvania Press, 1950.

Bourdieu, Pierre. *Distinction: A Social Critique of the Judgement of Taste*. Trans. Richard Nice. Cambridge, MA: Harvard University Press, 1984.

Boym, Svetlana. *The Future of Nostalgia*. New York: Basic Books, 2001.

Bozell, L. Brent. "'Family Hour' Landscape Is Moral Wasteland." *Human Events* 54.18 (1998): 10.

The Brady Bunch: The Complete Series. Prod. Sherwood Schwartz. Perf. Robert Reed, Florence Henderson, Ann B. Davis, et al. 1969–74. Paramount, 2007. DVD.

The Brady Bunch in the White House. Dir. Neal Israel. Perf. Shelley Long, Gary Cole, and Chad Doreck. 2002. TV.

The Brady Bunch Movie. Dir. Betty Thomas. Perf. Shelley Long, Gary Cole, and Christine Taylor. 1995. Film.

Bronstein, Carolyn. *Battling Pornography: The American Feminist Anti-pornography Movement, 1976–1986*. Cambridge: Cambridge University Press, 2011.

Brown, Les. "Elton's Rule: Be Different: ABC-TV Prez Puts Accent on Youth." *Variety*, 3 Apr. 1968, 33, 52.

Brown, Tammy L. "An Interview with John Amos." *African Americans on Television: Race-ing for Ratings*. Ed. David Leonard and Lisa Guerrero. Santa Barbara, CA: Praeger, 2013. 34–44.

Bruhm, Steve, and Natasha Hurley, eds. *Curiouser: On the Queerness of Children*. Minneapolis: University of Minnesota Press, 2004.

Buckingham, David. "Introduction: The Child and the Screen." *Small Screens: Television for Children*. Ed. David Buckingham. London: Leicester University Press, 2002. 1–14.

Budd, Mike, and Clay Steinman. "White Racism and *The Cosby Show*." *Jump Cut* 37 (1992): 5–12.

Butler, Judith. *Bodies That Matter: On the Discursive Limits of "Sex."* New York: Routledge, 1993.

———. "Critically Queer." *GLQ: A Journal of Lesbian and Gay Studies* 1.2 (1993): 17–32.

———. *Gender Trouble: Feminism and the Subversion of Identity*. 1990. New York: Routledge, 2006.

Butsch, Richard. "Five Decades and Three Hundred Sitcoms about Class and Gender." *Thinking Outside the Box: A Contemporary Television Genre Reader*. Ed. Gary Edgerton and Brian Rose. Lexington: University Press of Kentucky, 2005. 111–35.

Cameron, Kirk, with Lissa Halls Johnson. *Still Growing: An Autobiography*. Ventura, CA: Regal, 2008.

Capsuto, Steven. *Alternate Channels: The Uncensored Story of Gay and Lesbian Images on Radio and Television*. New York: Ballantine, 2000.

Carah, Nicholas. *Pop Brands: Branding, Popular Music, and Young People*. New York: Peter Lang, 2010.

Carlson, Joanne. *The Parent Effect: How Parenting Style Affects Adolescent Behavior and Personality Development*. Washington, DC: National Association of Social Workers Press, 2011.

Carmody, John. "The TV Column." *Washington Post*, 11 Dec. 1995. Web.

Carroll, Peter. *It Seemed Like Nothing Happened: The Tragedy and Promise of America in the 1970s*. New York: Holt, Rinehart and Winston, 1982.

Carter, Bill. "Lawyer Defends Cosby over Assault Claims." *New York Times*, 16 Nov. 2014. Web.

———. "NBC and Netflix Shelve Projects with Bill Cosby." *New York Times*, 19 Nov. 2014. Web.

Casablanca. Dir. Michael Curtiz. Perf. Humphrey Bogart, Ingrid Bergman, and Claude Rains. 1942. Film.

Chiaro, Delia. "Laughing At or Laughing With?" *Hybrid Humour: Comedy in Transcultural Perspectives*. Ed. Graeme Dunphy and Rainer Emig. Amsterdam: Rodopi, 2010. 65–83.

Chittenden, Gertrude. *Living with Children*. 1944. New York: Macmillan, 1951.

Christian, Margena. "The Death of James Evans, Sr." *Jet*, 28 Jan. 2008, 36.

———. "*A Different World* Twenty-Five Years Later: A Look at *The Cosby Show* Spin-Off That Educated Viewers." *Ebony*, Sept. 2012, 155+.

Cloarec, Nicole. Introduction to *Social Class on British and American Screens: Essays on Cinema and Television*. Ed. Nicole Cloarec, David Haigron, and Delphine Letort. Jefferson, NC: McFarland, 2016. 1–16.

Cohen, Cathy. *Democracy Remixed*. Oxford: Oxford University Press, 2010.

Cohen, Micah. "Gay Vote Proved a Boon for Obama." *New York Times*, 15 Nov. 2012. Web.

Coleman, Robin. *African American Viewers and the Black Situation Comedy: Situating Racial Humor*. New York: Garland, 2000.

Collins, Joan. *Second Act*. New York: St. Martin's, 1996.

Comstock, George, with Haejung Paik. *Television and the American Child*. San Diego, CA: Academic, 1991.
Confessions of a Teenage Drama Queen. Dir. Sara Sugarman. Perf. Lindsay Lohan. 2004. Film.
Coon, David. *Look Closer: Suburban Narratives and American Values in Film and Television*. New Brunswick, NJ: Rutgers University Press, 2013.
Coontz, Stephanie. *The Way We Never Were: American Families and the Nostalgia Trap*. New York: Basic Books, 1992.
———. *The Way We Really Are: Coming to Terms with America's Changing Families*. New York: Basic Books, 1997.
Cosby, Bill. *Childhood*. Introduction by Alvin F. Poussaint. New York: Putnam's, 1991.
———. *Fatherhood*. Introduction by Alvin F. Poussaint. New York: Doubleday, 1986.
Cosby, Bill, and Alvin F. Poussaint. *Come On, People: On the Path from Victims to Victors*. Nashville, TN: Thomas Nelson, 2007.
The Cosby Show: The Complete Series. Perf. Bill Cosby, Phylicia Rashad, Lisa Bonet, et al. 1982–94. Mill Creek Entertainment, 2015. DVD.
Coscarelli, Joe. "Miley Cyrus on Nicki Manaj and Hosting a 'Raw' MTV Video Music Awards." *New York Times*, 27 Aug 2015. Web.
Cowan, Geoffrey. *See No Evil: The Backstage Battle over Sex and Violence on Television*. New York: Simon and Schuster, 1979.
Cowell, Maria. "How *Two and a Half Men* Star Became a 'Paid Hypocrite.'" *Christianity Today*, 27 Nov. 2012. Web.
Cross, Gary. *The Cute and the Cool: Wondrous Innocence and Modern American Children's Culture*. Oxford: Oxford University Press, 2004.
Cyrus, Miley, with Hilary Liftin. *Miles to Go*. New York: Disney Hyperion, 2009.
Dalton, Mary, and Laura Linder, eds. *The Sitcom Reader: America Viewed and Skewed*. Albany: State University of New York Press, 2005.
De Casparis, Lena. "The Gender Debate: Miley Cyrus Gets the Conversation Started." *Elle UK*, Oct. 2015, 236+.
Deleuze, Gilles, and Félix Guattari. *Anti-Oedipus: Capitalism and Schizophrenia*. 1977. New York: Penguin, 2009.
Del Moro, Michael, and Dan Good. "TV Land Pulls *The Cosby Show* Reruns amid Sexual Assault Allegations." ABC News, 20 Nov. 2014. Web.
Deresiewicz, William. "Ready for Prime Time: Why TV Got Good." *Harper's*, Nov. 2016, 82–86.
Diamond, Dustin. *Behind the Bell*. Montreal: Transit, 2009.
Dicker, Rory, and Alison Piepmeier, eds. *Catching a Wave: Reclaiming Feminism for the Twenty-First Century*. Boston: Northeastern University Press, 2003.
Dinshaw, Carolyn. *How Soon Is Now?* Durham, NC: Duke University Press, 2012.
Donahue, Ann. "Tween Idol: After Almost Five Years Building *Hannah Montana* on TV, in Record Stores, and on Tour, Miley Cyrus Makes a Movie—and Maybe a Dance Craze." *Billboard*, 28 Mar. 2009, 16+. Web.
Doty, Alexander. *Making Things Perfectly Queer: Interpreting Mass Culture*. Minneapolis: University of Minnesota Press, 1993.
———. "*Modern Family*, *Glee*, and the Limits of Television Liberalism." *FlowTV* 12.9 (24 Sept. 2010). Web.
Douglas, Susan. *Where the Girls Are: Growing Up Female with the Mass Media*. New York: Random House, 1995.
Douglas, William. *Television Families: Is Something Wrong in Suburbia?* Mahwah, NJ: Erlbaum, 2003.

Dow, Bonnie. *Prime-Time Feminism: Television, Media Culture, and the Women's Movement since 1970*. Philadelphia: University of Pennsylvania Press, 1996.
Driscoll, Catherine. *Girls: Feminine Adolescence in Popular Culture and Cultural Theory*. New York: Columbia University Press, 2002.
Dunnewold, Anne. *Even June Cleaver Would Forget the Juice Box: Cut Yourself Some Slack (And Still Raise Great Kids) in the Age of Extreme Parenting*. Deerfield Beach, FL: Health Communications, 2007.
Dutka, Elaine. "Interview: Slightly to the Left of Normal." *Time*, 8 May 1989, 82+.
Dworkin, Susan. "Roseanne Barr: The Disgruntled Housewife as Stand-Up Comedian." *Ms.*, Jul.-Aug. 1987, 92+.
Dyson, Michael. "Bill Cosby and the Politics of Race." *Z Magazine*, Sept. 1989, 26–30.
Eagleton, Terry. *Walter Benjamin, or Towards a Revolutionary Criticism*. London: Verso, 1981.
Easy Rider. Dir. Dennis Hopper. Perf. Peter Fonda, Dennis Hopper, and Jack Nicholson. 1969. Film.
Ebenkamp, Becky. "Hannah and Her Boosters." *Brandweek*, 8 Sept. 2008, MO40–42.
Eberle, Paul, and Shirley Eberle. *The Abuse of Innocence: The McMartin Preschool Trial*. Buffalo, NY: Prometheus, 1993.
Ebert, Roger. "*Angel Heart* (1987)." 6 Mar. 1987. RogerEbert.com. Web.
Edelman, Lee. *No Future: Queer Theory and the Death Drive*. Durham, NC: Duke University Press, 2004.
Ehrenreich, Barbara. *Fear of Falling: The Inner Life of the Middle Class*. New York: HarperPerennial, 1990.
———. "The Wretched of the Hearth: The Undainty Feminism of Roseanne Barr." *New Republic*, 2 Apr. 1990, 28–31.
Ella Enchanted. Dir. Tommy O'Haver. Prod. Jane Startz. Perf. Anne Hathaway and Hugh Dancy. 2004. Film.
Ellis, John. *Visible Fictions: Cinema, Television, Video*. London: Routledge and Kegan Paul, 1982.
Endless Love. Dir. Franco Zeffirelli. Perf. Brooke Shields and Martin Hewitt. 1981. Film.
Eng, David, Jack [Judith] Halberstam, and José Esteban Muñoz. "What's Queer about Queer Studies Now?" *Social Text* 23.3–4 (2005): 1–17.
Erickson, Hal. *Television Cartoon Shows: An Illustrated Encyclopedia, 1949–1993*. Jefferson, NC: McFarland, 1995.
Farmer, Brett. *Spectacular Passion: Cinema, Fantasy, Gay Male Spectatorships*. Durham, NC: Duke University Press, 2000.
Feiler, Bruce. "What *Modern Family* Says about Modern Families." *New York Times*, 21 Jan. 2011. Web.
Feuer, Jane. "Narrative Form in American Network Television." *High Theory / Low Culture: Analysing Popular Television and Film*. Ed. Colin McCabe. Manchester: Manchester University Press, 1986. 101–14.
———. "Situation Comedy, Part 2." *The Television Genre Book*. Ed. Glen Creeber, Toby Miller, and John Tulloch. London: British Film Institute, 2001. 67–70.
Finke, Nikke. "The Blue-Collar Backgrounds behind a Blue-Collar Hit." *Los Angeles Times*, 26 Jan. 1989. Web.
Fiske, John. "British Cultural Studies." *Channels of Discourse: Television and Contemporary Criticism*. Ed. Robert C. Allen. Chapel Hill: University of North Carolina Press, 1987. 254–89.
———. *Media Matters*. Minneapolis: University of Minnesota Press, 1996.

Fleming, Anne Taylor. "Roseanne's Tough Act: Is It Too Harsh?" *New York Times*, 17 Jan. 1990. Web.

Foreman, Joel, ed. *The Other Fifties: Interrogating Midcentury American Icons*. Urbana: University of Illinois Press, 1997.

Foucault, Michel. *The History of Sexuality: Volume 1, An Introduction*. Trans. Robert Hurley. 1978. New York: Pantheon, 1990.

Frazer, June, and Timothy Frazer. "*Father Knows Best* and *The Cosby Show*: Nostalgia and the Sitcom Tradition." *Journal of Popular Culture* 27.3 (1993): 163–72.

Freaky Friday. Dir. Mark Waters. Perf. Lindsay Lohan and Jamie Lee Curtis. 2003. Film.

Freeman, Dan, and Stewart Shapiro. "Tweens' Knowledge of Marketing Tactics: Skeptical beyond Their Years." *Journal of Advertising Research* 54 (Mar. 2014): 44–55.

Freeman, Elizabeth. *Time Binds: Queer Temporalities, Queer Histories*. Durham, NC: Duke University Press, 2010.

Freud, Sigmund. "'A Child Is Being Beaten': A Contribution to the Study of the Origin of Sexual Perversions." *The Standard Edition of the Complete Psychological Works of Sigmund Freud*. Trans. and ed. James Strachey. London: Hogarth, 1953–74. 17:175–204.

Galenson, Walter. *The American Labor Movement, 1955–1995*. Westport, CT: Greenwood, 1996.

Gates, Gary, and Frank Newport. "Gallup Special Report: The LGBT Vote in the 2012 Presidential Election." Williams Institute of UCLA Law School. Oct. 2012. WilliamsInstitute.law.ucla.edu. Web.

Gates, Henry Louis, Jr. "TV's Black World Turns—But Stays Unreal." *Race, Class, and Gender: An Anthology*. Ed. Margaret Andersen and Patricia Hill Collins. Belmont, CA: Wadsworth, 1992. 310–17.

Gilson, D. "'Homonormativity' and Its Discontents." *Gay & Lesbian Review*, Jan.-Feb. 2016, 22–24.

"Going into November Sweeps, Members of Congress Last Week Urge Six Broadcast Networks to Bring Back the Family Hour." *Broadcasting & Cable*, 15 Nov. 1999, 113.

Gray, Ann. "Behind Closed Doors: Video Recorders in the Home." *Feminist Television Criticism: A Reader*. Ed. Charlotte Brunsdon, Julie D'Acci, and Lynn Spigel. Oxford: Clarendon, 1997. 235–46.

Gray, Herman. *Watching Race: Television and the Struggle for "Blackness."* Minneapolis: University of Minnesota Press, 1995.

Gray, Jonathan. *Television Entertainment*. New York: Routledge, 2008.

Green, Philip. *Primetime Politics: The Truth about Conservative Lies, Corporate Control, and Television Culture*. Lanham, MD: Rowman and Littlefield, 2005.

Greenberg, Clement. "Avant-Garde and Kitsch." *Clement Greenberg: The Collected Essays and Criticism. Vol. 1, Perceptions and Judgments, 1939–1944*. Ed. John O'Brian. Chicago: University of Chicago Press, 1986. 5–22.

Greene, Doyle. *Politics and the American Television Comedy: A Critical Survey from "I Love Lucy" through "South Park."* Jefferson, NC: McFarland, 2008.

Grier, Rosey. *Rosey Grier's Needlepoint for Men*. New York: Walker, 1973.

Gross, Larry. *Up from Invisibility: Lesbians, Gay Men, and the Media in America*. New York: Columbia University Press, 2001.

Grosz, Elizabeth. *Space, Time, and Perversion: Essays on the Politics of Bodies*. New York: Routledge, 1995.

Grote, David. *The End of Comedy: The Sit-Com and the Comedic Tradition*. Hamden, CT: Archon, 1983.

Gruenberg, Sidonie Matsner, ed. *Our Children Today: A Guide to Their Needs from Infancy through Adolescence*. New York: Viking, 1952.

Haimoff, Michelle. "Not So Modern Family: Top Sitcoms Make for Sexist, Inaccurate Television." *Christian Science Monitor*, 27 Jan. 2012. Web.

Halberstam, David. *The Fifties*. New York: Villard, 1993.

Hamamoto, Darrell. *Nervous Laughter: Television Situation Comedy and Liberal Democratic Ideology*. New York: Praeger, 1989.

Handy, Bruce. "Miley Knows Best." *Vanity Fair*, Jun. 2008. Web.

Hannah Montana Forever: Final Season. Walt Disney Studios, 2011. DVD.

Hannah Montana in the Mix. Book and Magnetic Set. New York: Disney Press, 2009.

Hannah Montana: Keeping It Real. Walt Disney Studios, 2009. DVD.

Hannah Montana: Life's What You Make It. Walt Disney Studios, 2007. DVD.

Hannah Montana: Miley Says Goodbye? Walt Disney Studios, 2010. DVD.

Hannah Montana: One in a Million. Walt Disney Studios, 2008. DVD.

Hannah Montana: Season 1. Walt Disney Studios, 2008. DVD.

Hannah Montana: The Movie. Walt Disney Studios, 2009. DVD.

Harper, Ralph. *Nostalgia: An Existential Exploration of Longing and Fulfillment in the Modern Age*. Cleveland, OH: Press of Western Reserve University, 1966.

Haste, Helen. *The Sexual Metaphor*. Cambridge, MA: Harvard University Press, 1994.

Hatch, David. "Lawmakers: Reinstate 'Family Hour.'" *Electronic Media* 16.20 (1997): 1.

Havrilesky, Heather. "*Parenthood* Fumbles, *Modern Family* Triumphs." Salon.com, 13 Mar. 2010. Web.

Hein, Jon. *Jump the Shark*. New York: Dutton, 2002.

Henderson, Florence, with Joel Brokaw. *Life Is Not a Stage: From Broadway Baby to Lovely Lady and Beyond*. New York: Center Street, 2011.

Henry, Matthew. "The Triumph of Popular Culture: Situation Comedy, Postmodernism, and *The Simpsons*." Morreale 262–73.

Hernandez, Greg. "Out Actor Tuc Watkins Challenges Hollywood to Create More Diverse Gay Characters." *Gay Star News*, 31 Dec. 2014. Web.

Heywood, Colin. *A History of Childhood: Children and Childhood in the West from Medieval to Modern Times*. Malden, MA: Polity, 2001.

Himmelstein, Hal. *Television Myth and the American Mind*. 2nd ed. Westport, CT: Praeger, 1994.

"H.I.V. Contributed to Death of Robert Reed, Doctor Says." *New York Times*, 20 May 1992.

Holdsworth, Amy. *Television, Memory, and Nostalgia*. Basingstoke, Hampshire: Palgrave Macmillan, 2011.

Hunt, Morton. *Sexual Behavior in the 1970s*. Chicago: Playboy Press, 1974.

Innis, Leslie, and Joe Feagin. "*The Cosby Show*: The View from the Black Middle Class." *Say It Loud: African-American Audiences, Media, and Identity*. Ed. Robin Coleman. New York: Routledge, 2002. 187–204.

It Happened One Night. Dir. Frank Capra. Perf. Clark Gable and Claudette Colbert. 1934. Film.

Jameson, Fredric. *The Political Unconscious: Narrative as a Socially Symbolic Act*. Ithaca, NY: Cornell University Press, 1981.

———. *Postmodernism, or, The Cultural Logic of Late Capitalism*. Durham, NC: Duke University Press, 1991.

Jerome, Jim. "Roseanne Unchained." *People Weekly*, 9 Oct. 1989, 87+.

Jhally, Sut, and Justin Lewis. *Enlightened Racism: "The Cosby Show," Audiences, and the Myth of the American Dream*. Boulder, CO: Westview, 1992.

Johnson, Merri Lisa. "Ladies Love Your Box: The Rhetoric of Pleasure and Danger in Feminist Television Studies." *Third Wave Feminism and Television: Jane Puts It in a Box*. Ed. Merri Lisa Johnson. London: I. B. Tauris, 2007. 1–27.

Johnson, Thomas. "The Decline of Television's Family Hour." *USA Today Magazine*, Nov. 1996. Web.

Jones, Gerard. *Honey, I'm Home! Sitcoms: Selling the American Dream*. New York: Grove Weidenfeld, 1992.

Joyrich, Lynne. "Epistemology of the Console." *Critical Inquiry* 27.3 (2001): 439–67.

———. "Queer Television Studies: Currents, Flows, and (Main)streams." *Cinema Journal* 53.2 (2014): 133–39.

Kackman, Michael, Marnie Binfield, Matthew Thomas Payne, Allison Perlman, and Bryan Sebok, eds. *Flow TV: Television in the Age of Media Convergence*. New York: Routledge, 2011.

Kallas, Christina. *Inside the Writers' Room: Conversations with American TV Writers*. Houndmills, Basingstoke: Palgrave Macmillan, 2014.

Kalu, Anthonia. "Bill Cosby, Blues, and the Reconstruction of African-American Literary Theory." *Literary Griot: International Journal of Black Expressive Cultural Studies* 4.1–2 (1992): 1–15.

Kaplan, Elaine. *Not Our Kind of Girl: Unraveling the Myths of Black Teenage Motherhood*. Berkeley: University of California Press, 1997.

Kassel, Michael. "Mayfield after Midnight: Images of Youth and Parenting in *Leave It to Beaver*." *Images of Youth: Popular Culture as Educational Ideology*. Ed. Michael Oliker and Walter Krolikowski. New York: Peter Lang, 2001. 112–29.

Katz, Barney. *How to Be a Better Parent: Understanding Yourself and Your Child*. New York: Ronald Press, 1953.

Keller, James, and Leslie Stratyner, eds. *The New Queer Aesthetic on Television: Essays on Recent Programming*. Jefferson, NC: McFarland, 2006.

Kendall, Diana. *Framing Class: Media Representations of Wealth and Poverty in America*. 2nd ed. Lanham, MD: Rowman and Littlefield, 2011.

Kennedy, Melanie. "Hannah Montana and Miley Cyrus: 'Becoming' a Woman, 'Becoming' a Star." *Celebrity Studies* 5.3 (2014): 225–41.

Kierkegaard, Søren. *Either/Or, Part 1*. Ed. and trans. Howard Hong and Edna Hong. Princeton, NJ: Princeton University Press, 1987.

Kimmel, Daniel. *The Fourth Network: How FOX Broke the Rules and Reinvented Television*. Chicago: Ivan R. Dee, 2004.

Kincaid, James. *Child-Loving: The Erotic Child and Victorian Culture*. New York: Routledge, 1992.

———. *Erotic Innocence: The Culture of Child Molesting*. Durham, NC: Duke University Press, 1998.

King of the Gypsies. Dir. Frank Pierson. Perf. Sterling Hayden and Brooke Shields. 1978. Film.

Kleinhans, Chuck. "The Change from Film to Video Pornography: Implications for Analysis." *Pornography: Film and Culture*. Ed. Peter Lehman. New Brunswick, NJ: Rutgers University Press, 2006. 154–67.

Kutulas, Judy. "Liberated Women and New Sensitive Men: Reconstructing Gender in the 1970s Workplace Comedies." Dalton and Linder 217–25.

Lahr, John. "Dealing with Roseanne." *Life Stories: Profiles from "The New Yorker."* Ed. David Remnick. New York: Random House, 2000. 441–67.

Lancioni, Judith. "Murder and Mayhem on Wisteria Lane: A Study of Genre and Cultural Context in *Desperate Housewives*." *Reading "Desperate Housewives": Beyond the White Picket Fence*. Ed. Janet McCabe and Kim Akass. London: I. B. Tauris, 2006. 129–43.

Lanser, Susan. "Queering Narratology." *Ambiguous Discourse: Feminist Narratology and British Women Writers*. Ed. Kathy Mezei. Chapel Hill: University of North Carolina Press, 1996. 250–61.

Larocca, Amy. "The Real Miley Cyrus." *Harper's Bazaar*, 6 Jan. 2010. Web.

Larson, Mary Strom. "Sibling Interaction in Situation Comedies over the Years." *Television and the American Family*. Ed. Jennings Bryant and Alison Bryant. 2nd ed. Mahwah, NJ: Erlbaum, 2001. 163–76.

The Last Picture Show. Dir. Peter Bogdanovich. Perf. Timothy Bottoms, Jeff Bridges, and Cybill Shepherd. 1971. Film.

Last Summer. Dir. Frank Perry. Perf. Barbara Hershey, Richard Thomas, and Bruce Davison. 1969. Film.

Laurent, Lawrence. "Commercial Television: What Are Its Educational Possibilities and Limits?" *Television's Impact on American Culture*. Ed. William Elliott. East Lansing: Michigan State University Press, 1956. 125–73.

LaVecchia, Christina. "Of Peerenting, Trophy Wives, and Effeminate Men: *Modern Family*'s Surprisingly Conservative Remediation of the Family Sitcom Genre." *Harlot: A Revealing Look at the Arts of Persuasion* 6 (Spring 2011): n. pag. Web.

Lears, T. J. Jackson. "Making Fun of Popular Culture." *American Historical Review* 97.5 (1992): 1417–26.

Leave It to Beaver. Dir. Andy Cadiff. Perf. Christopher McDonald, Janine Turner, and Barbara Billingsley. 1997. Film.

Leave It to Beaver: The Complete Series. Perf. Barbara Billingsley, Hugh Beaumont, Tony Dow, and Jerry Mathers. 1957–63. NBC Universal, 2010. DVD.

Lee, Janet. "Subversive Sitcoms: *Roseanne* as Inspiration for Feminist Resistance." *Women's Studies* 21 (1992): 87–101.

Lehman, Katherine. *Those Girls: Single Women in Sixties and Seventies Popular Culture*. Lawrence: University Press of Kansas, 2011.

Leibman, Nina. *Living Room Lectures: The Fifties Family in Film and Television*. Austin: University of Texas Press, 1995.

Lembo, Ron. *Thinking through Television*. Cambridge: Cambridge University Press, 2000.

Levin, Diane. "So Sexy, So Soon: The Sexualization of Childhood." *The Sexualization of Childhood*. Ed. Sharna Olfman. Westport, CT: Praeger, 2009. 75–88.

Levine, Elana. *Wallowing in Sex: The New Sexual Culture of 1970s American Television*. Durham, NC: Duke University Press, 2007.

Lewis, Richard Warren. "The Importance of Being Julia." *TV Guide*, 14 Dec. 1968, 24–28.

Linneman, Thomas. "How Do You Solve a Problem Like Will Truman? The Feminization of Gay Masculinities on *Will & Grace*." *Men and Masculinities* 10.5 (2008): 583–603.

"Lisa Bonet: How Bill Cosby Will Handle Return of His Prodigal Daughter." *Jet*, 19 Sept. 1988, 56+.

"Lisa Bonet Dropped from *The Cosby Show*." *Jet*, 15 Apr. 1991, 52.

Littler, Jo. "Making Fame Ordinary: Intimacy, Reflexivity, and 'Keeping It Real.'" *Mediactive* 2 (2004): 8–25.

Long, Rob. "Three Cheers." *National Review*, 7 Jun. 1993, 62–63.

Lords, Traci. *Underneath It All*. New York: HarperEntertainment, 2003.

Luscombe, Belinda. "How Disney Builds Stars." *Time*, 2 Nov. 2009, 50–52.

Macey, Deborah, Kathleen Ryan, and Noah Springer, eds. *How Television Shapes Our Worldview: Media Representations of Social Trends and Change*. Lanham, MD: Lexington, 2014.

Mann, Bonnie. "The Lesbian June Cleaver: Heterosexism and Lesbian Mothering." *Hypatia* 22.1 (2007): 149–65.

Marc, David. *Comic Visions: Television Comedy and American Culture*. 2nd ed. Malden, MA: Blackwell, 1997.

Marinucci, Mimi. "Television, Generation X, and Third Wave Feminism: A Contextual Analysis of *The Brady Bunch*." *Journal of Popular Culture* 38.3 (2005): 505–24.

Mayerle, Judine. "*Roseanne*—How Did You Get Inside My House? A Case Study of a Hit Blue-Collar Situation Comedy." *Journal of Popular Culture* 24.4 (1991): 71–88.

Mayes-Elma, Ruthann. "From Miley Merchandising to Pop Princess Peddling: The *Hannah Montana* Phenomenon." *Kinderculture: The Corporate Construction of Childhood*. Ed. Shirley Steinberg. Boulder, CO: Westview, 2011. 173–86.

Mayne, Judith. *Cinema and Spectatorship*. London: Routledge, 1993.

McCartin, Joseph. *Collision Course: Ronald Reagan, the Air Traffic Controllers, and the Strike That Changed America*. Oxford: Oxford University Press, 2011.

Mean Girls. Dir. Mark Waters. Perf. Lindsay Lohan and Rachel McAdams. 2004. Film.

Meehan, Diana. *Ladies of the Evening: Women Characters of Prime-Time Television*. Metuchen, NJ: Scarecrow, 1983.

Melville, Herman. *Moby-Dick; or, The Whale*. Ed. Harrison Hayford, Hershel Parker, and Thomas Tanselle. 1851. Evanston, IL: Northwestern University Press, 2001.

Meyerowitz, Joanne, ed. *Not June Cleaver: Women and Gender in Postwar America, 1945–1960*. Philadelphia: Temple University Press, 1994.

Miller, Quinn. "*The Dick van Dyke Show*: Queer Meanings." *How to Watch Television*. Ed. Ethan Thompson and Jason Mittell. New York: New York University Press, 2013. 112–20.

Mills, Brett. *The Sitcom*. Edinburgh: Edinburgh University Press, 2009.

———. *Television Sitcom*. London: British Film Institute, 2005.

Mintz, Lawrence. "Situation Comedy." *TV Genres: A Handbook and Reference Guide*. Ed. Brian Rose. Westport, CT: Greenwood, 1985. 107–29.

Mintz, Steven. *Huck's Raft: A History of American Childhood*. Cambridge, MA: Belknap, 2004.

Mitchell, Claudia, and Jacqueline Reid-Walsh. "Theorizing Tween Culture within Girlhood Studies." Mitchell and Reid-Walsh 1–21.

Mitchell, Claudia, and Jacqueline Reid-Walsh, eds. *Seven Going on Seventeen: Tween Studies in the Culture of Girlhood*. New York: Peter Lang, 2005.

Mittell, Jason. *Genre and Television: From Cop Shows to Cartoons in American Culture*. New York: Routledge, 2004.

Mock, Erin Lee. "The Horror of 'Honey, I'm Home!': The Perils of Postwar Family Love in the Domestic Sitcom." *Film & History* 41.2 (2011): 29–50.

Modern Family: The Complete Seasons 1–5. Perf. Ed O'Neill, Sofia Vergara, Julie Bowen, Ty Burrell, Jesse Tyler Ferguson, Eric Stonestreet, et al. Beverly Hills, CA: Twentieth Century Fox, 2009–14. DVD.

Morreale, Joanne, ed. *Critiquing the Sitcom: A Reader*. Syracuse, NY: Syracuse University Press, 2003.

Mulvey, Laura. *Visual and Other Pleasures*. Bloomington: Indiana University Press, 1989.

Nadel, Alan. *Television in Black-and-White America: Race and National Identity*. Lawrence: University Press of Kansas, 2005.

Newcomb, Horace. "The Opening of America: Meaningful Difference in 1950s Television." Foreman 103–23.

———. *TV: The Most Popular Art*. Garden City, NY: Anchor, 1974.

Nichelson, Ted, Susan Olsen, and Lisa Sutton. *Love to Love You Bradys: The Bizarre Story of "The Brady Bunch Variety Hour."* Toronto: ECW, 2009.

Norment, Lynn. "Lisa Bonet: The Growing Pains of a Rising Star." *Ebony*, 1 Dec. 1987, 150+.

O'Dell, Cary. *June Cleaver Was a Feminist! Reconsidering the Female Characters of Early Television*. Jefferson, NC: McFarland, 2013.

Orlando, Tony, with Patsi Bale Cox. *Halfway to Paradise*. New York: St. Martin's, 2002.

Osgerby, Bill. "'So Who's Got Time for Adults!': Femininity, Consumption, and the Development of Teen TV—from *Gidget* to *Buffy*." *Teen TV: Genre, Consumption, Identity*. Ed. Glyn Davis and Kay Dickinson. London: British Film Institute, 2004. 71–86.

———. *Youth Media*. London: Routledge, 2004.

Packard, Vance. *The Hidden Persuaders*. New York: McKay, 1957.

Palmer, Edward. *Television and America's Children: A Crisis of Neglect*. New York: Oxford University Press, 1988.

Parker, James. "Family Portrait." *Atlantic*, Nov. 2011, 42–44.

Pegg, Robert. *Comical Co-stars of Television: From Ed Norton to Kramer*. Jefferson, NC: McFarland, 2002.

Pelkey, Stanley. "Music, Maturity, and the Moral Geography in *Leave It to Beaver* (1957–1963)." *Anxiety Muted: American Film Music in a Suburban Age*. Ed. Stanley Pelkey and Anthony Bushard. Oxford: Oxford University Press, 2015. 107–18.

Peterson, Valerie. "*Ellen*: Coming Out and Disappearing." Dalton and Linder 165–76.

Poussaint, Alvin F. Afterword to *Fatherhood*, by Bill Cosby, 161–78. New York: Doubleday, 1986.

———. Introduction to *Fatherhood*, by Bill Cosby, 1–11. New York: Doubleday, 1986.

Poussaint, Alvin F., and James Comber. *Raising Black Children*. New York: Plume, 1992.

The Princess Diaries. Dir. Garry Marshall. Perf. Anne Hathaway and Julie Andrews. 2001. Film.

The Princess Diaries 2: Royal Engagement. Dir. Garry Marshall. Perf. Anne Hathaway and Julie Andrews. 2004. Film.

Provencher, Denis. "Sealed with a Kiss: Heteronormative Narrative Strategies in NBC's *Will & Grace*." Dalton and Linder 177–89.

Psych-Out. Dir. Richard Rush. Perf. Susan Strasberg, Dean Stockwell, and Jack Nicholson. 1968. Film.

Reagan, Ronald. "Inaugural Address (20 Jan. 1981)." American Presidency Project, www.presidency.ucsb.edu. Web.

Reiche, Arianna. "Does *Modern Family* Preach Blatant Sexism?" *Gawker*, 14 Apr. 2010. Web.

Roberts, Donald. "Adolescents and the Mass Media: From *Leave It to Beaver* to *Beverly Hills 90210*." *Teachers College Record* 94.3 (1993): 629–44.

Robins, J. Max. "The Robins Report: Feeling Frisky in Early Prime Time." *TV Guide*, 9 Nov. 2002, 53–54.

Robinson, Louie. "Redd Foxx." *Ebony*, Jun. 1974, 154+.

Robinson, Paul. *Queer Wars: The New Gay Rights and Its Critics*. Chicago: University of Chicago Press, 2005.

Rose, Lacey. "*Modern Family* at 100: As the Top Comedy Hits a Milestone, Creators Christopher Lloyd and Steve Levitan, along with Their Wickedly Funny Writing Staff, Reveal Their Writers Room Squabbles (Condoms!), What the Show Would Be Like on Cable, and More." *Hollywood Reporter*, 18 Oct. 2013, 62+. Web.

Roseanne: The Complete Series. Perf. Roseanne Barr, John Goodman, Laurie Metcalf, et al. 1988–97. Mill Creek Entertainment and Carsey-Werner Company, 2013. DVD.

Rosenthal, Phil. *You're Lucky You're Funny: How Life Becomes a Sitcom*. New York: Viking, 2006.

Rothmann, Jacques. "'Send in the (Gay) Clowns': *Will & Grace* and *Modern Family* as 'Sensibly Queer.'" *Acta Academica* 45.4 (2013): 40–83.

Rottenberg, Josh. "Lisa Bonet Doesn't Pray Everyday [*sic*]." *Us Weekly*, 17 Apr. 2000, 74–79.

Rowe, Kathleen. *The Unruly Woman: Gender and the Genres of Laughter*. Austin: University of Texas Press, 1995.

Rubin, Gayle. *Deviations*. Durham, NC: Duke University Press, 2011.

Rudolph, Ileane, and Mike Hammer. "The Family Hour: Imagine June Cleaver in a Bustier." *TV Guide*, 31 Jul. 1996, 18–21.

Sanneh, Kelefa. "The Eternal Paternal: Bill Cosby's Never-Ending Tour." *New Yorker*, 15 Sept. 2014. Web.

Schaller, Michael. *Right Turn: American Life in the Reagan-Bush Era, 1980–1992*. New York: Oxford University Press, 2007.

Schulman, Sarah. *Stagestruck: Theater, AIDS, and the Marketing of Gay America*. Durham, NC: Duke University Press, 1998.

Schwartz, Sherwood, and Lloyd J. Schwartz. *Brady Brady Brady: The Complete Story of "The Brady Bunch" as Told by the Father/Son Team Who Really Know*. Philadelphia: Running Press, 2010.

Sedgwick, Eve Kosofsky. *Between Men: English Literature and Male Homosocial Desire*. New York: Columbia University Press, 1985.

———. "Queer and Now." *The Routledge Queer Studies Reader*. Ed. Donald Hall and Annamarie Jagose. London: Routledge, 2013. 3–17.

Shabazz, Demetria Rougeaux. "Negotiated Boundaries: Production Practices and the Making of Representation in *Julia*." Dalton and Linder 151–62.

Shaft. Dir. Gordon Parks. Perf. Richard Roundtree and Moses Gunn. 1971. Film.

Shakespeare in Love. Dir. John Madden. Perf. Joseph Fiennes and Gwyneth Paltrow. 1998. Film.

Shriver, Lionel. *We Have to Talk about Kevin*. New York: Counterpoint, 2003.

Siegel, David, Timothy Coffey, and Gregory Livingston. *The Great Tween Buying Machine: Marketing to Today's Tweens*. Ithaca, NY: Paramount Market, 2001.

Simpson, Brian. *Children and Television*. New York: Continuum, 2004.

Skolnick, Arlene. *Embattled Paradise: The American Family in an Age of Uncertainty*. New York: Basic Books, 1991.

Smith-Shomade, Beretta. *Shaded Lives: African-American Women and Television*. New Brunswick, NJ: Rutgers University Press, 2002.

Solinger, Rickie. "Teen Pregnancy." *Girlhood in America: An Encyclopedia*. Ed. Miriam Forman-Brunell. 2 vols. Santa Barbara, CA: ABC-CLIO, 2001. 2:645–53.

Spigel, Lynn. *Make Room for TV: Television and the Family Ideal in Postwar America*. Chicago: University of Chicago Press, 1992.

Steinberg, Brian. "Swearing during Family Hour? Who Gives a S#*! CBS Has Little Concern about How Its Hottest New Sitcom Will Be Received, Despite Airing on the Early Side." *Advertising Age*, 31 May 2010, 2.

St. Elmo's Fire. Dir. Joel Schumacher. Perf. Rob Lowe and Emilio Estevez. 1985. Film.

Stockton, Kathryn Bond. *The Queer Child, or Growing Sideways in the Twentieth Century*. Durham, NC: Duke University Press, 2009.

Strauss, Valerie. "Campbell Brown Responds to Critics (Including Me)." *Washington Post*, 13 Aug. 2014. Web.

The Strawberry Statement. Dir. Stuart Hagmann. Perf. Bruce Davison, Kim Darby, and Bud Cort. 1970. Film.

Superfly. Dir. Gordon Parks Jr. Perf. Ron O'Neal, Carl Lee, and Sheila Frazier. 1972. Film.

Swarns, Rachel. "Trying to Separate Bill Cosby from Cliff Huxtable." *New York Times*, 31 Jan. 2016. Web.

Sweeney, Kathleen. *Maiden USA: Girl Icons Come of Age*. New York: Peter Lang, 2008.

Take the Money and Run. Dir. Woody Allen. Perf. Woody Allen and Janet Margolin. 1969. Film.

Talbot, Margaret. *The Entertainer: Movies, Magic, and My Father's Twentieth Century*. New York: Riverhead, 2012.

Tally, Peggy. "Re-imagining Girlhood: Hollywood and the Tween Girl Film Market." Mitchell and Reid-Walsh 311–29.

Taylor, Ella. *Prime-Time Families: Television Culture in Postwar America*. Berkeley: University of California Press, 1989.

That's So Suite Life of Hannah Montana. Perf. Miley Cyrus and Raven-Symoné. Walt Disney Studios, 2007. DVD.

This Is Spinal Tap. Dir Rob Reiner. Perf. Michael McKean and Christopher Guest. 1984. Film.

Tolstoy, Leo. *Anna Karenina*. Ed. Leonard Kent and Nina Berberova. Trans. Constance Garnett. 1877. New York: Modern Library, 1993.

Tong, Rosemarie. *Feminist Thought*. 3rd ed. Philadelphia: Westview, 2009.

Toomey, Alyssa. "What Happened to Miley Cyrus?! Her Biggest Controversies and Scandals." Eonline.com, 27 Aug. 2013. Web.

Trebay, Guy. "Miley Cyrus's Style: An Exuberant Sexuality." *New York Times*, 27 Aug. 2015. Web.

The Trip. Dir. Roger Corman. Perf. Peter Fonda, Susan Strasberg, and Bruce Dern, 1967. Film.

Tropiano, Stephen. *The Prime Time Closet: A History of Gays and Lesbians on TV*. New York: Applause Theatre, 2002.

"The TV Parental Guidelines." tvguidelines.org. Web.

"TV Producers: All in the Family Hour." *Broadcasting*, 15 Sept. 1975, 29–30.

Twilight. Dir. Catherine Hardwicke. Perf. Kristen Stewart and Robert Pattinson. 2008. Film.

United States Commission on Civil Rights. *Window Dressing on the Set: Women and Minorities in Television*. Washington, DC: United States Commission on Civil Rights, 1977.

United States Department of Health, Education, and Welfare. "Television and Growing Up: The Impact of Televised Violence: Report to the Surgeon General, United States Public Health Service from the Surgeon General's Scientific Advisory Committee on Television and Social Behavior." Rockville, MD: National Institute of Mental Health, 1971.

Uricchio, William. "Television's Next Generation: Technology / Interface Culture / Flow." *Television after TV: Essays on a Medium in Transition*. Ed. Lynn Spigel and Jan Olsson. Durham, NC: Duke University Press, 2004. 163–82.

Varian, Nanette. "*Penthouse* Interview: Roseanne Barr." *Penthouse*, Jan. 1991, 81+.

A Very Brady Christmas. Included in *The Brady Bunch: The Complete Series*. Prod. Sherwood Schwartz. Perf. Robert Reed, Florence Henderson, Ann B. Davis, et al. 1988. Paramount, 2007. DVD.

A Very Brady Sequel. Dir. Arlene Sanford. Perf. Shelley Long, Gary Cole, and Tim Matheson. 1996. Film.

Villarejo, Amy. *Ethereal Queer: Television, Historicity, Desire*. Durham, NC: Duke University Press, 2014.

Villez, Barbara. "Clair Huxtable, Meet Renée Raddick: How Long a Way Have You Really Come, Baby?" *Cercles: Revue pluridisciplinaire du monde Anglophone* 8 (2003): 136–47.

Vinovskis, Maris. *An "Epidemic" of Adolescent Pregnancy? Some Historical and Policy Considerations*. New York: Oxford University Press, 1988.

Walker, Jimmie, with Sal Manna. *Dyn-o-mite! Good Times, Bad Times, Our Times—A Memoir*. Boston: Da Capo, 2012.

Waller, Gregory. “Flow, Genre, and the Television Text.” *In the Eye of the Beholder: Critical Perspectives in Popular Film and Television*. Ed. Gary Edgerton, Michael Marsden, and Jack Nachbar. Bowling Green, OH: Popular Press, 1997. 55–66.

Walters, Suzanna Danuta. *All the Rage: The Story of Gay Visibility in America*. Chicago: University of Chicago Press, 2001.

Wee, Valerie. *Teen Media: Hollywood and the Youth Market*. Jefferson, NC: McFarland, 2010.

Werksman, Deborah, ed. *I Killed June Cleaver: Modern Moms Shatter the Myth of Perfect Parenting*. Naperville, IL: Hysteria, 1999.

Wheatley, Helen. *Spectacular Television: Exploring Televisual Pleasure*. London: I. B. Tauris, 2016.

Whitaker, Mark. *Cosby: His Life and Times*. New York: Simon and Schuster, 2014.

White, Patricia. *Uninvited: Classical Hollywood Cinema and Lesbian Representability*. Bloomington: Indiana University Press, 1999.

Wiese, Otis Lee. “Live the Life of *McCall's*.” *McCall's*, May 1954, 27.

The Wild Angels. Dir. Roger Corman. Perf. Peter Fonda, Nancy Sinatra, and Bruce Dern. 1966. Film.

Wild in the Streets. Dir. Barry Shear. Perf. Christopher Jones and Shelley Winters. 1968. Film.

Williams, Barry, with Chris Kreski. *Growing Up Brady: I Was a Teenage Greg*. New York: HarperPerennial, 1992.

Williams, Raymond. *Television: Technology and Cultural Form*. Ed. Ederyn Williams. 2nd ed. 1974. London: Routledge, 1990.

Wiltz, Teresa. “The Latest Ingenue To-Do.” *Washington Post*, 29 Apr. 2008. Web.

Winn, Marie. *The Plug-In Drug: Television, Computers, and Family Life*. Rev. ed. New York: Penguin, 2002.

Wizards on Deck with Hannah Montana. Perf. Miley Cyrus and Selena Gomez. Walt Disney Studios, 2009. DVD.

Wolfson, Evan. “The Hawaii Marriage Case Launches the US Freedom-to-Marry Movement for Equality.” *Legal Recognition of Same-Sex Partnerships: A Study of National, European, and International Law*. Ed. Robert Wintemute and Mads Andenæs. Oxford: Hart, 2002. 169–75.

Wong, Curtis. “Jesse Tyler Ferguson Responds after Tuc Watkins Deems *Modern Family* Couple the Gay Equivalent of ‘Blackface.’” *Huffington Post*, 22 Dec. 2014. Web.

Wyatt, Edward. “NBC Tests Family Hour Boundaries.” *New York Times*, 14 Apr. 2008. Web.

Yahr, Emily. “*Pretty Little Liars*: When Will the Show Stop with Its Creepy Underage Relationships?” *Washington Post*, 10 Jun. 2014. Web.

Young, Tracy. “The Return of the Housewife: Roseanne Barr, Domestic Goddess.” *Vogue*, Apr. 1987: 335+.

Index

$#! My Dad Says*, 12
30 Rock, 11, 173

ABC, 10, 11, 12, 55, 76, 123, 188
ABC Family, 12
abortion, 20, 109, 116, 133
According to Jim, 11, 136
Addams Family, The, 59
Adventures of Ozzie and Harriet, The, 15, 29, 30, 37, 84, 105
advertising, 2, 12, 20, 134, 140, 146
African Americans, 79–106
AIDS and HIV, 69
Airplane!, 48
All-American Girl, 76, 78, 170
All in the Family, 7, 9, 61, 167
American Psychiatric Association, 60
Amos, John, 82, 213n9
anal imagery and eroticism, 21, 122, 156, 161, 163, 180–88
Angel Heart, 19, 102–4
Arnaz, Desi, 9, 39
Arnold, Roseanne. *See* Barr, Roseanne
Arnold, Tom, 108
Asner, Ed, 23
Attallah, Paul, 5
audience reception, 23, 45, 81, 86, 191–94
Austerlitz, Saul, 163
authenticity, 20, 134–35, 138, 140–46, 155, 157–59

Baehr v. Miike, 122
Ball, Lucille, 9, 44, 142
Bank, Frank, 17
Barr, Roseanne, 20, 48–49, 106, 107–33
Baudrillard, Jean, 27
Baxter-Birney, Meredith, 90, 107
Beaumont, Hugh, 28, 43
Becker, Ron, 123, 170
Berle, Milton, 34
Bernhard, Sandra, 20, 108, 120, 121, 131
Bersani, Leo, 181
Beverly Hillbillies, The, 141
Bewitched, 59
Bickford, Tyler, 141
Big Time Rush, 137–38
Billingsley, Barbara, 18, 28–29, 46–49
blackface, 171, 173
blaxploitation, 99
Bloodworth-Thomason, Linda, 167
Blossom, 137
blue collar vs. working class, 216n4. *See also* social class
Bob Cummings Show, The, 32–33
Bogle, Donald, 89–90
Bonet, Lisa, 17, 19, 80–81, 102–5, 196
Bourdieu, Pierre, 21, 192
Boy Meets World, 84, 137
Bozell, L. Brent, 10
Brady Brides, The, 70
Brady Bunch, The, 3, 6, 7, 15, 17, 19, 22, 24, 50, 51–78, 108, 130, 164, 172, 195
Brady Bunch Movie, The, 70
Brady Bunch Variety Hour, The, 70

Brady Kids, The, 70
Bradys, The, 74–77
breastfeeding, 117
Bronstein, Carolyn, 117
Brown, Campbell, 207n36
Brownmiller, Susan, 117
Brzezinski, Mika, 156
Buckingham, David, 14

Cameron, Kirk, 1–2
carnivalesque humor, 41–42, 44, 163, 196, 208n49. *See also* comedy
Carroll, Diahann, 82
Carsey, Marcy, 79, 81
CBS, 9–10, 12, 169
chastity, 93, 101, 148, 170
child abuse, 18, 29, 39–43, 105
childraising, 38, 45, 81; as discursive concepts, 3, 7; framing children, 63–70; and gender, 2, 34, 40, 47, 52, 61, 63, 81, 89, 101, 130, 159, 176, 195; and genres, 2, 3, 7, 18, 52, 76, 80, 108, 130, 134, 191–92, 194; and innocence, 4, 14–15, 17–19, 22, 24, 51–52, 55–57, 60, 63, 67, 69–70, 76, 80–83, 125, 128, 134, 140, 148, 155, 159, 188–89, 192, 194–95; queerness of, 4, 13–18, 32, 52; and sex education, 96, 156; and sexual autonomy, 125–29; as target audience, 7, 8, 9, 12–14, 139; and television ratings, 11. *See also* "growing sideways"; tweens
children: abuse of, 18, 29, 39–41; as actors, 14–15, 17, 47, 63, 66, 69, 102, 125–26, 142; and advertising, 8, 134, 140
Chittenden, Gertrude, 34
chrononormativity, 18, 27–32, 34, 37–38, 41, 43, 47–50, 54, 195
Coach, 88–89
Collins, Joan, 131
comedy, 5, 23–24, 74–75, 80, 109, 120, 163, 169, 191
Coon, David, 30
Coontz, Stephanie, 27
Cosby, Bill, 79–106, 108, 132, 142, 196
Cosby Show, The, 3, 6, 9, 17, 19, 22, 24, 78, 79–106, 108, 167, 170, 171, 191, 195
Cross, Gary, 14
Crowley, Pat, 48
Crystal, Billy, 61, 170
Cyrus, Billy Ray, 135, 142, 155, 159
Cyrus, Miley, 17, 20, 135–60

Davis, Ann B., 54
DeGeneres, Ellen, 119–20, 170
Deleuze, Gilles, 40–41
Desperate Housewives, 75, 171
Diamond, Dustin, 17
Diff'rent Strokes, 15, 191
Different World, A, 104
Dinshaw, Carolyn, 28
Disney Channel, 12, 135, 137, 139, 140–41, 145, 155
divorce, 6, 29–30, 47, 51, 55, 132
domestic sitcom. *See* family sitcom
Donna Reed Show, The, 44–45
Doty, Alexander, 4, 176, 180
double entendre, 11, 74, 126, 148, 153
Dow, Bonnie, 43
drag, 62–63, 122, 125, 147
dramedy, 19, 70, 74, 76, 213n45
Driscoll, Catherine, 147
drugs, depictions of, 48, 55, 57, 112, 130, 137
Dyson, Michael, 84

Eagleton, Terry, 208n49
Earles, Jason, 135
Edelman, Lee, 52
Ehrenreich, Barbara, 216n4
Eisenhower, Dwight D., 27
Ellen, 10, 119, 163, 170
Eng, David, 2
Everybody Loves Raymond, 7, 17, 119, 168

Facts of Life, The, 99, 191
Fairchild, Morgan, 121
Fales-Hill, Susan, 104
Family Affair, 15–16, 141
family-friendly programming, 2–3, 7–14, 18, 26, 56, 63, 65, 69, 76, 80, 81, 86, 92–93, 108, 123, 134, 138, 140, 148, 195
Family Guy, 76, 78, 168, 191
family hour, 9–12, 48, 76, 92–93, 119, 123, 125, 188
Family Matters, 6, 76
family sitcom, 5–8, 14–15, 18, *passim*
Family Ties, 15, 90, 108, 110, 191
Farmer, Brett, 193
Father Knows Best, 29, 38, 44, 48, 126
feminism, 20, 23, 32, 52, 55, 90, 107, 109, 111,

113, 116, 130–31; second-wave feminism, 32, 109; third-wave feminism, 109
Feuer, Jane, 163–64
flow, 23–24
football and football players, 36, 38, 46, 54, 60, 61, 78, 87–88, 182–83
Foster, Jodie, 120
Foucault, Michel, 3
FOX, 8, 92, 215n29
Foxx, Redd, 82
Freeman, Elizabeth, 27
Friends, 123
Full House, 9, 15, 76

Gates, Henry Louis, Jr., 83
gay male characters, 101, 119, 120, 122
gay marriage, 122–23, 168–69, 172, 179, 181, 196
gender and gender roles, 2, 4, 6, 8, 26–27, 29, 31–32, 34–37, 40, 44–47, 54, 60–63, 82, 87–91, 101–2, 106–8, 117, 125, 130, 149, 164, 170–73, 175–77, 181, 195
genre, 2–7, 18, 21–23, 25, 26, 43–44, 52, 74, 76, 80, 84, 86, 107–8, 119, 130, 131, 132, 134–35, 137, 156, 161, 163–65, 168–69, 171–72, 179, 180, 189, 191, 192, 194, 195–96. *See also* comedy; dramedy; family sitcom; melodrama; mockumentary; "zitcom"
George Burns and Gracie Allen Show, The, 6, 44, 141
Goldbergs, The, 195
Good Times, 53, 79, 82, 90
Goranson, Lecy, 107, 108, 131
Gray, Herman, 82
Gray, Jonathan, 71
Greenberg, Clement, 71
Grier, Rosey, 61
Growing Pains, 1, 15, 90, 108, 191
"growing sideways," 28, 34, 36, 37, 49
Gruenberg, Sidonie Matsner, 31
Guattari, Félix, 40–41
Guntzelman, Dan, 15
"guppie" (gay urban professional) stereotype, 120

Halberstam, David, 29–30, 32
Halberstam, Jack, 2
Hannah Montana, 3, 6, 17, 20, 22, 24, 133, 134–60, 196
Hannah Montana: The Movie, 144–45, 152
Happy Days, 6, 9, 53, 141
Haste, Helen, 63, 65
Hathaway, Anne, 138
Havrilesky, Heather, 191
Hefner, Hugh, 32, 58, 118
Henderson, Florence, 51, 68, 75, 130
heteronormativity, 7, 18, 26, 36–37, 42, 52, 69, 101, 125, 162
Hickman, Dwayne, 33
Higginbotham, Abraham, 178, 180
Hite, Shere, 117
HIV and AIDS, 69
Holliday, Polly, 61
Hollingsworth v. Perry, 169
Home Improvement, 15, 132
homonormativity, 172, 176, 180
homophobia, 60, 101, 121–22, 166, 176–78
homosexuality, 33–34, 36, 60–61, 69, 108, 119–22, 124–25, 133, 162–63, 171–81, 185, 189, 196
homosocial relationships, 34–36, 42–43, 101–2, 151–52, 209n21
How I Met Your Mother, 5, 188
hypermasculinity, 88

I Dream of Jeannie, 59, 60, 130, 141
I Love Lucy, 6, 9, 39, 44, 169
I Married Joan, 44
impotency, 117
incest, 36, 66–67, 76, 155, 186, 187, 188
innocence, 3–4, 13–20, 22, 24, 25, 28, 32, 50–57, 60, 63, 66–70, 74, 76–78, 80–81, 91, 93, 103, 106, 125, 128, 134–35, 137, 140, 143, 148, 149, 152–55, 157, 159, 163, 188–89, 192, 194–96

Jackson, Autumn, 105
Jameson, Fredric, 27
Jennings, Claudia, 65
Jhally, Sut, 83
Jonas Brothers, 143
Jones, Angus T., 1, 143
Jones, Deacon, 60
Joyrich, Lynne, 4, 162
Julia, 81–82, 163, 170

Kalu, Anthonia, 86
Kanter, Hal, 82
Kaplan, Elaine, 93

Kaye, Danny, 92
Kendall, Diana, 110
Kierkegaard, Søren, 71
Kincaid, James, 52, 65
kitsch, 5, 19, 52, 70–78, 195
Knight, Christopher, 51, 67
Kovacs, Ernie, 34
Kulp, Nancy, 34

labor unions. *See* unions, labor
Lanser, Susan, 164
Larson, Mary Strom, 18
laughing at vs. laughing with, 23, 173
Laurent, Lawrence, 8
LaVecchia, Christina, 171, 176, 180
Leahy, Janet, 167
Lear, Norman, 9, 10, 167, 194
Leave It to Beaver, 3, 6, 17, 18, 21, 22, 26–50, 130, 141, 171, 195
Leibman, Nina, 29–30, 32
Leibovitz, Annie, 155
lesbians and lesbianism, 20, 49, 101, 120–24, 131, 170, 171, 176, 193
Levin, Diane, 148
Levittown, 30
Lewis, Justin, 83
Lieberman, Joe, 10
Lloyd, Christopher, 165
Lockhart, June, 48
Lohan, Lindsay, 138
Long, Rob, 167, 194
Lookinland, Mike, 51, 68
Lopez, George, 136, 142
Lords, Traci, 20, 118–19
Lowe, Rob, 166–67
Lundy, Lamar, 61
Lynde, Paul, 34, 59

Madonna, 157
Make Room for Daddy, 29, 44
Malcolm in the Middle, 136
"mammy" stereotype, 90
Many Loves of Dobie Gillis, The, 33, 137
Marc, David, 6, 54, 191
Marinucci, Mimi, 62
marketing, 2, 8, 20, 22, 134–36, 139–48, 155–60, 170, 196
Married with Children, 6, 108, 136
Mary Tyler Moore Show, The, 23, 55, 130, 163
*M*A*S*H*, 213n45
masturbation, 114, 128
Mathers, Jerry, 28, 46
Maude, 9, 55, 167
Mayes-Elma, Ruthann, 140
Mayne, Judith, 193
McCormick, Maureen, 51, 63, 68
Meehan, Diana, 44, 54
melodrama, 192
menstruation, 96, 126
Metcalf, Laurie, 108, 119, 121, 131
Middle, The, 136
Miller, Quinn, 24
Mills, Alley, 48
Mills, Brett, 170
Minow, Newton, 191
mise-en-scène, 126, 164
Mittell, Jason, 4
Mock, Erin Lee, 39
mockumentary, 164–65
Modern Family, 3, 6, 21, 22, 24, 160, 161–89, 195, 196
Monte, Eric, 82
Moonlighting, 74–75
Moore, Mary Tyler, 23, 55, 130–31, 163
Moorehead, Agnes, 34, 59
morals and moralizing, 1, 6, 54, 126, 130, 141, 147, 165, 167
Mulvey, Laura, 63, 65
Muñoz, José Esteban, 2
Munsters, The, 59

narratology, 18, 21, 54, 108, 130, 135, 147, 161–69
NBC, 10, 11, 82, 92
Nelson, Ozzie, 29, 37–38, 105
Newcomb, Horace, 6, 29, 30, 32, 193
New Normal, The, 195
Nickelodeon, 12, 137, 138
Nixon, Richard, 53, 172
nostalgia, 6, 18, 19, 22, 27, 31, 32, 52, 70–78, 182, 193

O'Donnell, Rosie, 120
Olsen, Merlin, 61
Olsen, Susan, 51, 68
One Day at a Time, 10, 53, 55
Orlando, Tony, 214n16
Our Miss Brooks, 34

Packard, Vance, 8
Paglia, Camille, 155
pansexuality, 155, 220n6
parents and parenting, 7–8, 12, 17, 31, 34–35, 38–41, 46, 53–54, 56, 58, 80, 87, 94, 96–99, 122, 125–26, 131, 134–37, 139, 148, 152–59, 176, 183, 188; androgynous parenting, 80–81, 89–91, 93, 102, 107; authoritarian vs. authoritative parenting, 45, 81, 213n5
Parker, James, 174
Parks and Recreation, 165, 167
Parton, Dolly, 143, 159
Partridge Family, The, 10, 53, 55
Peterson-Davis, Buffy, 15–16
Playboy, 32, 65, 100, 118, 123
Plumb, Eve, 17, 51, 67, 69
pornography, 20, 33, 107, 117–19, 133, 188
Poussaint, Alvin F., 85, 89, 92, 96
pregnancy and teen pregnancy, 81, 93–94, 99, 104, 105, 117, 153, 195
Presley, Elvis, 32
Pretty Little Liars, 12
Private Secretary, 34
propaganda, 8

queer theory, 2, 52, 172

Rainer, Peter, 132
Raising Hope, 195
Rashad, Phylicia Ayers-Allen, 80, 89
ratings, 10, 15, 70, 73, 74, 76, 108, 123
Raven-Symoné, 80, 138, 145
Reagan, Ronald, and Reagan Republicanism, 20, 22, 82, 88, 94, 107, 110, 111, 113, 128, 133, 194, 196
Reed, Donna, 44–45
Reed, Robert, 51, 69
Robinson, Paul, 172
Roseanne, 3, 6, 20, 22, 24, 48–49, 106–33, 136, 142, 167
Rosenthal, Phil, 108–9
Ross, Rich, 143
Rottenberg, Josh, 105
Rowe, Kathleen, 112
Rubin, Gail, 102
Rule, Elton, 55

Sanford, Isabel, 48
Sanford and Son, 79, 81–82
Sanneh, Kelefa, 80
Saved by the Bell, 17
Schlatter, George, 9–10
Schulman, Sarah, 170
Schwartz, Lloyd, 59, 63, 68, 69, 72, 73
Schwartz, Sherwood, 51, 55, 69, 72
scopophilia, 63, 113, 149
Sedgwick, Eve Kosofsky, 52, 102
Seinfeld, 5, 165
Sesame Street, 219n1
sex. *See* anal imagery and eroticism; chastity; gay male characters; gay marriage; gender and gender roles; heteronormativity; homonormativity; homophobia; homosexuality; homosocial relationships; impotency; incest; lesbians and lesbianism; masturbation; menstruation; pansexuality; pornography; pregnancy and teen pregnancy; sodomy; transvestism; virginity
Sex and the City, 148
Shields, Brooke, 135, 153–54
Shriver, Lionel, 190
Simpsons, The, 8, 13, 15, 92, 108, 136
sissies, 35, 37
sitcom. *See* family sitcom
Smith, Will, 142
Smith-Shomade, Beretta, 79
Soap, 10, 61, 170
social class, 27, 30, 82, 87, 109–10, 112–13, 119, 131, 176. *See also* blue collar vs. working class
sodomy, 122
Solinger, Rickie, 94
spectatorship, 21, 192–94
Spigel, Lynn, 5–6
Spin City, 10
Startz, Jane, 138
Steinem, Gloria, 117
stereotypes, 21, 27, 31, 44, 82, 86, 90, 93, 99, 103, 120–21, 123, 161, 163, 171–77, 180, 189, 196
Stockton, Kathryn Bond, 28, 34
Stone, Sharon, 218n20
Stonestreet, Eric, 162, 170
Stonewall Riots, 59, 180
suburbia, 6, 8, 26–30, 39, 43, 45, 48–49, 56–57, 70, 78, 110, 162, 168, 174, 195

surface vs. symptomatic readings, 2, 22–24, 52, 70, 83, 86, 87, 96, 108, 168, 192
Sutton, Lisa, 70
syndication, 5, 18, 19, 70, 105, 169

Teletubbies, 219n1
That '70s Show, 78
Thomas, Danny, 29
Thomas, Marlo, 130, 131
Thompson, Fred Dalton, 111
Thompson, Shawn Berkes, 105
Tolstoy, Leo, 190, 193, 196
Transparent, 195
transvestism, 62, 125
tweens, 20, 22, 133–35, 137–49, 152–54, 157, 159–60, 196
twerking, 156
Two and a Half Men, 1, 143

United States Commission on Civil Rights, 79
United States v. Windsor, 169
unions, labor, 110–13
Uricchio, William, 23

Varian, Nanette, 132
VCRs, 118
Very Brady Christmas, A, 19, 70–75
Vietnam War, 53, 56, 111
Villarejo, Amy, 34
virginity, 3, 53, 81, 97–99, 101–2, 106, 152–53, 188

Walker, Jimmie, 82
Watkins, Tuc, 171
Weld, Tuesday, 33
Werner, Mort, 82
Werner, Tom, 79, 81
What's Happening!!, 79–80, 82, 90
Wheatley, Helen, 63
whiteness, 8, 79, 99
Who's the Boss?, 48, 90, 92–93, 191
widows and widowers, 46, 51, 55, 66, 116, 210n2
Will & Grace, 119, 170
Williams, Barry, 51, 68
Williams, Matt, 112, 130, 132
Williams, Raymond, 23
Williams, Tennessee, 34, 169
Williams, Vanessa, 145
Winn, Marie, 17
Witt, Paul Junger, 10
Wonder Years, The, 48, 110

Young, Robert, 29

"zitcoms," 137
Zuker, Danny, 185, 189

About the Author

TISON PUGH is a professor of English at the University of Central Florida. His books include *Truman Capote: A Literary Life at the Movies*; *Precious Perversions: Humor, Homosexuality, and the Southern Literary Canon*; and *Innocence, Heterosexuality, and the Queerness of Children's Literature*.